Palgrave Studies in Economic History

Series Editor
Kent Deng
London School of Economics
London, UK

Palgrave Studies in Economic History is designed to illuminate and enrich our understanding of economies and economic phenomena of the past. The series covers a vast range of topics including financial history, labour history, development economics, commercialisation, urbanisation, industrialisation, modernisation, globalisation, and changes in world economic orders.

More information about this series at
http://www.palgrave.com/gp/series/14632

Klas Rönnbäck • Oskar Broberg

Capital and Colonialism

The Return on British Investments in Africa 1869–1969

Klas Rönnbäck
Department of Economy and Society
University of Gothenburg
Gothenburg, Sweden

Oskar Broberg
Department of Economy and Society
University of Gothenburg
Gothenburg, Sweden

Palgrave Studies in Economic History
ISBN 978-3-030-19710-0   ISBN 978-3-030-19711-7 (eBook)
https://doi.org/10.1007/978-3-030-19711-7

© The Editor(s) (if applicable) and The Author(s) 2019
This work is subject to copyright. All rights are solely and exclusively licensed by the Publisher, whether the whole or part of the material is concerned, specifically the rights of translation, reprinting, reuse of illustrations, recitation, broadcasting, reproduction on microfilms or in any other physical way, and transmission or information storage and retrieval, electronic adaptation, computer software, or by similar or dissimilar methodology now known or hereafter developed.
The use of general descriptive names, registered names, trademarks, service marks, etc. in this publication does not imply, even in the absence of a specific statement, that such names are exempt from the relevant protective laws and regulations and therefore free for general use.
The publisher, the authors and the editors are safe to assume that the advice and information in this book are believed to be true and accurate at the date of publication. Neither the publisher nor the authors or the editors give a warranty, express or implied, with respect to the material contained herein or for any errors or omissions that may have been made. The publisher remains neutral with regard to jurisdictional claims in published maps and institutional affiliations.

Cover illustration: Classic Image / Alamy Stock Photo

This Palgrave Macmillan imprint is published by the registered company Springer Nature Switzerland AG
The registered company address is: Gewerbestrasse 11, 6330 Cham, Switzerland

Acknowledgements

The research underlying this book would not have been possible without the economic support from Jan Wallanders och Tom Hedelius Stiftelse, Stiftelsen för Ekonomisk Forskning i Västsverige and strategic funding from the School of Business, Economics and Law at Gothenburg University.

The research would likewise not have been possible without access to primary sources in the archives. We would therefore like to thank all the staff at the London Guildhall Archive, as well as Julia Woolcott, archivists at the Barloworld Limited company archive.

A couple of research assistants have furthermore been most helpful for different parts of this research project: Jens Boberg (Chap. 5), Young Jang (Chap. 8), Stefan Hagberg (Chap. 12), Laura Phillips (Chap. 12), Dimitrios Theodoridis (Chap. 14) and Stefania Galli (Chap. 14). We thank you all for your assistance to this work.

A number of scholars that we have been in contact with over the years have generously shared their respective expertise with us, providing us crucial feedback on sources, the methods employed or the results we arrived at. We would therefore like to thank Johan Fourie, Jeremy Mouat, Arn Keeling, Mark Hendrickson, Fredric Quivik, Kip Curtis and John Turner for their help as well as participants in the audience at several conferences where parts of this research have been presented, including conferences organized by the African Economic History Network,

European Business History Conference, the European Historical Economics Society, Ekonomisk-Historiska Mötet and the LEAP-seminar at Stellenbosch University. We would also like to thank Moritz Schularick who generously shared data from his research with us.

Most importantly, we would like to extend our deepest gratitude to a number of scholars who generously shared their expertise with us by reading selected draft chapters of this book and providing much valuable feedback. This helped us develop these chapters substantially. Thank you to Tinashe Nyamunda, Robert L. Tignor, Charles Harvey, Gareth Austin, Sarah Stockwell, Mariusz Lukasiewicz, Ed Kerby, Grietjie Verhoef, Staffan Granér, Birgit Karlsson and Susanna Fellman. All remaining errors are, naturally, our responsibility.

Contents

1 Introduction — 3

Part I Research Design — 15

2 Historical Context — 17

3 Capital and Colonialism in Theory — 39

4 Previous Empirical Research — 55

5 Data and Methods — 69

Part II Aggregate Results — 99

6 The Rate of Return on Investment in Africa — 101

7 Risk and Return — 125

Part III Regional Studies — 147

8 North Africa — 149

9 West Africa — 175

10 Central/Southern Africa — 209

11 South Africa — 235

Part IV Thematical Studies — 281

12 On the Ground Floor: The Corner House Group — 283

13 Imperial Profit — 311

14 African Mining in Global Comparison — 339

15 Conclusions — 381

Index — 393

List of Figures

Fig. 2.1	British investments in mining by region, 1865–1914 (percentage of total capital called). Source: Stone (1999, table 57)	29
Fig. 2.2	Capital exports from the United Kingdom to the British Empire and to countries outside the British Empire, by year, 1865–1914 (£000 sterling, current prices). Source: Stone (1999, table 33–34)	31
Fig. 5.1	Number of companies in the African Colonial Equities Database, by year, 1869–1969. Source: African Colonial Equities Database (ACED)	82
Fig. 6.1	Market capitalization in the African Colonial Equities Database, by year and region, 1869–1969 (£ million, constant 1868 prices). Source: African Colonial Equities Database (ACED). Note: market capitalization calculated for the month of December every year of observation. East African investments are too small to be clearly discernible in the figure	102
Fig. 6.2	Three-firm concentration ratio of the market capitalization in the African Colonial Equities Database, by year and region, 1869–1969 (per cent, nine-year moving averages). Source: African Colonial Equities Database (ACED)	105
Fig. 6.3	Histogram of the nominal average return on investment in individual companies in Africa, 1869–1969 (geometric mean per year). Source: African Colonial Equities Database (ACED)	108

x   List of Figures

Fig. 6.4   Nominal and real return on investment in Africa, by decade, 1869–1969 (geometric mean per year). Source: African Colonial Equities Database (ACED)   109

Fig. 6.5   Accumulated return on investment in Africa, by year and region, 1869–1969 (index 1868 = 100, logarithmic scale). Source: African Colonial Equities Database (ACED)   111

Fig. 6.6   Nominal return on British investments in South Africa compared to previous research, by decade, 1900–1969 (geometric mean per year). Source: Our estimates based on African Colonial Equities Database (ACED); Dimson et al.'s estimate based on (Dimson et al. 2002, table 28-2)   114

Fig. 6.7   Nominal return on British and South African investments in South African gold mining compared to previous research, by year, 1919–1962. Source: Our estimates based on African Colonial Equities Database (ACED); Frankel's estimate based on (Frankel 1967, appendix C, Table 6)   117

Fig. 6.8   Nominal return on investment in Belgian Congo compared to previous research, by year, 1889–1962. Source: Our estimates based on African Colonial Equities Database (ACED); Buelens & Marysse's estimates from (Buelens and Marysse 2009, appendix 1)   118

Fig. 6.9   Real return on investment in Africa compared to previous research on British foreign investments, by year, 1862–1913 (five year moving average). Source: Our estimates based on African Colonial Equities Database (ACED); Edelstein's estimates from (Edelstein 1976, appendix 3); Davis & Huttenback's estimates extracted from the data in (Davis and Huttenback 1986, chart 3.1)   120

Fig. 6.10   Real return on investment in Africa compared to previous research on investments in the UK, by decade, 1870–1969 (geometric mean per year). Source: Our estimates based on African Colonial Equities Database (ACED); Edelstein's figures based on (Edelstein 1976, appendix 3); Dimson et al.'s figures based on (Dimson et al. 2002, Table 32–2). Note: Dimson et al.'s figures have here been adjusted by using the same data for UK inflation rate as is used throughout this study, so that any differences due to different estimates of the inflation rate are eliminated   121

List of Figures   xi

Fig. 7.1 Return on investment in Africa, by year and decade, 1869–1969 (per year and geometric mean by decade). Source: African Colonial Equities Database (ACED). Note: The y-axis is truncated at +60 per cent to show fluctuations throughout the period more clearly, so the outlier in the year 1881 (+118 per cent) is not visible in the figure   126

Fig. 7.2 Average nominal return on investment in Africa in relation to the number of years present in the sample, by company, 1869–1969. Source: African Colonial Equities Database (ACED). Note: the x-axis is truncated at +100 per cent. Four outliers are therefore excluded from the figure. All of these outliers were present only one year in our sample before they disappear again   134

Fig. 7.3 Survival estimates of African companies traded on the London Stock Exchange, 1869–1969. Source: African Colonial Equities Database (ACED). Note: The figure also shows censored observations   136

Fig. 8.1 Price quotations of the Suez Canal Company on the London and Paris Stock Exchanges, by month, 1862–1969 (£ sterling, current prices, logarithmic scale). Source: African Colonial Equities Database (ACED) and (Bonin 2010, tables 22–24)   153

Fig. 8.2 Real return on investment in North Africa, by decade, 1869–1969 (geometric mean per year). Source: African Colonial Equities Database (ACED)   170

Fig. 9.1 Real return on investment in West Africa, by decade, 1869–1969 (geometric mean per year). Source: African Colonial Equities Database (ACED)   200

Fig. 10.1 Real return on investment in Central/Southern Africa, by decade, 1869–1969 (geometric mean per year). Source: African Colonial Equities Database (ACED)   228

Fig. 11.1 Real return on investment in South Africa, by decade, 1869–1969 (geometric mean per year). Source: African Colonial Equities Database (ACED)   266

Fig. 12.1 Price quotations for the Rand Mines Limited in London, by month, 1893–1904 (£ sterling, current prices). Source: Letters (February 1893–February 1894), *Financial Times* (FT) (March 1894–May 1895), African Colonial Equities Database (ACED) (June 1895–December 1904). Note: The time series

xii   List of Figures

has been adjusted for the split of the stock in 1901. The series are interpolated February 1893 to February 1894 based on letters found in March 1893, June 1893, December 1893 and February 1894)   297

Fig. 13.1 Price quotations for Egyptian equity on the London Stock Exchange, by month, 1870–1885 (index 1881 m1 = 100, current prices). Source: African Colonial Equities Database (ACED)   312

Fig. 13.2 Accumulated return on investment in Egypt, by month, 1874–1890 (index, January 1882 = 100, logarithmic scale). Source: African Colonial Equities Database (ACED)   316

Fig. 13.3 Accumulated return on investment in South Africa, by month, 1895–1905 (index, September 1899 = 100). Source: African Colonial Equities Database (ACED). Note: The shaded area shows the period of the South African War, from October 1899 to May 1902   318

Fig. 13.4 Accumulated return on investment for the British South Africa and Royal Niger Companies during chartered and post-chartered periods, by year, 1883–1965 (index, year charter ended = 100, logarithmic scale). Source: African Colonial Equities Database (ACED). Note: In the case of RNC, 1899 is treated as the last year of the charter, whereas in the case of BSAC, 1923 is treated as the last year of the charter, as the charter in the latter case was revoked effectively first by the end of the year   322

Fig. 13.5 Accumulated return on investment by type of colony, by year, 1869–1969 (index, 1868 = 100). Source: African Colonial Equities Database (ACED)   324

Fig. 13.6 Accumulated return on investment prior to and following political independence in Egypt, Ghana and Nigeria, by year (index, year of independence = 100, logarithmic scale). Source: African Colonial Equities Database (ACED)   329

Fig. 13.7 Accumulated return on investment prior to and following political independence in Belgian Congo, Zambia and Southern Rhodesia, by year (index, year of independence = 100, logarithmic scale). Source: African Colonial Equities Database (ACED). Note: All data are for portfolios representing all equity investments in each respective colony/

country, except in the case of Belgian Congo, which is based on the sole company of Tanganyika Concessions. As was shown in Fig. 6.8, the return on investment in this particular company seems to match the return on investment for the Belgian portfolio of investments studied by Buelens and Marysse quite well   331

Fig. 14.1 Market capitalization of companies in the Global Mining Equities Database, by continent of operation, 1869–1929 (£ million, constant 1868 prices). Source: Global Mining Equities Database (GMED)   340

Fig. 14.2 Market capitalization of companies in the Global Mining Equities Database, by continent of operation, 1930–1969 (£ million, constant 1868 prices). Source: Global Mining Equities Database (GMED)   342

Fig. 14.3 Relative market capitalization of companies in the Global Mining Equities Database operating in British colonies, 1869–1969 (per cent of market capitalization of all companies in the database). Source: Global Mining Equities Database (GMED)   342

Fig. 14.4 Ore grades of gold mining in selected parts of the world, 1886–1969 (ounce gold per metric ton ore, weighted averages by year). Sources: for Ghana: (Afrifa-Taylor 2006, appendix 3); for South Africa: (Charles Sidney Goldmann (1895) South African Mines: Their Position, Results & Developments. London: Effingham Wilson & Co.; Notes and Proceedings of the House of Assembly; Vol. V, Colonial and Provincial Papers Transvaal; Mining Engineer, report for the year ending 30th June 1910, table 13; Annual report of Mining Engineer 1947, table 10; Annual report of Mining Engineer 1965, unnumbered table); for Canada: (Geological Survey of Canada. Annual Report 1886–1905; A General Summary of the Mineral Production of Canada 1910–1917); for Australia: (A Statistical Account of the Seven Colonies of Australasia, 1897–1898; The Wealth and Progress of New South Wales 1887–1901; Statistical Register of the Colony of Western Australia 1899–1905; Report of the Department of Mines, Western Australia, Mining Statistics 1906–1970); for Colorado and South Dakota in the United States: (Mineral

Resources of the US 1904–1928; United States Bureau of Mines—Minerals Yearbook 1932–1969). Note: The data from Ghana is based on only one company, the major producer Ashanti Goldfields 344

Fig. 14.5 Average annual real return on investment in mining, by decade and continent of operations, 1869–1969 (geometric mean per year). Source: Global Mining Equities Database (GMED) 349

Fig. 14.6 Real return on investment in mining in Africa, by decade and by type of ore mined, 1869–1969 (geometric mean per year). Source: African Colonial Equities Database (ACED) 365

Fig. 14.7 Return on investment in South African gold mining and ore grade of the gold deposits mined, by decade, 1886–1969 (geometric mean per year). Source: African Colonial Equities Database (ACED) and Fig. 14.4 368

List of Tables

Table 2.1	Accumulated capital exports from the United Kingdom, by country of destination, 1865–1914	27
Table 4.1	Summary of key previous research	62
Table 5.1	Descriptive statistics of sample of African companies, 1869–1969	83
Table 5.2	Descriptive statistics of sample of global mining companies, 1869–1969	87
Table 6.1	Nominal and real return on investment in Africa, 1869–1969 (average per year, per cent)	107
Table 6.2	Real return on investment in Africa, by region, 1869–1969 (geometric mean per year)	110
Table 6.3	Real return on investment in Africa, by sector, 1869–1969 (geometric mean per year)	112
Table 7.1	Average and volatility of real return on investment in Africa, by portfolio, 1869–1969	127
Table 7.2	Real return on government bonds and private equity in the United Kingdom, South Africa and Egypt, 1880–1913 (per cent, geometric mean per year)	132
Table 7.3	Cox regression of hazard ratios for the survival of African ventures, 1869–1969	138
Table 7.4	Real return on investment in Africa, by eventual fate of company during our period of study, 1869–1969 (geometric mean per year)	140

List of Tables

Table 8.1	Real return on investment in selected portfolios in North Africa, 1869–1969 (geometric mean per year)	157
Table 8.2	Real return on investment in selected companies in North Africa, 1862–1969 (geometric mean per year)	158
Table 9.1	Real return on investment in selected portfolios in West Africa, 1869–1969 (geometric mean per year)	182
Table 9.2	Real return on investment in selected companies in West Africa, 1869–1969 (geometric mean per year)	183
Table 10.1	Real return on investment in selected portfolios in Central/Southern Africa, 1890–1969 (geometric mean per year)	211
Table 10.2	Real return on investment in selected companies in Central/Southern Africa, 1890–1969 (geometric mean per year)	215
Table 11.1	Real return on investment in selected portfolios in South Africa, 1869–1969 (geometric mean per year)	238
Table 11.2	Real return on investment in selected companies in South Africa, 1869–1969 (geometric mean per year)	239
Table 14.1	Nominal and real return on investment in (non-ferrous) mining companies, 1869–1969 (geometric mean per year)	348
Table 14.2	Real return on investment for selected mining companies, 1869–1969 (geometric mean per year)	351
Table 14.3	Wages paid to mine workers in various places around the world in 1914 (British shillings per shift)	369

Illustration, A Song of the English, Lions. Illustration to 'A Song of the English', a jingoistic set of poems about the colonization in Southern Africa. The poems were written by Rudyard Kipling and first published in the English Illustrated Magazine. The illustration depicts two lions, in reference to the lions on the English royal arms, and human bones, in reference to the violent process of colonization. © The Sharp Collection/Mary Evans Picture Library

1

Introduction

*Snatched and bartered oft from hand to hand,
I dream my dream, by rock and heath and pine,
Of Empire to the northward. Ay, one land
From Lion's Head to Line!*
Rudyard Kipling: 'The Song of the Cities: Cape Town', *from* A Song of the English *(1893).*

Rudyard Kipling's short poem captures the British imperialist ambition—a dream of an ever-expanding Empire. In the case of the Cape Colony, Kipling hoped that the Empire would come to stretch northwards from Lion's Head—a mountain next to the more famous Table Mountain in Cape Town—to the equatorial line. The poem did indeed capture the imperialist ambition so perfectly that it was inscribed upon the foundation of a statue of the empire-builder Cecil Rhodes located at the centre of the University of Cape Town's campus. This is a statue which in recent years has become highly controversial in South Africa, as it is correctly perceived as a symbol of imperialism and colonialism.

An illustration to 'The Song of the Dead', an earlier part of the same poem by Kipling, can also be seen on an adjacent page. In the picture, two lions—the symbols of England and imperialism—stand atop a sanddrift, upon which lie some human remains. Looking at the picture alone, we are unable to determine who the victims might have been, but Kipling's poem clearly laments the English who died for the sake of the British Empire. Kipling, in contrast, shed few tears for all the others who suffered and died as a consequence of English imperialism. In reality, human remains that were found where the English lion chose to roam would most frequently have been those of the colonized people killed by the imperialist lion, rather than of Englishmen dying for the sake of imperialism.

Kipling's jingoistic poem was a product of its time, when the Scramble for Africa was still under way. Imperialism and colonialism were ubiquitous issues in cultural and political spheres in Victorian England, but what role did imperialism and colonialism play economically for the development of modern capitalism? This question has been debated for more than a century. Some scholars have argued that modern capitalism developed in symbiosis with imperialism and/or colonialism. Other scholars have argued to the contrary that the development of modern capitalism had little or nothing to do with imperialism or colonialism, but that these processes were essentially independent of each other. In this study, we engage in this debate by analysing the role of financial markets and actors as links between imperialism/colonialism and the development of modern capitalism. We are thus interested in the interaction between investors and investments, on the one hand, and imperial politics and colonial institutions, on the other—in short, between capital and colonialism.

The word imperialism will be used in this book in the broad sense of policies and interventions that were intended to extend and maintain a country's political and economic influence internationally. Such policies can range from diplomacy or cultural influence to military intervention and the creation and control of colonies. Colonialism is used in a narrower sense: a policy or policies aimed at acquiring and maintaining political and judicial control over certain territories, that is, colonies. Furthermore, the colonies are treated as separate entities from the imperial power through differences in legislation and institutions.

One hotly contested question in the debate on the role of imperialism and colonialism has been whether it was economically profitable for the imperial powers to acquire and maintain colonies overseas or whether possessing colonies was actually an economic burden for the imperial powers. To answer that question in full, one would need to look at the net social profits of colonialism, including both the private and public benefits and costs of colonialism. In this study, we will focus upon one part of this equation: the private benefits to be earned in the imperial power from colonies. Public benefits and costs will not be studied in this book, as this has been the topic of much other research in recent years. As the focus in this book is on the imperial power, we will furthermore not analyse the benefits and costs of colonialism for the colonies, or for the populations living there, as that is a field of study in its own right.

We use the return on investment as the lens for our study. In order to understand the changing dynamics of the rate of return on these investments, we analyse it against the backdrop of what is already known about colonialism's impact on other factors of production, such as labour and natural resources. Colonial policies can thus influence the return on investment in private business ventures in the colonies in different ways. In this book, we will focus upon three mechanisms in particular: access to land, access to labour and risks related to financial investments.

One frequent aspect of colonialism was that colonial powers appropriated land and other natural resources in their colonies. Land was then distributed to colonial settlers for free or at a low price. In some cases, the land was not in wide economic use prior to colonization, for example, due to low population densities. In other cases, the land was in use, but appropriated during the process of colonization from the people who lived there before. Through this process, land (including all the natural resources that could be extracted from it, ranging from agricultural produce to minerals) could become available to settlers and private colonial ventures much more cheaply than otherwise would have been the case.

A second aspect of colonialism was that it could provide access to low-paid labour. When large tracts of land were appropriated by settlers, it eventually limited the opportunities for local populations to support themselves through subsistence or commercial farming. Hence, such land policies forced many to find work elsewhere, often resorting to working for the settlers. In many colonies, the access to low-paid labour was also reinforced by various forms of coercive labour institutions, which remained in use well into modern times. In some cases, these institutions were a legacy from precolonial times, and colonial authorities for various reasons saw fit not to challenge these institutions. In other cases, new forms of coercive labour institutions were imposed in the colonies. Regardless of origin, coercive labour mechanisms had the objective of reducing the reservation wage of the population, so as to provide the settlers and other colonial agents with a labour force that was paid lower wages than would otherwise have been possible.

These two mechanisms together constitute the basis for what we will call here economic exploitation. In this book, we will employ what we consider a narrow definition of the term exploitation: as an economic relationship based on these types of coercive institutions or practices. It can be, and certainly has been, argued that capitalism in itself is exploitative in the sense that the distribution of the means of production in a capitalist society, and the state's power to uphold the property rights determining this distribution, can create coercive institutions or practices. Even though this is an important issue in its own right, we will not enter into that particular discussion in this book. Here, we will employ the term exploitation in a more specific sense, as signifying a form and a level of coercion imposed through colonial institutions beyond what would be considered 'normal' in a modern capitalist society.

A third mechanism that will be explored in this book, whereby colonial institutions and imperialist policies can influence the return on investment, is how colonial policies could reconfigure the risk for foreign direct investment. It could, for example, reduce the risk of local rulers expropriating privately held assets. This would have implications for how high the (risk-adjusted) return on investment needed to be in order to offer competitive investment opportunities compared to other investment opportunities elsewhere in the world. In the end, colonial institutions could also, as development during the twentieth century illustrates, spur independence movements and civil disorder that could translate into higher risk for private investors. Colonialism could also reconfigure the risk for private investors by introducing new financial institutions—banking legislation, rules for incorporation or the establishment of stock exchanges. The implementation of such institutions could contribute to the modernization of the financial markets in the colonized area, which in itself would allow individual actors to take on both higher and lower risk than before.

There is thus a variety of possible theoretical arguments as to how imperial policies and colonial institutions might influence the return on investment in private companies operating in colonies. Whether they actually did have any such impact is, however, an empirical question. This is a question which previous research has not been able to reach consensus on. One school of thought has it that there was much higher return on investment in the colonies than elsewhere. A competing school of thought has argued that there is no solid evidence that the return on investment was systematically higher in colonies than elsewhere. Among the latter, some would therefore argue that non-economic motives must have been the driving force. Economic motives could still be important, even if the return on investment in colonies was on a par with that elsewhere in the world. First, as noted already by some classical economists, investments in colonies might have counteracted any tendency for the return on investment to decrease in the capital-exporting country. This idea of falling marginal return on investment was later developed by Marxist economists emphasizing the tendency of a falling profit rate. Second, as argued by more recent economists, colonialism might have decreased the risk of investing in colonies (compared to non-colonies), and investing in colonies might have been a means for investors to diversify their investment portfolios, and thereby reduce their risks, all else being equal.

There are a number of different shortcomings in the previous literature studying this topic empirically, which motivate this study. The aim of our book is to examine the return on investment in Africa over a period of 100 years from 1869 to 1969. This period covers the colonial period for most of the countries that we will study at some depth. We use data on the total return on portfolio investments for a representative investor on the London Stock Exchange as the focal point for our quantitative estimates. Our study is based upon the equity of some 700 companies, operating in Africa and traded on the London Stock Exchange. This allows us to study the return on investment in a greater number of companies operating in Africa than have been studied in any previous research. We analyse investments in a number of colonies (and later independent countries) in Africa, although the focus will be upon a key group of British colonies—most importantly South Africa and Egypt, but also current-day Ghana, Nigeria, Zambia and Zimbabwe.

To our knowledge, all the companies that are studied in this book were established either by Europeans or by people of European descent living in the colonies. There was certainly considerable local entrepreneurship in Africa, which has also been increasingly highlighted in recent scholarship on African economic and business history. Since our focal point is the financial nexus of imperialism, this kind of entrepreneurship falls outside the scope of our study.

In Chap. 2, we outline the broad historical context of the period under study, from 1869 to 1969. This was a period of revolutionary changes in societies and cultures in many parts of the world. A new wave of European colonialism meant that most of Africa and much of Asia came under the control of one or another of the major European powers. The world also experienced dramatic growth in the international capital markets. Recent research in global financial history has emphasized the pivotal role of the City of London in this process during the latter part of the nineteenth century and the first decades of the twentieth century.

Chapter 3 describes how various theoreticians have argued around the relationship between imperialism, colonialism and capitalism. Several classical economists saw colonies as a vent for surplus capital in the United Kingdom. Capital exports could help to maintain profit rates in an economy facing decreasing marginal return on investment. This was later expanded upon by Marxists, who also believed that there were 'super-profits' to be made, particularly from what they considered the economic exploitation of the colonies. Other scholars have instead emphasized the role that special interests—rather than the average rate of return—played in the process of imperialism.

Chapter 4 describes in detail previous empirical research on the private return on investment in colonies. In this chapter, we argue that there are several flaws in this literature, for various reasons. Much of the older literature in the field has been based on limited samples of companies, in some cases potentially suffering from problems of bias. Furthermore, several studies cover comparatively short periods of time, with an emphasis on the late nineteenth century. The African continent has also been largely excluded from this research. In more recent research, investments in some particular African countries have been studied, but these studies instead suffer from a limited geographical scope.

Chapter 5 describes the data and methods employed in the present book. We mainly employ data on the total return on portfolio investments for an investor trading in equities on the London Stock Exchange for companies operating in Africa. Data on the trade in equities, as well as other variables related to such equities (dividends, shares outstanding, etc.), is therefore our key primary data. We use data for 702 companies traded on the London Stock Exchange and operating somewhere in Africa, during the period under study (1869–1969). We use data on a monthly basis and calculate a monthly market capitalization-weighted index over the total return on investment in Africa.

Chapter 6 provides an overview of the return on investment in Africa, comparing the rate of return across different regions of the continent and different sectors of the economy. We also analyse how the return on investment developed over time. In this chapter, we furthermore test the reliability of our results by comparing our estimates with the figures arrived at in previous research, where such comparisons are possible. We also put our estimates into a comparative perspective by relating them to other estimates of the return on investment elsewhere in the world, including domestically in the United Kingdom, during the same period.

In Chap. 7, we study a set of risk-related issues that pertained to investment in Africa during the period under study. We estimate the equity premium, the market risk in terms of volatility, possible diversification effects and the longevity on the stock exchange for different kinds of ventures in various parts of Africa and how they relate to the estimated return on these investments.

Chapters 8, 9, 10 and 11 are regional studies, focussing upon North, West, Central/Southern and South Africa, respectively. Both the targets of investment and the types of colonial institutions imposed were of very different character in the different regions. The aim of these chapters is therefore twofold: first, to provide a richer historical context to our data on the return on investment in each respective region. Here, we draw extensively on previous research in the field. Second, we provide empirical evidence on the return on investment in these regions, for various portfolios of investments, as well as for investments in particularly important companies. Chapter 8 deals with investments in North Africa, most importantly in Egypt. One company—the Suez Canal Company—completely dominates this regional sample and plays an important role in our chapter. Chapter 9 turns to studying investments in West Africa, most importantly in current-day Ghana and Nigeria. The investments in this region were more diversified than investments in all other regions of Africa that we study, targeting trading, shipping, banking, mining and a couple of other sectors. Chapter 10 studies investments in Central and Southern Africa (apart from South Africa), most importantly current-day Zambia and Zimbabwe, which initially were dominated by the British South Africa Company (BSAC) but where investments over time diversify into a couple of different companies, mostly in the mining sector. Chapter 11 turns to the region of current-day South Africa. In this chapter, most of the attention is given to mining companies, primarily diamond- and gold-mining companies, as they were the dominant recipients of equity investments from London during this period. Companies in our sample operating in East Africa were too few and too marginal to merit a chapter of their own in this context and will therefore only be dealt with in Chap. 6.

Chapter 12 merges our macro-oriented approach with a more micro-oriented business history approach. We use the data from our general dataset and from primary archival source material to analyse the formation of one of the leading mining houses of South Africa, the Corner House group. We specifically focus on how Corner House strategically built up inside positions and how these positions were used to manage the opportunities and threats during the 1880s and 1890s.

Chapter 13 turns to studying to what extent particular imperial policies, and colonial institutions in particular, played any role in the estimated return on investment. We study whether the process of colonization played any role in the estimated rate of return. We also examine whether the type of colony—using the common distinction between settler and non-settler colonies—mattered for the return on investment. We furthermore study what impact decolonization had upon the estimated return on investment in the colonies that achieved political independence during the period under study.

Some investors might have been less interested in specific geographical territories, be they colonies or not, and focussed more upon investing in ventures in certain sectors or commodities. Chapter 14 therefore focusses upon the mining industry in particular, as this was the most dominant target for investments in Africa. In this chapter, we estimate the return on investment in non-ferrous, non-coal-mining industries around the world, in order to put our estimates for the return on investment in African mining into a global perspective.

Chapter 15, finally, summarizes our main findings, and we provide a concluding discussion on how to interpret these findings and their implications in relation to our overall aim of studying the financial nexus in relation to imperialism, colonialism and the development of capitalism.

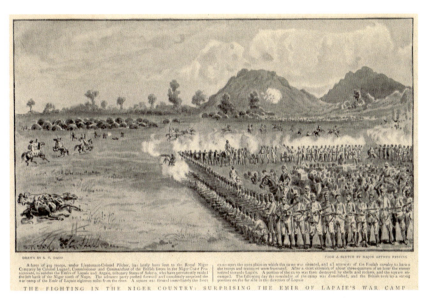

ROYAL NIGER CO. FIGHTING. British colonialism was often violent. In the picture, soldiers of the British Royal Niger Company form a square to attack the camp of the Emir of Lapaie and to subdue West African resistance to British colonial efforts. © Illustrated London News/Mary Evans Picture Library

Part I

Research Design

2

Historical Context

Classical Imperialism During the Nineteenth Century

The eighteenth century saw revolutionary changes around the world, including a population explosion and massive urbanization in many parts of the world, the industrial revolution taking off not only in the United Kingdom but also in other countries in Europe, and in the United States, a transport revolution that substantially decreased international transaction costs, increasing globalization of the world economy as a consequence of the transport revolution in combination with less protective trade barriers in many countries, increasing globalization of culture, modernization of socio-economic institutions, including the abolition of slavery and serfdom in many polities around the world, and rapid advances in the sciences (Berend 2013; Osterhammel and Camiller 2014; Baten 2016; Conrad and Osterhammel 2018).

One of the key changes during this century was also a drastic reordering of global political power. Some territories in the Americas that previously had been colonies under the old mercantilist-imperialist world order achieved independence, most importantly the United States of

America, followed by the Spanish and Portuguese colonies in South and Central America. Other territories, including large parts of Asia, and virtually the whole of Africa, instead became colonized by European powers at this time, especially during the latter half of the nineteenth century (Etemad 2007, table 7.2). During this nineteenth-century scramble for domination of as large part of the globe as possible, several of the large European nations competed.

Some scholars, the most prominent recent example is perhaps Professor Niall Ferguson, would have it that imperialism meant the introduction of the rule of law to the colonies by a relatively incorrupt government. Ferguson thereby suggests that the British Empire—which is what Ferguson is studying in particular—in essence was 'a Good Thing' (Ferguson 2003, xx). Other scholars would disagree with such a claim, both regarding British imperialism in particular and European imperialism in general. In many of their colonial possessions, the European colonial powers introduced highly exploitative institutions. The rule of law was often for the primary, not to say mere, benefit of the European settler population. Native authorities and native courts were instead common instruments of institutional segregation that amounted to little more than 'decentralized despotism' over the colonized, as Mahmood Mamdani has put it (Mamdani 1996, chaps. 2–3). In many colonies, there was dispossession of land from the indigenous populations through various legal means, such as limitations on landholding by the indigenous population and the introduction of special 'native reserves' (Alden Wily 2012; Mlambo 2014, 54–67; Laidlaw and Lester 2015; Bhandar 2018). In many cases, private property rights similar to the institutions found in the colonial powers had not developed in these societies prior to colonization, but rights to land were held in other ways, for example, communally. Such rights were, as a rule, not recognized by the colonial powers. The purpose of these land policies was simply to create territorial space for colonial settlers (Wolfe 2006). In several colonies, the European empires, furthermore, often turned a blind eye to various pre-existing coercive labour practices, including slavery-like institutions, and even (re-)introduced and/or strengthened several such coercive practices once colonial rule had been established (Lovejoy and Hogendorn 1993; Cooper 1996; Steinfeld 2001, 246–49; Hay and Craven 2004). The ultimate aim of accepting or introducing these exploitative institutions was to provide European agents with favourable conditions—cheap land and low-paid labour—if and when they wanted to establish economic activities in the colonies.

The United Kingdom—which will be in focus in the present study—became the leading European imperial power during this period. By the beginning of the twentieth century, the United Kingdom alone formally controlled one-quarter of the whole world's territory, and thereby, directly or indirectly ruled over more than one-fifth of the world's population (Etemad 2007, tables 7.1 & 7.3). It was not only the largest European empire but it also controlled some of the economically most important colonies of the time. The British Empire thus included Canada and several Caribbean islands in the Americas; Egypt, Ghana, Nigeria, Rhodesia, South Africa and several other territories in Africa; India and Malaya and several other territories in Asia; and territories such as Australia and New Zealand in the Pacific Ocean (Etemad 2007, table 10.1). The British colonies were of a number of different types. The most important distinction was between what came to be called the Dominions, on the one hand, and other types of colonial territories, on the other hand. The Dominions—most importantly Canada, Australia, New Zealand and South Africa—all had substantial European settler populations, largely as a consequence of a disease environment resembling what Europeans were used to (Acemoglu et al. 2001). Starting in the late nineteenth century, these Dominions were granted substantial self-rule in domestic matters. Other British colonies, protectorates and mandate areas, on the other hand, remained controlled by the British government, directly or indirectly (i.e. with the assistance of local elites) (Crowder 1964, 1968, 168–69, 217–35).

The European Colonization of Africa

The broad outlines of the European colonization of Africa are well known. Prior to the nineteenth century, only some limited parts of the African continent had been colonized by Europeans. This was not for lack of trying. The Portuguese, Dutch, French and British had made several attempts to colonize various parts of Africa ever since the first European explorers started to find their way south along the African coast. Two main factors prohibited European colonization of most parts of Africa for a long time. First, there existed already comparatively strong states in many parts of Africa. This was, for example, the case throughout North Africa, which was under the formal domination of the Ottoman Empire and in several parts of both East and West Africa. These states remained able to defend their respective territories from European penetration and occupation for a long period (Wilson 1977, 24–30; Scammell 1989, 46–48). Second, the tropical climate was hostile to European settlers. West Africa was famously dubbed 'the white man's grave', due to the extraordinarily high mortality rates that European settlers faced in the region from various tropical diseases. Any European army attempting to colonize the African interior would quickly be decimated without the indigenous population even having to meet the intruders in combat (Curtin 1961; Öberg and Rönnbäck 2015). European nations were therefore for a long time limited to establishing trading stations along the African coast, for example, in current-day Senegal, the Gambia, Ghana, Angola and Mozambique. These stations were generally established with the consent, and at the mercy, of local African rulers (Scammell 1989, 46–48, 71).

One exception to this pattern was the establishment of the Cape Colony, in current-day South Africa. The first foothold in this region was acquired already in the middle of the seventeenth century when the Dutch East India Company established a provisioning station there for its ships going to or coming from Asia. The provisioning station soon expanded geographically. The climate in the Cape region was considerably less hostile to European settlers than the tropical climate further north in Africa. The indigenous population in the region, the Khoisan, furthermore lived in decentralized societies and lacked a state strong enough to effectively organize resistance against European intrusion (Scammell 1989, 48–49; Thompson 2001, chap. 2; Feinstein 2005, 1–2). The Cape Colony became a British territory following the Napoleonic Wars and gradually came to expand its territory through a series of frontier wars between the British colonial forces and the local populations. As will be discussed further in this book (see in particular

Chap. 11), this expansion was in many cases directly related to the presence of economic resources.

Africa experienced drastic changes during the nineteenth century. Technological improvements, primarily in two areas, had substantial impacts upon the African continent. First, the development of tropical medicine meant a drastic reduction in the mortality rates of European settlers in Africa—most importantly, the development of quinine as a prophylactic against malaria (Headrick 1981, chap. 3; Curtin 1998). Second, the development of modern military technology introduced a major arms gap between the European colonizers and the indigenous African armies throughout most of Africa—most importantly, breech-loading guns and machine guns (Headrick 1981, chaps. 5–7).

There were many European interests at the time in favour of acquiring colonies in Africa. Geopolitical factors were important for the establishment of some colonies, as they were viewed as strategically important. Missionary and supposedly humanitarian interests were interested in getting state support, for example, for spreading their gospel to Africa. Nationalistic ideologies in Europe favoured geographical expansion as a matter of national pride. Several private agents were interested in securing protected markets for their output, in accessing raw materials for their inputs and in securing protection for their investments. Settlers in several colonies also pursued an agenda of their own, many times pushing for further colonization, for example, in order to enable the cultivation of new areas of land under European control (Platt 1968; Austen 1975; Sanderson 1975, 2–17; Wilson 1977, chap. 3; Schreuder 1980; MacKenzie 1983; Wickins 1986, 1–4; Boahen 1989, 30–31; Pakenham 1991, xvi–xvii; Chamberlain 2010; Laumann 2012, chap. 1).

Aside from the development of current-day South Africa, one of the first parts of Africa to be colonized by Europeans in the nineteenth century was Algeria, in the 1830s. Elsewhere, the process of colonizing the African interior often began from some of the European trading stations established along the African coast. The process picked up speed in the second half of the nineteenth century when the so-called Scramble for Africa took off. The scramble is generally considered to cover the period from around 1870 to the outbreak of First World War. European control over the African continent increased drastically during this period. In

1870, European control amounted to less than ten per cent of the continent (primarily in South Africa as well as some smaller enclaves along the African coast). By 1914, virtually the entire continent was colonized by Europeans (Chamberlain 2010, 3). The scramble occurred in several steps. The United Kingdom occupied Egypt in 1882. The Congo Free State was established around the same period. East Africa was colonized by Germany and the United Kingdom primarily during the second half of the 1880s, and West Africa was colonized by France and the United Kingdom primarily in the 1880s and 1890s, respectively. Other parts of southern Africa were also colonized in the 1880s and 1890s, including what became the British colony of Rhodesia. When the First World War broke out, only Ethiopia remained as an independent nation in Africa (Wilson 1977, chaps. 4–5; Schreuder 1980; Wickins 1986, 1–2; Wesseling 1996; Ferro 1997, 73–89; Iliffe 2007, chap. 9; Coquery-Vidrovitch 2009, chap. 6; Chamberlain 2010).

At the same time that European powers were scrambling for a share of the African continent, they wanted to do so at the lowest cost possible to the domestic treasury. As European military productivity had increased drastically in the nineteenth century, the 'incremental cost of territorial expansion was often relatively low' (Austin 2014, 307), at least in those parts of the world that had not kept up with nineteenth century military development. Further costs of imperialism were primarily paid for by revenues raised in the colonies (Gardner 2013; Huillery 2014). This was something that the imperial powers became more successful at over time. As Leigh Gardner has put it, regarding the British Empire, 'By the early twentieth century, the bulk of imperial expenditure was funded by revenue raised in the colonies rather than in the metropole' (Gardner 2013, 3). The pacification of local populations was often costly to an imperial power such as the United Kingdom during the first years of colonization (Gardner 2013, chap. 3). As resistance was crushed, and revenue-raising policies put in place, the net public costs of colonization to the imperial power quickly decreased to a tiny fraction of the colonies' total public finances (Gardner 2013, figs. 4.4–4.5).

The European colonization impacted the African societies in several ways—politically, economically, socially and culturally (Iliffe 2007, chaps. 9–10; Laumann 2012, chap. 2). While a transition to capitalist modes of production might have been initiated in parts of Africa already prior to colonization, some scholars argue that colonization speeded up that process (Warren and Sender 1980; Iliffe 1983; Sender and Smith 1986). Another, but to some extent related, economic consequence of the European colonization of Africa was dispossession of land. The impact differed among the colonies, to a large extent determined by the number of Europeans seeking to settle in a particular colony. Some colonies, such as several possessions in West Africa, saw few European settlers and comparatively little disruption of traditional systems of cultivation (Ochonu 2013). In settler colonies (such as Algeria in North Africa, Kenya in East Africa and current-day South Africa and Zimbabwe in southern Africa), on the other hand, the experience was very different. The infringements by the colonial authorities on permanently cultivated land could initially be limited. Land used for shifting cultivation or land dedicated to non-cultivation purposes (e.g. hunting or grazing) was, in contrast, more often declared to be unowned and 'vacant'. This allowed for European colonization primarily on some of these vacant lands first. As time went by, populations increased and consequently so did competition over increasingly scarce agricultural land. One common solution used in many of the European colonies in Africa, therefore, became to push the indigenous population onto specifically designated 'native reserves', limiting the cultivation of the rest of the land to the European settlers only (Arrighi 1970; Berry 1992; Bessant 1992; Paulin 2001, chap. 5; Feinstein 2005, chap. 2; Alden Wily 2012; Ochonu 2013).

Coerced labour became a cornerstone in many of the European colonies in Africa. Slaves were exploited in some of the early European colonies in Africa, such as in the Cape Colony (Ross 1983). When slavery eventually was abolished during the nineteenth century and early twentieth century, other means of acquiring labour had to be found. One common method, employed in several of the colonies in Africa, was corvée labour. In French and Portuguese colonies, the colonial subjects thus had to meet a yearly labour requirement for the colonial government (known as *prestation* in the French colonies and *indigenat* in the Portuguese colonies) (Cooper 1996; Fall 2002; Ash 2006). British colonial authorities instead commonly made use of, what they believed or claimed to be, customary law in order to acquire recruits. Under this system, the colonial authorities required that local chiefs provide a certain number of labourers regularly for various jobs, such as head porterage or the construction of roads and railroads. These local chiefs would, in turn, evoke customary laws supposedly giving them the right to coerce subjects into labouring for them (Cooper 1996; Ash 2006; Ochonu 2013). While these systems most generally were employed to acquire labourers for public works, colonial authorities occasionally also used them to provide private employers with low-paid labourers (e.g. Berman and Lonsdale 1980). The introduction of labour legislation, such as the Masters and Servants Acts in various British colonies in Africa, would further reduce the opportunities open for indigenous labourers (Van Der Merwe 1989; Raftopoulos 1997; Chanock 2004; Rathbone 2004; Anderson 2004).

This development was not something that the people living in Africa passively accepted. On the contrary, there was much resistance to the process of colonization. This resistance could take different forms, ranging from civil disobedience to outright rebellions and military conflicts (Ranger 1967; Crowder 1971; Crummey 1986; Crais 1992; Edgerton 1995; Coquery-Vidrovitch 2009, 172–84). By the early twentieth century, and particularly from the interwar period onwards, several of the colonies started to achieve some political influence, primarily over what was considered domestic affairs. In 1910, the Union of South Africa was established, and it was granted formal status as a Dominion within the British Empire. In practice, this meant almost complete political independence for the white minority that held political control over the colony (Thompson 2001, 148–53). Egypt was declared independent unilaterally by the United Kingdom in 1922, even though the United Kingdom kept control over certain strategic issues, including the right to maintain military troops around the Suez Canal in order to protect its interests in the canal (Vatikiotis 1991, chap. 12). In West Africa, elections were held to legislative councils in both the Gold Coast, Nigeria and Sierra Leone, although what powers these councils eventually came to wield varied between the colonies (Wickins 1986, 125). In southern Africa, the white minority regime of Southern Rhodesia was granted substantial self-rule once the administration by the British South Africa Company was abandoned in the 1920s (Mlambo 2014, 105–6).

Africa largely remained colonized until after the Second World War. Several of the North African colonies became independent in the early 1950s. In West Africa, the first country to achieve political independence was Ghana, in 1957. By the end of 1959, there were still only a handful of independent states on the African continent and the major wave of decolonization on the continent occurred during the 1960s. Virtually, all British, French and Belgian colonies on the continent had achieved political independence by 1969. Remaining Portuguese colonies achieved political independence in the 1970s. The process of decolonization unfolded differently. While some colonies managed to achieve independence peacefully, others achieved political independence after protracted wars of independence (Wickins 1986, 200–230; Iliffe 2007, 253–60; Laumann 2012, chaps. 3–4). South Africa and Southern Rhodesia (current-day Zimbabwe) are in this context somewhat of anomalies, as white minority rule continued for a long time after the countries had declared themselves to be politically independent from the British Empire (Welsh 2009, chaps. 1–2; Clark and Worger 2016, chap. 5; Mlambo 2014, chap. 7).

The City of London, Connecting the World

The second half of the nineteenth century was also a watershed in the development of international finance. Before 1850, international finance had been dominated by trade in government debt, and bonds had been the primary financial instrument of speculation. The limitations of the systems of communication furthermore inhibited the growth of a global financial market. After 1850, on the other hand, many factors changed. International finance became more geared towards the finance of private ventures. Stocks became the central vehicle for speculation during the heyday of industrialization. The introduction of new communication technologies (telegraph 1840–1870, telephone 1870–1900) conquered the problem of distance and relative political stability favoured the expansion of international finance (Michie 2001, 73–74, 2006). –The introduction of a comprehensive joint-stock legislation in the United Kingdom 1856–1862 also opened up the field for a new type of actor—the company promoter. After a slow start with a handful of active promoters, the market exploded during the 1880s and promoters became integrated in the expanding network of specialized financial services of the City of London (Chapman 1988, 32). Taken together, these trends propelled a rapid expansion of financial markets worldwide and the City of London came to be at the centre of the development of international finance. To some extent, this was paradoxical, since Germany and the United States were increasingly challenging the United Kingdom's role in terms of industrial strength. The City's growth was intimately connected with the growth of British international trade at the time and London's position, as the hub of international lending, trade and settlements was if anything strengthened after 1870 (Michie 2006, chap. 6; Cassis 2010, 83–89).

There were different kinds of investors trading on the London Stock Exchange. We know from the business history literature that the base of investors at the London Stock Exchange widened in the second half of the nineteenth century as new groups of the middle class were drawn into stocks investment. Clergymen, officers and shopkeepers more often appeared in the company's registers of shareholders than they had before (Michie 1981, pp. 149–50, see note 22). The literature is also clear that these new groups were marginal to the overall expansion of the financial sector at this time. The overrepresentation of the upper classes was massive in the 1850s and remained so in 1914. It is also clear that it was among these upper classes that a new investment culture was spreading all over Europe—the risk-appetite grew with an increased interest for international securities when bond yields were falling and stagnating agricultural prices made traditional domestic investments less attractive. This means that internationalization of the financial markets at this time was driven primarily by high-income groups in the United Kingdom, France and Germany (Van Helten 1990; Cassis 2010, 163–66).

The United Kingdom became the world's major exporter of capital during this period, particularly from the second half of the nineteenth century (Edelstein 1994, 174). During the period 1865–1914, roughly 20 per cent of all British capital exports went to the United States, and an almost as large a share went to various countries in Latin America—most importantly, Argentina and Brazil. As Table 2.1 also shows, a substantial share of British capital exports were also targeting British colonies,

Table 2.1 Accumulated capital exports from the United Kingdom, by country of destination, 1865–1914

		Capital called	
Rank	Country	Amount (£000)	Share of total (%)
1	United States	836,371	20.5
2	Canada	412,283	10.1
3	Argentina	349,243	8.6
4	Australia	339,001	8.3
5	India	317,174	7.8
6	South Africa	262,233	6.4
7	Brazil	172,742	4.2
9	New Zealand	84,495	2.1
13	Egypt	66,193	1.6
16	Rhodesia	46,232	1.1
	Fifteen other countries together	1,193,287	29.3

Source: Stone (1999, table 61)

including Canada, Australia, India, South Africa, New Zealand, Egypt and Rhodesia (see Table 2.1).

The major share of British capital exports was, by the early nineteenth century, primarily lent to governments. The turn towards also investing in private equity initially meant investments in the construction and operation of railroads around the world. Over the period 1865–1914, government lending and railroads were receiving roughly one-third each of total British capital exports. Other sectors, such as public utilities, mining and industrial investments, together received the remaining third of all British capital exports during the same period (Stone 1999, table 56). Geographical patterns of these capital exports varied by sector. Railroads were the most important sector for British investments in both North and South America. Lending to governments was important primarily in Europe and Asia (Stone 1999, table 60).

Investments in the mining sector came to play a decisive role for the development of the finance sector. This was due to several powerful and intertwined economic forces, such as increasing exploration for and findings of a number of different metals around the world, in combination with rising demand for base metals to satisfy the needs of industrialization and a concomitant rise in the demand for gold to meet the needs of increasing trade flows and the international Gold Standard (Harvey and

Press 1990; Dumett 2009b). Across all continents, and ranging from gold and diamonds to copper and oil, corporations were set up to explore and develop mineral resources (Michie 2006, 92). Between 1880 and 1913, no less than 8408 companies were registered in the United Kingdom for mining and exploration abroad. The majority of these companies were small and insignificant since they were formed on speculative basis without developing actual mining activity (Richardson and Van Helten 1982, 80, 1984, 335–36; Van Helten 1990, 161–63; Michie 2006, 11–18).

The discovery of diamonds in Kimberley in the 1860s and gold at the Witwatersrand in the 1880s turned things around. The development of these findings created a massive demand for capital. Within a few years after the first discoveries, a stock exchange opened in Johannesburg and several hundreds of companies were floated on the open market in Johannesburg (Jones 1988, 8; Lukasiewicz 2017, 724–25). The capital demands for this massive expansion of mining in South Africa could not be met by local capital supply. International capital markets therefore had to be tapped, and South Africa quickly became the focal point for international mining investments via the London Stock Exchange (Harvey and Press 1990, 106). This internationally financed expansion of the mining business fuelled several boom-and-bust cycles on the London Stock Exchange between 1870 and 1913 (Turrell and Van Helten 1986; Michie 2001, chap. 3). The pursuit for new mineral deposits was also a vital ingredient in the so-called Scramble for Africa. As earlier research has shown, the rapid expansion of the mining business hinged upon the interdependent development of the large-scale organization of resource exploitation, the workings of international finance and imperial policy (Davenport-Hines and Van Helten 1986; Dumett 2009b). After 1914, the Sturm und Drang characteristics of the earlier period faded and the mining business in Africa consolidated into large-scale organizations, in terms of production, exploration and finance (Phillips 2009, 215). British investments in foreign mining came to be particularly focussed on South Africa (and neighbouring Rhodesia), and to a lesser degree, Australia and the United States, as is shown in Fig. 2.1.

The London Stock Exchange could draw on several competitive advantages in relation to its continental and transatlantic counterparts during

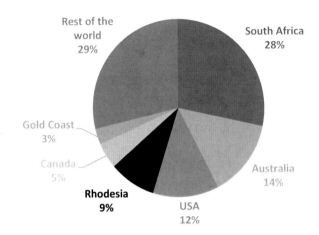

Fig. 2.1 British investments in mining by region, 1865–1914 (percentage of total capital called). Source: Stone (1999, table 57)

these expansive decades. The regulation of the London Stock Exchange was less strict than its primary competitors, such as New York, Paris, Frankfurt, Berlin and Amsterdam. This favoured the listing of companies in London and also meant that the City was more open to financial and organizational innovations. This differed markedly from competitors where Stock Exchange membership was restricted and the guarding of monopoly positions was key to the financial actors. During the period 1850–1900, the number of members at the London Stock exchange grew from 864 to 5567 (Turrell and Van Helten 1986; Michie 2001, 97–112, 2006, chap. 4). This created a productive undergrowth of financial actors in the City, specializing in different niches of the expanding financial markets—such as merchant banking, promoting, broker services, market intelligence and financing (Chapman 1985, 1988; Davenport-Hines and Van Helten 1986; Wilkins 1988).

The growth of regional exchanges all around the world during the second half of the nineteenth century further reinforced London's leading position. While New York, Paris and Amsterdam, to varying degrees, competed with London for the position as the leading centre for international finance, smaller exchanges acted more as peripheral nodes, which complemented London (Michie 2006; Newbury 2009). The formation of the stock exchange in Johannesburg in 1887, for example, stimulated the channelling of financial resources to the exploitation of diamonds and gold deposits in South Africa. Enabled by the advancement of new information and communication technology, the stocks of newly founded companies were often listed in both Johannesburg and London. This was a way to combine the much needed local knowledge about mining development with the general know-how of finance, management and engineering which could be tapped from a London connection (Chapman 1985; Harvey and Press 1990; Katzenellenbogen 1990; Lukasiewicz 2017).

Furthermore, London was able to draw on processes of path dependence in order to strengthen its leading role as an international financial centre. In part, this had to do with the powerful networks of firms and individuals which were centred in London. These networks had developed over several hundred years and extended in many directions, connecting domestic elites with financially resourceful interests both across the Atlantic and in continental Europe (Chapman 1985). The monetary arrangements of the international Gold Standard, which spread more widely from 1870 onwards, also benefitted the British pound as the undisputed currency in international trade. Furthermore, the political stability of the United Kingdom provided a fertile ground for investment.

Lastly, the growth of the British Empire and its imperial policy stimulated the growth of international finance and consolidated London's leading financial position. Capital exports to the British Empire were increasing over time in absolute terms, as is shown in Fig. 2.2. By 1914, 40 per cent of all British capital exports had thereby been exported to various colonies and dominions in the British Empire (Stone 1999, table 33–34; Twomey 2000, table 3.9).

This new pattern developed in tandem with the imperial policy. Cecil Rhodes' combination of politics and entrepreneurship in Southern Africa is a telling example, but for the Empire at large, the appointment of Joseph Chamberlain as Secretary of State for Colonies in 1895 was important. During Chamberlain's ten years in office, he developed a combination of strong nationalism with an expansionary global imperialism (Dumett 2009a, 66). A parallel development that was important in this respect was the changing British self-conception of the Empire in the late nineteenth century. Contemporary writers were distinguishing the

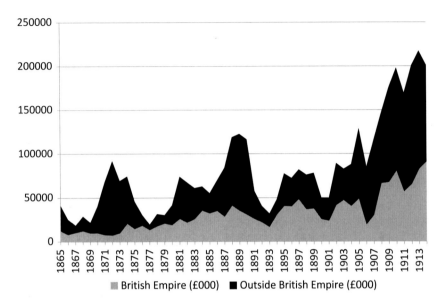

Fig. 2.2 Capital exports from the United Kingdom to the British Empire and to countries outside the British Empire, by year, 1865–1914 (£000 sterling, current prices). Source: Stone (1999, table 33–34)

settlement empire from areas of tropical colonial rule (e.g. India and tropical Africa). This issue became more pressing in the wake of the South African War 1899–1902 when the loyalty of settlers became a tangible strategic asset (Dilley 2012, 2).

Hence, the City of London managed to retain and even strengthen its role during the decades of rapid financial expansion in the late nineteenth and early twentieth centuries. This was accomplished not only because of its financial capabilities but also due to its ability to channel organizational and technical expertise to ventures around the globe. Furthermore, the City was helped by political forces, which developed the Empire by backing up private colonial ventures through investments in infrastructure and concessions to private corporations. The First World War marked a watershed in the development for the City of London, in general, and the Stock Exchange in particular. At the outset of the war, the London Stock Exchange was still the heart of a worldwide network of individual and institutional investors and borrowers. The war turned the expansion around and partially destroyed these networks. It also marked a new era of regulation and governmental control of the financial markets. The aftermaths of the war in terms of the financial distress of the interwar period shook the foundations of the global financial system which had emerged in the nineteenth century. Though London remained an important financial centre throughout the twentieth century, it was no longer the single hegemon it once had been (Michie 2006, chap. 6).

References

Acemoglu, Daron, Simon Johnson, and James A. Robinson. 2001. The Colonial Origins of Comparative Development: An Empirical Investigation. *American Economic Review* 91 (5): 1369–1401.

Alden Wily, Liz. 2012. Looking Back to See Forward: The Legal Niceties of Land Theft in Land Rushes. *The Journal of Peasant Studies* 39 (3–4): 751–775.

Anderson, David. 2004. Kenya, 1895–1939: Registration and Rough Justice. In *Masters, Servants, and Magistrates in Britain & the Empire, 1562–1955*, ed. Douglas Hay and Paul Craven, 498–528. Chapel Hill: University of North Carolina Press.

Arrighi, Giovanni. 1970. Labour Supplies in Historical Perspective: A Study of the Proletarianization of the African Peasantry in Rhodesia. *The Journal of Development Studies* 6 (3): 197–234.

Ash, Catherine B. 2006. Forced Labor in Colonial West Africa. *History Compass* 4 (3): 402–406.

Austen, Ralph A. 1975. Economic Imperialism Revisited: Late-Nineteenth-Century Europe and Africa. *The Journal of Modern History* 47 (3): 519–529.

Austin, Gareth. 2014. Capitalism and the Colonies. In *The Cambridge History of Capitalism. Volume II: The Spread of Capitalism: From 1848 to the Present*, ed. Larry Neal and Jeffrey Williamson, 301–347. Cambridge: Cambridge University Press.

Baten, Joerg. 2016. *A History of the Global Economy: From 1500 to the Present*. Cambridge: Cambridge University Press.

Berend, T. Iván. 2013. *An Economic History of Nineteenth-Century Europe: Diversity and Industrialization*. Cambridge: Cambridge University Press.

Berman, Bruce J., and John M. Lonsdale. 1980. Crises of Accumulation, Coercion and the Colonial State: The Development of the Labor Control

System in Kenya, 1919–1929. *Canadian Journal of African Studies/La Revue Canadienne Des Études Africaines* 14 (1): 55–81.

Berry, Sara. 1992. Hegemony on a Shoestring: Indirect Rule and Access to Agricultural Land. *Africa* 62 (03): 327–355.

Bessant, Leonard Leslie. 1992. Coercive Development: Land Shortage, Forced Labor, and Colonial Development in the Chiweshe Reserve, Colonial Zimbabwe, 1938–1946. *The International Journal of African Historical Studies* 25 (1): 39–65.

Bhandar, Brenna. 2018. *Colonial Lives of Property: Law, Land, and Racial Regimes of Ownership*. Durham: Duke University Press.

Boahen, A. Adu. 1989. *African Perspectives on Colonialism*. Baltimore: Johns Hopkins University Press.

Cassis, Youssef. 2010. *Capitals of Capital: The Rise and Fall of International Financial Centres, 1780–2009*. Cambridge: Cambridge University Press.

Chamberlain, M.E. 2010. *The Scramble for Africa*. 3rd ed. Harlow: Longman.

Chanock, Martin. 2004. South Africa, 1841–1924: Race, Contract, and Coercion. In *Masters, Servants, and Magistrates in Britain & the Empire, 1562–1955*, ed. Douglas Hay and Paul Craven, 338–364. Chapel Hill: University of North Carolina Press.

Chapman, Stanley. 1985. British-Based Investment Groups Before 1914. *The Economic History Review* 38 (2): 230–247.

———. 1988. Venture Capital and Financial Organisation: London and South Africa in the Nineteenth Century. In *Banking and Business in South Africa*, ed. Stuart Jones. Springer.

Clark, Nancy, and William Worger. 2016. *South Africa: The Rise and Fall of Apartheid*. 3rd ed. London: Routledge.

Conrad, Sebastian, and Jürgen Osterhammel. 2018. *An Emerging Modern World 1750–1870*. Cambridge: The Belknap Press of Harvard University Press.

Cooper, Frederick. 1996. *Decolonization and African Society: The Labor Question in French and British Africa*. Cambridge: Cambridge University Press.

Coquery-Vidrovitch, Catherine. 2009. *Africa and the Africans in the Nineteenth Century*. London: M.E. Sharpe.

Crais, Clifton C. 1992. *White Supremacy and Black Resistance in Pre-Industrial South Africa: The Making of the Colonial Order in the Eastern Cape, 1770–1865*. Cambridge: Cambridge University Press.

Crowder, Michael. 1964. Indirect Rule—French and British Style. *Africa* 34 (3): 197–205.

———. 1968. *West Africa under Colonial Rule*. London: Hutchinson.

———. 1971. *West African Resistance: The Military Response to Colonial Occupation*. London: Hutchinson.

Crummey, Donald. 1986. *Banditry, Rebellion and Social Protest in Africa*. London: Currey.

Curtin, Philip D. 1961. The White Man's Grave:' Image and Reality, 1780–1850. *The Journal of British Studies* 1 (1): 94–110.

———. 1998. *Disease and Empire: The Health of European Troops in the Conquest of Africa*. Cambridge: Cambridge University Press.

Davenport-Hines, R.P.T., and Jean-Jacques Van Helten. 1986. Edgar Vincent, Viscount D'Abernon, and the Eastern Investment Company in London, Constantinople and Johannesburg. *Business History* 28 (1): 35–61.

Dilley, Andrew Richard. 2012. *Finance, Politics, and Imperialism: Australia, Canada, and the City of London, c.1896–1914*. Basingstoke: Palgrave Macmillan.

Dumett, Raymond. 2009a. Edwin Cade and Frederick Gordon: British Imperialism and the Foundations of the Ashanti Goldfields Corporation, West Africa. In *Mining Tycoons in the Age of Empire, 1870–1945: Entrepreneurship, High Finance, Politics and Territorial Expansion*, ed. Raymond Dumett, 63–84. Farnham: Ashgate.

———. 2009b. *Mining Tycoons in the Age of Empire, 1870–1945: Entrepreneurship, High Finance, Politics and Territorial Expansion*. Farnham: Ashgate.

Edelstein, Michael. 1994. Foreign Investment and Accumulation, 1860–1914. In *The Economic History of Britain since 1700. Volume 2: 1860–1939*, ed. Roderick Floud and Donald McCloskey, 2nd ed., 173–196. Cambridge: Cambridge University Press.

Edgerton, Robert. 1995. *The Fall of the Asante Empire: The Hundred-Year War for Africa's Gold Coast*. New York: The Free Press.

Etemad, Bouda. 2007. *Possessing the World: Taking the Measurements of Colonisation from the Eighteenth to the Twentieth Century*. New York: Berghahn Books.

Fall, Babacar. 2002. *Social History in French West Africa: Forced Labor, Labor Market, Women and Politics*. Amsterdam: South-South Exchange Programme for Research on the History of Development.

Feinstein, Charles. 2005. *An Economic History of South Africa: Conquest, Discrimination and Development*. Cambridge: Cambridge University Press.

Ferguson, Niall. 2003. *Empire: The Rise and Demise of the British World Order and the Lessons for Global Power*. New York: Basic Books.

Ferro, Marc. 1997. *Colonization - A Global History.* Quebec: World Heritage Press.
Gardner, Leigh. 2013. *Taxing Colonial Africa: The Political Economy of British Imperialism.* Oxford: Oxford University Press.
Harvey, Charles, and Jon Press. 1990. The City and International Mining, 1870–1914. *Business History* 32 (3): 98–119.
Hay, Douglas, and Paul Craven. 2004. *Masters, Servants, and Magistrates in Britain and the Empire, 1562–1955. Studies in Legal History.* Chapel Hill: University of North Carolina Press.
Headrick, Daniel R. 1981. *The Tools of Empire: Technology and European Imperialism in the Nineteenth Century.* New York: Oxford University Press.
Huillery, Elise. 2014. The Black Man's Burden: The Cost of Colonization of French West Africa. *The Journal of Economic History* 74 (1): 1–38.
Iliffe, John. 1983. *The Emergence of African Capitalism.* London: Macmillan.
———. 2007. *Africans: The History of a Continent.* New ed. Cambridge: Cambridge University Press.
Jones, Stuart. 1988. *Banking and Business in South Africa.* New York: Palgrave Macmillan.
Katzenellenbogen, Simon. 1990. Southern African Mining Interests in Australia Before 1939. *Business History* 32 (3): 120–132.
Laidlaw, Zoë, and Alan Lester. 2015. *Indigenous Communities and Settler Colonialism: Land Holding, Loss and Survival in an Interconnected World.* Basingstoke: Palgrave Macmillan.
Laumann, Dennis. 2012. *African World Histories: Colonial Africa, 1884–1994.* New York: Oxford University Press.
Lovejoy, Paul E., and Jan S. Hogendorn. 1993. *Slow Death for Slavery: The Course of Abolition in Northern Nigeria 1897–1936.* Cambridge: Cambridge University Press.
Lukasiewicz, Mariusz. 2017. From Diamonds to Gold: The Making of the Johannesburg Stock Exchange, 1880–1890. *Journal of Southern African Studies* 43 (4): 715–732.
MacKenzie, John M. 1983. *The Partition of Africa 1880–1900 and European Imperialism in the Nineteenth Century.* London: Methuen.
Mamdani, Mahmood. 1996. *Citizen and Subject: Contemporary Africa and the Legacy of Late Colonialism.* Princeton, NJ: Princeton University Press.
Michie, Ranald C. 1981. Options, Concession, Syndicates, and the Provision of Venture Capital, 1880–1913. *Business History* 23 (2): 147–164.
———. 2001. *The London Stock Exchange: A History.* Oxford: Oxford University Press.

———. 2006. *The Global Securities Market a History*. Oxford: Oxford University Press.

Mlambo, A.S. 2014. *A History of Zimbabwe*. New York, NY: Cambridge University Press.

Newbury, Cecil. 2009. Cecil Rhodes, De Beers and Mining Finance in South Africa: The Business of Entrepreneurship and Imperialism. In *Mining Tycoons in the Age of Empire, 1870–1945: Entrepreneurship, High Finance, Politics and Territorial Expansion*, ed. Raymond Dumett, 85–108. Farnham: Ashgate.

Öberg, Stefan, and Klas Rönnbäck. 2015. *The White Man's Grave Revisited - Settler Mortality Rates in Pre-Colonial West Africa*. Working Paper, Gothenburg.

Ochonu, Moses. 2013. African Colonial Economies: Land, Labor, and Livelihoods. *History Compass* 11 (2): 91–103.

Osterhammel, Jürgen, and Patrick Camiller. 2014. *The Transformation of the World: A Global History of the Nineteenth Century*. Princeton: Princeton University Press.

Pakenham, Thomas. 1991. *The Scramble for Africa 1876–1912*. London: Weidenfeld and Nicolson.

Paulin, Christopher. 2001. *White Men's Dreams, Black Men's Blood: African Labor and British Expansionism in Southern Africa, 1877–1895*. Trenton: Africa World Press, Inc.

Phillips, John. 2009. Alfred Chester Beatty: Mining Engineer, Financier, and Entrepreneur, 1898–1950. In *Mining Tycoons in the Age of Empire, 1870–1945: Entrepreneurship, High Finance, Politics and Territorial Expansion*, ed. Raymond Dumett, 215–238. Farnham: Ashgate.

Platt, D.C.M. 1968. *Finance, Trade, and Politics in British Foreign Policy 1815–1914*. Oxford: Clarendon press.

Raftopoulos, Brian. 1997. The Labour Movement in Zimbabwe: 1945–1965. In *Keep on Knocking: A History of the Labour Movement in Zimbabwe 1900–97*, ed. Brian Raftopoulos and Ian Phimister, 55–90. Harare: Baobab Books.

Ranger, T.O. 1967. *Revolt in Southern Rhodesia 1896–7: A Study in African Resistance*. London: Heinemann.

Rathbone, Richard. 2004. West Africa, 1874–1948: Employment Legislation in a Nonsettler Peasant Economy. In *Masters, Servants, and Magistrates in Britain & the Empire, 1562–1955*, ed. Douglas Hay and Paul Craven, 481–497. Chapel Hill: University of North Carolina Press.

Richardson, Peter, and Jean-Jacques Van Helten. 1982. Labour in the South African Gold Mining Industry, 1886–1914. In *Industrialisation and Social Change in South Africa: African Class Formation, Culture, and Consciousness,*

1870–1930, ed. Shula Marks and Richard Rathbone, 77–98. New York: Longman.
———. 1984. The Development of the South African Gold-Mining Industry, 1895–1918. *The Economic History Review* 37 (3): 319–340.
Ross, Robert. 1983. *Cape of Torments: Slavery and Resistance in South Africa*. London: Routledge & Kegan Paul.
Sanderson, G.N. 1975. The European Partition of Africa: Coincidence or Conjuncture? In *European Imperialism and the Partition of Africa*, ed. E.F. Penrose, 1–54. London: Frank Cass.
Scammell, Geoffrey Vaughan. 1989. *The First Imperial Age: European Overseas Expansion c. 1400–1715*. London: Unwin Hyman.
Schreuder, D.M. 1980. *The Scramble for Southern Africa, 1877–1895: The Politics of Partition Reappraised*. Cambridge: Cambridge University Press.
Sender, John, and Sheila Smith. 1986. *The Development of Capitalism in Africa*. London: Methuen.
Steinfeld, Robert J. 2001. *Coercion, Contract, and Free Labor in the Nineteenth Century*. Cambridge: Cambridge University Press.
Stone, Irving. 1999. *The Global Export of Capital from Great Britain, 1865–1914: A Statistical Survey*. New York: Macmillan.
Thompson, Leonard. 2001. *A History of South Africa*. 3rd ed. New Haven: Yale University Press.
Turrell, Robert Vicat, and Jean-Jacques Van Helten. 1986. The Rothschilds, the Exploration Company and Mining Finance. *Business History* 28 (2): 181–205.
Twomey, Michael J. 2000. *A Century of Foreign Investment in the Third World*. London: Routledge.
Van Der Merwe, Derek. 1989. Not Slavery but a Gentle Stimulus: Labour-Inducing Legislation in the South African Republic. *Journal of South African Law*: 353–369.
Van Helten, Jean-Jacques. 1990. Mining, Share Manias and Speculation: British Investment in Overseas Mining, 1880–1913. In *Capitalism in a Mature Economy: Financial Institutions, Capital Exports and British Industry, 1870–1939*, ed. Jean-Jacques Van Helten and Youssef Cassis, 159–185. Aldershot: Edward Elgar.
Vatikiotis, P.J. 1991. *The History of Modern Egypt from Muhammad Ali to Mubarak*. 4th ed. London: Weidenfeld and Nicolson.
Warren, Bill, and John Sender. 1980. *Imperialism: Pioneer of Capitalism*. London: NLB.
Welsh, David. 2009. *The Rise and Fall of Apartheid*. Johannesburg: Jonathan Ball Publishers.

Wesseling, Hendrik Lodewijk. 1996. *Divide and Rule: The Partition of Africa, 1880–1914*. Westport, CT: Praeger.
Wickins, Peter. 1986. *Africa 1880–1980: An Economic History*. Cape Town: Oxford University Press.
Wilkins, Mira. 1988. The Free-Standing Company, 1870–1914: An Important Type of British Foreign Direct Investment. *The Economic History Review* 41 (2): 259–282.
Wilson, Henry. 1977. *The Imperial Experience in Sub-Saharan Africa since 1870*. Minneapolis: University of Minnesota Press.
Wolfe, Patrick. 2006. Settler Colonialism and the Elimination of the Native. *Journal of Genocide Research* 8 (4): 387–409.

3

Capital and Colonialism in Theory

Capital and Colonies in Classic Economic Theory

Several classical economists criticized the possession of colonies. Adam Smith, for example, argued that colonies were a net burden on the colonial power. Though colonial trade could lead to expanding markets for the colonial power, monopolies or preferential trade policies would reduce competition and lead to economic inefficiencies. These policies could at the same time increase the profit rate of investing in the colonies, which would lead capital being exported to the colonies rather than being put to productive use domestically. At the same time, Smith argued, there were large costs associated with controlling a colony, so in total, the possession of colonies would be costly to the colonial power (Winch 1965, 9–12).

Later, economists would come to debate the role that capital exports played for the British economy. Economists such as Edward Gibbon Wakefield, Jeremy Bentham and John Stuart Mill argued that capital exports could be explained by falling rates of return domestically, which occurred due to a shortage of profitable investment opportunities domestically (Winch 1965, 33, 77–80, 140–41). A fundamental assumption in the reasoning is that there are diminishing marginal returns to capital on a given market. Assuming that investors have full information about the investment opportunities available on the market, the rational investor would initially target the most profitable investment opportunities. As capital requirements for the most profitable ventures eventually are met, any further savings would have to be invested in less profitable investment opportunities.

Whenever larger parts of the world were integrated into a world capitalist system, during the nineteenth century, new investment opportunities opened up. To make economic use of all the new geographical territories opened up by European penetration, substantial capital investments were required. These investment opportunities bore the promise of high returns. Compared to the investment opportunities available domestically in Europe, and in the United Kingdom in particular, it therefore seemed rational for investors to invest capital in these new territories around the world, that is, to export capital from the United Kingdom. Wakefield and the other economists therefore saw capital exports as a relief for an economy suffering from a glut of capital, and therefore as something positive for the United Kingdom (Winch 1965, 78). This latter claim would cause disagreement with other classical economists. The most important proponent of an alternative interpretation was David Ricardo. Ricardo admitted that private investors might gain higher returns from foreign than from domestic investments. Any resulting capital exports would, in Ricardo's view, be detrimental to the British national economy, since the country then would be able to accumulate less capital and that the United Kingdom had ample opportunities for further capital investments (Winch 1965, 74–76).

Many modern-day scholars would agree with the basic ideas of the classical economists. Kevin O'Rourke and Jeffrey Williamson have, for example, argued that the most obvious explanation to the large capital exports from the United Kingdom was that investment demand was high due to 'capital requirements associated with frontier expansion' (O'Rourke and Williamson 1999, 229; see also Clemens and Williamson 2004). In time, as the frontiers closed and it became impossible to open up new areas to investment, the rate of return ought to converge globally.

Marxism, Capitalism and Imperialism

Marxists have a different interpretation of British capital exports. Karl Marx argued that colonialism provided a crucial impulse to the development of modern capitalism. In some of his early writings, he primarily stressed the importance of an expansion of markets for the output of capitalist industries (e.g. Marx 1969, 36). In later writings on colonial India, Marx arrived at a similar conclusion as Adam Smith once had: that while there might be several private parties that might gain economically from the colony of India, there were large military costs for the British East India Company—and thereby potentially for the British state—for controlling it (Marx 1969, 235–39). A substantial share of the debts accumulated due to these costs were eventually transformed into a debt of the Indian colony, rather than of the British state. Marx noted this and wrote about a 'bleeding process' whereby the Indian colony had been forced to pay large economic rents to the British colonial power (Marx 1969, 266–69, 471).

Other radical thinkers at that time also believed that there were various economic forces at play pushing the United Kingdom towards an imperialist policy, most importantly, interests aiming to achieve protection for British trade and industry (Hobson 1988; Porter 1968; Cain 2002). The fact that the two processes of growing British capital exports and the renewed expansion of the British Empire occurred more or less simultaneously has, to some theorists, suggested that there must be a causal link between the two. A highly influential work on this topic was published in 1902, John Hobson's book *Imperialism: A Study*. Hobson proposed a theory where imperialism was driven or directed not by trade interests but by financial interests. In this theory, income inequality leads to low purchasing power for the poorer classes in society, whereas the richer classes save a substantial part of their income. Capital saved at home in the United Kingdom had a hard time finding profitable opportunities to invest in domestically due to a combination of 'oversaving' and 'underconsumption'. Capital was, therefore, Hobson argued, exported to and invested in economically undeveloped parts of the world. The investors would then have strong incentives to try to protect their investments, and would therefore attempt to sway the British government towards imperialist policies. It would, however, only be a minority of capitalists that would stand to benefit from investment in colonies, and hence from these imperial policies (Hobson 1988; Etherington 1984, chap. 4; Cain 2002; Porter 1968, chap. 7).

Hobson's theories came to have a great influence on Marxist theories on imperialism. Here, a key idea taken from Marx was that there is a general tendency in capitalist systems for the profit rate to fall over time. This would in the long run lead to economic crises for the capitalist system. Hobson's theories were often combined with the Austrian Marxist Rudolph Hilferding's theory that finance capital increasingly sought state intervention on behalf of the wealth-owning classes (Fieldhouse 1973, chap. 3; Etherington 1984, chap. 7; Eckstein 1991; Noonan 2017, chap. 2). So far, this argument has been a variation on the argument by several classical economists that capital exports were rational, given diminishing marginal return on investment in a given economy and that capital exports could work opposite of any such tendency. Several Marxists came to extend the argument one step further, arguing that capital exports also would benefit from what came to be called 'super-profits' that supposedly were possible to attain within the confines of an exploitative imperial system. The key idea was that the various coercive institutions established in the colonies could drive down the costs of production and increase the rate of surplus value expropriated, and thereby increase the profit rates (Barratt Brown 1963, 96–97; Etherington 1984, chap. 7; Noonan 2017, chap. 2). The transfer of such super-profits has since continued to be popular in several Marxist theories of imperialism and underdevelopment of the so-called periphery. Some Marxists writers primarily emphasized how the export of capital could be a method of 'pumping surplus out of underdeveloped areas' (Baran and Sweezy 1966, 105; see also Noonan 2017, chap. 3). Walter Rodney, writing about the underdevelopment of Africa, on a similar note claimed that the return on colonial investments consistently was higher than the return on investment, for example, in Europe, and that this was attributable to colonial exploitation of African workers (Rodney 1972, 149, 152, 162).

Several contemporary Marxists still stress this issue. David Harvey, for example, maintains that capital exports were of crucial importance for imperialist politics in the nineteenth century. Starting around the 1870s, Harvey argues, surplus capital was exported from Europe in the form of speculative investments. These investments were, according to Harvey, clearly one factor driving imperialism: 'The need to protect these foreign ventures and even to regulate their excesses put pressure on states to respond to this expansionary capitalistic logic' (Harvey 2003, 43; see also Noonan 2017, 227–35). The imperialist policies developed in response to these pressures, Harvey further argues, meant 'the extraction of tribute from the colonies in some of the most oppressive and violently exploitative forms of imperialism ever invented' (Harvey 2003, 45). Capital exports were, in Harvey's theoretical framework, a 'spatial fix' to the tendency of the profit rate to fall in capitalistic societies (Harvey 2003, 87–88). Samir Amin has likewise emphasized the importance of what he calls 'imperialist rent' extracted from dominated peripheries of the world, for an analysis of the global accumulation of capital (Amin 2010, chap. 4, 2018, 110–11, 223–25; see also Noonan 2017, chap. 6).

The Hobsonian-Marxist theory of imperialism driven by financial interests has been heavily criticized by other scholars. Joseph Schumpeter famously saw imperialism as a legacy of precapitalist societies surviving within capitalist societies but in no way supporting the development of modern capitalism (Schumpeter 1951). Two other arguments have later turned out to be the most common ones: first, that most of the capital exported from Europe did not find its way to any exploited colonies in Asia or Africa. Instead, the largest recipients of overseas investment were independent nations such as the United States, or at most semi-independent dominions of white settlements like Canada and Australia. Second, the capital exported rarely earned any super-profits but faced returns more or less on par with those found, for example, in Europe (Fieldhouse 1961; Barratt Brown 1963, 87; Gann and Duignan 1968; Gann 1969; Hynes 1979; Warren and Sender 1980, 57–70; Davis and Huttenback 1982, 1985, 1986, 1988; O'Brien 1988; Davis 1999; Michie 2004). Several non-Marxist scholars would therefore arrive at the conclusion that there must have been other non-economic factors that were far more important in explaining imperialism than what the Hobsonian-Marxist theory allowed for (Fieldhouse 1961, 1973; Hyam 2010; see also Hillbom and Green 2010, 114–19).

Imperialism and Special Interests

Some scholars have suggested a return to economic interpretations of imperialism, but with deviating interpretations from previous theories. A popular theory for a long period was Ronald Robinson and John Gallagher's theory of 'informal empire', where they argued that the United Kingdom often preferred to abstain from formal colonialism, because of all the costs associated with actually colonizing another nation, but resorted to this if cheaper, informal methods of controlling or influencing another nation failed (Robinson and Gallagher 1968; see also Platt 1968).

Another theory has been suggested by Lance Davis and Robert Huttenback. They argue that to fully understand the drivers of imperialism, we must analyse both the benefits and costs of imperialism to the imperial power. On the one hand, there might be some gains to be made for the imperial country, for example, in the form of access to cheaper inputs or high return on some investments (Davis and Huttenback 1988, chap. 3). On the other hand, there were also substantial costs in the form of military expenditures or investment costs. These costs could many times dwarf any private economic gains from the Empire. On net, they therefore argue, imperialism was not very profitable for the imperial powers (Davis and Huttenback 1988, chaps. 4–6). Their argument is basically one of externalities, since the benefits and the costs were not enjoyed and borne by the same agents. Studying the British Empire, in particular, they found that most of the private investments in the British Empire were made by the British gentry and business elites, rather than by members of the middle or lower classes. These elite groups were hence the main beneficiaries from Empire (Davis and Huttenback 1988, chap. 7). A large share of the costs of Empire was, according to Davis and Huttenback, borne by the middle classes of the United Kingdom through heavy taxation (Davis and Huttenback 1988, chap. 8). Hence, the driving force behind imperial policies in Davis and Huttenback's interpretation was therefore special interests of various sorts. These special interests could be individual firms or trade associations, such as the Chambers of Commerce, lobbying on Parliament and the state bureaucracy (Davis and Huttenback 1988, chap. 9). Imperialism can therefore 'best be viewed as a mechanism for transferring income from the middle to the upper classes' (Davis and Huttenback 1988, 279).

Yet another, but related, theory has been suggested by P.J. Cain and A.G. Hopkins. They coined the term 'gentlemanly capitalism' for the nexus of the gentility, the financial interests and the British imperialist state (Cain and Hopkins 1980, 1987, 2001). Agricultural and financial interests all belonged to the group of British gentlemen. These gentlemen held considerable social prestige but also shared common, 'gentlemanly' ideals. The gentleman was supposed to earn an income from economic rents on land or from financial investments. As capital accumulated in British society over time, these gentlemanly capitalists constantly had to find new, culturally acceptable investment opportunities. Investing in British manufacturing industry would simply not do since that essentially was incompatible with the gentlemanly values. One solution was therefore to find investment opportunities suitable for a gentleman abroad (Cain and Hopkins 1986, 505, 1987, 1, 2001, 38–39). These gentlemen did, furthermore, have a considerable influence over British politics, including the Houses of Parliament as well as the Foreign and Colonial Offices, and commonly used this influence to shape imperial politics in their own favour, in order to safeguard any investments made (Cain and Hopkins 1980, 466, 469, 1986, 507, 1987, 4–5, 12, 2001, 43, 120–22, 422). Cain and Hopkins' theory has become popular among some scholars (see overview in Webster 2006; see also Darwin 2009) but has also received substantial critique from others. One critique, often forwarded by historians, has been that the theory is monocausal in that it reduces the whole issue of imperialism to one driving factor, whereas other interests also are influential (Fieldhouse 1994; Cannadine 1995; Kubicek 1999; Thompson 2000; Phimister 2002; see also response by Cain and Hopkins 2002; Hyam 2010). Another line of argumentation has it that the theory is too Anglo-centric; it might fit with the British experience but can hardly suffice as an explanation of imperialism in general (Porter 1990; Austin 2014).

One consequence of Cain and Hopkins' theory is that it was not necessarily relevant whether the rate of return on investing overseas was higher than the return on domestic investments (in manufacturing) or not; the cultural norms of these 'gentlemanly capitalists' supposedly prohibited them from investing in manufacturing, more or less, no matter how high the return on investment in domestic manufacturing was (Cain and Hopkins 2001, 57). The theory could be considered as a development of, or an alternative to, a long-running scholarly debate over whether there were imperfections, or irrational or unenlightened agents, operating in the British capital market. If that was the case, British capital might have been channelled abroad (rather than invested in domestic industries) to a greater extent than would have been rational in a perfectly functioning market (McCloskey 1970; Clemens and Williamson 2004; Parent and Rault 2004; Goetzmann and Ukhov 2006; Rota and Schettino 2011).

Whether one focusses on 'upper class' interests in general, or on 'gentlemanly capitalist' interests in particular, these theories arrive at similar conclusions: imperialism was not economically beneficial for the imperial power as a whole, but only for certain groups in the imperial powers (see also O'Brien 1988).

Risk, Return and the Empire Effect

The concept of risk and its relationship to expected return is central to finance. On a general level, the two concepts are always connected—it is difficult to envisage financial actors at any point in history that would not expect higher return in order to take higher risk. It was not until the 1950s and 1960s that this relationship was more thoroughly theorized. Harry Markowitz analysed investors' selection process and concluded that the risk could be defined as the variability of return (Markowitz 1959). If an investor can choose between two financial instruments with the same expected total return in the end, the rational investor would choose the instrument with the lowest expected variability of return. Hence, risk could be interpreted as the standard deviation of the return, that is, volatility. Since volatility can only be measured historically but has effects on investor behaviour in the present (based on expectations of the future), the idea of implied volatility became important. Hence, financial actors started to assemble figures of historical volatility of a specified financial instrument and used this data as a proxy for future volatility.

William Sharpe developed this theory further by mapping out the consequences of Markowitz's reasoning for the whole market (Sharpe 1970). Sharpe thereby laid the foundation for modern portfolio theory. A basic element of this theory is the power of diversification. No investor can escape the fact that financial markets fluctuate. By identifying assets whose price-movements are not correlated over time, investors can construct portfolios that (theoretically) optimize the risk/return-relationship. Hence, assets that systematically move in tandem carry the same kind of risk, while assets whose price-movements are not correlated over time can be used to decrease the overall volatility of a portfolio (Dimson et al. 2002, 54–60; MacKenzie 2006, 45–57).

For centuries, firms have invested in risky foreign environments, but the scale of international investments soared during the second half of the nineteenth century. Rapid technological development and the rise of globally interconnected financial markets set the scene not only for new profit opportunities but also for new types of risks (Wilkins 1988, 259; Michie 2006, 84–86). Based on the experience of foreign investments from Europe and the United States since the 1870s, Casson and Lopez identified six different types of risks in overseas investment, namely, unfamiliarity, political, social, business, financial, climatic and geological risk (Casson and da Silva Lopes 2013). Events like mining disasters, expropriations, strikes, patent infringements, capital losses due to bankruptcies and diseases are all examples of such risks, which threatened the stock market valuation of the companies in our sample.

Some of these risks were influenced by imperialism and colonialism. Since colonialism meant that the imperial power took over control from the local government, several risks associated with foreign investments could be reduced. This was not the least important when foreign investors were investing in foreign government bonds. Colonial institutions could reduce the risk of a government debt by default (Frieden 1994; Ferguson 2003, 305–6; Obstfeld and Taylor 2003, 2004, chap. 6; Flandreau and Zumer 2004; Ferguson and Schularick 2006; Accominotti et al. 2010; Accominotti et al. 2011). This 'Empire Effect', as it has been called, was not necessarily limited to government bonds. Colonial institutions and/or imperial policies could also impact other risks of investment, for example, by securing private property rights and by reducing the risk of nationalization of privately held assets. As Rajan Menon and John Oneal put it for the case of India, 'It was the security of investments in India which attracted investors and not the promise of exceptional returns' (Menon and Oneal 1986, 175). The implication would be that the required risk premium, and hence the total return on investment, that would be required in order to attract investors would be lower in the colonies than in comparable non-colonies. A logical consequence would also be that decolonization could be seen as a threat to investors' interests, as it could increase such country risks.

Asymmetric Flows of Information

One final theoretical perspective that will be dealt with in this book concerns information asymmetries. Eugene Fama's and George Akerlof's contributions on how to perceive efficiency in the face of asymmetric information were crucial for the development of the new financial theory of the 1960s and 1970s (Malkiel and Fama 1970; Akerlof 1970). The idea of efficient markets rests on the premise that prices fully reflect available information and therefore it would not be possible to make any systematic profits for financial speculators. In contrast to this idea of efficient markets, realized by actors having full access to information, we know that different agents on the financial markets have access to information of different quantity and quality. Fama showed how a distinction of three forms of market efficiency (weak/semi-strong/strong) could be related to market participants' access to different kind of information—such as prices, annual reports and corporate insiders (MacKenzie 2006, 65–67).

This line of thought within financial theory has proven to be fruitful for the study of financial history since the access and the distribution of information has always been the very essence of finance. Hence, asymmetric information has been an important theme in the historical studies of financial markets. For example, the role of inside investors and unscrupulous company-mongers has been a recurrent theme in descriptions of the City of London in the late nineteenth century (Davenport-Hines and Van Helten 1986, 45–47; Wilkins 1988, 266–67; Michie 2001, chap. 3).

The asymmetries originated from the fact that all steps of the value creation process were clouded in uncertainties and time-lags. Mining was, for example, inherently uncertain, due to the simple fact that it was difficult to assess the value of a mine due to the characteristics of the mineral deposits and due to technological development (which overnight could turn a seemingly hopeless deposit into a lucrative profit opportunity, or vice versa). This made mining stocks prone to speculation. Political processes also added uncertainties, which were met with lobbying and other strategies from financial actors in order to get access to and influence the flow of information. Asymmetries were further aggravated by the fact that information travelled relatively slowly from the places of operation around the world to the London Stock Exchange in the late nineteenth century. In situations with substantial time-lags, informational asymmetries emerged and depending on who managed to bring the information to the market first could use this information to speculate. From the 1850s onwards, a network of oceanic telegraph cables was successively being built around the world (Müller 2016). This radically changed the information flows for both financial actors and the international business press.

Conclusion

The overarching issue of the level of the return on investment in colonies will first be dealt with in Chap. 6, as well as in the geographical studies in Chaps. 8, 9, 10 and 11. Particular aspects related to imperial policies and colonial institutions will also be dealt with in Chaps. 13 and 14. The issue of risk will be dealt with in Chap. 7 on a more general level, and in Chap. 13 when it comes to some specific risks related to colonial policies and decolonization. We will touch upon the issue of asymmetrical information in Chaps. 8, 9, 10 and 11, but they will be specifically dealt with in the case study pursued in Chap. 12.

References

Accominotti, Olivier, Marc Flandreau, Riad Rezzik, and Frédéric Zumer. 2010. Black Man's Burden, White Man's Welfare: Control, Devolution and Development in the British Empire, 1880–1914. *European Review of Economic History* 14 (1): 47–70.

Accominotti, Olivier, Marc Flandreau, and Riad Rezzik. 2011. The Spread of Empire: Clio and the Measurement of Colonial Borrowing Costs. *The Economic History Review* 64 (2): 385–407.

Akerlof, George A. 1970. The Market for 'Lemons': Quality Uncertainty and the Market Mechanism. *The Quarterly Journal of Economics* 84 (3): 488–500.

Amin, Samir. 2010. *The Law of Worldwide Value*. New York: Monthly Review Press.

———. 2018. *Modern Imperialism, Monopoly Finance Capital, and Marx's Law of Value*. New York: Monthly Review Press.

Austin, Gareth. 2014. Capitalism and the Colonies. In *The Cambridge History of Capitalism. Volume II: The Spread of Capitalism: From 1848 to the Present*, ed. Larry Neal and Jeffrey Williamson, 301–347. Cambridge: Cambridge University Press.

Baran, Paul A., and Paul M. Sweezy. 1966. *Monopoly Capital: An Essay on the American Economic and Social Order*. New York: Monthly Review Press.

Barratt Brown, Michael. 1963. *After Imperialism*. London: Heinemann.

Cain, Peter J. 2002. *Hobson and Imperialism: Radicalism, New Liberalism, and Finance 1887–1938*. Oxford: Oxford University Press.

Cain, Peter J., and Anthony G. Hopkins. 1980. The Political Economy of British Expansion Overseas, 1750–1914. *The Economic History Review* 33 (4): 463–490.

———. 1986. Gentlemanly Capitalism and British Expansion Overseas I. The Old Colonial System, 1688–1850. *The Economic History Review* 39 (4): 501–525.

———. 1987. Gentlemanly Capitalism and British Expansion Overseas II: New Imperialism, 1850–1945. *The Economic History Review* 40 (1): 1–26.

———. 2001. *British Imperialism, 1688–2000*. Harlow: Longman.

———. 2002. The Peculiarities of British Capitalism: Imperialism and World Development. In *Gentlemanly Capitalism, Imperialism and Global History*, ed. Shigeru Akita, 207–255. New York: Springer. http://link.springer.com/chapter/10.1057/9781403919403_11.

Cannadine, David. 1995. The Empire Strikes Back. *Past & Present* 147: 180–194.

Casson, Mark, and Teresa da Silva Lopes. 2013. Foreign Direct Investment in High-Risk Environments: An Historical Perspective. *Business History* 55 (3): 375–404.

Clemens, Michael A., and Jeffrey G. Williamson. 2004. Wealth Bias in the First Global Capital Market Boom, 1870–1913. *Economic Journal* 114 (495): 304–337.

Darwin, John. 2009. *The Empire Project: The Rise and Fall of the British World-System, 1830–1970*. Cambridge: Cambridge University Press.

Davenport-Hines, R.P.T., and Jean-Jacques Van Helten. 1986. Edgar Vincent, Viscount D'Abernon, and the Eastern Investment Company in London, Constantinople and Johannesburg. *Business History* 28 (1): 35–61.

Davis, Lance. 1999. The Late Nineteenth-Century British Imperialist: Specification, Quantification and Controlled Conjectures. In *Gentlemanly Capitalism and British Imperialism: The New Debate on Empire*, ed. Raymond Dumett, 82–112. London: Longman.

Davis, Lance, and Robert Huttenback. 1982. The Political Economy of British Imperialism: Measures of Benefits and Support. *The Journal of Economic History* 42 (01): 119–130.

———. 1985. The Export of British Finance, 1865–1914. *The Journal of Imperial and Commonwealth History* 13 (3): 28–76.

———. 1986. *Mammon and the Pursuit of Empire: The Political Economy of British Imperialism, 1860–1912*. Cambridge: Cambridge University Press.

———. 1988. *Mammon and the Pursuit of Empire: The Economics of British Imperialism*. Abridged ed. Cambridge: Cambridge University Press.

Dimson, Elroy, Paul Marsh, and Mike Staunton. 2002. *Triumph of the Optimists: 101 Years of Global Investment Returns*. Princeton, NJ: Princeton University Press.

Eckstein, Arthur M. 1991. Is There a 'Hobson-Lenin Is' on Late Nineteenth-Century Colonial Expansion? *The Economic History Review* 44 (2): 297–318.

Etherington, Norman. 1984. *Theories of Imperialism: War, Conquest and Capital*. London: Croom Helm.

Ferguson, Niall. 2003. *Empire: The Rise and Demise of the British World Order and the Lessons for Global Power*. New York: Basic Books.

Ferguson, Niall, and Moritz Schularick. 2006. The Empire Effect: The Determinants of Country Risk in the First Age of Globalization, 1880–1913. *The Journal of Economic History* 66 (2): 283–312.

Fieldhouse, D.K. 1961. Imperialism': An Historiographical Revision. *The Economic History Review* 14 (2): 187–209.

———. 1973. *Economics and Empire 1830–1914*, World Economic History. London: Weidenfeld & Nicolson.

———. 1994. Gentlemen, Capitalists, and the British Empire. *The Journal of Imperial and Commonwealth History* 22 (3): 531–541.

Flandreau, Marc, and Frédéric Zumer. 2004. *The Making of Global Finance 1880–1913*. Paris: OECD.

Frieden, Jeffry A. 1994. International Investment and Colonial Control: A New Interpretation. *International Organization* 48 (4): 559–593.

Gann, Lewis H. 1969. Reflections on Imperialism and the Scramble for Africa. In *Colonialism in Africa 1870–1960. Volume 1: The History and Politics of Colonialism 1870–1914*, ed. L.H. Gann and Peter Duignan, 100–131. Cambridge: Cambridge University Press.

Gann, Lewis H., and Peter Duignan. 1968. *Burden of Empire: An Appraisal of Western Colonialism in Africa South of the Sahara*. London: Hoover Institution.

Goetzmann, William N., and Andrey D. Ukhov. 2006. British Investment Overseas 1870–1913: A Modern Portfolio Theory Approach. *Review of Finance* 10 (2): 261–300.

Harvey, David. 2003. *The New Imperialism*. Oxford: Oxford University Press.

Hillbom, Ellen, and Erik Green. 2010. *Afrika: En Kontinents Ekonomiska Och Sociala Historia*. Stockholm: SNS förlag.

Hobson, John Atkinson. 1988. *Imperialism: A Study*. London: Unwin Hyman.

Hyam, Ronald. 2010. *Understanding the British Empire*. Cambridge: Cambridge University Press.

Hynes, William G. 1979. *The Economics of Empire: Britain, Africa and the New Imperialism, 1870–95*. London: Longman.

Kubicek, Robert V. 1999. Economic Power at the Periphery: Canada, Australia, and South Africa, 1850–1914. In *Gentlemanly Capitalism and British Imperialism: The New Debate on Empire*, ed. Raymond Dumett, 113–127. London: Longman.

MacKenzie, Donald A. 2006. *An Engine, Not a Camera: How Financial Models Shape Markets*. Cambridge: The MIT Press.

Malkiel, Burton G., and Eugene F. Fama. 1970. Efficient Capital Markets: A Review of Theory and Empirical Work. *The Journal of Finance* 25 (2): 383–417.

Markowitz, H. 1959. *Portfolio Selection: Efficient Diversification of Investments*. New York: Wiley.

Marx, Karl. 1969. *On Colonialism & Modernization*. Edited by Shlmo Avineri. New York: Anchor.

McCloskey, Donald. 1970. Did Victorian Britain Fail? *Economic History Review* 23 (3): 446–459.
Menon, Rajan, and John R. Oneal. 1986. Explaining Imperialism: The State of the Art as Reflected in Three Theories. *Polity* 19 (2): 169–193.
Michie, Ranald C. 2001. *The London Stock Exchange: A History*. Oxford: Oxford University Press.
———. 2004. The City of London and the British Government: The Changing Relationship. In *The British Government and the City of London in the Twentieth Century*, ed. Ranald Michie and Philip Williamson, 31–55. Cambridge: Cambridge University Press.
———. 2006. *The Global Securities Market a History*. Oxford: Oxford University Press.
Müller, Simone M. 2016. *Wiring the World: The Social and Cultural Creation of Global Telegraph Networks*. New York: Columbia University Press.
Noonan, Murray. 2017. *Marxist Theories of Imperialism: A History*. London: I.B. Tauris.
O'Brien, Patrick K. 1988. The Costs and Benefits of British Imperialism 1846–1914. *Past and Present* 120 (1): 163–200.
O'Rourke, Kevin H., and Jeffrey G. Williamson. 1999. *Globalization and History: The Evolution of a Nineteenth-Century Atlantic Economy*. Cambridge: MIT Press.
Obstfeld, Maurice, and Alan M. Taylor. 2003. Sovereign Risk, Credibility and the Gold Standard: 1870–1913 versus 1925–31. *The Economic Journal* 113 (487): 241–275.
———. 2004. *Global Capital Markets: Integration, Crisis, and Growth*. New York: Cambridge University Press.
Parent, Antoine, and Christophe Rault. 2004. The Influences Affecting French Assets Abroad Prior to 1914. *The Journal of Economic History* 64 (2): 328–362.
Phimister, Ian. 2002. Empire, Imperialism and the Partition of Africa. In *Gentlemanly Capitalism, Imperialism and Global History*, ed. Shigeru Akita, 65–82. New York: Springer. http://link.springer.com/chapter/10.1057/9781403919403_4.
Platt, D.C.M. 1968. *Finance, Trade, and Politics in British Foreign Policy 1815–1914*. Oxford: Clarendon press.
Porter, Bernard. 1968. *Critics of Empire: British Radical Attitudes to Colonialism in Africa 1895–1914*. London: Macmillan.

Porter, Andrew. 1990. 'Gentlemanly Capitalism' and Empire: The British Experience since 1750? *The Journal of Imperial and Commonwealth History* 18 (3): 265–295.

Robinson, Ronald Edward, and John Gallagher. 1968. *Africa and the Victorians: The Climax of Imperialism*. New York: Anchor Books.

Rodney, Walter. 1972. *How Europe Underdeveloped Africa*. London: Bogle-L'Ouverture.

Rota, Mauro, and Francesco Schettino. 2011. The Long-Run Determinants of British Capital Exports, 1870–1913. *Financial History Review* 18 (1): 47–69.

Schumpeter, Joseph Alois. 1951. *Imperialism and Social Classes*. New York: Kelley.

Sharpe, William F. 1970. *Portfolio Theory and Capital Markets*. New York: McGraw-Hill.

Thompson, Andrew S. 2000. *Imperial Britain: The Empire in British Politics, c. 1880–1932*. New York: Longman.

Warren, Bill, and John Sender. 1980. *Imperialism: Pioneer of Capitalism*. London: NLB.

Webster, Anthony. 2006. *The Debate on the Rise of the British Empire*. Manchester: Manchester University Press.

Wilkins, Mira. 1988. The Free-Standing Company, 1870–1914: An Important Type of British Foreign Direct Investment. *The Economic History Review* 41 (2): 259–282.

Winch, Donald. 1965. *Classical Political Economy and Colonies*. London: London School of Economics and Political Science.

4

Previous Empirical Research

Estimating the Profitability of Colonial Ventures

There are competing theories claiming that the private return on foreign investment in general, and colonial investment in particular, ought to have been higher than the return on investment domestically (in the United Kingdom or in a wider group of core European countries). These include the classic theory that globalization opened up new, and potentially more profitable, investment opportunities in virgin areas of economic development (e.g. due to rich natural resources) and the neo-Marxist theory of super-profits from colonial exploitation. There are also theories suggesting that the private return on foreign investments might not need to be particularly high. These include a prediction of convergence of rates of return over time, different cultural values by different ('gentlemanly') investors and the fact that imperialism might reduce country risks (which would lead to a lower risk premium). It is important to note that these potential explanatory factors are not all mutually exclusive. They might reinforce or counteract each other. It is therefore by no means theoretically clear how high the return on foreign investments, and colonial investments in particular, would be compared to the domestic return on investment. The issue can therefore only be settled by empirical analysis.

What was then the actual historical rate of return on overseas investments compared to comparable investments in the United Kingdom? This issue has been debated in much previous research. In many monographs on particular companies, one can easily find information about how supposedly successful some of the more well-known companies operating in various colonies were. In the case of Africa, this includes companies such as the Suez Canal Company, the British South Africa Company, DeBeers Consolidated, Ashanti Goldfields or the Anglo-American Corporation (Chilvers 1939; Katzenellenbogen 1973; Hopkins 1976; Hansen and Tourk 1978; Cunningham 1981; Innes 1983; Afrifa-Taylor 2006; Tignor 2007; Newbury 2009; Bonin 2010). While these studies might shed light on the history of the individual companies, they are hardly enlightening on the issue of the general return on investment since there is a problematic selection bias of business history monographs. Those companies that have been the focus of such research were rarely chosen at random among all companies, but have been chosen particularly because they happened to be successful. For every successful company, one can also find failures. J. Forbes Munro has, for example, argued that many companies that invested in plantations in Africa failed economically, for various reasons (Munro 1981, 1983, 1984, 28–29; see also Mollan 2009).

There have been attempts to analyse the general return on foreign versus domestic investment, or the return on investment in particular colonies. One of the first and most influential studies, undertaken by Herbert Frankel, studied the return on investment in the South African mining industry from 1887 to 1965, comparing these to the return on investment in the United Kingdom around the same time (Frankel 1935, 1967). Frankel's original study was based on a sample of 576 South African mining companies, but his later study on the return on investment was limited to a smaller subsample of more 'important' South African companies. The study collected data from the South African Stock Exchange for an analysis of what he calls the internal rate of return. The method is not described transparently but seemingly includes both net capital gains and dividends paid out, thus amounting to estimates of the total return on the investments, using annual data. The author does furthermore not report explicitly how the data from the individual companies was weighted in order to arrive at an average rate of return, but the estimates seem to have been weighted. Frankel's results from these estimates suggest that the return on investing in South African mining was not particularly high if compared to the return possible from investing in British equity (Frankel 1967, 7–9). These results were later questioned by other scholars. Simon Katzenellenbogen studied the dividends paid out on South African mining equity, arguing that these dividends were extremely high on average (Katzenellenbogen 1975). Since Katzenellenbogen did not include capital gains or losses in his estimates, the figures are not comparable to Frankel's estimates. Robert Kubicek too criticized Frankel's estimates, arguing that the return on investing in South African mining actually was higher than the return on other comparable investments, but the empirical evidence in favour of this argument is not presented clearly and methodically (Kubicek 1979).

Michael Edelstein contributed with an often-cited study comparing the rate of return on British foreign and domestic investments. The study estimated the total rate of return, including both net capital gains and dividends paid out, for a sample of 566 'high-class' securities. The study covered the period from 1850 to 1914 using data primarily from *The Investors' Monthly Manual* (a publication from *The Economist* started in 1864). Mining companies were explicitly excluded from the study—thereby excluding virtually all investments in colonial Africa—and only one single company (a bank) operating in Africa was included in the sample. Unweighted sectoral average total return on investment was calculated, and an aggregate estimate of the total return on investment was arrived at by weighting the sectoral averages by their shares of national income. Edelstein's results show that the total rate of return was systematically higher on foreign investments than on domestic investments, even when adjusting for risk (Edelstein 1970, 1976, 1982). Important for the purpose of the present book, Edelstein did not distinguish between colonies and non-colonies in his aggregate estimates but tried to deal with this issue by separate case studies on investments in Canada, Australia and the United States.

The most often-cited studies on this topic have been the research undertaken by Lance Davis and Robert Huttenback (Davis and Huttenback 1982, 1986, 1988). In their research, the authors studied the return on British investments in colonies in particular. They compared this rate of return to the return on domestic investment, during the period 1860–1912. The authors make no distinction between different parts of the British Empire. The study is based on three different samples of companies merged together: one sample of 241 companies selected at random among companies traded on the London Stock Exchange, one non-random sample of 234 companies selected 'because some portion of their original records exist and are available for analysis', and one sample of seven British railway companies selected on unclear grounds and included 'to gain a modicum of regional representation' (Davis and Huttenback 1986, 81–82). Davis and Huttenback used data from the internal accounts of these companies to estimate the companies' rate of reported profits relative to physical assets (explicitly refraining from estimating the total rate of return on the investments) and calculated an unweighted average rate of return for the merged sample. The conclusion they arrived at is that the return on investing in colonies was somewhat higher than the return on investing in Britain during the early part of their study, from the 1860s to 1880s. After this period, the rate of return from colonial investment was similar to (or even lower than) the rate of return on domestic investment (Davis and Huttenback 1986, table 3.15, 1988, figs. 3.3–3.5). Because of the different selection criteria, there was a high risk of bias in the selection. Some reviewers have questioned the representativity of the study since virtually all of the well-known (and hence potentially most profitable) colonial companies were missing from the samples (Hopkins 1988; Porter 1988).

Peter Svedberg studied the profitability of British investments overseas during the period 1938–1974 using data from the Bank of England on capital stocks and income from affiliates or branches of British-controlled companies. Comparing the profits from companies operating in British colonies to those operating in non-colonized Least Developed Countries during this period, Svedberg found that the colonial branches or affiliates were much more profitable for the controlling company (Svedberg 1982).

In more recent years, there has been much more work on the return on investment in various countries using updated methodologies and more representative samples of data. Many of these studies have studied developed countries in particular (e.g. Goetzmann et al. 2001; Dimson et al. 2002; Grossman 2002; Eitrheim et al. 2004; Acheson et al. 2009; Esteves 2011; Waldenström 2014; Jordà et al. 2019).

There is some recent research studying the return on overseas investments in less developed countries (i.e. many former colonies). In 1999, Philippe Jorion and William Goetzmann published a study of the return on investment in 39 stock markets around the world, including 15 markets in Asia, Africa and Latin America. Data was assembled from various sources including the International Monetary Fund (IMF) and League of Nations' Statistical Yearbooks, for—at best—the period 1921–1996. For many of the developing markets, the time-series was much shorter, such as in the case of South Africa, where data was reported only for the period 1947–1996. Data on dividends paid out was furthermore missing for several of their series, essentially leading to a substantial downward bias of those estimates (Jorion and Goetzmann 1999).

In 2002, Elroy Dimson, Paul Marsh and Mike Staunton published *Triumph of the Optimists: 101 Years of Global Investment Returns* (Dimson et al. 2002). In the book, the authors created estimates for the total rate of return on investment in a number of countries during a whole century, from 1900 to 2000. Despite the subtitle, the data they present is not global in coverage. The data is reported by nation, but only one country in Africa (South Africa) and no Latin American or Asian countries were initially included in the analysis.[1] The data collection procedure varied between the countries and the time periods studied. For example, the data for the United Kingdom is based on a sample of 247 companies for the period 1900–1954 and of 604 companies for the period thereafter. The sample for the first period is made up of all companies present on the FTSE-100 list for six benchmark years (Dimson et al. 2002, 299–301). Since this list would include only the most traded and potentially most successful companies, it might introduce a considerable selection bias to

---

[1] In a later publication, these authors also included data on the return on investment in China and Japan, see Dimson et al. (2016).

these estimates. The dataset for South Africa is another example which is of interest as a point of comparison to this study. The dataset was spliced together from two different sources of data, based on a seemingly arbitrary weighting. This data might therefore also suffer from selection bias (Rönnbäck and Broberg 2018). The results that the authors arrive at suggest that the return on investment in a country such as South Africa was somewhat higher in both nominal and real terms than the return on investment in the United Kingdom during their period of study (Dimson et al. 2002, figs. 4–5).

Frans Buelens and Stefaan Marysse have published a study of the total return on investment in 158 companies operating in Belgian Congo, using the same basic methodology as Dimson et al. (2002), and compared the figures to total return on investment in Belgium during the same period (Buelens and Marysse 2009; see also Annaert et al. 2012). Their results indicate that return on investment in Belgian Congo was higher than the domestic return on investment in Belgium. This was true throughout the period except for the 1950s, the last decade of colonialism in Belgian Congo. If the 1950s are included in the estimate, the average return on investment in Belgian Congo decreases to low levels. The realization of country risk can thus have substantial impact even on the long-term average return on investment. In another study, Frans Buelens and Ewout Frankema studied return on investment in plantation agriculture in the Netherlands Indies using the same methodology. Return on investment there was in general somewhat higher than return on domestic investment, but investing in the colony was also somewhat riskier (Buelens and Frankema 2015).

Benjamin Chabot and Christopher Kurz published a study of the 'foreign bias' in English investment during the period 1886–1907 using monthly data for all securities reported in publications such as the *Money Market Review* and the *Investors' Monthly Manual* as listed on the London and US Stock Exchanges. These publications did not always manage to include all companies listed on the respective stock exchange but increasingly excluded smaller and less traded companies (Hannah 2018). All leading companies listed on the Stock Exchanges would have been included in the publications. Their data shows that high returns were not necessarily the only (or even the main) benefit of investing overseas. The real benefit, they argue, was instead that the diversification of portfolios from holding overseas assets increased the investors' utility (Chabot and Kurz 2010).

The most recent study of the historical return on investment has been published by Richard Grossman, studying the total return on British investments both domestically and overseas in the period 1869–1928 using data on all companies reported in the *Investors' Monthly Manual* published by *The Economist* (Grossman 2015, see also 2017). In contrast to Dimson et al., Grossman's data covered British investments in countries all over the globe, but a drawback is that the data was reported only by continent (with the exception of data for the United Kingdom in particular) and was based only on annual data. Grossman has received criticism for the data he had assembled (Hannah 2018), to which he responded by concluding that there seemingly are substantial problems with the estimated results, so that they might require revision (Grossman 2018).

Limitations of Previous Research in the Field

Table 4.1 summarizes the main previous research in the field.

There has been substantial amount of research conducted in this field, but there are several limitations to this previous research. First, there are chronological delimitations. The older studies of the profitability of imperialism were all limited to studying the period prior to the outbreak of the First World War, and they are therefore not able to study what happened to the return on investment in the colonies once the colonial economies started to mature in the interwar period. Chabot and Kurz's more recent study is similarly delimited to a short period prior to the First World War. Richard Grossman's study covers a longer time period, including the years until 1928, in his study. Any development after this time is not included in the analysis. But, as shown by Dimson et al. (2002), in order to handle exogenous events and market volatility, the length of the data series is crucial when analysing the average return on investment. This issue becomes even more acute for the African context, where risk and volatility historically have been high. The case of Belgian

Table 4.1 Summary of key previous research

Scholar(s)	Time period	Geographical coverage	Sample selection	Method	Frequency of data	Weighting of sample
Frankel (1935, 1967)	1887–1965	South African mining investments.	116 most important South African mining companies.	TRR	Annual	Not reported, but seemingly weighted by market capitalization.
Edelstein (1970, 1976, 1982)	1850–1914	British domestic versus 'overseas' investments.	566 high-class securities (excluding the mining sector).	TRR	Annual	Unweighted sectoral average figures, aggregate figures then weighted by size of each sector.
Davis and Huttenback (1982, 1986, 1988)	1860–1912	British versus British Empire investments.	482 companies selected in various ways (see text).	RP	Annual	Unweighted.
Dimson et al. (2002, 2016)	1900–2000	'Global' investments (in reality limited to investments in a number of key countries).	Varies by country studied.	TRR	Varies by country studied.	Varies by country studied.
Buelens and Marysse (2009)	1889–1962	Belgian domestic investments versus investments in Belgian Congo.	All 158 companies traded on the Brussels Stock Exchange reported to be operating in Belgian Congo.	TRR	Monthly	Weighted by market capitalization.

(continued)

Table 4.1 (continued)

Scholar(s)	Time period	Geographical coverage	Sample selection	Method	Frequency of data	Weighting of sample
Chabot and Kurz (2010)	1866–1907	British domestic versus foreign investments.	All 2242 main companies traded on London and US Stock Exchanges.	TRR	Monthly	Weighted by market capitalization.
Grossman (2015, 2018)	1869–1928	British investments globally, reported by continent.	All main companies traded on the London Stock Exchange, exact sample size not reported.	TRR	Annual	Weighted by market capitalization.

Note: *TRR* Total rate of return, including capital gains and dividends paid out; *RP* Reported profits in company accounts

Congo is illustrative, where the choice of limiting the data series to 1955 (rather than to 1960, when the country risk was realized under the process of independence) doubles the long-term average return on investment (Buelens and Marysse 2009, 152–53). Dimson et al., on the other hand, only started their study in 1900. For the purpose of our study, they thereby miss the important years of the 'Scramble for Africa', at the end of the nineteenth century. Apart from Buelens and Marysse's study of Belgian Congo, there is no previous research trying to study the return on investment in Africa covering the whole of the colonial period.

Second, there are geographical limitations. While some of the older studies of the profitability of imperialism had a clear focus upon studying the return on investment in colonies, none of them made any distinction between different types of colonies or their different geographical locations and treated all colonies and dominions similarly. Due to the way their samples were constructed, they furthermore missed out key African companies. Buelens and Marysse's study was, in contrast, limited to companies operating in one specific colony, Belgian Congo. Dimson et al. claimed to estimate return on global investments, but the only African country included in their dataset was South Africa. Belgian Congo and South Africa need not be representative of other African countries. One would expect that the historical return on investment could differ substantially between different colonies over time, as the economies in the colonies developed along different trajectories.

Third, there are issues of sample size and selection bias. As was noted in the previous chapter, older studies on the profitability of imperialism all suffer from a substantial selection bias. Edelstein totally excluded the main sector of investments in colonial Africa (mining). Davis and Huttenback created a sample based on three different (and not unproblematic) methods of selection. Dimson et al. based their study mainly on a limited number of larger companies in the mining and financial sectors, creating a potential survival selection bias. Grossman's sample of companies operating in Africa is seemingly larger than that of Dimson et al.'s, but it is still comparatively limited (further limited by only using annual data).

The present study will, in contrast to the previous research, study a whole century, from 1869 to 1969. We can thereby cover much of the process of colonization and decolonization in several of the countries studied. Our study will furthermore be based on a larger sample of companies compared to previous research on investments in Africa. Though our sample is not completely free from selection bias, we believe it suffers considerably less from such bias than previous research—an issue we will discuss further in the following chapter. We also employ data of a higher frequency using monthly data, allowing us to conduct a more detailed and robust analysis of the rate of return on investment. Finally, the present study will have a broader geographical coverage, studying British investments in several different parts of Africa. Because of the overall nature of the flow of these investments, the sample is biased towards South Africa and Egypt, but it also contains a substantial number of companies operating in current-day Ghana, Nigeria, Zambia and Zimbabwe as well as a smaller number of companies operating in 14 other colonies/countries in Africa.

References

Acheson, Graeme G., Charles R. Hickson, John D. Turner, and Qing Ye. 2009. Rule Britannia! British Stock Market Returns, 1825–1870. *The Journal of Economic History* 69 (4): 1107–1137.

Afrifa-Taylor, Ayowa. 2006. *An Economic History of the Ashanti Goldfields Corporation, 1895–2004: Land, Labour, Capital and Enterprise*. Ph.D. Dissertation, London School of Economics and Political Science.

Annaert, Jan, Frans Buelens, and Marc J.K. De Ceuster. 2012. New Belgian Stock Market Returns: 1832–1914. *Explorations in Economic History* 49 (2): 189–204.

Bonin, Hubert. 2010. *History of the Suez Canal Company 1858–2008*. Geneva: Droz.

Buelens, Frans, and Ewout Frankema. 2015. Colonial Adventures in Tropical Agriculture: New Estimates of Returns to Investment in the Netherlands Indies, 1919–1938. *Cliometrica*, May, 1–28.

Buelens, Frans, and Stefaan Marysse. 2009. Returns on Investments during the Colonial Era: The Case of the Belgian Congo. *The Economic History Review* 62 (s1): 135–166.

Chabot, Benjamin R., and Christopher J. Kurz. 2010. That's Where the Money Was: Foreign Bias and English Investment Abroad, 1866–1907. *The Economic Journal* 120 (547): 1056–1079.

Chilvers, Hedley A. 1939. *The Story of De Beers: With Some Notes on the Company's Financial, Farming, Railway and Industrial Activities in Africa and Some Introductory Chapters on the River Diggings and Early Kimberley*. London: Cassell and Co.

Cunningham, Simon. 1981. *The Copper Industry in Zambia: Foreign Mining Companies in a Developing Country*. New York: Praeger.

Davis, Lance, and Robert Huttenback. 1982. The Political Economy of British Imperialism: Measures of Benefits and Support. *The Journal of Economic History* 42 (1): 119–130.

———. 1986. *Mammon and the Pursuit of Empire: The Political Economy of British Imperialism, 1860–1912*. Cambridge: Cambridge University Press.

———. 1988. *Mammon and the Pursuit of Empire: The Economics of British Imperialism*. Abridged ed. Cambridge: Cambridge University Press.

Dimson, Elroy, Paul Marsh, and Mike Staunton. 2002. *Triumph of the Optimists: 101 Years of Global Investment Returns*. Princeton, NJ: Princeton University Press.

———. 2016. *Credit Suisse Global Investment Returns Sourcebook 2016*. Credit Suisse Research Institute.

Edelstein, Michael. 1970. *The Rate of Return to U.K. Home and Foreign Investment, 1870–1913*. Ph.D. Dissertation, University of Pennsylvania.

———. 1976. Realized Rates of Return on UK Home and Overseas Portfolio Investment in the Age of High Imperialism. *Explorations in Economic History* 13 (3): 283–329.

———. 1982. *Overseas Investment in the Age of High Imperialism: The United Kingdom, 1850–1914*. London: Methuen.

Eitrheim, Øyvind, Jan T. Klovland, and Jan F. Qvigstad. 2004. *Historical Monetary Statistics for Norway 1819–2003*. Vol. 35. Oslo: Norges Bank.

Esteves, Rui. 2011. *The Belle Epoque of International Finance: French Capital Exports, 1880–1914*. SSRN Working Paper.

Frankel, S. Herbert. 1935. Return to Capital Invested in the Witwatersrand Gold-Mining Industry, 1887–1932. *The Economic Journal* 45 (177): 67–76.

———. 1967. *Investment and the Return to Equity to Capital in the South African Gold Mining Industry 1887–1965: An International Comparison*. Oxford: Basil Blackwell.

Goetzmann, William N., Roger G. Ibbotson, and Liang Peng. 2001. A New Historical Database for the NYSE 1815 to 1925: Performance and Predictability. *Journal of Financial Markets* 4 (1): 1–32.

Grossman, Richard S. 2002. New Indices of British Equity Prices, 1870–1913. *The Journal of Economic History* 62 (1): 121–146.

———. 2015. Bloody Foreigners! Overseas Equity on the London Stock Exchange, 1869–1929. *The Economic History Review* 68 (2): 471–521.

———. 2017. *Stocks for the Long Run: New Monthly Indices of British Equities, 1869–1929*. CEPR Discussion Paper No. DP12121.

———. 2018. Revising 'Bloody Foreigners! *The Economic History Review* 71 (4): 1357–1359.

Hannah, Leslie. 2018. The London Stock Exchange, 1869–1929: New Statistics for Old? *Economic History Review* 71 (4): 1349–1356.

Hansen, Bent, and Khairy Tourk. 1978. The Profitability of the Suez Canal as a Private Enterprise, 1859–1956. *The Journal of Economic History* 38 (4): 938–958.

Hopkins, Anthony G. 1976. Imperial Business in Africa Part II. Interpretations. *The Journal of African History* 17 (2): 267–290.

———. 1988. Accounting for the British Empire. *The Journal of Imperial and Commonwealth History* 16 (2): 234–247.

Innes, Duncan. 1983. *Anglo American and the Rise of Modern South Africa*. London: Heinemann Educational.

Jordà, Oscar, Katharina Knoll, Dmitry Kuvshinov, Moritz Schularick, and Alan Taylor. 2019. *The Rate of Return on Everything, 1870–2015*. Quarterly Journal of Economics. Forthcoming.

Jorion, Philippe, and William N. Goetzmann. 1999. Global Stock Markets in the Twentieth Century. *The Journal of Finance* 54 (3): 953–980.

Katzenellenbogen, Simon. 1973. *Railways and the Copper Mines of Katanga*. Oxford: Clarendon press.

———. 1975. The Miner's Frontier, Transport and General Economic Development. In *Colonialism in Africa, 1870–1960: The Economics of Colonialism*, ed. P. Duignan and L.H. Gann, 360–426. Cambridge: Cambridge University Press.

Kubicek, Robert. 1979. *Economic Imperialism in Theory and Practice*. Durham, NC: Duke University Center for International Studies Publication.

Mollan, S.M. 2009. Business Failure, Capital Investment and Information: Mining Companies in the Anglo-Egyptian Sudan, 1900–13. *The Journal of Imperial and Commonwealth History* 37 (2): 229–248.

Munro, J. Forbes. 1981. Monopolists and Speculators: British Investment in West African Rubber, 1905–1914. *The Journal of African History* 22 (2): 263–278.

———. 1983. British Rubber Companies in East Africa before the First World War. *The Journal of African History* 24 (3): 369–379.

———. 1984. *Britain in Tropical Africa, 1880–1960: Economic Relationships and Impact.* London: Macmillan.

Newbury, Cecil. 2009. Cecil Rhodes, De Beers and Mining Finance in South Africa: The Business of Entrepreneurship and Imperialism. In *Mining Tycoons in the Age of Empire, 1870–1945: Entrepreneurship, High Finance, Politics and Territorial Expansion*, ed. Raymond Dumett, 85–108. Farnham: Ashgate.

Porter, Andrew. 1988. The Balance Sheet of Empire, 1850–1914. *The Historical Journal* 31 (3): 685–699.

Rönnbäck, Klas, and Oskar Broberg. 2018. All That Glitters Is Not Gold: The Return on British Investments in South Africa, 1869–1969. *Studies in Economics and Econometrics* 42 (2): 61–79.

Svedberg, Peter. 1982. The Profitability of UK Foreign Direct Investment under Colonialism. *Journal of Development Economics* 11 (3): 273–286.

Tignor, Robert. 2007. The Business Firm in Africa. *Business History Review* 81: 87–110.

Waldenström, Daniel. 2014. Swedish Stock and Bond Returns, 1856–2012. In *Historical monetary and financial statistics for Sweden, vol. 2*, ed. Rodney Edvinsson, Tor Jacobson, and Daniel Waldenström, 223–292. Stockholm: Sveriges Riksbank and Ekerlids förlag.

5

Data and Methods

Company Profits and Return on Investment

In this book, we study the return on portfolio investments in ventures operating in Africa. Portfolio investments are investments in assets such as equity, bonds and debentures. Portfolio investments are linked to foreign direct investments (FDI), but even though they are overlapping at times, not all portfolio investments count as FDI. The initial public offering (IPO) of a company or new issues of shares are associated with FDI when the capital assembled is used for new economic activity internationally (i.e. greenfield investments). IPOs and new issues can likewise be associated with FDI through mergers and acquisitions in already existing ventures (i.e. brownfield investments). Other portfolio investments can have little or no relation to any direct investments by the company, but may, for example, be transactions undertaken solely between different investors: one shareholder selling equity to another, without any further capital being injected into the company. The two are related, as FDI in terms of greenfield and brownfield investments has an impact on the return of portfolio investment.

The historical analysis of company profits and/or the return on investment is complicated by a fundamental informational dilemma: what kind of data can we use to actually say something about company performance? We know that annual reports include important information, but we also know that they are communicative products of the company management. In several cases, annual reports include numbers that are optimized to lower the tax burden, for example, by profit shifting (such as earnings stripping or transfer pricing), rather than to reveal value creation.

The strategy employed in this book is to use share prices as an external valuation of companies. We thereby turn to contemporary financial markets for help in assessing company information. Hence, we assume that investors in London, on average, were relatively well informed about their investment objects. This does not mean that they were always correct; we know that asset price bubbles were at least as common then as they still are today. An optimistic valuation in the short run will be smoothed out in the long run, if (or when) management fails to meet the expectations and share prices consequently fall.

Our method acknowledges that contemporary actors invested a lot of time, energy and money to keep up to date with their investments. We know that the informational processing capacity of the international financial markets increased dramatically during the latter half of the nineteenth century. The combination of steamship deliveries of post, transoceanic telegraph cables, global business press and disclosure clauses in limited liability legislation had the effect that unforeseen events around the world affected share prices in London within days (at the beginning of our study period) and within minutes (at the end of our study period). Hence, a fundamental assumption in this book is that the yield (the dividends actually paid out) together with a monthly market valuation (the share price) gives a reasonable proxy for company performance in the long run.

In the book, we furthermore focus upon portfolio investments in *equity* in companies operating in Africa, and specifically upon equity investments channelled through the *London Stock Exchange* (LSE). This was an important channel for investments in Africa but not the only one available.

Firstly, there were several other stock exchanges both in the United Kingdom and in other countries during the time studied that channelled capital to Africa—though the London Stock Exchange dominated on the global financial market at least until the 1920s. Despite the rise of New York Stock Exchange in the twentieth century, the London Stock Exchange remained one of the key stock exchanges in the world, throughout the period under study. Secondly, the equity of all companies operating in Africa was not necessarily traded on official exchanges, such as the London Stock Exchange, but could have been traded on unofficial exchanges. This trade involved both larger (which also were listed on official exchanges) and smaller companies (which were not listed on any formal exchange). For companies also listed elsewhere, the most important issue for this study is that there was a close relationship in terms of prices between the official and unofficial market. We find no reasons to believe that this was not the case. The trade in non-listed securities falls outside this study, but due to its smallness, we assume that its impact on a market-weighted return would have been marginal, had it been possible to include them. Thirdly, even though some companies might have been registered formally on an exchange, they might have been too small or too rarely traded to be included in the sources employed for this study. This is an issue we will return to below in this chapter, but again, their smallness would not impact the overall results due to the market capitalization-weighted average estimates. Fourthly, many investments were using financial instruments other than equity, including bonds and debentures. The return on bonds in various colonies, including several in Africa, has already been studied in much previous research on the 'Empire effect' on bond spreads (discussed in Chap. 3), and this previous research will form the basis for a comparison of the return on investment in bonds and equity, respectively, undertaken in Chap. 7 of this book.

Finally, and perhaps most importantly, substantial investments were raised not through stock exchanges but were channelled from capital-exporting countries to Africa in other ways. Capital was raised on a completely private basis, in the form of private companies whose shares were not publicly traded, or through informal credit arrangements. This includes, for example, substantial investments made by settler farmers in several parts of Africa, most importantly in Southern Africa. Another channel of investments was through companies wholly owned by a parent company, and therefore not traded on a stock exchange in their own rights. One example of this would be several of the oil companies that were established in Nigeria after the Second World War (see Chap. 9). The overall importance of such alternative channels for raising capital is not estimated in this book.

It is therefore beyond the scope of this book to estimate the total amount of foreign capital invested in Africa during the period under study. What we do study is the return on investment using data on the return on investment channelled through the London Stock Exchange. We see this capital as a proxy for British investments in general—a reasoning in line with the previous research referred to in Chap. 4. The reader must, nonetheless, be aware that this delineation creates a certain bias in regard to the sectoral distribution of our sample. Equity was more commonly used when investing in certain sectors, such as mining or manufacturing. Other sectors, such as the construction and running of railroads, more often employed bonds and debentures. Yet other sectors, such as agriculture, made more use of non-publicly traded companies. Hence, the sectoral composition in our sample cannot be used as an indicator of the sectoral composition of the whole economy in the colonies/countries studied. As the rate of return on investment varied substantially between the sectors that we are able to study (see Chap. 6), it is furthermore not possible to draw any conclusions about the rate of return in the sectors that are not well represented in our sample.

Delimitation

Geographically, the study is focussed upon investments in the African continent. Any company traded on the London Stock Exchange and operating anywhere in Africa during our time period would be eligible for inclusion in our study. One of the chapters will broaden the geographical coverage, in order to compare the return on investment in African mining to the return on investment in (non-ferrous, non-coal) mining elsewhere in the world. The geographical coverage of Chap. 14 is therefore global—any mining company that traded on the London Stock

Exchange is eligible for inclusion in this sample (excluding iron or coal as they would have been sorted under a different heading in the primary sources).

Delineation in time is not easy since the study covers a comparatively large number of countries on the African continent. In order to capture as much as possible of the British imperial history in Africa, the current book is delineated to the period 1869–1969. It covers a period from well before the main 'Scramble for Africa', to some years into independence for (most of) the former colonies. The delineation thereby leaves out some of the early investments in the British Cape Colony, prior to 1869, including, for example, some of the early mining ventures and some early banks. These investments were, however, limited in scale and scope.

Different countries as well as different parts of countries became colonized at different points in time. Colonization was furthermore often a drawn-out process, extending over several decades or even centuries. The outline of this history is described in greater detail in Chap. 4. Suffice to say here that, during the age of imperialism, the African continent—with the sole exception of Ethiopia—became colonized by European powers at some point or another. The main so-called Scramble for Africa occurred primarily during the 1880s. In principle, the African continent remained colonized until after the end of the Second World War, after which the process of decolonization started. All the colonies studied in the book had formally achieved independence in one way or another by the time our study ended in 1969. Two of the countries—South Africa and Southern Rhodesia (current-day Zimbabwe)—were still ruled by white minority regimes at this time, even though the countries formally had achieved independence from the United Kingdom. The economic and social order, and thereby many of the key institutions for foreign investors—ranging from property rights to labour market arrangements—which had been imposed under colonial rule, still remained essentially the same under these white minority regimes. White minority rule would, in these cases, not be overturned until well after the end of our period of study—in 1980 in Zimbabwe and in 1994 in South Africa. Some people have therefore suggested characterizing these white minority-run countries as still being under 'colonialism of a special type' (Visser 1997).

Estimating the Return on Investment in Equity

In this study, we will calculate the total return on investment in equity in ventures operating in Africa. We will, for that purpose, include both the yield (i.e. the dividend paid out in the case of equity) and the net capital gain (i.e. the change in the price of the equity). Following standard practice, our data is also weighted by market capitalization (the aggregate market valuation of all issued shares in the company), so as to reflect the stock market as a whole or to reflect specific portfolios (by geography, sector, etc.) (Dimson et al. 2002; Jordà et al. 2019). The market capitalization of the companies in the sample can also be employed to estimate how concentrated various market (sectors, countries) were, for example, by estimating a three-firm concentration ratio (3CR) of the sample.

The monthly return on the investments in an individual company is calculated based on the following formula (Eq. 5.1).

$$mp_t = \frac{(p_t - p_{t-1}) + d_t}{p_{t-1}} \tag{5.1}$$

where mp_t is the monthly return in year-month t, p is the closing price of the share (after controlling for any splits) and d is the dividend paid to the shareholder.

Market capitalization of the individual company was calculated as the product of the number of shares outstanding and the closing price of the stock for each month. The company's market capitalization is calculated by (Eq. 5.2).

$$mc_t = p_t * s_t \tag{5.2}$$

where mc_t is the company's market capitalization at time t, p the closing price of the share and s is the number of shares outstanding. The data for the individual companies was assembled into a joint database and a weighted return index was created. The index was weighted by the relative market capitalization of each company using the following formula (Eq. 5.3).

$$pi_t = \sum_{x=1}^{n}\left(\left(\frac{mc_{xt}}{\sum_{x=1}^{n} mc_{xt}}\right) * (1 + mp_{xt})\right) \qquad (5.3)$$

where pi_t is the weighted monthly index of the return on investment at time t, for all companies x. By using monthly data, it is possible to calculate the market capitalization every month, and thereby distribute weights to each company on a monthly basis, which should give a more precise estimate of the return on investment.

The monthly index, pi_t, was annualized into pi_T as the sum of the logarithmic values of the monthly index by year (Eq. 5.4).

$$pi_T = \exp\sum_{t=1}^{12} \ln(pi_t) \qquad (5.4)$$

Special indices have also been constructed by sector, region and country of incorporation, following the same basic model. The estimates are based on portfolios weighted by the market capitalization of each company listed on the London Stock Exchange and operating somewhere in Africa. Before the development of index funds, few individual investors would have invested in a weighted portfolio in this way in reality. Several investors might instead have invested in one or a handful of particular companies, often companies that they might have had some connection with. Intuitively, the calculations can therefore best be interpreted as showing the return on investment that an abstract investor, representative of investment strategies of all the investors on the London Stock Exchange, might have gained. In some previous research, there have been attempts to study more concretely who the shareholders in imperial enterprises were (Davis and Huttenback 1988, chap. 7). In this study, we make no such attempt apart from discussing some of the key entrepreneurs when looking at greater depth at one particular company, the Rand Mines Corporation (see more on this below, and the study in Chap. 12).

The development of the total rate of return over a period can be expressed in the form of either arithmetic or geometric mean. The arithmetic mean answers the question: if I chose a year at random, what return should I expect? Hence, it functions as a starting point for analysing the volatility of markets. When analysing a time series of data, arithmetic mean will systematically overestimate the actual mean achieved: if during the first period of observation, you lose 50 per cent of the value of an investment and in the second period gain 50 per cent on the capital you had left after the loss during the first period, you have still lost money in total—but the arithmetic mean will be zero. The arithmetic mean is therefore not a good measure to estimate the historical rate of return in a time series of data.

The geometric mean, on the other hand, represents the compounded annualized rate of return that equates the initial investment to the final value of a portfolio. In this book, we will therefore primarily use geometric mean when we analyse the long-term performance of investments. This is important to remember when comparing our results to previous research. Some of this (primarily the older) literature does not always clearly state whether it uses arithmetic or geometric mean but seems to be reporting arithmetic mean figures. In some cases, the arithmetic mean will therefore be reported in this book, in order to show the difference between the two measures and enable a comparison with literature using the arithmetic mean figures.

The nominal return of an investment might furthermore be influenced by the rate of inflation. A nominal rate of return of 5 per cent per year might be an ordinary rate of return during some periods, when the rate of inflation is low, but would, during some other periods, not even be on par with inflation. In order to account for this, we estimate the real rate of return on investment. Real return on investment has been calculated using data on the inflation rate in the United Kingdom (O'Donoghue et al. 2004), as this would be the most relevant inflation rate for the British investors in focus of our study.

In some years during our period of study, most importantly for a couple of months during the First World War, finally, the stock markets closed their operations. In our dataset, data has been interpolated for these periods of missing data, similar to other previous research (Jordà et al. 2019).

Sources Employed

This book makes use of data from the UK Stocks database, owned by the company Global Financial Data (GFD) and available by subscription. The database contains historical data on the prices of the stocks and bonds on the London Stock Exchange. GFD data has been used in previous economic-historical research, for example, studying the return on government bonds or the international integration of equity markets (see, e.g. Obstfeld and Taylor 2003, 2004; Reinhart and Rogoff 2009; Schularick and Taylor 2012; Campbell and Rogers 2017; Hauner et al. 2017).

When it comes to share prices, GFD has collected monthly data on the London share prices for companies from the *Investors' Monthly Manual* (IMM) published by *The Economist*. Much previous research has made use of the data from this source, not the least since digitized data for the period 1869–1929 was published online by the International Center for Finance at Yale School of Management (some examples with bearing on the current study include Edelstein 1970, 1976, 1982; Chabot and Kurz 2010; Grossman 2015, 2017; Jordà et al. 2019). Publication of the IMM begun already in 1864. It soon became one of the key channels of information for London investors. In the beginning, the ambition was to cover all traded securities in the IMM. As the number of securities listed on the London Stock Exchange increased in number, the task became impossible for the team at *The Economist*. Already by the 1880s, the IMM started to limit its coverage of junior markets, and by the interwar period, only a minority of the securities officially listed on the London Stock Exchange appeared regularly in the IMM (Hannah 2018). The exact criteria for inclusion in the IMM therefore changed over time, and it increasingly focussed on the more regularly traded companies. It is important to note that the IMM only reports a sample of all companies traded on the London Stock Exchange. There were, furthermore, a number of companies given permission to be traded on the Exchange, but not officially quoted on the London Stock Exchange Daily List but put on a separate Supplementary List (Michie 2001, 275)—and for that reason potentially excluded from publications such as the *IMM* or *The Times* that made use of the data from the London Stock Exchange Daily List. There might consequently be a problem of selection bias, so that smaller (and potentially not as successful) companies were not included on the lists. Since the list included all the larger companies traded on the London Stock Exchange, a market capitalization-weighted index would probably not suffer any major problems from this potential selection bias.

As a complement to the data from the IMM, GFD has also collected daily share price data from *The Times of London*. *The Times of London* published daily data on the prices for a large sample of equity traded on the London Stock Exchange, starting in the late nineteenth century. Prior to GFD's collection of this data, this source has not been used in previous historical research, possibly due to the major investment needed in order to create a database from it, prohibiting any such use prior to modern-day methods of digitizing historical data. The exact criteria for inclusion on *The Times*' listings are not clear, but it seems safe to assume that the publication focussed upon the mainly traded stocks, as this would have been the interest of the readership of these pages. The selection might therefore suffer from a similar selection bias as the companies in the IMM, even if it, too, probably would have little effect on a market capitalization-weighted index.

As not all companies were reported both in *The Times* and in the *IMM*, the periodicity of the data varies by company depending on from which source GFD has gathered the data for that particular company. For our purposes, monthly data is of sufficient density.

The data in the IMM is neither consistently nor always transparently reported. Reporting on some variables, such as the number of shares outstanding or the price of the security, is quite consistent. Most problematic is the data on dividends paid out. The IMM was supposed to report data on the last four dividend payments. The dates of these payments are frequently unclear. How the dividends were reported did furthermore vary: sometimes they were reported as the per-year equivalent percentage of the par value (thus requiring knowledge of the number of dividend payments during the year); at other times, they were reported in pounds, shillings and pence (Grossman 2017, appendix 1).

We have checked the reliability of the share price data from GFD's database manually against the main primary source, the *London Stock*

Exchange Daily Lists, available in the Guildhall Library in London. The reliability was checked by extracting the whole time series of data for a couple of selected companies from the sample as well as by randomly selecting specific data points from a number of other companies in the sample. The data on the closing price of the stocks every month did for these companies match extremely well, with correlations of more than 99 per cent. Since we can expect that the share prices generally are characterized by serial correlation, random omissions or errors would not be highly problematic. If the share price for one particular day by some mistake, for example, was reported as higher than it really was, that would lead to an erroneous estimate of a positive capital gain that day. If the price data in the data series is correct the following day, the mistake would be adjusted in the form of an estimated capital loss the following day. Aggregating the changes in the price data over time periods (months and/or years) would tend to adjust for any random errors in the share price series. Any such errors would therefore only tend to create problems if the errors were extreme. Estimates of extreme values (defined here as an annual return of more than 100 per cent or losses of more than 50 per cent) have been checked manually against the data source to ensure that there were no errors in the calculations or in the entries in the database.

The GFD database also contains information on dividends, number of shares outstanding, the country of incorporation, sector in which the company is operating and other variables. Data on shares outstanding as well as for dividends was also assembled by GFD, based on the *Investors' Monthly Manual* through 1930, and from the London Stock Exchange Yearbook from 1930 onwards. When checking the reliability of the data for these variables, we found that GFD's data on some of these variables occasionally was incomplete or erroneous. Since the data for these variables is not characterized by serial correlation in the same manner as the share prices are, any errors here will not be cancelled out when aggregating the data over time. The errors were in some cases substantial. We therefore assembled the data for these variables manually ourselves from the primary sources (the Stock Exchange Yearbooks and/or the *Investors' Monthly Manual*) for all companies in our sample, thereby correcting any errors we found in the GFD data series.

Sample of Data for African Companies

Companies were selected to be included in our study if they met any of the following four criteria:

1. Companies traded on the London Stock Exchange anytime during this period with 'Country of Incorporation' somewhere in Africa. This amounts to 654 companies in total.
2. Companies with the word 'Africa' (or derivations of this, e.g. 'African') in their company name, incorporated in a non-African country. Aside from those already selected according to the first criteria, this criteria yielded a further 15 companies in total, all of them registered in the GFD database as being incorporated in the United Kingdom.
3. Companies with the name of an African country or distinct region (e.g. 'Gold Coast', 'Rhodesia', 'Nigeria', 'Transvaal' and 'Tanganyika') in the company name, incorporated in a non-African country. This yielded a further 23 companies in total, all of them registered in GFD as incorporated in the United Kingdom.
4. Mining companies that, when scrutinized in the Stock Exchange Yearbooks for the comparative study of mining companies globally (see Chap. 14 of this book), were found to be operating in Sub-Saharan Africa. This yielded a further 34 companies.

The total number of companies selected in this way thus amounted to 728. Of these 728 companies identified for our study, we were able to find 704 companies in the primary sources for the whole period for which GFD had data on the price of the share, in order to assemble the necessary data for the other variables in our database. Any errors or omissions found in the GFD database for these companies were corrected and the company was included in our dataset. One company was excluded from the sample as there was conflicting data in the primary sources. Another company was excluded because there was only one single share price observation in the GFD database, and thereby impossible to calculate capital gain or loss.

We were unable to find the remaining 24 companies in the primary sources (neither in the Stock Exchange Yearbooks nor in the Investors

Monthly Manual). The most plausible reason that we can think of is either that the company had a different name formally than what, for example, was reported in *The Times* or the *Investors Monthly Manual* (e.g. *IMM* or *The Times* using an abbreviated name) in contrast to the Stock Exchange Yearbook or that the company at some point in time changed name without this being noted in the GFD database. Judging from the data in the GFD database, most of these companies were registered in the London Stock Exchange during a handful of years only. Data for the companies that we were unable to verify in any of primary sources consulted was therefore excluded from the sample. Excluding this data had marginal effects upon our results. Only one of the excluded companies (South Shields Consolidated Mine Co.) had a market capitalization large enough to have any measurable impact at all upon our estimates, and even in this particular case, the impact is on the whole negligible: for a few particular years during the early twentieth century, the estimated return on investment would be marginally lower (at most one half to one percentage point) if these excluded companies instead were included in the sample under the assumption that the data available from GFD for these particular companies is essentially correct. Excluding this data does therefore not change the overall picture obtained from our estimates.

The sample that we actually use is therefore made up of 702 unique companies, including data for 135,548 company-months. This database will henceforth be called the *African Colonial Equities Database (ACED)*. Figure 5.1 shows how the sample size develops over time.

As can be seen in the graph, the sample is limited prior to the 1890s, with around 15–30 companies. The 1890s experienced a drastic increase in the number of companies operating in Africa, registered on the London Stock Exchange—the number of companies in our sample increased to 136 companies in the year 1899 and increased further to reach a peak of 246 companies in our sample in the year 1909. Most of these companies were mining companies operating in South Africa. After 1909 follows a period when a number of companies were either taken over by or merged with other companies or faced bankruptcy. The sample size also decreased substantially between the years 1929 and 1930. This might partly be an effect of the global financial crisis of 1929 having an impact upon the number of African companies regis-

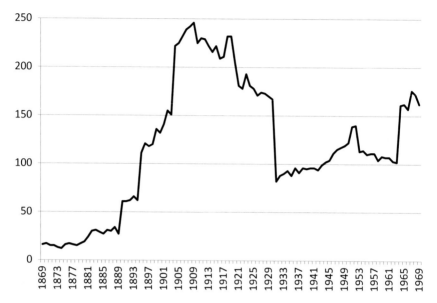

Fig. 5.1 Number of companies in the African Colonial Equities Database, by year, 1869–1969. Source: African Colonial Equities Database (ACED)

tered on the London Stock Exchange. It is also an effect of a change in the primary data: the IMM was not published after 1929, so from 1930 onwards the GFD database is based solely upon *The Times of London*. Since the two publications had different selection criteria for including companies in their monthly/daily stock listings, the end of the IMM meant that a number of companies previously reported only in this publication simply disappear from the sample without necessarily disappearing from the London Stock Exchange. All the major companies that have a notable influence on our market capitalization-weighted indices remain in our sample over this break.

The number of observations per company varies substantially, whereas the stocks of some companies were traded for almost the entire period of the study and other companies disappear from the sample after a couple of months or years. In total, the database contains 135,548 company-month observations. In Table 5.1, our dataset is described both in terms of country and region of operation and by the industrial sector it was operating in.

5 Data and Methods

Table 5.1 Descriptive statistics of sample of African companies, 1869–1969

	Companies		Company-months	
	No.	Per cent	No.	Per cent
By country				
Algeria	2	0.3	94	0.1
Angola	1	0.1	78	0.1
Botswana	3	0.4	730	0.5
Egypt	37	5.3	8831	6.5
Ethiopia	1	0.1	174	0.1
Ghana	42	6.0	6792	5.0
Kenya	9	1.3	881	0.6
Malawi	1	0.1	62	0.0
Mauritius	5	0.7	1225	0.9
Mozambique	5	0.7	621	0.5
Namibia	4	0.6	902	0.7
Nigeria	62	8.8	7094	5.2
Sierra Leone	2	0.3	275	0.2
South Africa	450	64.1	92,275	68.1
Sudan	2	0.3	366	0.3
Swaziland	2	0.3	71	0.1
Tanzania	1	0.1	46	0.0
Uganda	2	0.3	303	0.2
Zambia	12	1.7	4215	3.1
Zimbabwe	59	8.4	10,513	7.8
By region				
North Africa	42	6.0	9465	7.0
West Africa	106	15.1	14,161	10.4
East Africa	17	2.4	2455	1.8
Central/Southern Africa	87	12.4	17,192	12.7
South Africa	450	64.1	92,275	68.1
By sector				
Consumer Products	32	4.6	5387	4.0
Finance	43	6.1	10,928	8.1
Industrials	22	3.1	2766	2.0
Materials (non-mining)	22	3.1	2162	1.6
Mining	518	73.8	98,684	72.8
Real Estate	24	3.4	5453	4.0
Transports	15	2.1	4223	3.1
Utilities & Energy	26	3.7	5945	4.4

Source: African Colonial Equities Database (ACED)

As can be seen in the table, South African companies clearly dominate the sample in terms of numbers of companies as well as the number of company-month observations. In terms of sector, mining companies clearly dominate the sample.

Geographical Location

As Table 5.1 shows, the sample includes companies operating throughout most parts of Africa. For the vast majority of the companies in the sample, designating a geographical location is unproblematic since they only have operations in a single country. In some cases, there are companies that run operations in several different countries. One possibility is that the companies have operations in several different locations in Africa. One example would be the Bank of (British) West Africa, which, during some periods of time, had operations in several different British colonies in West Africa but also in North Africa (see Chap. 9). Another possibility is that a company might have operations not only in one or more African countries but also in other parts of the world. One such company would, for example, be the Rio Tinto Company—originally a mining company based in Spain, but as time went by, increasingly globalized with operations in many parts of the world, including in Africa and Australia (see Chap. 14).

The methodological approach employed here essentially treats all the companies as black boxes, as their internal distribution of revenue from and costs for different countries or regions of operations is not known to us. In cases where a company was operating in multiple countries, primary sources (primarily the Stock Exchange Yearbook) and secondary literature have been employed in order to try to determine the country where the company in question had most of its activities. Determining this was in many such cases problematic. The geographical disaggregation must, for that reason, be considered to be crude. This might in some cases also create a problem with biased estimates when the data is disaggregated geographically (if a company is classified as having their main operations in one country but make much of their profits from or experience most of the losses in another). This must be kept in mind when interpreting the geographically disaggregated results.

Different Types of Colonies

Several scholars have suggested making a distinction between different types of colonies, for example, Myint's classification of settler colonies and peasant colonies (Myint 1967). In the peasant economies, economic activities were dominated by the native population, and colonial ventures were mainly involved in activities such as merchant trading and banking. In the settler colonies, in contrast, larger numbers of European settlers were interested in acquiring labourers to work on European-owned mines and plantations, and thereby often imposed policies to ascertain access to low-paid labour (Myint 1967, chaps. 3–4). This distinction is of importance for this study as some theoretical schools (discussed in Chap. 3) have argued that the latter type of policies increased the rate of return on investment. If that is the case, we would expect to find systematic differences in the rate of return on investment depending on the type of colony the investments were made in.

The distinction between settler and peasant (or as some scholars have put it more recently, non-settler) colonies has been used in much previous research on the history of colonial Africa (see, e.g. Mosley 1983; Austin 2007, 2008; Bowden et al. 2008; Bowden and Mosley 2012; Austin 2016, 324–25). In this literature, South Africa, Southern and Northern Rhodesia (modern-day Zimbabwe and Zambia), Mozambique, Angola, Kenya, Belgian Congo (Democratic Republic of Congo), Bechuanaland (Botswana) and Algeria are generally categorized as settler colonies (Mosley 1983, 5), and other African colonies as peasant/non-settler colonies. The classifications are crude, as it, for example, does not take into account the fact that the share of land alienated by or reserved for Europeans differed vastly between what then are considered to be settler colonies (Bowden and Mosley 2012, table 1). The classification can nonetheless shed some further light on the factors at play. Samir Amin has instead suggested a different classification distinguishing between 'African trading colonies' on the one hand and 'Africa of the labor reserves' on the other (Amin 1972). His classification, on the other hand, only covers 'black Africa', so it does not explicitly include North Africa.

For the purposes of this book, the differences between Myint's and Amin's schemes of classification are small and will have no substantial impact upon our results. Both schemes lead to the same distinction between colonies for virtually all the colonies that carry any weight in our sample. South Africa and the two Rhodesias are categorized as settler/labour reserve colonies, while Ghana and Nigeria are categorized as peasant/trading colonies. Since the choice of classification will not impact the categorization to any substantial degree, the choice between them is merely a choice of terminology. Here, we will employ the terminology of settler versus non-settler economies, as this has become standard practice among scholars in recent years.

The only problematic issue is whether to classify Egypt as belonging to the peasant/non-settler colonies (if using Myint's scheme) or as a trading colony (if using Amin's scheme) or to instead treat it as a completely different type of colony. In this book, we make a distinction between the colonies of labour reserves/settler colonies, on the one hand, and other colonies, on the other hand, in order to analyse if the low-paid labour policies that Myint describes as characteristic of settler colonies could have had any impact upon the estimated return on investment. We therefore classify Egypt as a non-settler colony.

Sectoral Division

For sectoral classification of companies, we have primarily relied upon the information from the GFD database, which in turn is based upon the classifications made in the primary source employed (the IMM and *The Times of London*). In most cases, the classification is straightforward. We have on several occasions merged some of the sectors under one joint heading. Mining (including gold mining) has, on the other hand, been reclassified as a sector independent of other 'Materials' industries under which it was classified in the GFD.

Chapter 14 of the book is furthermore devoted to putting the African mining industry into an international, comparative perspective. In order to do so, a second sample of global mining companies was created. All companies registered in the GFD database as being involved in mining (including the subcategory of gold mining) during the period 1869–1969 were included in the sample. As iron-mining and coal-mining companies generally were classified under other headings in the primary sources used by GFD (e.g. under the heading of 'Iron, Coal and Steel Companies' in

Table 5.2 Descriptive statistics of sample of global mining companies, 1869–1969

	Companies	Company-months
Africa	511	96,155
Asia	88	18,093
Europe	144	22,537
Latin America	59	8677
North America	84	9492
Oceania	142	20,786
Total	*1028*	*175,740*

Source: Global Mining Equities Database (GMED)

the IMM together with smelters and other similar companies), any such mines have not been included in this analysis. The sample consequently only includes non-ferrous, non-coal-mining companies.

The selection criteria led to a total of 1097 non-ferrous, non-coal-mining companies found in the GFD database. A procedure of verifying the data was undertaken similar to the one described for the African sample of companies above. During this process, we were unable to verify the data for a smaller number of companies in the primary sources employed here. These companies were therefore excluded from the sample. In total, our sample of mining companies therefore includes a total of 1028 companies operating around the world. This database will henceforth be called the *Global Mining Equities Database (GMED)*. The geographical distribution of the companies in this sample is shown in Table 5.2.

Company Longevity

We furthermore analyse the longevity of the African ventures in our sample. Longevity of a company can be defined and analysed in several ways depending on what one is interested in. We define longevity as the duration for which a company was traded on the stock exchange. This is not a measurement of the formal lifespan of these companies, as companies could have been incorporated prior to being publicly traded (and they could survive after delisting). We believe that such a measurement is a reasonable proxy for how many years each company was a viable investment object for the general public, which is the focus of this study.

In order to analyse longevity, we need to know which companies failed to survive. For that purpose, we made use of the 1989–1990 edition of the Register of Defunct Companies (RDC). This register contains over 25,000 notices of companies removed from *The International Stock Exchange Official Yearbook* and its predecessors since 1875. The publication gives us the possibility to find information on when companies in our sample were listed on LSE but also information on the timing and conditions for delisting. Companies delisted from the London Stock Exchange, for whatever reasons, were classified as having failed to survive. In the first part of the analysis, we define failure to survive without any distinction as to the reasons for delisting. We return to the causes of delisting in the latter part of the analysis.

In the RDC, we have identified 328 companies that were formally delisted during the period of our study. This is slightly less than half of our total sample. A comparatively large number of the other companies (263) disappear from our sample without being recorded in the RDC as having been delisted from the London Stock Exchange. The most plausible reason for this is that the company formally remained listed on the LSE, but for some reason was not traded regularly enough (e.g. too small, or no stocks traded on the open market) to be included in the primary sources underlying our database. These companies are here treated as censored in the longevity analysis.

Geographically, the 328 companies that were delisted are broadly representative of the total sample, as South Africa make up the lion part (with 206 registered companies), followed by Ghana (32), Northern Rhodesia (27), Nigeria (27), Egypt (17) and a number of other minor countries (19).

Our measure of company longevity is not perfect. For example, many companies had been private ventures before their IPO. Our method cannot capture any private precursors to the companies listed on the LSE. More important for our analysis, though, is that some companies were listed on the London Stock Exchange before they were included in the sources underlying our database. Among the companies found in the RDC, the median companies had been listed on the LSE for a few years before they appear in the primary sources underlying our database. Only a handful of companies had been traded publicly any longer period than that before starting to appear in our database. In some cases, furthermore, companies disappear from our sample some time before being delisted from the LSE. In such cases, the companies most probably disappear from our sample because they were too small to be included in the primary sources underlying our database, only to be delisted some time later. Among the companies found in the RDC as delisted, the median companies were traded on the LSE at most one year between disappearing from our sample and being formally delisted. These minor errors will introduce a slight downward bias in our longevity estimates, which must be kept in mind when interpreting the data.

The reasons for companies to delist were categorized based on the data in the RDC. In the introduction to the RDC, the formal reasons for bringing a company to its end are explained, compulsory wind-up, voluntary liquidation or subject to court supervision (London Stock Exchange 1990, 6–7). This formal classification is not helpful for our purposes since almost all of the companies ended their days by voluntary liquidation. Instead, based on the additional information supplied in the RDC, we constructed three categories on our own, namely, *shutdown*, *reconstruction* and *takeover*. A delisting was coded as a shutdown if the RDC mentioned a final meeting with shareholders. Sometimes, but not always, there was also a sentence stating 'capital back to contributories'—yet a further indication that the company actually ceased to exist in its current form. To be coded as a reconstruction, the RDC needed to state that either (1) company was reconstructed or (2) that the undertaking was acquired by a new company after a specified amount of the shares' value were written down. In nearly all of these cases, the new company name was mentioned. To be coded as a takeover, the RDC needed to state that either (1) the delisted company was amalgamated with another company or (2) that the delisted company was acquired by another company.

Complementary Qualitative Microdata

The construction of the African Colonial Equities Database is at the heart of this project. In order to make use of the database, we have also used several other types of sources and materials. Secondary literature have of course been highly relevant to put the estimated levels of return in its proper historical context. This literature includes business history, financial history and general economic history. The secondary literature is particularly important for Chaps. 8, 9, 10 and 11, where we aim to contribute to the historiography of the region by providing evidence on the total return on investment there, which generally has been lacking in the previous research. With its focus on the link between the financial market in London and the companies' actual operation in Africa, we also connect literature that previously has not been analysed together.

Furthermore, secondary literature is also important in order to identify specific factors that could explain the return on investment—the spread of new mining techniques, the development of monopolies or access to political influence. The literature offers insights in the assessment of these factors' relative importance since they were time-specific and context-bound. In some cases, authors of company monographs have dealt in-depth with such issues. Furthermore, this is also important because this literature has seldom treated these factors quantitatively and rarely related them to the overall question of the total return to investment. One typical example is the diamond company De Beers Consolidated, where there exists an abundant literature ranging from critical popular accounts to in-depth scholarly studies on the role of Cecil Rhodes. We have used this literature in combination with our database in Chap. 11. Here, we show how the return on investments in De Beers Consolidated was important for the long-term return of a London-based investor, but at the same time, we show how the negative profitability of De Beers during the interwar years must be understood in the context of a structural transformation process of the global diamond industry.

In Chap. 12, we take one step further in the analysis of specific factors behind the total return on investment. Based on the notion that all investors are not equal in terms of access to relevant information, we study the case of the leading gold company of the 1890s—Rand Mines Limited. We specifically analyse the flow of information pertaining to Rand Mines and the role played by asymmetric information. In order to do this, we trace the roots of the company in the late 1880s and follow its development during the 1890s, through a variety of historical sources. The archives of Rand Mines Limited (and important parts of the Corner

House Group) are maintained in a corporate archive, located at the head office of Barloworld, in Johannesburg. The archive is well preserved and contains roughly 700 linear metres of company documents. The material covers Rand Mines Ltd, but since the Johannesburg office was the central node of the Corner House Group, the archive also contains a lot of material from individual mines and a whole range of subsidiaries.

The archives reveal internal perspectives through both memos and substantial correspondence between the offices in Johannesburg and London. It also reveals the company's external communication in the form of annual reports. Annual reports between 1893 and 1899 were used for the construction of spreadsheets of information in order to follow the company during its initial years of existence. The next step in the process was to go through the extensive correspondence material. We concentrated on the years from 1887 to 1898. Photocopies were taken of letters and internal documents which were coded in a spreadsheet according to the themes of the chapter.

In order to get an external contemporary view of the company, we have collected data from the business press. The business press was an important transmitter of information relating to international investments in the late nineteenth century. Since the South African mining market was a hot topic in London during the 1890s, the reports in the business press were widely spread among investors. Therefore, we used the historical archives of *The Economist* and *The Financial Times*, which are available through www.gale.com. It is clear that these two journals gathered information from many different sources, not least from the local South African press.

We made a search for Rand Mines and found 30 articles in *The Financial Times* and *The Economist* from December 1893 to September 1895. These articles shed light on how the business press perceived and discussed Rand Mines in the mining boom of 1894–1895. Specifically, it also provided us with valuable information on the role played by the business press in critically discussing the issues analysed in the chapter. There was valuable information in both of these journals, even though Rand Mines appeared more frequently in *The Financial Times* than in *The Economist*. This can be explained by the fact that *The Financial Times* had a regular section called *The Mining Market* where Rand Mines appeared, but then most of the times only to report the price of the share. In 1894, Rand Mines appeared throughout the year in texts where the journals analysed the South African mining market. This was a time when gold shares were at the centre of attention in the City of London (as will be discussed further in Chap. 12).

The company's relationship to the business press is also frequently referred to in the archival materials from the company, for example, when the press became engaged in reporting on conflicts where the company was involved. The company was occasionally also involved in trying to influence the management of the local press, for example, when editors were appointed.

A Note on Terminology

In this book, we will use the terminology of 'white' and 'black' populations in several of the colonies, most importantly regarding the colonies in Southern Africa. The terms are far from unproblematic or uncontroversial, as they were commonly used by racist colonial regimes during the colonial period, and today also carry racist connotations. The simple reason to make a distinction between different groups of the population in this book in the first place is because the British colonial power—as well as many of the other colonial powers in Africa—imposed policies in favour of (many members of) the 'white' population and discriminating against (all or most of) the 'black' population (see more on this in Chaps. 8, 9, 10 and 11). Many of these discriminatory policies, we argue in the book, were imposed with the direct intention of having—and in reality often turned out to have—consequences for companies' bottom-line, for example, by lowering the cost of labour.

There are other terms that have been used to describe essentially the same distinction between different groups. One alternative term for the 'black' population is, for example, to call them 'Africans', in contrast to 'Europeans'. This division might be suitable when describing some of the colonies, such as some of the colonies in West Africa, where many of the 'Europeans' most probably considered themselves just as that, European, rather than as natives of the country they indeed were living in at the time. For other parts of the continent, such a terminology could be much less suitable. In settler colonies, such as South Africa, many of the 'white' population might be of European descent, but a substantial share of this population had an ancestry of people that had been living on the African continent for generations, and therefore, considered themselves as 'African' as 'black' people living in the same region. It would be possible, but perhaps not always as short, to make a distinction between 'people of African descent' or 'people of European descent', respectively. The fact that people also might be of a mixed African/European descent further complicates such a distinction. Colonial policies would, in such cases, often stipulate determining the descent by the colour of the skin, that is, whether they were considered to be 'black' or 'white' (or 'coloured', as many of mixed background came to be called).

References

Amin, Samir. 1972. Underdevelopment and Dependence in Black Africa: Historical Origin. *Journal of Peace Research* 9 (2): 105–119.

Austin, Gareth. 2007. Reciprocal Comparison and African History: Tackling Conceptual Eurocentrism in the Study of Africa's Economic Past. *African Studies Review* 50 (3): 1–28.

———. 2008. Resources, Techniques, and Strategies South of the Sahara: Revising the Factor Endowments Perspective on African Economic Development, 1500–20001. *The Economic History Review* 61 (3): 587–624.

———. 2016. Sub-Saharan Africa. In *A History of the Global Economy 1500 to the Present*, ed. Joerg Baten, 316–350. Cambridge: Cambridge University Press.

Bowden, Sue, and Paul Mosley. 2012. *Politics, Public Expenditure and the Evolution of Poverty in Africa 1920–2009*. Working Paper. Department of Economics, University of Sheffield. Sheffield.

Bowden, Sue, Blessing Chiripanhura, and Paul Mosley. 2008. Measuring and Explaining Poverty in Six African Countries: A Long-Period Approach. *Journal of International Development* 20 (8): 1049–1079.

Campbell, Gareth, and Meeghan Rogers. 2017. Integration between the London and New York Stock Exchanges, 1825–1925. *The Economic History Review* 70 (4): 1185–1218.

Chabot, Benjamin R., and Christopher J. Kurz. 2010. That's Where the Money Was: Foreign Bias and English Investment Abroad, 1866–1907. *The Economic Journal* 120 (547): 1056–1079.

Davis, Lance, and Robert Huttenback. 1988. *Mammon and the Pursuit of Empire: The Economics of British Imperialism*. Abridged ed. Cambridge: Cambridge University Press.

Dimson, Elroy, Paul Marsh, and Mike Staunton. 2002. *Triumph of the Optimists: 101 Years of Global Investment Returns*. Princeton, NJ: Princeton University Press.

Edelstein, Michael. 1970. *The Rate of Return to U.K. Home and Foreign Investment, 1870–1913*. Ph.D. Dissertation, University of Pennsylvania.

———. 1976. Realized Rates of Return on UK Home and Overseas Portfolio Investment in the Age of High Imperialism. *Explorations in Economic History* 13 (3): 283–329.

———. 1982. *Overseas Investment in the Age of High Imperialism: The United Kingdom, 1850–1914*. London: Methuen.

Exchange, London Stock. 1990. *Register of Defunct and Other Companies Removed from the Stock Exchange Official Year-Book*. London: Macmillan.

Grossman, Richard S. 2015. Bloody Foreigners! Overseas Equity on the London Stock Exchange, 1869–1929. *The Economic History Review* 68 (2): 471–521.

———. 2017. *Stocks for the Long Run: New Monthly Indices of British Equities, 1869–1929*. CEPR Discussion Paper No. DP12121.

Hannah, Leslie. 2018. The London Stock Exchange, 1869–1929: New Statistics for Old? *Economic History Review* 71 (4): 1349–1356.

Hauner, Thomas, Branko Milanovic, and Suresh Naidu. 2017. *Inequality, Foreign Investment, and Imperialism*. Stone Center Working Paper.

Jordà, Oscar, Katharina Knoll, Dmitry Kuvshinov, Moritz Schularick, and Alan Taylor. 2019. *The Rate of Return on Everything, 1870–2015*. Quarterly Journal of Economics. Forthcoming.

Michie, Ranald C. 2001. *The London Stock Exchange: A History*. Oxford: Oxford University Press.

Mosley, Paul. 1983. *The Settler Economies: Studies in the Economic History of Kenya and Southern Rhodesia 1900–1963*. Cambridge: Cambridge University Press.

Myint, Hla. 1967. *The Economics of Developing Countries*. London: Hutchinson.

O'Donoghue, Jim, Louise Goulding, and Grahame Allen. 2004. Consumer Price Inflation Since 1750. *Economic Trends* No. 604.

Obstfeld, Maurice, and Alan M. Taylor. 2003. Sovereign Risk, Credibility and the Gold Standard: 1870–1913 versus 1925–31. *The Economic Journal* 113 (487): 241–275.

———. 2004. *Global Capital Markets: Integration, Crisis, and Growth*. New York: Cambridge University Press.

Reinhart, Carmen M., and Kenneth S. Rogoff. 2009. *This Time Is Different: Eight Centuries of Financial Folly*. Princeton, NJ: Princeton University Press.

Schularick, Moritz, and Alan M. Taylor. 2012. Credit Booms Gone Bust: Monetary Policy, Leverage Cycles, and Financial Crises, 1870–2008. *American Economic Review* 102 (2): 1029–1061.

Visser, Nicholas. 1997. Postcoloniality of a Special Type: Theory and Its Appropriations in South Africa. *The Yearbook of English Studies* 27: 79–94.

Diamond mines workers 1887. The illustration contains various scenes showing the treatment of black workers in the mines of Kimberley in South Africa in 1887, including an attempt to stop a worker from swallowing a diamond. © Illustrated London News/Mary Evans Picture Library

Part II

Aggregate Results

6

The Rate of Return on Investment in Africa

Growing Investments in Africa

Investments in Africa differed considerably between the colonies and over time. Figure 6.1 shows the market capitalization of our total sample of companies operating in Africa and traded on the London Stock Exchange. The total market capitalization increased substantially over time, starting at around £6.5 million in 1869 and ending at over £5100 million a century later. A substantial part of this increase was due to inflation. Figure 6.1 therefore reports the market capitalization in the sample using 1868 constant prices. The increase in market capitalization is still impressive, increasing from £6.5 million to almost £750 million in 1868 constant prices. The increasing market capitalization is, naturally, a combination of inflows of new companies traded on the market and an increase in the market valuation of companies already established on the market.

The growth of total market capitalization occurred in a couple of different stages. Market capitalization increased substantially in real terms during the last decade of the nineteenth century and the first years of the twentieth century, peaking in 1904. The collapse of the South African

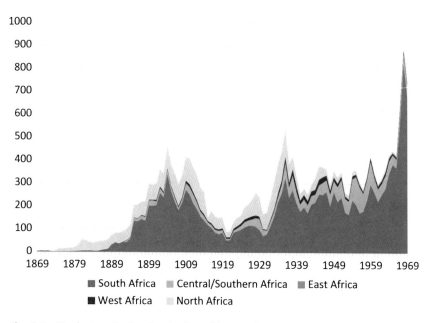

Fig. 6.1 Market capitalization in the African Colonial Equities Database, by year and region, 1869–1969 (£ million, constant 1868 prices). Source: African Colonial Equities Database (ACED). Note: market capitalization calculated for the month of December every year of observation. East African investments are too small to be clearly discernible in the figure

mining boom (see Chap. 11), followed by the collapse of the Suez Canal Company's share price associated with the outbreak of the First World War (see Chap. 8), led to major losses in the capital values of African investments. These losses were, on an aggregate level, not recuperated until the 1930s, and then through a major growth in the value of mining stocks—particularly so for many of the gold-mining companies (see Chaps. 11 and 14). The market, finally, experienced a drastic growth in the last decade of our study.

Geographically, the sample is dominated by two regions: North and South Africa, as is also evident from Fig. 6.1. North African companies (primarily some banks along with the Suez Canal Company) initially dominated the sample. From the 1890s onwards, South African companies started to take on an increasingly dominant position in the sample, a dominance which increased even further at the end of the period of our study.

6 The Rate of Return on Investment in Africa

Cain and Hopkins have famously argued that the United Kingdom's involvement in Africa developed along two different axes: on the one hand, a north-south axis reflecting financial interests and, on the other hand, an east-west axis reflecting manufacturing interests (Cain and Hopkins 2001, 311). Their argument is partially supported by our data. One indication of this is that investments channelled through the London Stock Exchange were clearly of a much smaller magnitude in Eastern and Western Africa compared to investments in Northern and Southern Africa.

There were, on the other hand, no similarly clear-cut qualitative differences in the types of operations invested in the different regions. The Egyptian sample of companies is completely dominated by one particular company—Compagnie Universelle du Canal Maritime de Suez, the Suez Canal company. This company alone accounted for between 60 and 90 per cent of total market capitalization of the Egyptian portfolio of equity traded on the London Stock Exchange. Aside from this company, the investments in Egypt were indeed largely focussed upon the financial sector, as Cain and Hopkins argued. The South African sample of companies is, for its part, highly dominated by a number of mining companies—initially the diamond-mining companies established around Kimberley from the 1860s, followed by the gold-mining companies established around Witwatersrand from the 1880s onwards—as well as a couple of banks and other financial institutions. In Central-Southern Africa, mining companies also dominate the sample completely, most importantly Cecil Rhodes' British South Africa Company, followed by the development of a couple of larger mining companies established on the Copperbelt in current-day Zambia, particularly from the 1920s onwards. The question is: should these investments be considered to be dominated by financial interests? Interpreted liberally, financial interests were deeply involved in the Suez Canal Company (see Chap. 8), and mining companies in Southern Africa were clearly a bridge between mining and financial interests (see Chaps. 11 and 12). Hence, the data could be said to fit with Cain and Hopkins' claim.

The West African sample of companies is more diverse. The sample was initially dominated by a few steamship companies operating in West Africa. The chartered Royal Niger Company (RNC) (later renamed the Niger Co. Ltd) is also one of the major companies in the sample. To the extent that Cain and Hopkins' east-west axis based on 'manufacturing interests' is interpreted to have been associated with such trading companies, this could be said to fit with their characterization. The mining company Ashanti Goldfields did, however, grow and became the most important company in the West African companies traded on the London Stock Exchange for a long period. Furthermore, a number of other West African mining ventures—tin mining in Nigeria, diamond mining in both Sierra Leone and on the Gold Coast—also became important for foreign investors. If mining interests are considered to have been an important part of the nexus of financial interests, this does not fit squarely with Cain and Hopkins' characterization of the east-west axis based on manufacturing interests. There were finally a small number of companies traded on the London Stock Exchange operating in East Africa, and the companies never achieved any substantial market capitalization, if compared to companies operating elsewhere in Africa. The companies were largely involved in mercantile activities of various sorts, and might therefore be interpreted as fitting into Cain and Hopkin's axis.

In summary, Cain and Hopkins' characterization of British involvement in Africa as following either of the two axes—east-west (manufacturing interests) or north-south (finance interests)—is, on the one hand, a fitting description of the magnitude of the investments in the different regions of Africa, and on the other hand, it is too simplified to explain the character of the investments in this way. It neither captures the major investments in the single most important company in the sample (the Suez Canal Company), nor does it fully take into account the historical change occurring in the investments in British West Africa (from mercantile to mining interests).

Decreasing Market Concentration

With a market capitalization-weighted index, some companies in the sample will be of much greater importance than the others. Our African portfolio is dependent on a limited number of companies. This is illustrated in Fig. 6.2, showing the share of the total market capitalization of the three largest companies, in total and in different African regional portfolios.

Figure 6.2 shows the three-firm concentration ratio of market capitalization of the companies in the sample. The concentration was high during the 1870s and 1880s, with the three largest firms in the sample accounting for 70–80 per cent of the sample's total market capitalization. The explanation was the Compagnie Financiere de Suez, which singlehandedly accounted for around 75 per cent of the market capitalization of all companies in our sample and more than 95 per cent of the market capitalization of the North African portfolio. The aggregate return on investment during this period does therefore to a large extent depend upon the fate of this particular company.

A decrease in market concentration started in the 1880s, primarily in the West and South African portfolios. The overall market concentration decreased rapidly from the outset of the 1890s. New companies were also

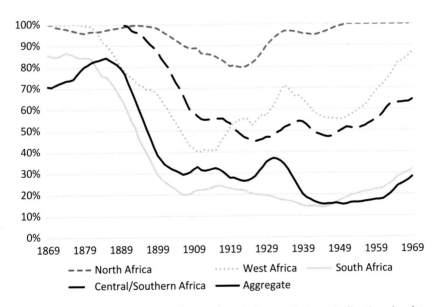

Fig. 6.2 Three-firm concentration ratio of the market capitalization in the African Colonial Equities Database, by year and region, 1869–1969 (per cent, nine-year moving averages). Source: African Colonial Equities Database (ACED)

established and gained importance in North Africa from around this time, though the Suez Canal Company remained dominant in that regional portfolio. Several of the newly established companies are well known from previous literature—including the British South Africa Company, De Beers Consolidated Mining, Consolidated Gold Fields of South Africa, Ashanti Goldfields and Anglo-American Corporation of South Africa (see Chaps. 8, 9, 10 and 11). By the early twentieth century, the three largest companies in the sample together accounted for around 35 per cent of total market capitalization, leaving the remaining 65 per cent to a large number of smaller companies.

The trend shifted in West Africa around the time of the First World War, when a few companies again started to become of increasing importance. The trend also shifted in North Africa around a decade later. Meanwhile, the trend towards decreased market concentration continued in Central and Southern Africa, including in South Africa. By this time, the latter regions were of much greater importance in terms of market capitalization than the North and West African equity markets. By the interwar period, therefore, the total market concentration had dropped even further, so that the large companies together accounted for around 30 per cent of the total market capitalization of the investments. After the Second World War, the market concentration of the aggregate African portfolio reached its lowest point during our period of study, when the three largest companies only accounted for around 15 per cent of total market capitalization in the whole sample. From around the 1950s, the trend shifted upwards, and by the late 1960s, it once again was around 30 per cent.

Total Return on Investment in Africa

Table 6.1 reports data on the aggregate nominal and real return on investment for the whole period of our study, 1869–1969. In order to enable comparisons with previous studies, this table reports data on both geometric and arithmetic mean, even though it was argued in Chap. 5 that arithmetic mean is basically flawed when estimating historical rates of return on investment.

6 The Rate of Return on Investment in Africa

Table 6.1 Nominal and real return on investment in Africa, 1869–1969 (average per year, per cent)

	Nominal return (%)	Real return (%)
Arithmetic mean	10.0	8.0
Geometric mean	8.3	5.9
Standard deviation	20.8	22.0

Source: African Colonial Equities Database (ACED)
N = 702

As expected, the estimated arithmetic return on investment was higher than the geometric mean return. Over the whole century studied, the average return on investment in Africa was a respectable 8.3 per cent per year in nominal terms (geometric mean), translating into a real return on investment of 5.9 per cent per year. The figures are, to a large extent, driven by the very high return on investment exhibited by some of the largest companies in the sample, for example, 10 per cent per year for Anglo-American Corporation of South Africa, 12 per cent for De Beers Consolidated and 22 per cent per year for Consolidated African Selection Trust. There were also a substantial number of highly unsuccessful investments in Africa. In Fig. 6.3, we show the distribution of the estimated average return on investment in each particular company in the sample (in nominal terms). The capital losses incurred from the substantial amount of companies that on average had a negative return on investment substantially reduced the average return on the total portfolio.

Figure 6.3 shows the distribution of the average nominal return on investment in a particular company over the whole 'lifetime' of that particular company. As can be seen in the graph, the distribution is similar to a normal distribution, centred around a median company achieving a return on investment of 1.2 per cent per year in nominal terms. A large number, 237 of the companies in the sample, fall into the range of a return on investment between 0 and 10 per cent per year. A smaller number of companies—137 in total—exhibit an average nominal return on investment higher than 10 per cent per year. There were finally a handful of companies exhibiting an average return on investment exceeding 100 per cent per year. These outliers are in all cases present in our sample for a single year before they disappear from our sample, generally after being acquired by another company. There are at the same time a large number

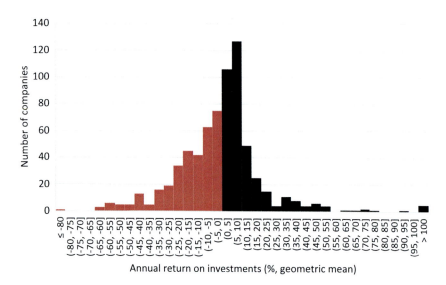

Fig. 6.3 Histogram of the nominal average return on investment in individual companies in Africa, 1869–1969 (geometric mean per year). Source: African Colonial Equities Database (ACED)

of companies that fail economically, from the perspective of the investor. No less than 328 of the companies in the sample actually exhibit a negative average nominal return on investment. Furthermore, if the real return on investment had been calculated, even fewer companies would have made a positive return to begin with. The return on investment of the individual company is to some extent associated with the length of time a company is present in our sample, an issue we will return to in Chap. 7.

Changing Rate of Return over Time

Figure 6.4 shows our estimates of the return on investment by decade. The data reveals considerable changes in return on investment over time. This can be explained, on the one hand, by differences in the nominal return on investment and, on the other hand, by the impact of inflation. There were also substantial fluctuations—volatility—between the years, an issue we will return to in Chap. 7.

6 The Rate of Return on Investment in Africa

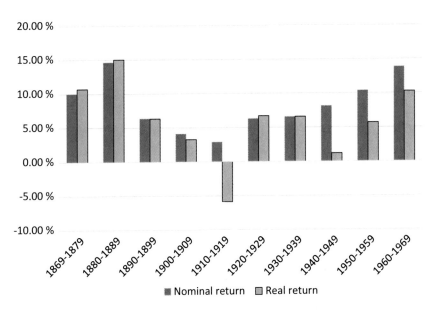

Fig. 6.4 Nominal and real return on investment in Africa, by decade, 1869–1969 (geometric mean per year). Source: African Colonial Equities Database (ACED)

The early years of the Scramble for Africa, in the 1870s and 1880s, exhibited very high return on investment in Africa, on average some 10–15 per cent per year. This was attributable to the development of the Suez Canal, on the one hand, and the development of the South African mining industry, on the other. The 1890s still exhibited high returns on investment than the previous decades, on average around 6 per cent per year, as the South African mining industry required increasing amounts of capital investments without generating particularly high returns in its initial phase. As the rate of inflation was close to zero (or even slightly negative) during these first decades of our study, these high nominal rates of return translated into a high real rate of return. When a number of these companies failed in the early 1900s, the average nominal return on investment decreased to a modest level of 3 per cent per year.

This was followed by the outbreak of the First World War which was a period of substantial losses in nominal terms for investments in Africa. The results are in line with global securities markets at the time. The information of the outbreak of the war also had direct effects on African investments: in July 1914, the weighted index fell by 8.4 per cent. Investors had experienced other periods of even higher losses before. In parallel to the fall of share prices was the onset of substantial inflation. By the end of the First World War, inflation temporarily increased to more than 20 per cent per year. This combination effectively lowered the total return on investment to negative levels.

The interwar period exhibited a recovery of the nominal rate of return on African investments during the 1920s and 1930s to around 7 per cent per year on average. As the rate of inflation in the United Kingdom decreased to low levels during this time, this reflected a real rate of return of a similarly high magnitude. After the Gold Standard was abandoned in the 1930s, inflation increased again. Inflation reached high levels, particularly during the Second World War—even though the real rate of return at least stayed positive, but most modest, during the decade (+1 per cent per year), in contrast to during the First World War.

In the 1950s and 1960s, finally, the nominal rate of return on investment in Africa increased further—reaching 10 per cent per year in the 1950s and 14 per cent per year in the 1960s. At the same time, the rate of inflation decreased. The consequence was that the real rate of return on African investments again reached historically very high levels, exceeding 10 per cent per year during the final decade of our study.

Table 6.2 shows the real annual average rate of return on investment by region of operation. As can be seen in the table, there were substantial differences between the regions. The real total return on investment was not even positive in all regions: whereas the real return for investments in South Africa amounted to 6.2 per cent per year, it was almost exactly

Table 6.2 Real return on investment in Africa, by region, 1869–1969 (geometric mean per year)

Region	Real return (%)	Number of companies
North Africa	2.5	42
East Africa	−2.5	17
West Africa	−0.1	106
Central/Southern Africa (excl. South Africa)	2.2	87
South Africa (colony/republic)	6.2	450
Total	*5.9*	*702*

Source: African Colonial Equities Database (ACED)

zero for investments in West Africa, and actually negative for what little investments there were in East Africa. The total average over the whole period, from 1869 to 1969, covers most substantial shifts within each region, so that return on investment, for example, was very high in Egypt during the early decades of our study but subsequently decreased. Investments in Central/Southern Africa, in contrast, remained low during the first decades of our study but increased to high levels by the end of the period of our study. Figure 6.5 therefore shows an index over the accumulated return on investment by region of operation in Africa over the period under study.

As is shown in the figure, the return on investment in North and South Africa was initially high. The two series also follow similar trajectories over several decades. A major divergence started to occur in the middle in the 1930s. By this time, the accumulated return in North Africa peaked at an index-value of almost 16,000 and then entered a downwards trajectory—so that the index ended up at around 1200 by the end of the period

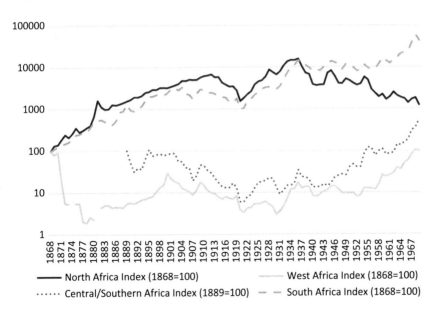

Fig. 6.5 Accumulated return on investment in Africa, by year and region, 1869–1969 (index 1868 = 100, logarithmic scale). Source: African Colonial Equities Database (ACED)

of our study. The return on investment in South Africa, in contrast, continued to be positive throughout the period under study—so that it had risen to an index-value of around 42,000 by the end of the period under study. The few early investors in West African equity experienced major losses during the first decade of our study with the index dropping from 100 at our starting point to a nadir of 2, just nine years later. These initial losses were of such magnitude that, at the end of the period of our study, the accumulated index did not even manage to reach the starting level (index-value 100), despite the fact that the real return on West African investments in the following nine decades actually approached normal levels (4.1 per cent per year for the period from 1880 to 1969). Investments in central/southern Africa started later than in the other regions. As in West Africa, the investors were initially experiencing major losses, so that the accumulated index went down from 100 to 6 in 1921, just a few years before the administration of Northern and Southern Rhodesia was handed over from the British South Africa Company to local or colonial authorities, respectively. From this time onwards, the accumulated return on the central/southern African portfolio increased rapidly, thereby reaching an index-value of 550 by the end of the period of our study. We will return to this issue at greater length in Chaps. 8, 9, 10 and 11.

Table 6.3 reports data on the real rate of return on investment disaggregated by industrial sector. Again, the average figure for the whole century of data masks important shifts over time, so that the estimate for the transport sector, for example, is determined by the fate of the

Table 6.3 Real return on investment in Africa, by sector, 1869–1969 (geometric mean per year)

	Real return (%)	Number of companies
Consumer products	1.9	32
Finance	3.4	43
Industrials	0.7	22
Materials (non-mining)	−1.1	22
Mining	7.1	518
Real estate	1.1	24
Transports	3.9	15
Utilities & Energy	2.3	26
Total	5.9	702

Source: African Colonial Equities Database (ACED)

Suez Canal Company, described in Chap. 8. Regardless, mining was the largest sector in our sample both in terms of number of companies and in terms of the market capitalization of the companies throughout most of the period under study. It was also undoubtedly the sector with the highest return on investment of them all, with an average real rate of return on investment at 7.1 per cent per year. All other sectors—such as industrials, non-mining materials production, utilities and energy production—were not very profitable in comparison, but exhibited a low (or in one case, even negative) return on investment.

Testing the Reliability of Our Results

Two previous studies allow us to test the reliability of our dataset. The first of these studies is the work by Dimson, Marsh and Staunton. As was noted earlier (see Chap. 4), the only country on the African continent that Dimson et al. incorporated in their study is South Africa. Similar to ours, their study also rests primarily on data from the London Stock Exchange. Their data suggests that the return on investment in South Africa might have been higher than the return both on domestic investments in the United Kingdom and on investments in their 'world'–portfolio.

In Fig. 6.6, our estimates for South Africa are compared to the South African estimates by Dimson et al. The comparison is based upon the nominal return on investment, as Dimson et al. used a South African price index for arriving at their estimated real rate of return on investment. We report decadal average data, as this is how Dimson et al. reported their data. Reassuringly, the two estimates show similar patterns over time. The main difference between the two estimates is that our estimate is lower than Dimson et al.'s estimate for the first decades of the twentieth century. As has been argued in a previous publication (Rönnbäck and Broberg 2018), we believe the differences are attributable to sample selection (where our sample is substantially larger and potentially suffers less from survival bias), and the weighting of the sample (where Dimson et al. seem to give improper weights when merging two different indices).

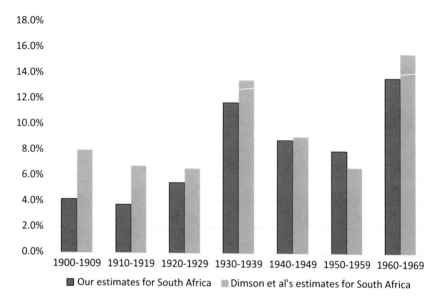

Fig. 6.6 Nominal return on British investments in South Africa compared to previous research, by decade, 1900–1969 (geometric mean per year). Source: Our estimates based on African Colonial Equities Database (ACED); Dimson et al.'s estimate based on (Dimson et al. 2002, table 28-2)

Another point of comparison is the work of Richard Grossman in which he studied the return on British investments worldwide during the period 1879–1928, essentially using the same underlying source of data—the Investor's Monthly Manual. As the underlying dataset is the same as in our study and the methods are similar (with the exception that Grossman employs annual data, whereas we employ monthly data), the results should essentially also be similar. This is also the case: with two exceptions, the data series exhibit a high correlation (correlation coefficient = 0.60, but increasing to a correlation coefficient of 0.89 if the two exceptional years are excluded), so there is a great overlap between the two series. The two exceptional years are 1881 and 1893, respectively. In 1881, our estimates suggest a much higher return on investment than Grossman's estimates (+117 per cent in our sample versus +49 per cent in Grossman's sample). This is most probably attributable to the fact that we employ monthly data for calculating the market capitalization-weighted index, in contrast to Grossman's estimates, which are weighted based on annual data only. In 1881, the capital value of the Suez Canal Company's shares boomed, particularly in connection to the anticipated occupation of Egypt (see Chap. 8). As the share price increased gradually over the year prior to the boom at the end of the year, it also gains an increasingly larger weighting in our sample, which it cannot do in Grossman's sample of annual data due to the method employed. When the final boom in the share's price occurred at the end of the year, this also impacts our sample more because of the greater weight attributed to this particular stock. There is also a major difference in the year 1893. In this year, Grossman's data suggested a very high positive return on investment (+119 per cent), in contrast to our estimates (+3 per cent). We have, unfortunately, not been able to determine for certain what might have caused such a major difference in this year.[1] Overall, our figures match previous estimates using similar data and methods well. This allows us to turn to comparing our estimates to previous estimates using other samples of data in order to draw conclusions about the rates of return on investment that we estimate for Africa.

Return on British Investments in Africa Versus Other Investments

As was described in Chap. 4, previous research has studied different time periods and different geographical units. Furthermore, different methods have been employed (e.g. reporting nominal or real returns, reporting annual data or averages over periods and calculating averages in different ways using either geometric or arithmetic means). Authors do furthermore not always report all the underlying data that would be necessary for constructing a coherent approach, enabling a comparison between all previous studies. Therefore, we cannot easily compare our results to all previous research at once, but are forced to compare our estimates to previous research in different stages.

---

[1] After a request to Grossman in December 2018, we have still been unable to determine which company/companies are driving the high return estimated in his data.

The first study in the field was the pioneering research by Herbert Frankel. Frankel studied the return on investment in South African mining, essentially using a method similar to the one employed in this study, but relying on data from the Johannesburg Stock Exchange. Previous research by Gareth Campbell and Meeghan Rogers, studying the integration of the London and New York Stock Exchanges from 1825 to 1925, has showed that there was a high degree of international integration in the pricing of the securities of companies that were listed on both stock exchanges (Campbell and Rogers 2017). As most of the major gold-mining companies included in Frankel's study were also traded in London, we might expect that the pricing of securities on these two markets were well integrated.

For the whole period 1887–1965, Frankel estimated that the average return on investment in South African gold mining amounted to 5.2 per cent per year. This is considerably higher than the figures from our dataset for the same period; the equivalent figure for South African investments in gold mining during this period is only 2.6 per cent per year in our dataset. Given that Frankel's book unfortunately is untransparent about the details of the methods he employed, it has not been possible to determine to what extent the difference between the estimates is attributable to differences in method (including sample selection and the weighting of the companies in the sample) and to what extent it is attributable to real differences between the two markets in Johannesburg and London, respectively. Frankel only reported annual data for the period from 1919 to 1962. This is reported in Fig. 6.7.

As was expected, there is a high degree of correlation between the two series during this period (correlation coefficient = 0.67, and increasing to 0.82 if we exclude the particular outliers in 1932–1933). The prices on the stock markets in Johannesburg and London were thus highly integrated during this period. A British investor would not have been any better off from investing on the Johannesburg Stock Exchange instead of investing in London. One exception could be the particular years 1932 and 1933. Much of the difference seen in these particular years is attributable to the details of how the data is calculated. Frankel's data is based on the Johannesburg Stock Exchange share prices from the month of October every year (Frankel 1967, 11, footnote 7). This particular choice of month

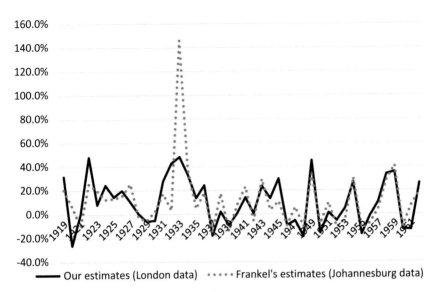

Fig. 6.7 Nominal return on British and South African investments in South African gold mining compared to previous research, by year, 1919–1962. Source: Our estimates based on African Colonial Equities Database (ACED); Frankel's estimate based on (Frankel 1967, appendix C, Table 6)

is important in this case, as South Africa left the Gold Standard in December 1932 (see Chap. 11). This change would not be captured in Frankel's data for the year 1932, but instead captured in the data for the year 1933, and would, in our dataset—based on monthly data—start to be captured already for the year 1932. This contributes to explaining why the figures differ both for 1932 (higher in our estimate than in Frankel's) and for 1933 (lower in our estimate than in Frankel's). Estimating the average return for these two years together therefore evens out most of this difference.

Another point of comparison when it comes to the return on investment in Africa is Buelens and Marysse's study of the return on investment in Belgian Congo (Buelens and Marysse 2009). In their study of Belgian Congo, they argue that return on investment in Belgian Congo was high, when compared to domestic investments in Belgium—at least until country risk became a reality in Belgian Congo in the late 1950s. The final years of colonialism, on the other hand, resulted in substantial losses for investors in Belgian Congo.

In Fig. 6.8, we compare the results from Buelens and Marysse's study with our estimate for one single company in our sample—Tanganyika Concessions. This company was the only company in our sample involved in Belgian Congo. Its involvement was however substantial, as it held about 40 per cent of the shares of the major Congolese mining company Union Minière du Haut-Katanga (UMHK) (see Chap. 10). This was Tanganyika Concessions' major holding, and since the UMHK was one of the major companies operating in Belgian Congo, we should expect the estimates for this company to be correlated with Buelens and Marysse's aggregate estimates. The return on investment in the Congo Free State was high several years prior to when the UMHK was born. It does, for example, seem as if return on investment in the Congo Free State boomed during the last years of the nineteenth century, possibly attributable to a boom in exports (particularly of rubber exports) from the colony at this

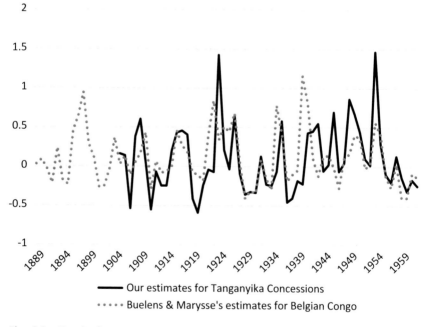

Fig. 6.8 Nominal return on investment in Belgian Congo compared to previous research, by year, 1889–1962. Source: Our estimates based on African Colonial Equities Database (ACED); Buelens & Marysse's estimates from (Buelens and Marysse 2009, appendix 1)

time (Renton et al. 2007, 37). From the time the UMHK was born in 1906, our figures on the return on investment in the major owner Tanganyika Concessions are reassuringly similar to the figures from Buelens and Marysse's previous research. On a statistical level, the two estimates show a quite high degree of correlation (correlation coefficient = 0.48). The major differences between the series seem to be attributable to two factors: slight differences in the volatility of the series and a minor time lag. First, the series for Tanganyika Concessions fluctuates more than the portfolio figures estimated by Buelens and Marysse (approximately 9 percentage points higher standard deviation for our data series for Tanganyika Concessions than for Buelens and Marysse's portfolio of all Belgian companies operating in Congo). This is hardly surprising as we, in this case, compare the return on investment in one single company to the return on investment for a portfolio of investments. This is, indeed, a key reason for the development of portfolio investments: fluctuations can be smoothed if the holdings in the portfolio fluctuate independently of each other. Second, there seems to be a time lag where some of the fluctuations in Buelens and Marysse's data only appear in the following year in our dataset.

Further points of comparison are with the research by Michael Edelstein, on the one hand, and Lance Davis and Robert Huttenback, on the other. It is important to bear in mind that their studies essentially exclude Africa—Edelstein's study because he excludes the mining sector completely from the study, and Davis and Huttenback's study because their constructed sample of non-domestic firms essentially virtually misses all the major African companies. There are furthermore other issues complicating any comparisons of the data (see Chap. 4). Nonetheless, Fig. 6.9 reports the results from such a comparison, putting our estimates for the return on investment in Africa relative to Edelstein's estimates for the return on equity investments overseas, and Davis and Huttenback's estimates for the return on investment in the British Empire. As Davis and Huttenback report their data in the form of a series of five-year moving averages, the data in the other two series in this figure are also reported in this way in order to enable a comparison. In aggregate, the figures amount to similar long-term average return on investment. Edelstein's data amount to an estimated real rate of return on

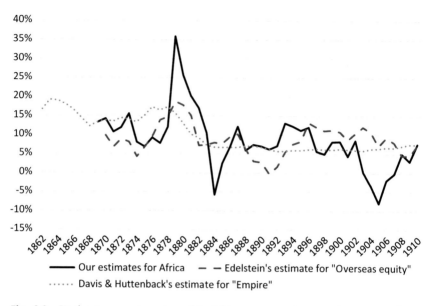

Fig. 6.9 Real return on investment in Africa compared to previous research on British foreign investments, by year, 1862–1913 (five year moving average). Source: Our estimates based on African Colonial Equities Database (ACED); Edelstein's estimates from (Edelstein 1976, appendix 3); Davis & Huttenback's estimates extracted from the data in (Davis and Huttenback 1986, chart 3.1)

investment in overseas equity of 8.3 per cent per year during the period 1870–1913. Our data for the return on investment in Africa during the same period is slightly lower, 7.5 per cent per year. Davis and Huttenback's data suggest that the return on investing in the British Empire amounted to an average of 9.0 per cent per year during the period 1869–1910. Again, our estimates for the return on investing in Africa during the same period are somewhat lower, 8.5 per cent per year. While our estimates on average are somewhat lower than the estimates by Edelstein and Davis and Huttenback, they are definitely of a similar magnitude.

While the magnitude of the rates of return from investing in these different investment portfolios might be similar, this does not automatically mean that the markets were well integrated. In the previously mentioned research by Campbell and Rogers, they find that the pricing of most securities during the nineteenth century was still driven primarily by local factors (Campbell and Rogers 2017). As there is little overlap between the companies included in our sample and the samples assembled by Edelstein or Davis and Huttenback, we might expect to find comparatively little correlation between the series. This is also the case: the data suggests a comparatively low degree of correlation in the annual data (correlation coefficient = 0.35, increasing to 0.40 if we exclude the particular outlier of 1881) between our estimates for Africa and Edelstein's estimates for UK 'overseas' equities.

A final point of comparison is with the rate of return on investing domestically in the United Kingdom. This is shown in Fig. 6.10. As the data by Dimson et al. is reported by decade, this is also how the data is reported in the figure.

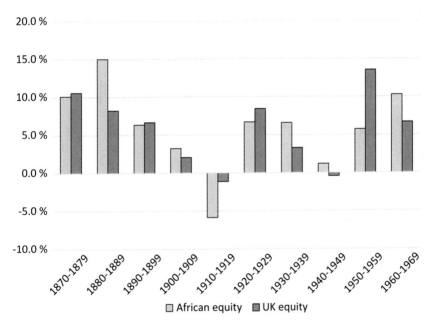

Fig. 6.10 Real return on investment in Africa compared to previous research on investments in the UK, by decade, 1870–1969 (geometric mean per year). Source: Our estimates based on African Colonial Equities Database (ACED); Edelstein's figures based on (Edelstein 1976, appendix 3); Dimson et al.'s figures based on (Dimson et al. 2002, Table 32–2). Note: Dimson et al.'s figures have here been adjusted by using the same data for UK inflation rate as is used throughout this study, so that any differences due to different estimates of the inflation rate are eliminated

The comparison is not perfect, as there might be issues, for example, of survival bias in the UK data (as Dimson et al.'s data from the United Kingdom was based on the largest, and presumably, most successful domestic companies on the London Stock Exchange, see Chap. 4). The most striking result of comparing our estimates to previous estimates is how similar the long-term patterns are. The rate of return on investing in domestic equities in the United Kingdom decreased from around 10 per cent per year in the 1870s to negative figures during the First World War. Our African estimates do, during this period, exhibit an increasing rate of return from 10 per cent per year in the 1870s to around 15 per cent in the 1880s. After this, the rate of return started to decrease. Had our study ended in 1913, as many of the previous studies of the relationship between imperialism and the return on investment have done (see Chap. 4), the average rate of return of investments would have seemed higher in Africa than in the United Kingdom. Following events would change this pattern. During the First World War, the rate of return on investment in Africa was lower than the rate of return on investing domestically in the United Kingdom. The two series continued to exhibit a similar development, a recovery after the war (stronger for the UK portfolio than for the African portfolio of investments) to drop again during the Second World War. The recovery in the 1950s was stronger in the United Kingdom than for our African portfolio, but during the 1960s, finally, the relationship shifted again so that the rate of return on investing in Africa was higher than the rate of return on investing domestically in the United Kingdom. Overall, the higher rate of return on investment in Africa than in the United Kingdom during the period prior to the First World War was therefore followed by a period of slightly lower rate of return on investment in Africa than in the United Kingdom from the First World War to the end of the period of our study.

Conclusion

In this chapter, we have analysed the aggregate rate of return on investment in Africa. The median company operating in Africa and traded on the London Stock Exchange was not generating a particularly high

6 The Rate of Return on Investment in Africa

rate of return on investment—in nominal terms, yielding an average rate of return of around 1 per cent per year. A nominal rate of return of that magnitude would not even match the average inflation rate during the period under study. Almost half of the companies in the sample failed even in nominal terms, from the perspective of the investors, in that they exhibited a negative average rate of return on investment. Unsurprisingly, a large number of the companies in the sample, therefore, wound up or were acquired by competitors. Investing in Africa was a risky business, an issue we will return to in the next chapter.

There were periods when investing in Africa was a profitable option, including during the Scramble for Africa in the late nineteenth century and in the period after the Second World War. The latter is surprising, given that this is the time of decolonization of Africa. This is an issue we will return to in Chap. 13. Investments in several other parts of the world, including domestically in the United Kingdom, exhibited similar patterns over time. The return on investment in Africa was therefore not particularly high when compared to the alternatives open to investors at the London Stock Exchange. The rate of return was, for example, on average more or less on par with the rate of return on investing in domestic equity in the United Kingdom. The return on investing in South Africa was higher than the return on investing elsewhere in Africa, but the rate of return from investing in that particular part of the continent was still not much higher than alternative investment opportunities. From the perspective of the ordinary investors on the London Stock Exchange, there were over the whole period seemingly no 'super-profits' to be made from investing in the African colonies. There were, however, occasions when investors were able to achieve a higher return on their investments than the average London equity investor. We will return to this issue in Chaps. 12 and 13. One sector, mining, dominated the investments both in terms of the number of companies involved and—for most of the period under study—in terms of the market capitalization of the companies in question. This sector was also the most profitable sector to invest in Africa. We will return to African mining and analyse this sector comparatively in Chap. 14.

References

Buelens, Frans, and Stefaan Marysse. 2009. Returns on Investments during the Colonial Era: The Case of the Belgian Congo. *The Economic History Review* 62 (s1): 135–166.

Cain, Peter J., and Anthony G. Hopkins. 2001. *British Imperialism, 1688–2000*. Harlow: Longman.

Campbell, Gareth, and Meeghan Rogers. 2017. Integration between the London and New York Stock Exchanges, 1825–1925. *The Economic History Review* 70 (4): 1185–1218.

Davis, Lance, and Robert Huttenback. 1986. *Mammon and the Pursuit of Empire: The Political Economy of British Imperialism, 1860–1912*. Cambridge: Cambridge University Press.

Dimson, Elroy, Paul Marsh, and Mike Staunton. 2002. *Triumph of the Optimists: 101 Years of Global Investment Returns*. Princeton, NJ: Princeton University Press.

Edelstein, Michael. 1976. Realized Rates of Return on UK Home and Overseas Portfolio Investment in the Age of High Imperialism. *Explorations in Economic History* 13 (3): 283–329.

Frankel, S. Herbert. 1967. *Investment and the Return to Equity to Capital in the South African Gold Mining Industry 1887–1965: An International Comparison*. Oxford: Basil Blackwell.

Renton, Dave, David Seddon, and Leo Zeilig. 2007. *The Congo: Plunder and Resistance*. London: Zed.

Rönnbäck, Klas, and Oskar Broberg. 2018. All That Glitters Is Not Gold: The Return on British Investments in South Africa, 1869–1969. *Studies in Economics and Econometrics* 42 (2): 61–79.

7

Risk and Return

Volatility

Several factors—ranging from price fluctuations to geopolitical conflicts or technological development—continuously change the outlook for individual companies. The inherently uncertain future creates a fundament for a financial market, trading on the relationship between risk and return.

The relationship between risk and return is crucial when we try to put yield figures in their proper context. The basic theoretical reasoning, as described in Chap. 3, is that a higher expected risk is associated with a higher expected return, otherwise no rational investor would choose to invest in more risky ventures. Risk in the form of market volatility can only be measured historically. Therefore, the distinction between implied and realized volatility becomes important when we study risk in specific historical contexts (Edelstein 1976, 299). We know from the literature that colonial ventures—particularly in mining—became popular investment objects at the London Stock Exchange (LSE) during the last decades of the nineteenth century. At the same time, due to market risks and asymmetric information, they also gained a reputation of being very risky for investors (Van Helten 1990, 176–77). To what extent was this reputation well deserved?

To approach this question, we start out by giving a helicopter perspective on the variability of returns in our sample between 1869 and 1969. Figure 7.1 shows the annual market capitalization-weighted annual real return on investment in Africa. The figure also includes the decadal average real rate of return, which has been reported in the previous chapter (see Fig. 6.4). As can be seen in the figure, the volatility of the weighted index was considerable. The market capitalization-weighted real return on investment often changed more than 20 percentage points, up or down, in a single year. The year 1881 was extreme, as the return on investment was 118 per cent in this year alone, mainly due to developments in the Suez Canal Company (see Chap. 13).

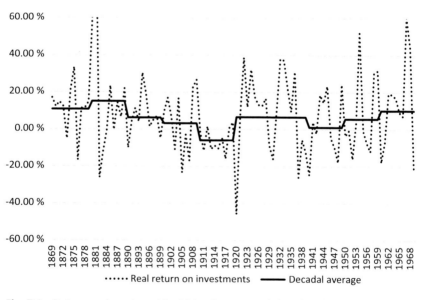

Fig. 7.1 Return on investment in Africa, by year and decade, 1869–1969 (per year and geometric mean by decade). Source: African Colonial Equities Database (ACED). Note: The y-axis is truncated at +60 per cent to show fluctuations throughout the period more clearly, so the outlier in the year 1881 (+118 per cent) is not visible in the figure

Over the long run, we cannot discern any clear trend for the overall volatility, even though the return on investment fell from high levels during the last decades of the nineteenth century to low/negative levels during the first decades of the twentieth century. Paradoxically, the most stable share prices were to be found during the 1910s, the only decade with negative returns. This was, at least partly, due to limited trade and the partial close-down of the London Stock Exchange during the First World War (Michie 2006, 155–76).

Table 7.1 shows the average and the standard deviation of annual returns for the total sample of companies in our study. The table also disaggregates the data by regions, by economic sectors and by time periods. The overall average real rate of return for the whole period was 5.9 per cent and the standard deviation of annual return was 22 percentage points. The impression of an unchanged level of volatility throughout the century under study is confirmed when the data is subdivided into two periods. The volatility for the period prior to First World War was 23.1

Table 7.1 Average and volatility of real return on investment in Africa, by portfolio, 1869–1969

	Average annual real rate of return (geometric mean, %)	Standard deviation of annual rate of return (percentage points)
By region		
North Africa	2.5	26.2
East Africa	−2.5	27.9
West Africa	−0.1	28.3
Central/Southern Africa (excl. South Africa)	2.2	33.8
South Africa (colony/republic)	6.2	20.9
By sector		
Finance	2.8	16.3
Mining	7.1	25.9
Other	4.2	26.9
By time period		
1869–1913	7.4	23.1
1914–1969	4.7	21.3
Total	*5.9*	*22.0*

Source: African Colonial Equities Database (ACED)

percentage points, while for the remaining years it was 21.3 percentage points—a small, but relatively insignificant, decline. The only sector where there was a somewhat larger shift was in mining, where volatility declined from 29 to 23 percentage points—a decrease that fits well with the picture of a mining sector that by the 1910s had left its first, formative period.

In order to put our results in context, we need to compare them to earlier research. Since there are no figures that match our geographical and temporal coverage completely, our comparison can at best be tentative at this stage. Edelstein had studied the return on investment between 1870 and 1913. In his work, the level of volatility of the realized return on British domestic investments for this period is below 10 percentage points (Edelstein 1976, 294). These figures seem to be confirmed by the recent work by Richard Grossman (Grossman 2015, Table 1). Dimson, Marsh and Staunton for their part studied the return on investment in 16 countries—most of them developed economies—during the twentieth century. They report volatility figures for this period ranging from 16.8 percentage points (Canada) to 30.3 (Germany). For the United Kingdom, they report an annual volatility of 20.0 percentage points. They furthermore found no clear relationship between the realized average rate of return and the level of volatility during their period of study (Dimson et al. 2002, 60).

As for African investments, Grossman reports a volatility of 23.6 percentage points for his portfolio of African ventures during the early period, 1879–1928 (Grossman 2015, table 1). Dimson et al.'s estimates (for South Africa only) exhibit a volatility of the same order of magnitude, at 22.8 percentage points, during the twentieth century. In the first half of their period (1900–1950), their volatility figures are a couple of percentage points higher than in the second half of the period (Dimson et al. 2002, 110). Buelens and Marysse's work on Belgian Congo exhibits a somewhat higher volatility in the annual return on investment of 31.8 percentage points (Buelens and Marysse 2009, 153). Hence, our aggregate results are in line with previous estimates for the risk and return from investing in Africa, both when comparing our estimates to previous estimates for Africa as a whole by Grossman, but also for specific regions—either when comparing our estimates for South Africa with those by

Dimson et al., or our estimates for Central/Southern Africa with those by Buelens and Marysse (see Table 7.1).

One conclusion that can be drawn when comparing these figures to the risk and return from investing elsewhere in the world is that the volatility in the return on investment was higher for African ventures than for investments on the larger and more mature market for investments in British domestic ventures, at least until the First World War. During this period, the average rate of return on investment was, on the other hand, also higher on average for investments in Africa than the return on investment domestically in the United Kingdom (see Fig. 6.10). During the twentieth century, the volatility of the return on investment in the United Kingdom increased, so that our African portfolio by this time exhibit no major difference in volatility compared to that of domestic investments in the United Kingdom. As a whole, the aggregate figures therefore seem compatible with the theoretical predictions of risk premia for investing in more risky portfolios.

As Table 7.1 demonstrates, the regional and sectoral variation was considerable in our sample. What is striking is that the realized rate of return for a specific portfolio of investments is not positively associated with its actual market risk, as theory would predict, when we disaggregate the data by sector or by region in Africa. By region, the average return on investment was, on the contrary, the highest in South Africa, which at the same time carried the lowest market risk (lowest volatility) over time. For the other regions in Africa, the risk of investing there—as measured by the volatility of the annual return—was in all cases considerably higher, but the average rate of return was substantially lower than when investing in South Africa. By sector, financial companies (including real estate) displayed comparatively low figures of volatility (a standard deviation of 16.3 percentage points), but also comparatively low real average rate of return. Mining was the sector in Africa with the highest average rate of return on investment, but it also had a markedly higher volatility (a standard deviation of 25.9 percentage points). Comparing these two sectors, investors in the more risky African mining sector seem to receive a risk premium on their investments, compared to the return on investment in the African finance sector. This is an issue we will return to in Chap. 11, where we will show that South African banks delivered more stable returns than, for example, the more speculative mining sector. The relationship between risk and return again becomes problematic when we look at other African investments: the highest volatility was to be found among companies operating in sectors other than mining or finance (standard deviation of 26.9 percentage points), even though the total return on investment was not as high as for the mining companies.

One important explanation to this seeming paradox is, of course, the distinction between expected and realized return on investment. *Ex ante*, investors might have hoped for, or expected to, earn a high return when investing in some specific region or sector. In hindsight, it is possible to see that their expectations were not met, as the return on investment was even negative in some cases. Many investors did at the time simply not possess full and accurate information about all potential objects of investments but had to base their expectations on information that could be of varying quality—an issue we will return to in Chap. 12.

These were all relatively young markets from the perspective of a London investor. The market for British domestic equity was much larger both in terms of market capitalization and in terms of the number of equity issues. External shocks influencing particular companies would not have as large an effect upon the market capitalization-weighted average rate of return as they would in a less diversified portfolio. Furthermore, as has been shown previously (see Fig. 6.1), the vast majority of all investments in African ventures went to South Africa, primarily into the mining sector. The relationship between and risk and return on investment in South Africa converged with more mature financial markets in the core economies during the twentieth century. This did not happen for investments in other sectors or regions of Africa. Investing in Africa outside of South Africa meant investing in portfolios based on a small numbers of companies, some of which could be highly profitable during certain periods, but they were also portfolios that were highly sensitive to external shocks.

If investments in Africa on average did not outperform investments in the United Kingdom significantly in terms of the risk/return relationship, why did Victorian United Kingdom send so much capital abroad? In their paper on foreign bias and English investment abroad, Chabot and Kurz showed that foreign assets significantly expanded the mean-variance frontier and thereby lowered the total risk that faced an investor (Chabot and Kurz 2010, 1056). They based their conclusions on a dataset from the United Kingdom and the United States that covered the period 1866–1907. Financial markets around the world became successively more integrated throughout the twentieth century. For example, the correlation of the annual return on investment between the four largest international financial markets has gone up from 0.09 in the late nineteenth century to 0.4 hundred years later. Hence, the benefit of diversification was stronger in the first half of the twentieth century than in the second half. This also means that there was high marginal utility, in terms of diversification, to invest in markets with lower correlation. The annual return on investment in South Africa, for example, had a correlation to the annual return on investment in the United Kingdom of 0.49. South African investment returns correlated more strongly with Australia (0.56) and Canada (0.54), which can be explained by the importance of the mining industry in all of these three countries (Dimson et al. 2002, 116; Goetzmann and Ibbotson 2006). Within our African sample, the correlation was the highest between South Africa and Central/Southern Africa (0.54), while North Africa was not particularly correlated with either Central/Southern (0.21) or South Africa (0.33). A tentative conclusion from our results is that investors in London did not treat Africa as one entity but that they managed to adjust their investments according to developments of different regions. Our results also indicate that there were gains of diversification to be reaped within the overall African portfolio. A illustrative example is that companies like the Suez Canal and the Standard Bank of South Africa both provided their investors with stable long-term returns, based on circumstances different from the average conditions of the London Stock Exchange, but also different from each other.

Equity Risk Premium

In order to make it worthwhile for an investor to invest in highly volatile stocks, there ought to have been some form of risk premium involved. As we showed above, the correlation between volatility and return in our sample was low throughout the hundred years. Another way of measuring the historical rewards that investors enjoyed for bearing risk is the equity risk premium—that is, the difference between the return on equity and a comparable risk free investment. What can be considered risk free is of course an open question, but typically, government bills or bonds are used as a proxy (Dimson et al. 2002, 163).

Previous research on the historical equity risk premium in the United States has arrived at different results regarding the long-term trends to the return on investment in equity and bonds. The results from this research nonetheless suggest that the historical equity risk premium in the United States was around 3–5 percentage points (Siegel 1992; Goetzmann and Ibbotson 2005). In Dimson et al.'s global estimates, the world equity risk premium for the entire twentieth century was 4.6 per cent. The variation between the 16 studied countries ranged from 2.0 for Denmark to 6.7 for Germany; South Africa had a premium of 5.4 per cent (Dimson et al. 2002, 173).

It is important to note that the equity risk premium—like volatility—can only be measured historically, though what investors really care about is future risk. When we measure and interpret the equity risk premium, we must therefore take into account that it is just a proxy for future risk. Especially in times of greater financial instability, it can be a poor guide for investors (Goetzmann and Ibbotson 2006, 7). The equity risk premium can potentially serve the purpose of answering a basic question: does this kind of risk-adjustment change the overall picture of the return to investment? In order to do this, we made an analysis for the years

Table 7.2 Real return on government bonds and private equity in the United Kingdom, South Africa and Egypt, 1880–1913 (per cent, geometric mean per year)

	Government bonds	Equity	Equity risk premium
United Kingdom	1.71	5.15	3.45
South Africa	2.74	5.53	2.79
Egypt	3.24	8.40	5.16

Source: UK government bonds: GFD Database United Kingdom Consol Government Bond Total Return Index; UK equity: (Edelstein 1976, appendix 3); South African and Egyptian government bonds: data underlying (Ferguson and Schularick 2006); South African and Egyptian equity: African Colonial Equities Database (ACED)

1880–1913 where comparable data is available for South Africa and Egypt. Hence, Table 7.2 shows the total average annual return on government bonds and private equity in the United Kingdom, South Africa and Egypt.

It has been argued in the previous literature that the British Empire gave certain actors a competitive edge on the financial market because market participants treated foreign borrowers differently than they treated borrowers associated with the British Empire (Edelstein 1994, 240; Cain and Hopkins 2001). Ferguson and Schularick studied the period 1880–1913 and they found that the yield on government bonds from British colonies was on average 3.89 per cent, compared to 6.30 for independent countries (Ferguson and Schularick 2006, 290). There could, of course, be several reasons for these differences. Cain and Hopkins pointed to the role of legislation which specifically encouraged investors to buy colonial bonds (Cain and Hopkins 2001, 439). Another reason that has been put forward is that direct imperial interventions could reduce borrowing costs for poorer peripheries of the empire (Gardner 2017, 236). Ferguson and Schularick's own argument was that colonial status reduced the perceived risk of default by investors (Ferguson and Schularick 2006, 283).

Our data does not exhibit any similar clear-cut 'Empire effect' on the return on investment in equity, as is shown in Table 7.2, in contrast to the effect that being a colony of the British Empire seemingly had on colonial government borrowing. On the contrary, the return on investment in South African equity was roughly on par with the return on investments in the United Kingdom equity around the turn of the century 1900. The return on Egyptian equity was in contrast markedly higher. It is important to note that the high return of the Suez Canal Company, which dominated the Egyptian sample, rests heavily on a single year, the year 1881 (see Chaps. 8 and 13). If this outlier is excluded from the analysis, the return on the entire Egyptian portfolio converges to roughly the same levels as that of the United Kingdom and South Africa in Table 7.2. Hence, the underlying data not only explains the difference, but it also concretely illustrates the higher risk that faced investors in Egyptian equity. In consequence, the equity premium differed substantially: while the premium for Egyptian equity was substantially higher than the British equity premium, the premium for South African equity was actually somewhat below the figures for the United Kingdom.

Survival and Death of African Ventures

One of the greatest risks when investing in a company was the risk that the company would go bankrupt, so that the investor would lose all of the capital invested. A large number of the companies in our sample did in fact lose all of their investors' capital, but there were also other reasons why they disappeared from the sample. In our panel dataset, only one single company is present throughout the whole period under study and only a minority (around 16 per cent of the sample) survived at the end of the period of our study. The vast majority of the companies that entered our sample also disappeared from our sample for one reason or another. Companies entered and exited the stock exchange at different points in

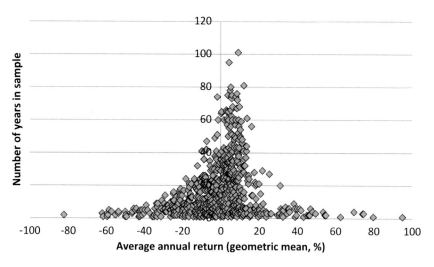

Fig. 7.2 Average nominal return on investment in Africa in relation to the number of years present in the sample, by company, 1869–1969. Source: African Colonial Equities Database (ACED). Note: the x-axis is truncated at +100 per cent. Four outliers are therefore excluded from the figure. All of these outliers were present only one year in our sample before they disappear again

time. While some companies introduced on the stock exchange were newly established, others had been run privately for a time prior to their transformation into publicly traded companies. Companies also exited the stock exchange for various reasons such as bankruptcy, mergers or ownership changes. Very short periods of observation might, therefore, be due to a company failing economically soon after the introduction on the stock exchange or because it in contrast was highly successful and taken over by another company. The relationship between the return on investment and longevity in our sample is illustrated in Fig. 7.2.

As can be seen in Fig. 7.2, there is a large number of companies that essentially did not return anything but losses to their investors during their time in our sample. The median company in our sample exhibited a meagre nominal return of 1.2 per cent per year on average. The rate of return is furthermore clearly related to the longevity of the company. Virtually all the long-lived companies were able to produce a reasonably high return on investment of around 5–10 per cent per year in nominal terms. A smaller number of companies exhibit extreme average rates of return on investment—either positive or negative—but all of these are present only one or at most a few years in our sample before they disappear for one reason or another. The vast majority of companies that exhibit a negative average rate of return over the whole period that they were traded on the LSE did not survive more than two decades. It is hardly surprising that companies failing to meet the investors' expectations over any longer period would be delisted from the LSE. There were, however, a number of companies that managed to stay listed for several decades despite the fact that the average return on investment was negative. These companies experienced different trajectories. In some cases, such companies experienced a slow decline throughout much of the period, with investors possibly hoping that the performance of the company eventually would improve. In other cases, the company experienced a positive rate of return for much of the period, but major losses during a short period (e.g. due to external shocks) were of such magnitude that it created a negative average rate of return for the whole period.

A large number of companies in our sample were thus unable to survive for any longer period of time. Figure 7.3 illustrates the risk of failing to survive in the form of a Kaplan-Meier survival function for the

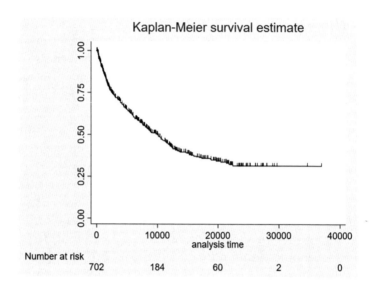

Fig. 7.3 Survival estimates of African companies traded on the London Stock Exchange, 1869–1969. Source: African Colonial Equities Database (ACED). Note: The figure also shows censored observations

companies in our sample. All companies that were delisted from the London Stock Exchange, according to the Register of Defunct Companies (see Chap. 5), are here treated as having failed to survive. We will return to the issue of why these companies failed below. All companies that disappeared from our sample without having been delisted formally are treated as censored from our sample. As discussed in Chap. 5, this could most importantly include the possibility that companies became too small, or too rarely traded, to be included in the reporting of the sources employed for our database, such as the *Investors' Monthly Manual*.

The estimates in Fig. 7.3 suggest that the median company survived in our sample for around 10,000 days, or roughly a quarter of a century. The estimate might be too low since our data, as was noted in the discussion on the methodology (see Chap. 5), might miss some years when a company was traded on the London Stock Exchange before or after being included in the primary sources underlying our database. Many companies were, furthermore, present in our sample for a shorter period than this, but they disappear from the sample for unknown reasons. Our results are in concord with the general observation of the firm survival literature—that roughly 5–10 per cent of the firms in a given market leave the market in any single year (Agarwal and Gort 2002, 184). Hence, one important conclusion is that our companies in general have a lifespan this is at least as long as what could be expected from the literature.

In the previous literature, some key factors have been acknowledged to influence the exit of firms: individual factors relating to the entrepreneurs, structural factors of the firm like age and size and finally macroeconomic and institutional conditions and constraints (Box 2008, 379–80). The first refinement of our analysis is, therefore, to investigate the latter. One way to capture macroeconomic and institutional conditions in firm survival analysis is to analyse cohort effects (Box 2008, 383). We categorized our sample into five cohorts of equal length, according to when the companies were floated at the LSE: 1869–1889, 1890–1909, 1910–1929, 1930–1949 and 1950–1969. We also categorized the sample geographically into two groups, namely, South African ventures and ventures in other parts of Africa, as our expectation is that the South African market would turn out to be more mature and that ventures there faced a better chance of surviving. We finally also categorized our sample in terms of sector of operation: mining companies versus non-mining companies, as our expectation is that mining ventures were more risky than other ventures. Simple bivariate analyses suggest that the cohort mattered (so that the cohorts around the mining booms in the late nineteenth century exhibited a much shorter longevity than other cohorts), that geography on the other hand did not matter and that there indeed were sectoral differences (with mining ventures less chance of surviving than non-mining ventures). Several of these variables might be associated. Table 7.3, therefore, shows the results from a Cox regression analysing these factors in combination in a multivariate regression. In a first model, we only include the sector and country of operation as variables. In a second model, we also include the cohort that the company belonged to as well as dummy variables controlling for the decade of observation (as some decades, e.g. exhibited more substantial external shocks).

Table 7.3 shows that mining companies had a much lower chance of surviving than non-mining companies (i.e. higher risk of 'failing'). South African ventures had—when taking into consideration that they to a

Table 7.3 Cox regression of hazard ratios for the survival of African ventures, 1869–1969

Variable	Model 1	Model 2
Mining	2.070***	2.344***
	(0.313)	(0.379)
South African	0.758**	0.871
	(0.088)	(0.111)
Cohort		
Cohort 1 (1869–1889)		Ref.
Cohort 2 (1890–1909)		0.943
		(0.296)
Cohort 3 (1910–1929)		1.577
		(0.641)
Cohort 4 (1930–1949)		0.822
		(0.530)
Cohort 5 (1950–1969)		4.402*
		(3.442)
Decade		
1869–1879		
1880–1889		1.504
		(0.675)
1890–1899		0.769
		(0.180)
1900–1909		Ref.
1910–1919		1.005
		(0.187)
1920–1929		0.886
		(0.213)
1930–1939		0.649
		(0.208)
1940–1949		0.150***
		(0.074)
1950–1959		0.140***
		(0.075)
1960–1969		0.068***
		(0.039)

Source: African Colonial Equities Database (ACED)
Notes: Standard errors in parentheses. 'Mining' estimates versus non-mining; 'South African' estimates South African ventures versus ventures operating somewhere else in Africa. ***Statistically significant at 1 per cent confidence level. **Statistically significant at 5 per cent confidence level. *Statistically significant at 10 per cent confidence level

large extent were mining companies—no statistically significant higher chance of surviving than equivalent ventures in other parts of Africa. The cohort when the company was introduced on the LSE, in contrast, might have had a marginal impact upon the chances of survival for the last cohort in the sample but exhibited no statistically significant results for other cohorts. The final decades of our study, from the 1940s onwards, on the other hand, exhibited a considerably lower risk of failure among the companies in the sample than the reference decade, possibly suggesting a more stable environment for the companies that had managed to survive thus far. What the two latter results taken together suggest is that—by the Second World War—a number of companies had managed to survive a long period of time, and had by then developed into secure objects of investment, with good chances of continued survival.

But why were some companies delisted from the London Stock Exchange? All of the delisted companies were clearly not failures in terms of the return on investment in them. The Register of Defunct Companies noted (in most cases) whether the winding-up of the company was voluntary or compulsory. A majority of the companies that were delisted ceased to exist through a process of voluntary liquidation. The formal reasons for delisting do unfortunately not give us many clues as to the underlying reasons for the delisting. In order to move beyond this formal answer to the question of delisting, we used the information in the Register of Defunct Companies (RDC) to classify the underlying reasons for delisting into four categories (see Chap. 5 on the method for this classification). Firstly, there were 149 companies which were described as shutdown, either in direct connection to when it disappeared from our sample or some time shortly thereafter. Secondly, 127 companies were delisted because they were taken over by or amalgamated with one or more other companies. In a limited number of cases, this was part of a nationalization process (see Chap. 14). Thirdly, 42 companies were reconstructed and operations continued under a different name. Finally, there were 10 companies which could not be classified in this scheme for lack of information in the RDC.

Table 7.4 reports data on the return on investment for all these categories of companies—companies that survived in our sample, companies that were censored from the sample and companies that were delisted from the LSE for various reasons.

Table 7.4 Real return on investment in Africa, by eventual fate of company during our period of study, 1869–1969 (geometric mean per year)

	Real return (%)	Standard deviation (percentage points)	N
Not in Register of Defunct Companies			
Remaining in sample by end of our study	7.2	24.0	111
Censored from sample	3.8	23.6	263
In Register of Defunct Companies			
Shutdown	6.3	23.8	149
Reconstruction	−3.1	25.2	42
Takeover	1.4	29.0	127
Delisted, reason unknown	3.2	26.3	10

Source: African Colonial Equities Database (ACED); Register of Defunct Companies

The data in the table shows that the company that survived in our sample to the end of our study also exhibits the highest real return on investment of all the categories of companies, at 7.2 per cent per year. This is unsurprising as a company exhibiting a high average return also would seem more likely to survive. The companies that were censored from the sample, that is, those that disappear from our sample without having been formally delisted from the LSE, exhibit a lower average return on investment. Still, the return on investment is not catastrophically low for this group of companies, so many of them clearly disappeared from our sample even though they were performing well from the perspective of the investor. More surprising is the result that the companies that were reported as shutdown exhibit such a high rate of return (6.3 per cent per year). The evidence provided in the RDC suggest that this group was made up of a large number of companies that were shut down in an orderly fashion, with much initially invested capital being returned to the investors, for example, when a mine was running out of ore that could be processed economically.

The companies that were delisted because they were taken over or amalgamated were much more diverse. Some of these companies were clearly doing well and were acquired and integrated into larger companies. A typical example of this is the South African Trust & Finance, which was delisted in 1895 when it was taken over by the Johannesburg Consolidated Investment Company, after having exhibited an annual nominal return on investment exceeding 30 per cent per year for several years. Others were in contrast taken over because they were not turning a profit, for example, because capital shortages prohibited many mining companies from starting up or pursuing actual mining operations. Out of the 127 companies that were either taken over or amalgamated, the vast majority were active in mining. This is not surprising given that the mining sector was volatile with a continuous process of reorganization in terms of operation and ownership. Among the companies taking over other companies, we see both large players like De Beers and Consolidated Goldfields and smaller companies like the African & European Investment Co and City Deep. In some cases, we see companies actively taking over several other mines in a short time. For example, the East Rand Proprietary Mines took over seven other mines in 1908 and the London and Rhodesian Mining and Land (Lonrho) acquired four mines around 1920. Even though the reasons for takeovers were diverse, the average return on investment for the group of companies that eventually were taken over by others was low—at 1.4 per cent per year.

Reconstruction, finally, was apparently the end for several of the most unsuccessful companies. The average real return for the companies that eventually ended up as reconstructions exhibited a negative return of −3.1 per cent per year. Some of these might have been short-lived companies where the initial founders had no ambition other than to float and exit. These types of companies never started any production, and they were most common during mining booms when the investing public showed an apparently insatiable demand for new investment objects. They did nonetheless influence the return on portfolio investments in certain sectors, particularly in mining, during certain periods. There were also reconstructed companies in our sample which experienced protracted economic problems. As mentioned earlier, a number of companies did actually have a negative average return over several decades (see Fig. 7.2). In the end, they were generally either voluntarily entered into liquidation or more commonly delisted and reorganized outside the stock exchange.

Conclusions

Investors faced different types of risks in Africa during our period of study. What we have been able to show in this chapter is that the general market risk of investing in South Africa, as measured by the volatility of the return, might have been higher than the risk of investing domestically in the United Kingdom during the late nineteenth century. During this period, there was also a somewhat higher average return on investment in Africa than in the United Kingdom, suggesting that investors actually earned a certain risk premium. During the twentieth century, the risk/return relationship seems to have converged between these two markets.

In contrast, investments in other parts of Africa exhibit a much lower average rate of return—but at the same time a much higher volatility in the return on investment. These results might seem contradictory from a theoretical perspective, as the investors apparently received no risk premium. One key to this paradox is the difference between expected and realized return, where the realized return on investment in many parts of Africa must have been much below what the investors expected to earn *ex ante*. Another key to the paradox is that the ventures operating in some regions were highly sensitive to external shocks and that the small number of ventures on some of these young markets allowed for little smoothing of the shocks impacting individual companies in the portfolios.

We also show that investing in Africa might have been a way of diversification, in order to spread risk. The fluctuations of the South African portfolio of investments show a low correlation with the fluctuations of a portfolio of investments domestically in the United Kingdom. The South African portfolio, in turn, shows a low correlation with the portfolios for other regions in Africa.

The chapter, furthermore, shows the great width of our sample. Some of the companies, that we might call Imperial Blue Chips, were highly successful. These companies exhibited a stable return on investment over long periods. Other ventures were short-lived examples of company mongering, where the founders might have little intention of actually starting real operations. Such practices were often based on asymmetrical information where investors had limited information about (fraudulent) claims made about the venture's prospects. Other companies initiated real operations, but for one reason or another, they faced structural problems or major external shocks that undermined their operations. In between all of these were a number of vanilla investments that exhibited ordinary levels of both risk and return. The vast majority of these companies never got their monograph written, but they were still integral parts of the economic-political landscape that emerged in the British Empire during the period of our study.

The operations of the African ventures concerned with in this chapter illustrate the varieties of risks that were faced by company management and international investors during the nineteenth and twentieth centuries (Casson and da Silva Lopes 2013). These risks were only occasionally connected to imperial policies and colonial institutions, though they form a backdrop for an analysis of that issue. In Chap. 13, we will therefore return to this issue when we look at some of the particular risks associated with (or averted by) imperialist policies or colonial institutions, such as the risk of nationalization of assets by independent regimes, either before or after colonial rule.

References

Agarwal, Rajshree, and Michael Gort. 2002. Firm and Product Life Cycles and Firm Survival. *American Economic Review* 92 (2): 184–190.

Box, Marcus. 2008. The Death of Firms: Exploring the Effects of Environment and Birth Cohort on Firm Survival in Sweden. *Small Business Economics* 31 (4): 379–393.

Buelens, Frans, and Stefaan Marysse. 2009. Returns on Investments during the Colonial Era: The Case of the Belgian Congo. *The Economic History Review* 62 (s1): 135–166.

Cain, Peter J., and Anthony G. Hopkins. 2001. *British Imperialism, 1688–2000*. Harlow: Longman.

Casson, Mark, and Teresa da Silva Lopes. 2013. Foreign Direct Investment in High-Risk Environments: An Historical Perspective. *Business History* 55 (3): 375–404.

Chabot, Benjamin R., and Christopher J. Kurz. 2010. That's Where the Money Was: Foreign Bias and English Investment Abroad, 1866–1907. *The Economic Journal* 120 (547): 1056–1079.

Dimson, Elroy, Paul Marsh, and Mike Staunton. 2002. *Triumph of the Optimists: 101 Years of Global Investment Returns*. Princeton, NJ: Princeton University Press.

Edelstein, Michael. 1976. Realized Rates of Return on UK Home and Overseas Portfolio Investment in the Age of High Imperialism. *Explorations in Economic History* 13 (3): 283–329.

———. 1994. Foreign Investment and Accumulation, 1860–1914. *The Economic History of Britain Since* 1700: 173–196.

Ferguson, Niall, and Moritz Schularick. 2006. The Empire Effect: The Determinants of Country Risk in the First Age of Globalization, 1880–1913. *The Journal of Economic History* 66 (2): 283–312.

Gardner, Leigh. 2017. Colonialism or Supersanctions: Sovereignty and Debt in West Africa, 1871–1914. *European Review of Economic History* 21 (2): 236–257.

Goetzmann, William N., and Roger G. Ibbotson. 2005. History and the Equity Risk Premium. In *Handbook of the Equity Risk Premium*, ed. Rajnish Mehra, 515–529. Amsterdam: Elsevier.

———. 2006. *The Equity Risk Premium: Essays and Explorations*. New York: Oxford University Press.

Grossman, Richard S. 2015. Bloody Foreigners! Overseas Equity on the London Stock Exchange, 1869–1929. *The Economic History Review* 68 (2): 471–521.

Michie, Ranald C. 2006. *The Global Securities Market a History*. Oxford: Oxford University Press.

Siegel, Jeremy J. 1992. The Equity Premium: Stock and Bond Returns since 1802. *Financial Analysts Journal* 48 (1): 28–38.

Van Helten, Jean-Jacques. 1990. Mining, Share Manias and Speculation: British Investment in Overseas Mining, 1880–1913. In *Capitalism in a Mature Economy: Financial Institutions, Capital Exports and British Industry, 1870–1939*, ed. Jean-Jacques Van Helten and Youssef Cassis, 159–185. Aldershot: Edward Elgar.

Map of Africa. The African continent was partitioned between the European powers during the late nineteenth century. The map shows European annexations and claims in 1888. British possessions are coloured in pink. © Mary Evans Picture Library

Part III

Regional Studies

8

North Africa

The Modernization of Egypt Until Middle of the Nineteenth Century

By the nineteenth century, Egypt had, for several centuries, been a province of the Ottoman Empire. In 1805, Muhammad Ali was appointed the *wāli* (governor) of Egypt. During Ali's reign as a governor, Egypt experienced considerable modernization in many fields—socially, culturally and economically. The Egyptian state was also modernized, including the administration and military (Owen 1981, 64–76; Toledano 1990; Sherbiny and Hatem 2015, 34–40). Population increased, but data is scarce before the end of the nineteenth century. In 1882, the population was estimated to be around 7–8 million people. By 1917, the population had risen to 12.8 million (Owen 1981, 216–17). The country was also experiencing substantial urbanization during the period (Toledano 1990, 196). Egypt embraced expansionist policies of its own, independent of the central policies of the Ottoman Empire—first in Sudan, and later in the Levant, even threatening to invade the capital of the empire, Constantinople, itself. In order to appease Ali, the Ottoman regime was forced to recognize Mohammed Ali's line as hereditary rulers of Egypt (Harrison 1995, 36).

Economically, agriculture dominated in nineteenth-century Egypt. One key agricultural output was cotton. The Egyptian cotton was of the highest quality, among the best in the world, and sold at high prices. Egypt had since ancient times been a producer of short-staple cotton. By the early nineteenth century, a variety of long-staple cotton suitable for Egyptian agriculture had been introduced. Following this development, cotton production in Egypt expanded rapidly during the first half of the nineteenth century. Production boomed particularly during the American Civil War. The country thereby became increasingly dependent upon cotton for its exports (Tignor 1966, 227; Issawi 1982, 30–31).

There were also considerable efforts put into trying to industrialize Egypt, starting under Muhammad Ali and continued by several of his successors. State-run industries in the textile or armaments sectors were, for example, established (Owen 1981, 69–73; Issawi 1982, 154; Sherbiny and Hatem 2015, 34–40). The construction of railways expanded, particularly during the second half of the century. In the 1850s, there was a total 353 kilometres of railways in the country. By 1869, the railway network had expanded to 1338 kilometres, and by 1905, Egypt had around 3000 kilometres of railways (Issawi 1982, 54). The industrialization was comparatively successful under Muhammad Ali and his first successors. The modernization required substantial amount of capital. There were therefore close connections between several European bankers and the pashas of Egypt, throughout the nineteenth century. Several bankers were more than willing to provide the Egyptian government with credit (Landes 1958; Sherbiny and Hatem 2015, 41–48).

Investments, Indebtedness and Foreign Control, 1859–1882

The Suez Canal

One crucial development for Egypt was the construction of the Suez Canal. The idea of constructing such a canal across the Suez isthmus was not new, but it had previously not been considered feasible. The United Kingdom was furthermore initially hostile towards the construction of such a canal for the simple reason that this might empower France as well as Egypt. The latter would, in term, it was thought at the time, undermine the power of the Ottoman Empire, which at the time was a British ally (Farnie 1969, 40; Karabell 2003, 95; Mangold 2016, 41).

In 1854, the Frenchman Ferdinand de Lesseps managed to acquire a concession for the establishment of such a canal (Farnie 1969, 33; Karabell 2003, 78–79). A new concession, in January 1856, specified the route the canal was to take across the isthmus. According to this concession, furthermore, 15 per cent of all profits from the operations of the canal would accrue to the Egyptian government, 10 per cent would accrue to the founders of the Suez Canal Company and 75 per cent were to be divided among the ordinary shareholders. The concession would last for 99 years and could then be renewed (Farnie 1969, 40; Karabell 2003, 112–13; Piquet 2004, 109). In total, 166 people were provided with founders' shares, including both founding investors, special advisers and generally powerful and influential people who had acted in favour of the project (Farnie 1969, 53; Karabell 2003, 82).

Once the concessions had been issued, de Lesseps could establish the Suez Canal Company. The floating of shares in the company would wait until 1858 since it took some time to establish that it actually was technically feasible to build the canal and to persuade potential investors of buying shares. In October of that year, the shares were finally floated (Karabell 2003, 132, 137). Despite all preparations, the initial public offering of the shares in the Suez Canal Company turned out to be a major failure. Few people outside France—with the exception of the governor of Egypt, Sa'id Pasha, himself—were willing to invest in the company. In consequence, Sa'id Pasha was forced, by an earlier agreement, to purchase the remaining shares of the company. The resulting increase in Egyptian government debt (around £1.13 million) was not insignificant (Farnie 1969, 50; Karabell 2003, 140–43).

The work of constructing the canal began the following year, in 1859. The construction required massive numbers of labourers. As had been stipulated in the original concession to de Lesseps, the labourers were to be Egyptian, supposedly supplied by the Egyptian government. At the time, corvée (forced) labour was common practice in Egypt. Under this system, the government required all people in Egypt to contribute to work, for example, in large-scale construction works. The workers were paid some, but comparatively low, wages for their work. Many of the labourers therefore attempted to avoid the work by running away or by outright protests (Toledano 1990, 188–95). Corvée labour also provided the Suez Canal with labourers. For the construction of the Suez Canal, some 12–22,000 corvée labourers were employed for every shift (Bonin 2010, 68). The corvée labourers working on the construction of the Suez Canal were paid 2–3 piasters per day of work (Karabell 2003, 113). As a comparison, a contracted, unskilled, male construction labourer was normally paid 6 piasters per day around this time, whereas a female worker generally was paid around 4 piasters (Tucker 1985, 90). The use of corvée labour would therefore drastically reduce the wage cost for the construction of the canal. When criticized by British authorities for exploiting corvée labourers for the construction of the canal, de Lesseps defended this practice by simply stating that labour coercion remained an accepted phenomenon in many parts of the world (Harrison 1995, 46).

The construction costs were, nonetheless, enormous—estimated to £17–18 million. A not insignificant cost was that the shareholders had been promised an annual dividend of 5 per cent of the capital invested throughout the period of construction, something that would cost the company almost £3 million (Farnie 1969, 83–84; Bonin 2010, 190).

In the end, half of the construction costs had been paid by the Egyptian government—partly in the form of purchasing equity, but also in the form of cash provided directly by the government to the company during the final years of the construction. The remainder had been raised on the international (primarily French) capital markets through equity and bonds (Bonin 2010, table 19).

One of the key cash payments by the Egyptian government to the Suez Canal Company was due to a modification in the original concessions to the Suez Canal Company during 1854–1856. The modification included that the use of corvée labour was to be abolished in Egypt, including for the construction of the Suez Canal. The Egyptian government also wanted to regain territory surrounding the canal, which had been handed over to the company in the original concession, to be used as farmland. Unsurprisingly, the company did not want to agree to any such modifications voluntarily and managed to get the French emperor Napoleon III

8 North Africa   153

to intervene in Egyptian politics on its behalf. The French emperor sided with the Suez Canal Company arguing that while Egypt might have the right to change its legislation and abolish the use of coerced labour, the decree stating that the Egyptian government was to provide labour for the construction of the canal meant that the company was entitled to corvée labourers and that any change on this account would have to be compensated for economically (Saul 1997, chap. VIII; Karabell 2003, 203). Under such pressure, the governor Isma'il Pasha gave in, and agreed to pay compensation to the company. The compensation amounted to £3.4 million. Of this sum, £1.5 million was paid in compensation for the company's loss of corvée labour and £1.9 million for other changes in the concession (Owen 1981, 127; Harrison 1995, 46; Bonin 2010, 261).

Figure 8.1 shows the price of the Suez Canal Company shares on the Paris and London Stock Exchanges, with prices from London starting to appear regularly in the source used in 1875 (once the British government

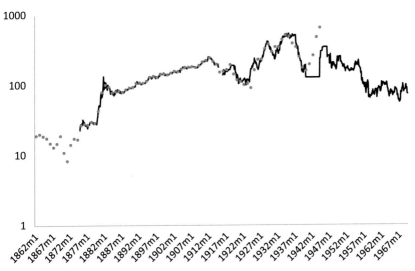

—— Stock price on London Stock Exchange (£)   • Stock price on Paris Stock Exchange (£)

Fig. 8.1 Price quotations of the Suez Canal Company on the London and Paris Stock Exchanges, by month, 1862–1969 (£ sterling, current prices, logarithmic scale). Source: African Colonial Equities Database (ACED) and (Bonin 2010, tables 22–24)

had purchased the Egyptian government's shares in the company, see more on this below). Data from the Paris stock exchange, as reported by Hubert Bonin, had been assembled already from 1862. At this time, the share price was still roughly equivalent to the par value of 500 francs (£20) per share. By the middle of the 1860s, many investors seemed to have started to doubt whether the company ever would be able to finish constructing the canal: starting in 1864, the stock lost substantially in value, despite the fact that the company still honoured the promise to pay dividends during the construction period. In 1867, the share reached a low of 326 francs (£13) per share, 35 per cent below par, on the Paris stock exchange, as is shown in the figure.

As construction progressed, the investors became more hopeful of seeing the project come to fruition: in 1868, the share price reached 368 francs. After a construction period of ten years, the Suez Canal was finally opened for traffic (Karabell 2003, 10; Bonin 2010, 74). The declaration of an opening date for the Canal to the 17 November 1869 meant a rapid increase in the share price to 23 per cent above the par value, or 615 francs per share, in August that year (Farnie 1969, 81).

In 1869, the Suez Canal was opened for traffic. The Suez Canal Company was off to a most challenging start. Even though the number of ships passing through the canal increased quickly during the first years of operations, the absolute numbers were much lower than hoped for (Karabell 2003, 260). Revenues were consequently below the expected, so that the costs—most importantly the capital costs for bonds issued—dwarfed the revenues earned. The company therefore suffered a deficit every year until 1871. In June 1870, the company suspended all payments of dividends and interests on shares due to urgent financial difficulties (Farnie 1969, 108). The costs still trumped revenues, so by 1872, the company was on the verge of bankruptcy. This is also reflected in a major drop in the share price, as can be seen in Fig. 8.1. The company was saved from bankruptcy by an emergency loan by a major shareholder and by successfully renegotiating debts with some creditors (Farnie 1969, 213; Bonin 2010, 194). By the middle of the 1870s, the company had overcome the most immediate financial challenges. The number of passages through the canal also increased steadily. Dividend payments were therefore resumed in January 1875 (Farnie 1969, 228).

Given the fluctuations in the share price during the construction of the canal, the return on investment in the canal company varied substantially between the years. In the end, the investors who continued to hold the shares of the Suez Canal Company until the canal actually was finished and had started to operate should have been more than satisfied with their investment: the average real return on investment in Paris amounted to 12.0 per cent per year for the period 1862 (when the available data starts) to 1882, when Egypt was occupied by the United Kingdom, as can be seen in Table 8.2. The data also suggests a remarkable return on investment of 24 per cent per year on the London Stock Exchange (30 per cent on the Paris stock exchange) for the period 1875–1882 in particular.

Banking

In the 1860s—starting under the reign of Sa'id Pasha, and intensified under his successor Isma'il Pasha—Egyptian government spending substantially outpaced revenue. The costs for building the Suez Canal, railroads and other investments were not matched by government revenues, but had to be paid for by the government lending money on international capital markets (Landes 1958, appendix D; Tignor 1966, 23; Cain 2006, 180). Another important contributor to Egyptian government debt was that the country was forced to pay tribute to the Ottoman Empire. These tributes were, in turn, used as collateral for loans that the Ottoman Empire took from European bankers, so the payment of these tributes became a matter of concern for European-Egyptian relations (Tignor 1984, 85). Yet another important aspect behind the budget deficit was also that the Egyptian state started to face increasing costs for raising loans in Europe—Charles Issawi even characterized the terms as 'usurious' (Issawi 1961, 10). The Egyptian treasury thereby only came to receive a fraction of the nominal amounts borrowed internationally. The loans floated during 1862–1873, for example, amounted to a total face value of £68.5 million, but the Egyptian treasury only received £46.6 million of these—the rest was kept by bankers and agents (Owen 1981, 127; Issawi 1982, 66). That, in effect, also meant a substantially higher real interest on the money actually received than what had been calculated with when the loan was disbursed (Chamberlain 2010, 37).

The Egyptian government's lending spree was profitable for several of the European-owned banks established in Egypt. Investors in the Bank of Egypt—which had been established in 1856 and mainly was engaged in lending to the Egyptian government (Baster 1934, 78–79; National Bank of Egypt 1898–1948, 13; Jones 1993, 21, 404)—would have to make do with an extraordinary average real return of 14.7 per cent per year, while investors in the competing Anglo-Egyptian Bank—founded in 1864 and was also mainly doing business related to Egyptian government lending (Baster 1934, 80–81; Jones 1993, 26, 403)—experienced a real average return of a stunning 23.5 per cent per year during the years 1869–1874, as shown in Table 8.2.

This bonanza soon ended when the Egyptian government's finances were coming into ever greater disarray. By 1875, debt payments had become too large to handle for the Egyptian government. The *khedive*, as the governor now titled himself, therefore found it necessary to sell the Egyptian government's own shares in the Suez Canal Company in November 1875. The purchaser was the British government. The British government could thereby acquire 44 per cent of the shares in the Suez Canal Company, for the price of £4 million (Farnie 1969, 231–32; Owen 1981, 127; Hopkins 1986, 380; Vatikiotis 1991, 128–29; Harrison 1995, 52; Piquet 2004, 112; Bonin 2010, 160–64). The announcement that the British government had purchased shares in the Suez Canal Company led, according to Douglas Farnie, to a massive rush for Egyptian stocks on the London Stock Exchange in November 1875. As Farnie put it, 'Everyone rushed to buy Egyptian stocks as though England had just announced that she would pay the Egyptian Debt' (Farnie 1969, 233).

The Egyptian foreign debts were still huge, and British and French capital interests were afraid that the Egyptian government would default on their loans. In 1875, some bondholders were starting to raise the idea that Egypt ought to be put under European control, so as to ensure the repayment of debts (Farnie 1969, 230). In no small part due to these fears of a default, 1876 exhibited major capital losses for investments in the Egyptian financial sector. The shares in the largest of bank in our sample of companies, the Anglo-Egyptian Bank, were the worst hit, losing more than half of their market value. The shares in the other banks in our sample also experienced a substantial reduction in value.

Under international pressure, Isma'il Pasha, in November 1876, finally accepted that an international body—the *Caisse de la Dette Publique*, made up of representatives of European financial interests—was to control the government revenues in order to operate a debt-repayment scheme. Two representatives—the British and the French—came to have the most influence, thereby establishing what became called the 'Dual Control' of Egypt (Tignor 1966, 11; Harrison 1995, 52; Hunter 1998, 195). The Dual Control would remain in place until the British occupation in 1882 (Chamberlain 2010, 39).

Despite the massively fluctuating value of the equity in the Egyptian financial sector over this first time period, before British control of the country, the companies operating in the Egyptian financial sector were successful investments, with an average real return in the range of 7–9 per cent per year, as can be seen in Table 8.1. That the return on investment differed so much over time, and the fact the Suez Canal Company entered our sample in 1875 also leads to a composition effect when calculating the return on investment for the total sample, which can be seen in the table: while the return on financial equity was very high during the first half of the 1870s, it was substantially lower during the second half of the decade. At this time, the Suez Canal Company enters our sample,

Table 8.1 Real return on investment in selected portfolios in North Africa, 1869–1969 (geometric mean per year)

Portfolio	Period of data	Real return (%)
Total sample	*1869–1969*	*2.5*
	1869–1882	18.9
	1883–1914	5.3
	1915–1956	−1.8
	1957–1969	−6.5
Financial sector	*1869–1969*	*4.7*
	1869–1882	9.6
	1883–1914	5.1
	1915–1956	0.6
	1957–1969	−6.5

Source: African Colonial Equities Database (ACED)

Table 8.2 Real return on investment in selected companies in North Africa, 1862–1969 (geometric mean per year)

Company	Period of data	Real return (%)
Compagnie Universelle du Canal Maritime de Suez	1875–1969	1.5
	1875–1882	24.1
	(1862–1882 on Paris stock exchange)	(12.0)
	1883–1914	5.6
	1915–1956	−2.6
	1957–1969	−6.7
Agricultural Bank of Egypt	*1903–1937*	*3.9*
	1903–1914	1.8
	1915–1937	4.9
Anglo-Egyptian Banking Co Ltd.	*1869–1920*	*7.0*
	1869–1882	9.3
	1883–1914	8.0
	1915–1920	−3.2
Bank of Abyssinia	*1907–1924*	*−7.9*
Bank of Egypt	*1869–1911*	*8.3*
	1869–1882	6.2
	1883–1911	9.3
Franco-Egyptian Bank	*1872–1882*	*7.4*
National Bank of Egypt	*1899–1958*	*0.6*
	1899–1914	1.3
	1915–1956	0.9
Sudan Plantation Syndicate	*1919–1947*	*2.9*

Source: African Colonial Equities Database (ACED)

dwarfing the market capitalization of the investments in the financial sector. The total weighted average return on investment therefore exceeds that of the individual companies in the sample.

The financial administration of the country by the Caisse only allowed marginal public spending on education, public health or productive investments, for example, in irrigation projects. For several years, around 60 per cent of total government revenue raised was used to repay the foreign debt (Tignor 1966, 78–79; Cain 2006, 187). Aside from crippling tax levels, another way of raising additional revenue was to sell government land (Tignor 1966, 243; Vatikiotis 1991, 128). There was therefore increasing disapproval of the European control of Egyptian state finances, for example, in some of the independent press (Blunt

1907, 164). In April 1879, Isma'il Pasha attempted to regain control over the government's finances by exploiting a revolt among military officers in February to dismiss the government, including its international advisers from the Caisse, with the key argument that the government had failed to uphold political stability in the country (Vatikiotis 1991, 132–33; Pakenham 1991, 78). Several observers feared that the khedive was about to repudiate all of Egypt's foreign debts. The British government therefore intervened with the Ottoman authorities and managed to get them to depose the Egyptian khedive on 26 June 1879. In his place, his son Tewfik was appointed as the new khedive of Egypt (Vatikiotis 1991, 135–41; Harrison 1995, 55).

The harsh financial regime imposed on Egypt could thereby continue unabated. In 1880, the khedive was even required to relinquish the Egyptian state's share of the profits of the Suez Canal Company. As per the original concessions to the Suez Canal Company, the Egyptian government was to receive 15 per cent of profits (prior to the payment of dividends) from the operations of the canal. In order to urgently acquire capital for the repayment of the foreign debts, this right was relinquished to a private company, Crédit foncier de France, in return for the company paying off some of Egypt's foreign debts (Piquet 2004, 112; Bonin 2010, 261). Since the period of construction had meant substantial investments costs, followed by several years of operating losses during the canal's initial years of operations, the Egyptian government thereby received virtually no economic benefits from the Suez Canal, despite having invested massively in the project (Issawi 1982, 51).

A nationalist movement did increasingly come to oppose the Dual Control over Egyptian government finances. In the European establishment, a fear was growing that this nationalist movement would spell disaster not only for the European bondholders, if the Egyptian government would default on loan payments, but also for strategic interests in the control over the Suez Canal. In November and December 1881, French and British ministers were discussing taking 'vigorous action' against the Egyptian nationalist movement (Blunt 1907, 183–84). The discussions led to the two countries issuing the famous Joint Note of 6 January 1882, where they expressed support for the khedive Tewfik, and stated that they would not accept the khedive being deposed by nationalist interests (Tignor 1966, 20–21; Chamberlain 1976, 233, 2010, 40).

During the spring of 1882, events unfolded fast. Throughout the spring, the French and British governments were explicitly threatening to intervene militarily in Egypt if that would become necessary to protect British or French interests. In May 1882, the British sent warships to Alexandria to awe the Egyptian population and government. Their presence only increased tensions in the Egyptian society. On 11 June 1882, the British started bombarding the nationalist army which had been camped outside of Alexandria. In August the same year, the British finally and swiftly occupied Egypt militarily (Pakenham 1991, 132; Chamberlain 2010, 41–42). We will return to discussing the driving forces behind this occupation further in Chap. 13.

Economic Development During the British Occupation of Egypt, 1883–1914

Under the British occupation, Egypt experienced a period of substantial economic growth, primarily in the rural economy (Yousef 2002, table 5; Pamuk 2006, table 1). This would have some positive consequences for public finances. The British chose to maintain Tawfiq as new khedive since he had been opposed to the nationalist movement, but the khedive's authority had been undermined by the occupation (Tignor 1966, 66). The Dual Control was furthermore replaced by a single British financial 'adviser' to the khedive. While formally not a British colony, the financial adviser would in practice have substantial power over the Egyptian government (Owen 1981, 220). The British-run government proceeded to stabilize Egyptian government finances in order to be able to repay the accumulated foreign debts (Tignor 1966, 94; Daly 1998, 239). Nonetheless, the debt burden remained crippling for the Egyptian economy. In the 1880s, around 40 per cent of gross government revenue was used for repaying the debts. By the early twentieth century, the debt burden had been reduced, but roughly 25 per cent of government revenue was still used for repaying debts (Issawi 1982, 67).

The Suez Canal

In the meantime, the Suez Canal experienced a steady increase in traffic passing, rising from around 5 million tons in 1882 to about 20 million tons before the outbreak of the First World War (Farnie 1969, appendix table 1). This growth of trade through the Suez Canal does, to a large extent, mirror the development of the world economy of the time both in terms of size and structure (Bonin 2010, 124). One crucial factor for the success of the Suez Canal Company was that steamships took over from sailing ships. When construction of the canal began, it was not obvious that this would be the case. The company's gamble paid off, as the tonnage of steamships increased fast, particularly from the 1880s onwards (Bonin 2010, 95). The operation of the Suez Canal also improved over time. The canal was, for example, successively made safer to use so that fewer accidents occurred. Transit times improved substantially: decreasing from 48 hours for an average passage in 1870 down to 12.6 hours for an average passage in 1939. Further investments in broadening the canal also enabled increasingly larger ships to pass through (Bonin 2010, 142–43). While some of the gross revenue was used for further investments in the canal, around 50–60 per cent of total revenue was dedicated to paying dividends to the shareholders (Farnie 1969, appendix table 4).

The increase in traffic is reflected in a steady increase in the value of the stock for several decades, until the 1910s. Since the value of Suez Canal shares had increased so drastically already in advance of and in connection with the British occupation of Egypt (as discussed in the previous section), the real return on investment was not enormous during this period, but amounted to around 5.6 per cent per year on average (see Table 8.2). The volatility of the return on these investments was, at the same time, very low. Prior to the 1910s, the return on investment in the Suez Canal Company turned negative only during some odd years. The period was thus one of not particularly remarkable but, on the other hand, very stable, return on this investment to its investors.

Banking

During the occupation, British authorities in Egypt largely practiced laissez-faire policies towards banks and other businesses (Owen 1981, 224). The yield spreads between Egypt and European financial markets did furthermore decrease substantially during the period, largely due to investor confidence that debts were going to be repaid (Hansen 1983). The major banks that had been established in Egypt already before the British occupation of Egypt, such as the Anglo-Egyptian Banking Company and the Bank of Egypt, nonetheless flourished during this period. As can be seen in Table 8.2, with an average return on investment of 8.0 per cent per year for the Anglo-Egyptian Banking Corporation, and an average return of 9.3 per cent for investments in the Bank of Egypt. The return on these investments did furthermore generally not exhibit as drastic fluctuations, neither positive nor negative, as the previous period had done. However, important events impacted the operations of these banks. The international financial crisis of the early 1890s (Jones 1993, 63–69) did, for example, impact the Egyptian banks too, with a large negative return on investment for both of the major banks, particularly in the year 1891. Unlike several other banks at the time, the Egyptian banks were nonetheless able to recover from this crisis. The Bank of Egypt did furthermore experience some substantial losses during the final years of its existence, according to Geoffrey Jones due to 'incautious mortgage-lending on property', and was wound up in 1912 (Jones 1993, 79, 404).

Newly established banks were, in contrast, not very successful at all. The National Bank of Egypt was founded in 1898 as a state bank of Egypt but with foreign investments involved. It was formally established by a khedival decree, but this was issued with the support of the British occupation authorities. The bank issued notes and served as the Egyptian government's banker, alongside operating a commercial banking business (National Bank of Egypt 1898–1948, 16–17; Thane 1986, 92; Jones 1993, 109–10, 411; Tignor 1984, 70). The Agricultural Bank of Egypt was formed some years later, in 1902, largely as an affiliate to the National Bank of Egypt, to lend money to small farmers in particular. None of these two newcomers were doing particularly well during the period until the First World War. The return on investment in the National Bank of Egypt was particularly volatile, ranging from positive return of up to 40 per cent for one year, to a negative return of almost −30 per cent another year. The fate of the Agricultural Bank of Egypt would, for its part, be determined by a change in the Egyptian legislation in 1911, whereby small landholdings could not be seized for debt. Small landholders thereby generally became unable to provide security for loans, since their most important asset—land—no more could be used as such (Jones 1993, 110). The change in legislation is reflected in the data from the London Stock Exchange. In its first years of operation up until 1910, the bank was providing investors with a healthy real return of around 8 per cent per year. Following the change in legislation in 1911, until the outbreak of the First World War, this changed to a negative return of minus 10 per cent per year on investments in the company. The National Bank of Egypt had in 1905 also been granted a concession to establish a bank in Ethiopia, the Bank of Abyssinia, whose shares were introduced on the London Stock Exchange in 1907. The bank experienced substantial turmoil during its initial years of existence (Schaefer 1992, 367–78), which is also reflected in major losses for the investors, amounting to an average return on investment of −16.5 per cent per year for the years leading up to the First World War, as can be seen in Table 8.2.

North Africa from the First World War to Independence, 1915–1956

The relationship between the United Kingdom and Egypt after the British occupation had for a long period not been formalized. In 1914, Egypt was finally transformed into a British protectorate (Mangold 2016, 70–71). After a brief nationalist revolt of 1919, the United Kingdom formally declared Egypt independent in 1922—even though British military forces remained in the country. Egypt did, on the one hand, gain more political power after the First World War (Tignor 1984, 4; Daly 1998, 251; Goldberg 1992, 201–2, 211), but it has at the same time been argued that the relationship nonetheless remained colonial in essence (Owen and Pamuk 1998, 33). The country also underwent a more liberal political period during the interwar years (Botman 1998, 304–7; Sherbiny and Hatem 2015, 56–63). Some outstanding issues in Anglo-Egyptian relations remained and were not solved until the Anglo-Egyptian treaty of 1936, which formally legitimized the continued British occupation in Egypt by calling it an 'alliance' between the two countries and allowed the United Kingdom to continue to station military troops in the vicinity of the Suez Canal. The civil administration of Egypt was completely turned over to the Egyptian authorities (Vatikiotis 1991, 293; Mangold 2016, 118).

The Suez Canal

Among the Egyptian companies traded on the London Stock Exchange during this period, the Suez Canal Company remained by far the largest. The period was not favourable for the investors in the company. After temporary decrease in traffic during the First World War, the total volume of traffic passing through the Canal continued to increase during the interwar period. The outbreak of the Second World War did lead to a drastic reduction in the tonnage passing through the canal, but the traffic soon resumed after the end of the War. The structure of the traffic did also change considerably during this period, with a most important increase in the volume of energy products (oil and fuel) carried through the canal (Bonin 2010, 317).

Despite this increase in traffic, the Suez Canal Company exhibited a negative return on investment (−2.6 per cent per year) on the London Stock Exchange during this period, as is shown in Table 8.2. This was largely an effect of major fluctuations in the share price, as can be seen in Fig. 8.1 (with no net gain in the value of the stock seen over the whole period), in combination with the onset of inflation as the Gold Standard collapsed.

Shortly before the First World War, the share price had reached a peak of almost £250 per share—more than 12 times the par value of the share. The outbreak of the war was negative for the company, even though the share price recovered from the start of 1917. The price of Suez Canal shares fell again in the autumn of 1919 and in the early 1920s. The second half of the 1920s was a period of rapid creation of value for the investors. One key aspect for this was the exchange rate fluctuations during the interwar period, with an appreciation of the British pound. This meant a bonanza for the Suez Canal Company since its earnings in French francs thereby increased substantially (Farnie 1969, 574–75; Bonin 2010, 198). The share price increased until the financial crisis of 1929, and the following Great Depression, and peaked in the early 1930s at around £500 per share. During the 1920s, the company therefore exhibited a very high return on investment of 10.9 per cent per year.

The growth of nationalist tendencies in Egypt forced the Suez Canal Company to renegotiate the terms of its concession. Having paid no revenue to the Egyptian state after the original 15 per cent share of profits had been relinquished in 1880 (see more on this above), the company in 1937 agreed to henceforth pay a certain share of its profits to the Egyptian government (Piquet 2004, 119; Bonin 2010, 263–64). At the same time, the Second World War drew closer. Investors in the Suez Canal Company therefore seemed to have become more afraid of losing their investments completely. Starting in June 1937, the share price experienced a most drastic decline on the London Stock Exchange, reaching a low of £128 per share before trade in the stock was stopped by the stock exchange in early 1940. As the tides of war turned in North Africa, the investors' faith in the Suez Canal Company did too. Since the London Stock Exchange apparently had stopped all trading in the Suez Canal Company during the war, the share price was officially reported as constant until June 1944. Only in 1941 did the share price of the Suez Canal on the Paris Stock Exchange start to increase again (as can be seen in Fig. 8.1), after a drastic decline following the outbreak of the Second World War. Peace in Europe would not spell the end of problems for investors in the Suez Canal Company. Despite the renegotiation of the concession, the share of revenues going to Egypt was meagre: during the years 1947–1955, total revenue amounted to 2348 million gold francs. Of this, the Egyptian government received 77 million francs, that is, 3.3 per cent, whereas shareholders received 815 million, that is, 35 per cent

(Bonin 2010, Table 55). The changes to the concession were, in the words of Hubert Bonin, merely 'cosmetic', and largely without substance (Bonin 2010, 456). Both the 1930s and 1940s were nonetheless in total negative for the investors in the company, with a negative average rate of return (on average −2 and −3 per cent per year for the two decades, respectively).

More important for the company was instead the fact that the original concession was coming to an end. The Suez Canal Company had been granted a concession for operating the canal for a period of 99 years, which would end in 1968. As the company's main (virtually only) real asset would be lost, the value of the stock must have fallen as that date approached. Theoretically, the concession could have been renewed. The chances of a renewal of the concession occurring in practice must have seemed bleak to informed investors. This ought to have contributed to a downward pressure on the value of the stock—and thereby to explaining the major capital losses for the investors at this time. The non-renewal of the concession was furthermore not the investors' only worry. They furthermore had to worry about the company losing its asset prematurely. During and following the Second World War, nationalist movements increasingly gained political ground in Egypt. The years immediately after the war saw increasing numbers of demonstrations and protests against what was still perceived as British colonial rule, including British control over the Suez Canal. This would culminate in the military coup of 1952, overthrowing the old regime (Tignor 1998, 45–54; Botman 1998, 304–7; Owen and Pamuk 1998, 128; Bonin 2010, 409–14). The fact that the Suez Canal Company had failed to Egyptianize their operations to any great extent made the company a particular target for much protest (Tignor 1987, 497). In 1954, the United Kingdom and Egypt agreed to a treaty which stipulated that all British troops would withdraw from Egypt within 18 months (Mangold 2016, 212). As the risk of nationalization increased over time, canal shares must have seemed increasingly less attractive to British investors, also contributing to the major capital losses experienced at the time, with an average return on investment of −10.6 per cent per year during the 1950s.

Banking

As for the main financial institutions, the Bank of Egypt had been wound up already in 1912. In 1920, the Anglo-Egyptian Bank was instead taken over by the Barclays Bank and merged with some other banks into the Barclays (Dominion, Colonial and Overseas) (Jones 1993, 149). It therefore too disappears from our sample. The National Bank of Egypt did not fare much better than during the period prior to the First World War: the return on this investment fluctuated much during the period. From the outbreak of the Second World War, the company was experiencing a negative trend, which culminated following the nationalization of foreign companies in 1956 (Bonin 2010, 478), when the investors experienced a negative return of −40 per cent in one single year. As for the Agricultural Bank of Egypt, Geoffrey Jones has claimed that business for the bank 'evaporated' following the change in legislation in 1911 (see more on this above) (Jones 1993, 110). The formulation might seem to be too drastic since the company apparently could continue to operate for several decades. Our evidence also suggests that the company actually seems to have been able to recuperate to some extent after the First World War, so that the real return during the interwar period actually was comparatively high.

The Bank of Abyssinia would continue to face severe challenges. The First World War and the recession experienced in Ethiopia after the end of the war hindered the growth of commercial activities (Schaefer 1992, 381–83), so that return on investment in the bank for the period up until the mid-1920s was practically zero, as can be seen in Table 8.2. Data for the company from the London Stock Exchange ends in 1924, at the time when banking in Ethiopia finally started to takeoff (Schaefer 1992, 383–84).

Plantations

The interwar years also saw the expansion of cotton production in Anglo-Egyptian condominium of Sudan, led by the Sudan Plantation Syndicate Company (Mollan 2008, 3). The company had been founded already in

1899 and was to a large extent financed from the Corner House (Mollan 2008, 85)—who also was involved in the Rand Mines in South Africa (see Chap. 12), among other business ventures. The Sudan Plantation Syndicate started to be traded regularly on the London Stock Exchange once the company attempted to increase the capital to expand activities, once preparations for plantations had been completed in the so-called Gezira Scheme, and the area under cultivation began to increase (Mollan 2008, 192–95). The company was comparatively successful during the 1920s, with an average return on investment of 8.7 per cent during the decade. The company experienced major difficulties during the first years of the Depression, one of the major problems being crop diseases reducing output for many years (Mollan 2008, 202; Ross 2017, 60–61). The return on investment would therefore remain moderate throughout the 1930s and early 1940s. In 1944, the company was informed that the Sudanese government would not renew its concession to the plantations on the Gezira plains, and the company eventually liquidated voluntarily (Mollan 2008, 275–79). In total, over the period for which the company's shares were traded on the London Stock Exchange, the real return on investment was therefore a modest 2.9 per cent per year, as is noted in Table 8.2.

The Transformation of the Suez Canal Company, 1957–1969

Robert Tignor has argued that most businessmen operating in Egypt in the 1950s had a realistic view of Egyptian nationalism and favoured a gradual withdrawal of the British troops from Egypt in order to be able to conduct business in the country in future. However, Tignor claims, these interests failed to persuade decision makers in the United Kingdom who paid more attention to British strategic interests than to financial interests (Tignor 1987, 505). While this might be so, the analysis cannot neglect the substantial economic values involved for the British government itself: the British government was in the 1950s still the single largest shareholder in the Suez Canal Company (Tignor 1987, 483–84; Bonin 2005, 100). The British government therefore had much to lose not just strategically, but also financially, from losing control over the Suez Canal and the Suez Canal Company. The company directors do not seem to have worried much about the national movement and subscribed to the same strategy of Egyptianizing their business as other companies at the time tried (Tignor 1987, 497).

Eventually, nationalization of the Suez Canal became a reality. The military regime that had taken control of the Egyptian government would not be satisfied with letting the Suez Canal Company remain in the hands of European owners. An Egyptian Law of July 1956 decreed the nationalization of the Suez Canal Company's assets in Egypt, including the Canal per se (Farnie 1969, 723; Tignor 1998, 115). The British and French responded with military aggression, the so-called Suez War, but were under international pressure soon forced to withdraw (Vatikiotis 1991, 392; Tignor 1998, 126–28; Porter 2012, 267). After the war, the Egyptian government continued with the nationalization of other foreign assets that had been confiscated during the war (Tignor 1998, 136).

The nationalization was a catastrophe for the investors, as share prices tumbled: the Suez Canal Company experienced a drop in the share price from around £224 each in August 1955 down to around £65 by December 1958—a loss of more than 71 per cent of the capital value in a few years' time. Most of the remaining companies in our sample also disappear from the London Stock Exchange within a few years after the nationalization, being liquidated or wound up.

The most important company in the sample, the Suez Canal Company, continued to exist as a corporate entity, and the shares of the company continued to be traded on the London Stock Exchange. With the assistance of the World Bank, the company negotiated with the Egyptian government to settle the accounts for the Egyptian nationalization of the Suez Canal. As a consequence of these negotiations, the canal company got to keep £5 million that had been paid to the company in transit fees for passages that occurred after the canal formally had been nationalized. It also received payments of £23 million as compensation for the loss of expected profits for the remainder of the concession. All liabilities in Egypt (valued to £15 million) were furthermore taken over by the Egyptian government (Tignor 1998, 147; Bonin 2010, 488–89). The compensation paid meant a substantial liquidization of assets and stopped the company from going completely bankrupt. This was also reflected by the share price, which at least ceased to fall. The new liquid assets would also enable the company to completely shift field of operations, turning itself into a holding company involved in financial investments, rather than a company operating a canal (Tignor 1998, 101, 146; Bonin 2010, 495). As a whole, the 1960s was still a period of negative return on investment for investors in the Suez Canal Company, averaging −4.7 per cent per year during the decade.

Return on Investment in North Africa in the Long Run, 1862–1969

Figure 8.2 shows the development of the return on investment in North Africa over time. As can be seen in the figure, the return on investment varied most considerably over time.

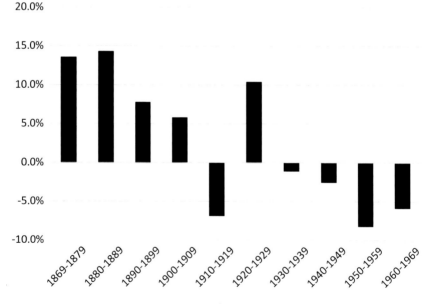

Fig. 8.2 Real return on investment in North Africa, by decade, 1869–1969 (geometric mean per year). Source: African Colonial Equities Database (ACED)

As was made clear from the outset, the North African sample was—in terms of market capitalization—completely dominated by investments in one particular country, Egypt, and in one particular company, the Suez Canal Company. This company remained the single most important company in our sample throughout the period under study.

Over the whole period, investments in the company were not very successful: the average real return on investment was a mere 1.5 per cent per year over the whole period for which there is data from the London Stock Exchange. This is substantially lower than previous estimates by Hansen and Tourk, who estimated an average nominal return on investment of around 8.7 per cent per year during a period for which our estimates suggest a nominal return of 5.5 per cent (Hansen and Tourk 1978, table 1). Hansen and Tourk do not report any disaggregated data, by year or by specific time periods, which would enable us to determine more clearly when differences occur. The difference might potentially be explained by the different methods employed when calculating the return. Hansen and Tourk assume that shareholders purchased shares at the initial value and sold it in 1956 at market prices (Hansen and Tourk 1978, 945–46). Presumably, then, they calculated the yield (dividend payments) relative to the initial share price, in contrast to our figures which calculate the yield relative to the present value of the stock. As the share prices increased over several decades, there were capital gains to be made (later followed by capital losses when the share price tumbled). Depending on when dividends were and were not paid out, this might explain the differences between the two estimates.

Most importantly, the long-term average figure covers different trends for different shorter periods. For several decades, the company was very successful. Once the Canal had opened for business, the number of passages boomed for a number of years, which is reflected in very high return on investment these years, after which followed a period of normal, but remarkably steady, return on investment for two further decades. This turned into major losses during the First World War due to decreasing international shipping through the Canal. The company was able to recover after the war. Any investor that had invested in Egyptian shares up until the 1920s, but then stepped out of this market, would have walked away having earned a substantial average rate of return. These results were overturned from the 1930s onwards. The onset of the Second World War, followed by the threat of nationalization of the Canal, which was also realized once Egypt achieved real political independence after the Second World War, created insecurities and major losses for the company's investors.

The fate of several of the financial companies operating in Egypt mirrored, to a large extent, the general trend experienced by the Suez Canal Company: very high return on investment during the period leading up to the British occupation, and in the early years of the occupation, followed by declining rate of return over the following period, until nationalization of the company's assets created major losses for the financial companies still surviving at that time.

References

Baster, Albert. 1934. The Origins of British Banking Expansion in the Near East. *The Economic History Review* 5 (1): 76–86.

Blunt, Wilfred Scawen. 1907. *Secret History of the English Occupation of Egypt*. London: T. Fisher Unwin.

Bonin, Hubert. 2005. The Compagnie Du Canal de Suez and Transit Shipping, 1900–1956. *International Journal of Maritime History* 17 (2): 87–112.

———. 2010. *History of the Suez Canal Company 1858–2008*. Geneva: Droz.

Botman, Selma. 1998. The Liberal Age, 1923–1952. In *The Cambridge History of Egypt. Volume 2: Modern Egypt, from 1517 to the End of the Twentieth Century*, ed. M.W. Daly, 285–308. Cambridge: Cambridge University Press.

Cain, Peter J. 2006. Character and Imperialism: The British Financial Administration of Egypt, 1878–1914. *Journal of Imperial and Commonwealth History* 34 (2): 177–200.

Chamberlain, M.E. 1976. Sir Charles Dilke and the British Intervention In Egypt, 1882: Decision Making In a Nineteenth-Century Cabinet. *Review of International Studies* 2 (3): 231–245.

———. 2010. *The Scramble for Africa*. 3rd ed. Harlow: Longman.

Daly, Martin W. 1998. The British Occupation, 1882–1922. *The Cambridge History of Egypt* 2: 239–251.

Farnie, D.A. 1969. *East and West of Suez: The Suez Canal in History 1854–1956*. Oxford: Clarendon Press.

Goldberg, Ellis. 1992. Peasants in Revolt—Egypt 1919. *International Journal of Middle East Studies* 24 (2): 261–280.
Hansen, Bent. 1983. Interest Rates and Foreign Capital in Egypt under British Occupation. *The Journal of Economic History* 43 (4): 867–884.
Hansen, Bent, and Khairy Tourk. 1978. The Profitability of the Suez Canal as a Private Enterprise, 1859–1956. *The Journal of Economic History* 38 (4): 938–958.
Harrison, Robert. 1995. *Gladstone's Imperialism in Egypt: Techniques of Domination*. Westport: Greenwood press.
Hopkins, Anthony G. 1986. The Victorians and Africa: A Reconsideration of the Occupation of Egypt, 1882. *The Journal of African History* 27 (2): 363–391.
Hunter, F.R. 1998. Egypt under the Successors of Muhammad Ali. In *The Cambridge History of Egypt. Volume 2: Modern Egypt, from 1517 to the End of the Twentieth Century*, ed. M.W. Daly, 180–197. Cambridge: Cambridge University Press.
Issawi, Charles. 1961. Egypt since 1800: A Study in Lop-Sided Development. *The Journal of Economic History* 21 (1): 1–25.
———. 1982. *An Economic History of the Middle East and North Africa*. London: Methuen.
Jones, Geoffrey. 1993. *British Multinational Banking, 1830–1990*. Oxford: Clarendon Press.
Karabell, Zachary. 2003. *Parting the Desert - The Creation of the Suez Canal*. London: John Murray.
Landes, David. 1958. *Bankers and Pashas: International Finance and Economic Imperialism in Egypt*. London: Heinemann.
Mangold, Peter. 2016. *What the British Did - Two Centuries in the Middle East*. London: I.B. Tauris.
Mollan, Simon. 2008. *Economic Imperialism and the Political Economy of Sudan: The Case of the Sudan Plantations Syndicate, 1899–1956*. Durham: Durham University.
National Bank of Egypt 1898–1948. 1948. Cairo: National Bank of Egypt.
Owen, Roger. 1981. *The Middle East in the World Economy 1800–1914*. London: Methuen.
Owen, Roger, and Sevket Pamuk. 1998. *A History of Middle East Economies in the Twentieth Century*. London: I.B. Tauris.
Pakenham, Thomas. 1991. *The Scramble for Africa 1876–1912*. London: Weidenfeld and Nicolson.

Pamuk, Şevket. 2006. Estimating Economic Growth in the Middle East since 1820. *The Journal of Economic History* 66 (3): 809–828.

Piquet, Caroline. 2004. The Suez Company's Concession in Egypt, 1854–1956: Modern Infrastructure and Local Economic Development. *Enterprise & Society* 5 (1): 107–127.

Porter, Bernard. 2012. *The Lion's Share - A History of British Imperialism 1850 to the Present.* 5th ed. London: Routledge.

Ross, Corey. 2017. *Ecology and Power in the Age of Empire: Europe and the Transformation of the Tropical World.* Oxford: Oxford University Press.

Saul, Samir. 1997. *La France et l'Egypte de 1882 à 1914: Intérêts Économiques et Implications Politiques.* Paris: Institut de la gestion publique et du développement économique.

Schaefer, Charles. 1992. The Politics of Banking: The Bank of Abyssinia, 1905–1931. *The International Journal of African Historical Studies* 25 (2): 361–389.

Sherbiny, Naiem, and Omaima Hatem. 2015. *State and Entrepreneurs in Egypt: Economic Development since 1805.* New York: Palgrave Macmillan.

Thane, Pat. 1986. Financiers and the British State: The Case of Sir Ernest Cassel. *Business History* 28 (1): 80–99.

Tignor, Robert. 1966. *Modernization and British Colonial Rule in Egypt, 1882–1914.* Princeton: Princeton University Press.

———. 1984. *State, Private Enterprise, and Economic Change in Egypt, 1918–1952.* Princeton: Princeton University Press.

———. 1987. Decolonization and Business: The Case of Egypt. *The Journal of Modern History* 59 (3): 479–505.

———. 1998. *Capitalism and Nationalism at the End of Empire: State and Business in Decolonizing Egypt, Nigeria, and Kenya, 1945–1963.* Princeton: Princeton University Press.

Toledano, Ehud. 1990. *State and Society in Mid-Nineteenth Century Egypt.* Cambridge: Cambridge University Press.

Tucker, Judith. 1985. *Women in Nineteenth-Century Egypt.* Cambridge: Cambridge University Press.

Vatikiotis, P.J. 1991. *The History of Modern Egypt from Muhammad Ali to Mubarak.* 4th ed. London: Weidenfeld and Nicolson.

Yousef, Tarik M. 2002. Egypt's Growth Performance Under Economic Liberalism: A Reassessment with New GDP Estimates, 1886–1945. *Review of Income and Wealth* 48 (4): 561–579.

9

West Africa

The Scramble for West Africa Until 1900

West Africa has been in contact with European traders for several centuries, mainly through trading stations and forts along the West African coast. For a long time, the slave trade dominated this exchange. During the early nineteenth century, the trade in slaves gradually came to be replaced by the so-called legitimate commerce in various commodities, such as palm oil (Hargreaves 1963; Hopkins 1973, 125–35; Agbodeka 1992, chaps. 4–5; Lynn 1997). A number of European trading companies came to be involved in this growing trade (Pedler 1974, chaps. 1–8).

These trading stations on the West African coast also became stepping stones for further colonial expansion in the region. The expansion accelerated particularly from the 1870s and culminated in several wars of colonial occupation (Kimble 1963, 192–201, 270–95; Crowder 1968, chaps. 3–4; Falola 1999, 54–59; Chamberlain 2010, chap. 5). Similar to the discussion about the partition of other parts of Africa, there has been a debate about motives for the scramble for West Africa in particular. There were no strategic motives for the United Kingdom's push to acquire colonies in the region. Several scholars have instead emphasized economic

© The Author(s) 2019
K. Rönnbäck, O. Broberg, *Capital and Colonialism*, Palgrave Studies in Economic History, https://doi.org/10.1007/978-3-030-19711-7_9

motives, most importantly an interest in protecting trade routes and traders operating in the region or in acquiring more favourable terms of trade (Robinson and Gallagher 1968, 379–95; Hopkins 1968, 1973, 164; Flint 1973; Reynolds 1975; Howard 1978, 30; Cain and Hopkins 2001, 327–35; Porter 2012, 18, 142; Frankema et al. 2018).

One crucial consequence of the colonization of West Africa was institutional changes. In West Africa, the new colonial authorities introduced new legislation relating to both land tenure and labour relations. Slavery was formally abolished throughout the British Empire in 1833. When new colonies were added to the Empire by the late nineteenth century, slavery was formally abolished there too, such as on the Gold Coast in 1874 (Getz 2004, 54–68). At the same time, a Masters and Servants Act was introduced in the Gold Coast Colony. The aim was officially to ease the transition from slavery. The idea was that by relying on the institution of servitude, masters could forego ownership over the labour force in the form of slavery and instead turn to recruiting legally free, but in practice semi-coerced, labour (Rathbone 2004, 492). When Asante was conquered in 1896, slave trading was formally forbidden there too. Domestic Asante slavery still remained recognized in practice by the colonial authorities until 1908, when the governor of the Gold Coast Colony imposed a ban on this institution throughout Asante (Austin 2005, 206–7). The colonial authorities in several of the British colonies would keep on exploiting coerced (often labelled 'communal') labour, for example, for infrastructure development. Local chiefs were obliged to contribute a certain amount of labour for a specific infrastructure project. Contributing the required labour became compulsory for the chief's subjects (Rathbone 2004, 488; Ash 2006; Ochonu 2013). It would therefore take a long time for slavery and other forms of labour coercion to actually disappear from the region (Phillips 1989, 26–33; Lovejoy and Hogendorn 1993; Austin 2005, chap. 11).

Forms of land tenure were also changed by colonial authorities, but less so in West Africa than in several other colonies in sub-Saharan Africa (Austin 2005, chap. 5; Ochonu 2013). In the Gold Coast Colony, for example, colonial authorities attempted to impose the introduction of bills, whereby all mineral and forest lands would be vested in Crown hands. The native population could continue to farm land that they traditionally had farmed but did not hold ownership to the land in question and could therefore not sell the land if they so wanted. Any concessions were to be granted by the British government (Kimble 1963, 334–40; Howard 1978, 37–43; Phillips 1989, 60). The bills were eventually defeated by a vocal (but unarmed) opposition—an indication that the colonial administration had less motivation to push through such reforms here than in many settler colonies (Kimble 1963, 355–57; Crowder 1968, 421–22; Agbodeka 1971, 137–46). The institution of special land reserves, imposed in many colonies in Southern Africa, was furthermore rarely used in West African colonies (Rathbone 2004, 484). Agricultural lands, and hence also production, would therefore largely remain in African hands throughout the region (Phillips 1989, chaps. 4, 6).

Shipping

New possibilities for trading opened up already before the region was colonized, when the first steam shipping line between the United Kingdom and West Africa was established by the African Steam Ship Company in 1852. This was followed by the establishment of a competitor, the British & African Steam Navigation Company, in 1868. One year later, the two competitors divided up the market between them (Davies 1969, 215–19, 1977, 6–7, 2000, 7, 23–29). As can be seen in Table 9.2, both companies also exhibited a high return on investment during the period—5 per cent per year for the African Steam Ship Company and 10 per cent per year for the British & African Steam Navigation Company. The difference between the two is attributable to when there is data available; in a single year—1877, before data becomes available from the latter company—investors in the African Steam Ship Company experienced substantial losses. During the period for which we have data for both companies, 1883–1900, the return on investment is almost the same for both companies: 9.7 per cent per year for the African Steam Ship Company, compared to 10 per cent per year for the British & African Steam Navigation Company (see Table 9.2).

The 1890s exhibited an oligopolization of shipping to West Africa. A newly established company, Elder Dempster & Company, had over time come to control both shipping companies operating on West Africa, even though the companies formally remained independent. By the 1890s, the Elder Dempster & Company achieved effective control over all shipping companies, including non-British companies, operating in the region once the West African Shipping Conference had been established as a cartel (Leubuscher 1963, 16–19; Davies 1969, 222–23; Sherwood 1997, 260; Davies 2000, 72). Unsurprisingly, the return on investment achieved during the 1890s was consequently extraordinarily high for the involved shipping companies—almost 12 per cent per year for the African Steam Ship Company and 16 per cent per year for the British & African Steam Navigation Company (see Table 9.2). The Elder Dempster & Company was also involved in the main bank in the region. The first bank to be established in the region, in 1891, was the African Banking Corporation. After experiencing losses for a couple of years, this bank was rescued by a group of businessmen led by the shipping magnate controlling the Elder Dempster Lines, Alfred Jones. In 1894, it was turned into a joint-stock company and renamed the Bank of British West Africa, but it was not quoted on the London Stock Exchange until 1901 (Fry 1976, 23–26; Jones 1993, 76–77; Uche 1999, 672–73).

Trading

The establishment of shipping lines contributed to higher competition in the trade on West Africa. It enabled many small traders, including indigenous entrepreneurs (Dumett 1983), to enter a market which previously had been restricted due to the high capital cost of owning or chartering a whole ship of one's own. In order to limit such competitive pressures, several of the trading companies started to amalgamate (Lynn 1989, 231, 245, 1992, 27). In 1879, the United African Company (UAC) was established, with the aim to take over all British trading companies operating on the Niger River. This led to the UAC acquiring a monopsony position on the local markets, and thereby was able to drive down the price of the West African exports purchased (Flint 1960, 31; Pedler 1974, 117; Baker 1996, 34). To achieve control over all British trading companies would, however, not suffice if competitors from other European nations could enter the

West African market. In 1882, the founders of the United African Company therefore established the National African Company. The aim was to negotiate monopoly treaties with local rulers in Africa, as well as to acquire a British royal charter for a complete monopoly on all economic activities in the Niger river region (Flint 1960, 44–45; Hargreaves 1963, 271–78; Pedler 1974, 118; Baker 1996, 40). The company was successful at negotiating treaties with local African rulers, and it had, by 1886, entered into 327 such treaties (Flint 1960, 60–61; Hargreaves 1963, 329–30).

In July 1886, the company was granted a royal charter, and consequently, changed its name into the Royal Niger Company (Flint 1960, 85–87; Pedler 1974, 123; Baker 1996, 53–54). The charter did not contain any clause granting the company a legal monopoly on trade in the Niger River region, which must have been a disappointment for many investors. The main advantage of the charter was instead that it allowed the company to profit from agreements entered into with local rulers in that region (Flint 1960, 87). At the same time, the charter mandated the company the administration of the territory in question. As most of current-day Nigeria was not yet colonized at this time, this aspect of the charter was potentially a big step forward for investors. The company thereby became responsible for police and military operations, including 'punitive expeditions' against the local population when someone from those populations was accused of a crime (Baker 1996, 70–72), or military campaigns against local populations, often under the official banner of fighting slave trade (Flint 1960, chaps. 9–10; Pedler 1974, 134–35; Baker 1996, 164–87).

The return on investment in the Royal Niger Company fluctuated much between the years. The granting of the royal charter did not have any immediate, substantial impact upon the share price, which fluctuated around £1–1.25 per share throughout the year 1886 and only started to increase in the following year, reaching a peak of £2 per share in December 1887. In 1889, a competing company named the African Association was established, by the merger of eight companies trading on the Oil Rivers (Pedler 1974, 139; Jones 1993, 77–78). The immediate effect for the Royal Niger Company was that the share price started to fall back. The price reached a low of £1 per share in June 1892, as the investors seemingly feared that the new competitor could challenge the Royal Niger Company's de facto monopsony position in the region.

The two companies would soon come to agree on a geographical division of territories in which each company would trade, with the effect that the African Association in 1893 sold all trading stations it had on the Niger River to the Royal Niger Company (Pedler 1974, 145). For the investors in the Royal Niger Company, the agreement with the African Association was very profitable. The annual average real return on investment between 1883 and 1900 was an extraordinary 15.8 per cent per year (see Table 9.2). Similarly, the data for the African Association also reveals very high return on investment, though it was only reported in the *Investors' Monthly Manual* from the end of the 1890s.

Telegraph

In 1868, the British government nationalized all domestic telegraph lines. Investors in these companies thereby had substantial liquid capital to invest abroad (Headrick and Griset 2001, 560). Telegraph connections were expanding rapidly around the world during the second half of the eighteenth century, including in West Africa. The industry came to be characterized by intimate connections and crossholdings between the major telegraph companies (Müller 2016, chaps. 1–2). In 1885, the African Direct Telegraph Company was established, but only served British colonies. The West African Telegraph Company was later established, also serving French, Spanish and Portuguese colonies (Headrick and Griset 2001, 562). In 1889, West African Telegraph Co was acquired by the Eastern and South African Telegraph Co, and amalgamated under British control (Davies 2002, 228). The company seems to have struggled to make ends meet economically, and the return on investment until the end of the century was on average negative (as can be seen in Table 9.2). In 1902, the French government became a major owner of the West African Telegraph Company (Headrick and Griset 2001, 565). It is from around this time that the company started to exhibit positive return on investment on average and continued to do so until the company was delisted from the London Stock Exchange.

Mining

One West African sector particularly targeted by early European investments was mining. Mining had been undertaken by local entrepreneurs in the region for centuries (Dumett 1998, chap. 3; Hilson 2002). The 1870s included a veritable European 'gold rush', starting in 1877 when a French company first established operations in the Wassa region on the Gold Coast. This was followed by a number of other European companies, negotiating for concessions in an attempt to join the rush for gold (Howard 1978, 63; Agbodeka 1992, 106; Dumett 1998, chap. 4; Afrifa-Taylor 2006, 44). Labour had to be recruited from afar, as the mining regions were sparsely populated (Dumett 2012, 38–39). The early mines generally failed economically. Studying the companies involved in the gold rush, Jim Silver has argued that most were not profitable at all: of the 25 companies established during the period 1877–1900, a single one paid out some dividends (Silver 1981). This is also reflected in our data, as can be seen in the return on investment in the mining sector in the region, shown in Table 9.1. There were a handful of West African mining companies whose shares were traded regularly enough on the London Stock Exchange to be included in the sources used for our study, but the weighted average for the return on these investments during the period 1869–1900 was a massive loss of −10.9 per cent per year. This is a reflection of the fact that most of the companies failed to make any profits at all and that several of them consequently went bankrupt. To that extent, our data support Raymond Dumett's claim that the companies during this period 'probably pumped more into the country [...] than they ever took out of it in direct profits' (Dumett 1998, 262).

One key reason why the companies were unable to become profitable was that they failed to attract enough labourers. While much of Africa, including West Africa, generally was characterized by a scarcity of labour, there was a seasonal abundance of labour during the slack season in agriculture, which enabled mining to take place during this part of the year (Austin 2005, 73–77). Mining had traditionally also been an activity to a large extent undertaken by coerced labour, including slaves and corvée labourers (Dumett 1998, 70–72). To the extent that the local population

Table 9.1 Real return on investment in selected portfolios in West Africa, 1869–1969 (geometric mean per year)

Portfolio	Time-period	Real return (%)
Total West Africa	*1869–1969*	*−0.05*
	1869–1900	−4.0
	1901–1929	−6.2
	1930–1959	6.0
	1960–1969	13.8
Ghana	*1869–1969*	*0.8*
	1869–1900	−2.8
	1901–1929	−7.0
	1930–1959	8.0
	1960–1969	15.2
Nigeria	*1869–1969*	*0.6*
	1869–1900	−4.1
	1901–1929	−2.1
	1930–1959	4.1
	1960–1969	9.8
Mining sector	*1869–1969*	*−1.12*
	1869–1900	−10.9
	1901–1929	−9.0
	1930–1959	7.2
	1960–1969	13.2

Source: African Colonial Equities Database (ACED)

had a choice over whether to get involved in mining or not, they seemed to have preferred not to voluntarily seek employment with the European companies established in the region (Silver 1981; Dumett 1998, 147–48). The labourers required therefore had to be recruited from elsewhere, primarily from among the Kru, on the Liberian coast (Dumett 1998, 144). Some companies also resorted to using a tributary sharing system, rather than seeking to employ them as labourers. Under this arrangement, members of the local population were allowed to mine on a company's concession, provided that the company received a share of the output (Dumett 1998, 153–54). In addition, some of the mining companies suffered further from some early strikes among employed labourers, even though the mineworkers at this time generally were not successful in their struggles (Crisp 1984, 18–19).

One mining company eventually became highly successful: the Ashanti Goldfields Corporation. Its predecessor, the Côte d'Or Mining Company,

Table 9.2 Real return on investment in selected companies in West Africa, 1869–1969 (geometric mean per year)

Company	Time-period	Real return (%)
African Association/African and Eastern Trade Corporation	*1897–1932*	−2.2
African Steam Ship Company	*1869–1930*	2.1
	1869–1900	4.8
	1901–1929	1.1
Amalgamated Tin Mines of Nigeria	*1939–1969*	5.1
	1939–1959	7.7
	1960–1969	−0.1
Ashanti Goldfields Corporation	*1901–1968*	5.8
	1901–1929	−0.3
	1930–1959	10.9
	1960–1968	9.7
Bank of (British) West Africa	*1901–1965*	7.5
	1901–1929	5.2
	1930–1959	8.9
	1960–1965	13.1
British & African Steam Navigation Co.	*1883–1900*	10.0
Consolidated African Selection Trust	*1941–1969*	16.9
	1941–1959	14.7
	1960–1969	21.4
National African/Royal Niger/Niger Company	*1883–1919*	8.5
	1883–1900	15.8
	1901–1919	1.6
West African Telegraph Co. Ltd.	*1886–1908*	2.9
	1886–1900	−4.4
	1901–1908	18.0

Source: African Colonial Equities Database (ACED)

was established by Edwin Cade to acquire mining rights on the Gold Coast. In 1895, the company acquired a mining lease in the Obuasi region from three African entrepreneurs. Cade further managed to get two local rulers—the chiefs of the Bekwai and Adanse—to agree to a mining concession covering 100 square miles in the region for a period of 99 years (McCaskie 1978, 38–40; Ayensu 1997, 11–12; Afrifa-Taylor 2006, 62–64, 69; Dumett 2009, 64, 70–72). The concession was later contested by the *asantehene*, the Asante monarch (Austin 2005, 136). That would come to nothing, due to the British occupation of Asante that took place in 1896, which in effect deposed the *asantehene*. This was a development that Edwin Cade was well-informed of in advance, so that he considered it unnecessary to acquire any concessions from the, at the time, soon-to-be deposed *asantehene* (McCaskie 1978, 41–42). As of 1 January 1897, the British colonial government granted a new concession for the company's lease. On 11 June 1897, finally, Côte d'Or transferred all its assets and liabilities to the newly established Ashanti Goldfields Corporation, which also was registered on the London Stock Exchange the same day (McCaskie 1978; Ayensu 1997, 11–12; Afrifa-Taylor 2006, 71–72, 163; Dumett 2009, 72). The mining operations at Obuasi began for real in 1898, and in March of that year, the first gold was produced (Afrifa-Taylor 2006, 76).

Ashanti Goldfields' concession included not only the right to mine for minerals but also a right to use the land for agricultural production, a right to exploit forest resources within the concession for timber, as well as a monopoly on trade within the concession area (Howard 1978, 66; Afrifa-Taylor 2006, 164). At the same time, there were many outstanding issues regarding the mining concession that the Ashanti Goldfields Corporation never managed to acquire (at least not formally). One issue was whether the British colonial authorities had the legal right to grant such a concession in the first place. At the time when the concession was issued, there was no legislation in place in the colony allowing for such action. It was not until the Concessions Ordinance was introduced in Asante in 1903 that the colonial institutions regulating land tenure were established (Afrifa-Taylor 2006, 168, 171). The company would choose not to have outstanding issues clarified, so that the company's behaviour 'had a consolidating effect on their perceived rights and established a sort of accepted corporate custom' (Afrifa-Taylor 2006, 187). The Ashanti Goldfields Corporation was floated on the London Stock Exchange in 1897, with an authorized share capital of 250,000 shares at £1 par value. Of these shares, 64,000 were allocated to friends and families of the founding directors, and a further 50,000 shares were allocated to the shareholders of the Côte d'Or Company, in exchange for the concession rights in Asante (Afrifa-Taylor 2006, 223). The first shares offered to the public, in August 1898, traded for £2 each (Afrifa-Taylor 2006, 241).

High Imperialism in West Africa, 1900s to 1920s

The first years of the twentieth century spelled substantial changes in West Africa. On the Gold Coast, orders in Council issued in 1901 brought Ashanti and the Northern Territories under direct rule and protection, respectively, and made them—together with the already established Gold Coast Colony—effectively into one single colony (Kimble 1963, 325).

The Royal Niger Company lost its chartered status, effective from 1 January 1900, since the British government had decided it wanted to separate administrative functions from commercial activities. The Northern Territories of Nigeria was thereby declared a British protectorate (Ekundare 1973, 104; Pedler 1974, 138). In 1914, a number of different territories were amalgamated into the single colony of Nigeria (Falola 1999, 68–69).

Trading

Once the Royal Niger Company lost its royal charter, it was renamed the Niger Company (Pedler 1974, 164; Baker 1996, 202–4). As compensation for its loss of charter, the British government paid a major economic compensation, £865,000, to the company (Flint 1960, 307–8; Pedler 1974, 137). In 1899, the Royal Niger Company, the African Association and two other independent trading companies also agreed to establish a cartel (entering into effect in 1900) and to divide up the market between the companies (Pedler 1974, 147). By 1913, the Niger Company had grown into one of the largest British trading companies in the world (Jones 2000, table 3.1).

Geoffrey Jones has claimed that the Niger Company flourished once it lost its administrative responsibilities (Jones 2000, 77). This is not the case from the investors' point of view. Over the whole period from 1901 to 1929, the trading companies were not very successful investments at all, as is shown in Table 9.2, with average real return amounting to 1.6–2.8 per cent per year. The return on investment in these companies shifted dramatically over time. The period up until the First World War was comparatively successful for the trading companies, with average real return on investment of around 3 per cent per year for the Royal Niger Company and 8 per cent per year for the African Association. The outbreak of the war led in contrast to major losses for investors in the Royal Niger Company, in particular, with the price of the shares falling from £3.2 in January 1914 to £1.15 one year later. The war also spelled the collapse of the cartel agreement between the major trading companies (Martin 1988, 93). The process of oligopolization of trade in the region, which had started already during the late nineteenth century, would, on the other hand, continue in the interwar period. In 1919, the African Association merged with a couple of other trading companies to form the African & Eastern Trade Corporation. The assets of the Niger Company were purchased by the Lever Brothers in 1920 (Bauer 1954, 106–8; Pedler 1974, 2; Howard 1976, 73, 1978, 94–97; Jones 2000, 91). For a while, the market experienced fierce monopolistic competition, which was also reflected in the return on investment. The estimated return on investment in the African & Eastern Trade Corporation amounted to an average of −12 per cent per year during the 1920s (see Table 9.2). Since the Niger Company had been taken over by the Lever Brothers, it does not figure as an independent company traded on the London Stock Exchange during the interwar period. The competition finally ended in 1929 when the Niger Company was merged with the African & Eastern Trade Corporation to form the United Africa Company (Pedler 1974, 2; Howard 1976, 73, 1978, 94–97; Fieldhouse 1994, 9–18; Baker 1996, 246; Jones 2000, 91). The United Africa Company (not to be confused with the previously mentioned United African Company formed in 1879) developed into one of the major businesses of the recently formed Unilever Corporation (Fieldhouse 1978, 46).

Shipping

The shipping industry continued to be dominated by the West African Shipping Conference cartel for the initial years of the twentieth century (Howard 1978, 116–27; Sherwood 1997). The average real return for the whole of the period from 1901 to 1929 was not high, as is shown in

Table 9.1—a mere 1.1 per cent per year. But as for the trading companies, the return changed drastically over the period. The return on investment in the shipping companies remained high up until the First World War. Investments in the African Steam Ship Company did, for example, exhibit an average return of 7.9 per cent per year until 1913. The shipping cartel collapsed during the First World War (Davies 2000, 164). As a consequence of the war, Elder Dempster managed to acquire a complete monopoly on West African trade when the sole competitor, a German shipping line, was forced out of the trade (Olukoju 1992). The end of the First World War saw new entrants in the shipping market by companies from countries other than the United Kingdom. This in turn increased shipping competition to and from West Africa. For investors, these years implied substantial losses: the price of the shares in the African Steam Ship Company was, for example, halved in 1920, as investors fled the stock. A new shipping conference was established in 1924, operating successfully for a period (Leubuscher 1963, 32–33; Davies 2000, 185). The main challenge for the shipping companies during this period was to keep their customers satisfied enough, so that they would not choose to start operating shipping of their own. Since the trade in the region was dominated by a handful of companies, the risk of losing any of these major clients posed a major challenge for the shipping lines. In 1923, the African & Eastern Trade Corporation started shipping on its own. In 1929, the United African Company did likewise. This meant a drastic blow to the volumes handled by the dedicated shipping lines, and hence, on their profitability—especially so in combination with major losses, following the collapse of international trade in the wake of the 1929 stock market crash. As a consequence, the African Steam Ship Company was wound up the following year, after exhibiting major negative return on investment during its last two years of existence (Leubuscher 1963, 46–52; Davies 1969, 231–32, 2000, 187–210).

Banking

The Bank of British West Africa was introduced on the London Stock Exchange in 1901. At this stage, the bank was not only a commercial bank but also the sole distributor of silver coins in the British West

African colonies. There were many complaints against the company for how they were managing this task. In 1912, the West African Currency Board was established by the government to overtake this task (Jones 1993, 114–16). The bank expanded rapidly during the first decades of the twentieth century. The return on investment in this company reflects that of the trading companies operating in West Africa (see Table 9.2). This is hardly surprising, given that there was a lot of crossholding between the companies and that the bank at the time was engaged almost exclusively in lending to European trading companies (Fry 1976, chap. 9; Jones 1993, 92). Alfred Jones' policy was furthermore that it was less important whether the bank itself made large profits—the most important task for the bank was to assist the trading companies in the region with banking services (Fry 1976, 61), presumably, most importantly, the trading companies where Jones himself held a position. A competitor, the Anglo-African Bank, was established in Nigeria in 1899, in 1905 renamed the Bank of Nigeria (Fry 1976, 42). In 1912, the Bank of British West Africa acquired a monopoly position in Nigeria again when it merged with the rival bank (Uche 1999, 670). Until the outbreak of the First World War, the return on investment was high with an average real return of 7 per cent per year (see Table 9.2). Data on the price of the bank's shares is unfortunately missing in the source employed during the First World War. The monopoly position the bank had acquired was challenged already in 1917 when the Colonial Bank (later part of Barclays, too) established branches in the region, first in Nigeria (Fry 1976, 91–93). The return on investment in the Bank of British West Africa was therefore relatively high during the 1920s, averaging to 6.3 per cent per year. Throughout the interwar period, the relationship between the two banks was characterized by both rivalry and collusion, including price-fixing, with the tacit acquiescence of the colonial authorities (Austin and Uche 2007). No doubt, a consequence of this collusion was high bank charges in the region (Austin and Uche 2007, 18–19).

Mining

Colonial status also entailed substantial institutional changes, with implications most importantly for the mining industry. The mining boom that had taken place on the Gold Coast during the last decades of the nineteenth century petered out during the first decades of the twentieth century, with several of the companies failing to make any profits (Howard 1978, 64; Agbodeka 1992, 106). Mineral exports did regardless become comparatively important for the British colonies in West Africa during this period: gold and diamonds from the Gold Coast, tin from Nigeria and diamonds from Sierra Leone (Hopkins 1973, 177). Institutional changes were imposed in several colonies to support the mining industry. On the Gold Coast, for example, attempts to introduce a Land Bill had been defeated in the 1890s, but an amended Concessions Ordinance was enacted in the Gold Coast Colony in the year 1900, followed by a similar ordinance in Asante in 1903 (Kimble 1963, 355–57; Phillips 1989, 69–70). The Concessions Ordinance stipulated that mining concessions could be granted to private mining companies. The mining companies did not acquire ownership of the land from such a concession but would have to pay rent to the landowner. The ordinance limited the size of the concessions in order to limit companies acquiring such huge concessions as the Ashanti Goldfields Corporation had been able to acquire in the preceding years (Howard 1978, 48).

Wage costs continued to be a major issue for the labour-intensive mining industry. The first decades of the twentieth century exhibited the first genuine attempts to abolish slavery in the new colonies in the region, even though slavery in some cases continued to be tolerated on the ground well into the 1920s (Phillips 1989, 26–33; Lovejoy and Hogendorn 1993; Austin 2005, chap. 13). Several mining companies instead participated in attempts to establish a monopsony recruitment organization, as had been done in South Africa earlier (see Chap. 11). A Mine Managers' Association was, for example, established on the Gold Coast and in 1903 agreed on fixed wages. This attempt did not bear fruit in the Gold Coast Colony because the agreement to fix wages was in practice reneged upon by some of the mines mere weeks after the agreement. When Consolidated Gold Fields of South Africa became a major owner of mines in the Tarkwa region of the Gold Coast Colony from 1909, they also attempted—but again failed—to establish similar institutions (Crisp 1984, 26–28, 38–39; Phillips 1989, 44). Another, and from the perspective of the mine owners, more successful solution was instead to recruit migrant labourers (Cooper 1996, 43–50). These recruits were not always migrating of their own choice. By the early twentieth century, for example, the system of semi-coerced, 'communal labourers' came to be exploited in a recruitment scheme operated by the colonial authorities in order to recruit labourers from the Northern Territories of the Gold Coast Colony (Thomas 1973; Crisp 1984, 35; Agbodeka 1992, 108–9; Dumett 2012, 42–45).

Investments in mining in the region were dominated by the Ashanti Goldfields Corporation. In contrast to several other mining companies, Ashanti Goldfields did not use the colonial authorities' communal labour recruitment scheme. According to Ayowa Afrifa-Taylor, this was not due to any different opinion about coerced labour among the company management. On the contrary, the founder of the company—Edwin Cade—clearly embraced racist stereotypes about Africans as being lazy and lacking ambition and even seems to have found chattel slavery of Africans acceptable (quoted in Afrifa-Taylor 2006, 68). However, the company had ample access to labourers locally and management therefore did not need to enrol migrant labourers to any great extent. This was a consequence of the geographically large concession that the company had managed to acquire, and that there consequently were no other major companies in the immediate vicinity which Ashanti Goldfields had to compete with when recruiting labour. Starting in 1913, Ashanti Goldfields experienced some labour shortages, primarily due to a competing demand for labour from cocoa plantations. An immediate consequence was that the company was forced to raise the wages paid in order to be able to attract labourers. The company also planned to start recruiting coerced, communal labour through the colonial authorities' recruitment scheme, but the plans do not seem to have been set in motion (Afrifa-Taylor 2006, 86–89; Dumett 2012, 45).

In the previous scholarly literature, this particular company has sometimes been referred to as a major failure. For example, Lance Davis and Robert Huttenback used Ashanti Goldfields to contrast the story of Cecil Rhodes and as an example of an unsuccessful company leading a 'beleaguered existence' (Davis and Huttenback 1988, 82). This is indeed also the impression one might get from studying the estimated return on investment based on data from Investors Monthly Manual. In the period from 1901 to 1929, the average return per year was −0.3 (see Table 9.2).

The company exhibited particularly large losses during the period studied by Davis and Huttenback, up until 1914—a negative real return on investment of −11 per cent per year on average. This development was largely a reflection of what had occurred before the company started to appear in the main source for our dataset, the *Investors' Monthly Manual*. As was noted previously, the first shares offered to the public in August 1898, traded for £2 each. In January 1900, shares were traded at £10 and in May 1901, the share price reached £25 (Afrifa-Taylor 2006, 241). Ashanti Goldfields Corporation was only considered worthy of being included in the *Investors' Monthly Manual*, and thereby entered our main dataset, starting in June 1901. By this time, the share price had risen to a spectacular £31 15s. Eventually, this was the peak price of the share which it would never recover at any time throughout the period under study in this book. From the Initial Public Offering (IPO) in August 1898, to the first occurrence in the *Investors' Monthly Manual* in June 1901, the initial shareholders had thereby made a total capital gain of 1488 per cent on their investment. The drop in the share price exhibited from June 1901, continuing until the spring of 1908, was consequently a backlash after this initial speculative wave. This was exacerbated by declining ore recovery rates from 1904 onwards, which is reflected in the price of the shares dropping drastically this year in particular (Afrifa-Taylor 2006, 79). The long-term development of the share price of Ashanti Goldfields thereby affected investors differently. Those who had invested in the early stages of company, largely insiders of the controlling network of the company, could enjoy a high return on investment. Investors who jumped on the opportunity later would, in contrast, experience substantial losses for many years, as the share price declined after the initial speculative wave. The development of the Ashanti Goldfields thereby resembles the development of the Rand Mines Limited (see Chap. 12). The company started to exhibit very high average return on investment again during the 1920s (+12 per cent per year during this decade). The return on investment became negative some years during this period as well, for example, in 1920, when the threat of a major strike forced the Ashanti Goldfields Corporation to increase wages to the labourers (Afrifa-Taylor 2006, 93). In total, the company exhibited a very high average return on investment, of 10.7 per cent per year, from 1915 to 1929. Taking into account that these years included the First World War, the company could hardly be characterized as suffering from any beleaguered existence.

The 1920s was also the period when the first diamonds were found on the Gold Coast. Several mining companies were established to explore and exploit these diamond resources. Land and mining rights were by this time well established in the colony, so the newly established diamond-mining companies had to negotiate with local rulers for mining concessions (Greenhalgh 1985, 95). The major company became the Consolidated African Selection Trust, the result of a merger in 1924 of the African Selection Trust and Anglo-African Exploration Limited. As such, it became a part of the of the finance house Selection Trust Limited (Greenhalgh 1985, 24, 44; Ofosu-Mensah 2016, 28). The Selection Trust companies did not appear in the sources used for this study until the interwar period.

In Nigeria, there was a tin-mining boom during the first decades of the century. The National African Company had already in 1884 discovered that tin was mined by the African population in the Bauchi region of Nigeria (Fell 1939, 246). As compensation for losing its royal charter, the Niger Company retained half a share to all mineral rights to a vast area of land in what eventually became Nigeria. In 1906, the company therefore initiated tin-mining operations (Ekundare 1973, 177; Shenton and Freund 1978, 15; Freund 1981, 33). Starting in 1909, the Niger Company started to sell prospecting rights to other companies, such as Champion Tin Fields, Naraguta, Rayfield, Bisichi Tin Company and the Kaduna Syndicate. As a consequence of it owning the mineral rights, the Niger Company also came to receive royalties from these other mining companies (Fell 1939, 246; Freund 1981, 36–38). Many of the early establishments probably suffered from speculation and company-mongering on the London Stock Exchange (Phimister 2000), but many of them eventually initiated actual mining operations. The mining companies were not always welcomed by the local population, but the colonial state 'destroyed with considerable brutality local resistance to the penetration of miners' on the Jos Plateau in Nigeria (quote from Shenton and Freund 1978, 15; see also Freund 1981, 43–44). As the mining industry on the Gold Coast sought means to acquire low-paid labour, so did the Nigerian mining industry. The Nigerian mining companies were much more successful at this, and had, after a few years, started to operate a cartel, acting as a monopsonist to keep wage costs for unskilled labourers low (Newbury 1978, 561; Freund 1981, 54–55). During the First World War, tin prices temporarily boomed, thereby increasing profits of tin-mining companies at the time. In 1920, in contrast, prices dropped drastically, and with them the return on investment, which is also reflected in the estimated return on investment in the mining sector, as is shown in Table 9.2. This also contributed substantially to the economic hardships faced by the Niger Company, and why it eventually was taken over by the Lever Brothers (Newbury 1978, 570; Ingulstad 2015, 99–100).

Towards Political Independence, 1930s to 1950s

The period from the 1930s to the 1950s spelled substantial changes in West Africa. Slavery was finally abolished throughout the region. Limits on the amount of labour that traditional chiefs could extract by coercion were furthermore imposed in the 1930s (Rathbone 2004, 488–89). In several West African colonies, political organizations striving for independence were established in the 1940s. By the 1950s, many of these organizations had—according to some historians—become rather conciliatory towards the European imperialist powers (Hopkins 1973, 270–71; Porter 2012, 264–65). Starting during the Second World War, the British government also came to accept import-substituting industrial development in its West African possessions (Butler 1997). Ghana achieved political independence in March 1957 and was followed by the political independence of several other colonies in the region, including Nigeria in October 1960 (Porter 2012, 274).

In the final years of colonial rule after the Second World War, when it started to become obvious to an increasing number of people that colonial rule was coming to an end, several of the companies operating in the colonies became active participants in the process of decolonization. They thereby attempted to look after their own interests in maintaining business in the former colonies even after decolonization. One way of doing this was to 'Africanize' their operations: employing a larger number of Africans in their operations, including in managerial positions (Jones 1993, 318; Stockwell 1995, 2000, 2004; Decker 2007, 2008; Murillo 2011). Some companies also changed their names. The Bank of British West Africa, for example, simply dropped the word 'British' from the name in 1957 (Fry 1976, 208). A further adaptation to decolonization was to find new markets for the company's services. This was most markedly the case for the colonial banks. In the case of the Bank of British West Africa, European-owned trading companies had continued to be the main customers of the bank's services throughout the 1950s. The banks expanded rapidly in the 1950s, primarily through the opening of new branches (Fry 1976, 197; Stockwell 2000, 161–62). In the late 1950s, when political decolonization already had started to happen, did the company first start to lend money to African firms to any substantial degree (Jones 1993, 303–4, 308). A final option for several companies was to 'redeploy' capital from the colonies, for example, to the Americas and Europe, to safeguard it from expropriation after decolonization (Jones 2000, 151–53, 320–21).

Trading and Banking

The process of oligopolization of the economy, which had started already in the 1920s, continued throughout the 1930s and 1940s. Trading companies had, to a large extent, disappeared from our sample after being amalgamated into the United Africa Company in 1929. The trading companies that remained in operation entered into cartel agreements in the 1930s (Bauer 1954, 77–78). The Great Depression had serious repercussions for trade with West Africa. It thereby also impacted West African banking, as lending to trading companies was a key activity for the banks in the region (Fry 1976, 135–36; Jones 1993, 188). The two rival banks in the region continued to collude, particularly from 1933 onwards (Austin and Uche 2007). There were several attempts to start competing banks in the region after the Second World War, but all these attempts failed (Fry 1976, 215–20). Given this, the bank was able to achieve a high return on investment, amounting to a real average return of 8.9 per cent per year during the period, as can be seen in Table 9.2.

Mining

British investments in the West African colonies became even more dominated by the extractive sector during this period. In Nigeria, exploration for petroleum oil had been going on from the start of the twentieth century, but was for a long time largely fruitless. Large wells were located in 1956, and the country started to export oil two years later. The operations were managed by a company wholly owned by the multinational companies British Petroleum and Royal Dutch Shell, and several of the later established competitors were likewise wholly owned by major multinational oil companies (Uche 2010, 170–71). As these companies were not traded on the London Stock Exchange, they do not, unfortunately, figure in our sample of African companies.

Several of the mining companies traded on the London Stock Exchange also experienced substantial growth in capital value during this period. The most prominent example was Ashanti Goldfields, which grew to such an extent during this period that it turned into the single most important company in our West African sample—for a time during the 1930s, it accounted for around half of the total market capitalization of the regional portfolio. Similar to how the fall of the Gold Standard in the early 1930s impacted the gold-mining companies in South Africa (see Chap. 11), this also increased the profitability of the Ashanti Goldfields Corporation (Afrifa-Taylor 2006, 98). The 1930s therefore into a fabulously successful time for the company, returning some 37.5 per cent per year to its investors. The 1940s and 1950s, in contrast, presented substantial challenges for the company. At this time, the mineworkers started to organize themselves into unions, and they staged a number of strikes, including two major general strikes in 1945 and 1956. These strikes became turning points for the further unionization of the labour force (Crisp 1984, 58–59, 76, 80, 86, 115; Afrifa-Taylor 2006, 197). This was something that the company fiercely attempted to oppose, fearing that successful unions would increase labour costs. Strikers were dismissed and blacklisted from further work. Detectives were employed to infiltrate and spy upon union meetings (Stockwell 2000, 185–87). The company also tried to encourage loyalty towards the company through various bonuses and other incentives (Afrifa-Taylor 2006, 207–8, 213). The attempts were generally not successful, and the share price exhibited a sharp downward trend, particularly from 1946 to 1952, after which the price of the share continued to fall in total, but at a less dramatic rate and with at least some periods of recovery. In total, therefore, the 1940s and 1950s were negative for the company's investors: the average rate of return on investment in the Ashanti Goldfields Corporation was −9.6 per cent per year from 1940 until Ghana became independent in 1957. The substantial fall in share price might partly be attributed to a fear of decolonization and what then would happen to the company's investments in the Gold Coast. Once political independence was a fact, many investors seemed to have become less alarmed, at least for a period, as the share price recovered in the immediate aftermath of Ghana's political independence.

Diamond mining also increased in importance during the period. The Consolidated African Selection Trust (CAST) established subsidiaries abroad, most importantly the Sierra Leone Selection Trust (SLST). As for the gold-mining companies, diamond mines, to a large extent, recruited migrant labourers, often from the poorer Northern Territories (Greenhalgh 1985, 122). One incentive used for recruiting labour for the diamond-mining companies was to provide social benefits such as housing and healthcare for the workers (Ofosu-Mensah 2011, 2016). CAST participated in the international diamond cartel established by the South African company De Beers (see Chap. 11). Participation included an agreement to sell all of its diamonds to the Central Selling Organization (CSO) (Greenhalgh 1985, 232). Peter Greenhalgh has estimated that the Consolidated African Selection Trust and its subsidiaries consequently were extraordinarily profitable: the CAST exhibited retained profits (relative to net assets) averaging 24 per cent per year during the period 1925–1960, while the subsidiary SLST exhibited profits averaging 33 per cent per year during the period 1934–1960 (Greenhalgh 1985, table 7). This is also reflected in our estimates. Between 1941 and 1969, the estimated average real return on investment amounted to an extraordinary 16.9 per cent per year (see Table 9.2).

In Nigeria, tin mining expanded substantially, and Nigeria became a major international producer of tin during the interwar period (Ingulstad et al. 2015, 5). The development of the Nigerian mining industry resulted in high royalties to the United Africa Company, especially in the interwar period (Freund 1981, 213–14). The late 1920s and early 1930s saw considerable consolidation of the tin-mining industry in the colony. Associated Tin Mines of Nigeria (ATMN), controlled by the Anglo-Oriental Trust, was established in 1926 and acquired several smaller companies in the colony. The Anglo-Oriental Trust also controlled the London Tin Corporation, established in 1929 to operate tin mines in Nigeria. Remaining tin-mining companies were in 1945 further merged into the Amalgamated Tin Mines of Nigeria, which became the world's largest tin-mining company at the time (Shenton and Freund 1978, 16; Freund 1981, 117–18, 126; Borok et al. 2015, 325). London Tin Corporation would later invest little in its Nigerian operations, but instead switch focus to its Malaysian mines (Freund 1981, 222–23; Thoburn 2015, 225–27).

As for several of the other mining companies, the supply of labour was a crucial concern for the Nigerian tin mines. During the Second World War, tin was considered a strategic product, leading the British government to allow the use of 'conscript' (i.e. coerced) labour in the Nigerian tin mines (Freund 1981, chap. 5). During this time, the first unions were also allowed in Nigeria, and the first union among ATMN workers was established in 1941 (Freund 1981, 175, 178). The tin-mining companies for a long time persisted in trying to counteract union organization in order to keep wages down (Borok et al. 2015, 325). A first strike in Nigerian tin mines occurred at the Gold and Base Metal Mining Company in 1947 (Freund 1981, 182), followed by new strikes in the Nigerian tin fields in 1950 and 1955 (Freund 1981, 183–88).

The major tin-mining companies in the world agreed on the International Tin Agreement in 1931. The agreement aimed to restrain competition on the market in order to control prices in the interests of the producers (Hopkins 1973, 259; Ekundare 1973, 178; Freund 1981, 122). In Nigeria, the agreement limited the output of tin. This led to many migrant workers leaving the minefields, with the long-run consequence of a lack of labour once output started to increase again (Fell 1939, 249). The agreement was no unqualified success for the companies involved, seeing that the real average returns on investments in tin-mining companies in the 1930s were low, for example, 2.3 per cent per year for the London Tin Corporation. A new International Tin Agreement was agreed to in 1954 and renewed several times (Freund 1981, 206). For a time, the tin-mining companies seemed to have profited substantially from this, with average rates of return exceeding 10 per cent per year on average during the remainder of the 1950s for investments in both two surviving Nigerian tin-mining companies.

Political Independence in West Africa, 1960–1969

Political decolonization had different effects in different countries and in different sectors of the economy. For old shipping lines, it initially meant more competition, at least in theory, as some of the newly independent West African countries established shipping lines of their own, such as the Black Star Lines, based in Ghana, or the Nigerian National Shipping Line. In practice, these companies remained members of the established shipping conference cartels, and thereby did not threaten the profitability of the already established shipping companies (Leubuscher 1963, 66; Davies 2000, 299–300). The banking sector was able to find new markets among African firms interested in borrowing money, making the initial years of the 1960s successful for investors in what was now called the Bank of West Africa. In 1965, the bank was acquired by the Standard Bank (Fry 1976, 253–58; Jones 1993, 262).

Political independence had a substantial impact upon the mining sector in West Africa. Once Ghana achieved independence in 1957, the Convention People's Party (CPP) under Kwame Nkrumah came into power. The CPP was officially a pan-Africanist, socialist party. The new government attempted to control much of the economy in order to reduce foreign control (Hutchful 1979, 36–38). Although professedly a socialist country, foreign companies were initially allowed to continue their operations. Certainly, several mines were purchased in 1960 by the Ghanaian government, but these were mines that were under threat of closure and the government purchased them in order to keep them in operation (Crisp 1984, 133; Afrifa-Taylor 2006, 111).

Nkrumah's rule of Ghana put heavy political pressure on the mine workers' unions to reduce their militant tactics in support of the national cause (Crisp 1984, 125). The Industrial Relations Act of 1958 required all unions to submit to arbitration rather than take strike action of their own, in practice making it illegal to strike. Under the new laws, furthermore, the union's leadership was no longer elected by the rank-and-file members but imposed from above by the state and chosen from supporters of the ruling CPP (Afrifa-Taylor 2006, 216–17). At Ashanti Goldfields Corporation, for example, the union essentially became part of the management of the corporation (Afrifa-Taylor 2006, 216). Ashanti Goldfields was taken over by the Lonrho corporation in 1968 (Ayensu 1997, 18; Afrifa-Taylor 2006, 122–23). The Nkrumah government was ousted by a pro-capitalist, military coup in 1966. This led to renewed militancy among the mine workers' unions from 1968 onwards (Crisp 1984, 150–51). This was in turn followed by another military coup in 1972, which started to take substantially greater control over the economy, taking over controlling shares in several timber and mining companies (including the Ashanti Goldfields Corporation and the Consolidated African Selection Trust), as well as others, including the United Africa Company (Hutchful 1979, 36–38). Despite the political turbulence, the decade was a successful one for the Ashanti Goldfields Corporation, with an average return on investment amounting to 9.7 per cent per year.

Unrelated to the political development in Ghana, the Selection Trust companies in 1960 decided to break ranks with the CSO, with which they had cooperated since the 1920s. The break was caused by the perception that they were paid too little for their diamonds, especially for their Sierra Leonean gem diamonds. This initiated the so-called Diamond War between the companies; it ended with a new deal between the companies which assured higher prices for the Sierra Leone diamonds (Greenhalgh 1985, 255–58). Unsurprisingly, therefore, the Consolidated African Selection Trust exhibits an extraordinary return on investment during the 1960s, on average 21.4 per cent per year.

At the same time, the tin-mining companies in Nigeria struggled economically. Despite the fact that the International Tin Agreement was formally still in operation, the real return on investment in a company such as the Amalgamated Tin Mines of Nigeria was in practice zero.

Return on Investment in West Africa in the Long Run, 1869–1969

Figure 9.1 shows the return on investment in the region by decade. As can be seen, investments in the region were off to a catastrophically bad start, with major losses experienced by some of the early investors, most importantly in gold mining on the Gold Coast. Return on investment would, in the following decades, fluctuate considerably over time, ranging from −5 per cent per year during some decades to +10 per cent per year during some other decades. All in all, it needs to be borne in mind that the initial losses were of such magnitude that it significantly impacted the total return over the full hundred years. If total return instead is calculated from 1880 to 1969, the annual average amounts 4.1 per cent. Some companies fared very well, most prominently the Consolidated African Selection Trust, exhibiting an extraordinary average annual return on investment of almost 17 per cent for the 28 years for which we have data. Several other major companies, such as the Royal Niger Company

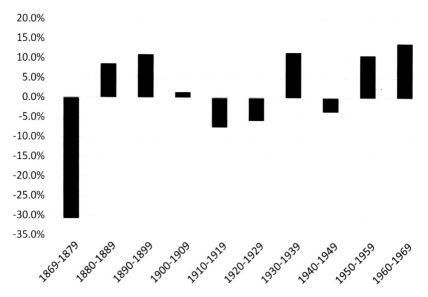

Fig. 9.1 Real return on investment in West Africa, by decade, 1869–1969 (geometric mean per year). Source: African Colonial Equities Database (ACED)

and its successor or the Bank of (British) West Africa, also exhibited very high return over an extended period. Investments in some companies might furthermore have fared even better than what our estimates suggest. In particular, as was shown previously, estimating the return on investment for the Ashanti Goldfields Corporation based on data from the *Investors' Monthly Manual* does in reality lead to a serious underestimation of the average return on investment, due to data only being reported from 1901 in the source employed. At this time, the share price peaked after having experienced a major rise in previous years and the share price turned to a major decline. Total average real return over the whole period studied is, according to these figures, 5.8 per cent per year. If we include the period from the first public offering, the total average real return is substantially higher, at 9.8 per cent per year.

Several companies—even some of the largest ones in the sample—in contrast exhibited negative return on investment for one reason or another, or major losses during some periods. As has been described previously in this chapter, this was due to a number of different factors, such as shorter or longer stints of fierce monopolistic competition between rivals, mining operations that never showed the expected return, increased labour costs following labour unionization and fears among investors of what decolonization could imply. In consequence, the average real return on investment in the complete sample of companies operating in the region of West Africa was practically zero over the whole period under study in this book.

References

Afrifa-Taylor, Ayowa. 2006. *An Economic History of the Ashanti Goldfields Corporation, 1895–2004: Land, Labour, Capital and Enterprise.* Ph.D. Dissertation, London School of Economics and Political Science.

Agbodeka, Francis. 1971. *African Politics and British Policy in the Gold Coast 1868–1900.* London: Longman.

———. 1992. *An Economic History of Ghana.* Accra: Ghana Universities Press.

Ash, Catherine B. 2006. Forced Labor in Colonial West Africa. *History Compass* 4 (3): 402–406.

Austin, Gareth. 2005. *Labour, Land and Capital in Ghana: From Slavery to Free Labour in Asante, 1807–1956*. Rochester, NY: University of Rochester Press.

Austin, Gareth, and Chibuike Ugochukwu Uche. 2007. Collusion and Competition in Colonial Economies: Banking in British West Africa, 1916–1960. *Business History Review* 81 (1): 1–26.

Ayensu, Edward. 1997. *Ashanti Gold*. Accra: Ashanti Goldfields Corporation.

Baker, Geoffrey. 1996. *Trade Winds on the Niger: The Saga of the Royal Niger Company, 1830–1971*. London: The Radcliffe Press.

Bauer, P.T. 1954. *West African Trade: A Study of Competition, Oligopoly and Monopoly in a Changing Economy*. Cambridge: Cambridge University Press.

Borok, A.M., A. Suleiman, and Charles Azgaku. 2015. The Politics of Labour Control and Inter-Group Relations in the Jos-Plateau Mining Camps 1945–1960. *International Journal of Humanities & Social Science Studies* 2 (1): 322–333.

Butler, L.J. 1997. *Industrialisation and the British Colonial State: West Africa 1939–1951*. London: Frank Cass.

Cain, Peter J., and Anthony G. Hopkins. 2001. *British Imperialism, 1688–2000*. Harlow: Longman.

Chamberlain, M.E. 2010. *The Scramble for Africa*. 3rd ed. Harlow: Longman.

Cooper, Frederick. 1996. *Decolonization and African Society: The Labor Question in French and British Africa*. Cambridge: Cambridge University Press.

Crisp, Jeff. 1984. *The Story of an African Working Class: Ghanaian Miners' Struggles 1870–1980*. London: Zed Books.

Crowder, Michael. 1968. *West Africa under Colonial Rule*. London: Hutchinson.

Davies, Peter N. 1969. The African Steam Ship Company. In *Liverpool and Merseyside: Essays in the Economic and Social History of the Port and Its Hinterland*, ed. J.R. Harris, 212–238. London: Frank Cass.

———. 1977. The Impact of the Expatriate Shipping Lines on the Economic Development of British West Africa. *Business History* 19 (1): 3–17.

———. 2000. *The Trade Makers: Elder Dempster in West Africa, 1852–1972, 1973–1989*. St John's, Newfoundland: International Maritime Economic History Association.

———. 2002. The Impact of Improving Communications on Commercial Transactions: Nineteenth-Century Case Studies from British West Africa and Japan. *International Journal of Maritime History* 14 (1): 225–238.

Davis, Lance, and Robert Huttenback. 1988. *Mammon and the Pursuit of Empire: The Economics of British Imperialism*. Abridged ed. Cambridge: Cambridge University Press.

Decker, Stephanie. 2007. Corporate Legitimacy and Advertising: British Companies and the Rhetoric of Development in West Africa, 1950–1970. *Business History Review* 81 (1): 59–86.

———. 2008. Building Up Goodwill: British Business, Development and Economic Nationalism in Ghana and Nigeria, 1945–1977. *Enterprise and Society* 9 (4): 602–613.

Dumett, Raymond. 1983. African Merchants of the Gold Coast, 1860–1905—Dynamics of Indigenous Entrepreneurship. *Comparative Studies in Society and History* 25 (4): 661–693.

———. 1998. *El Dorado in West Africa: The Gold-Mining Frontier, African Labor, and Colonial Capitalism in the Gold Coast, 1875–1900*. Athens: Ohio University Press.

———. 2009. Edwin Cade and Frederick Gordon: British Imperialism and the Foundations of the Ashanti Goldfields Corporation, West Africa. In *Mining Tycoons in the Age of Empire, 1870–1945: Entrepreneurship, High Finance, Politics and Territorial Expansion*, ed. Raymond Dumett, 63–84. Farnham: Ashgate.

———. 2012. Parallel Mining Frontiers in the Gold Coast and Asante in the Late 19th and Early 20th Centuries. In *Mining Frontiers in Africa: Anthropological and Historical Perspectives*, ed. Katja Werthmann and Tilo Grätz, 33–54. Köln: Rüdiger Köppe Verlag.

Ekundare, Olufeni. 1973. *An Economic History of Nigeria 1860–1960*. London: Methuen.

Falola, Toyin. 1999. *The History of Nigeria*. Westport: Greenwood Press.

Fell, Godfrey. 1939. The Tin Mining Industry in Nigeria. '*Journal of the Royal African Society* 38 (151): 246–258.

Fieldhouse, D.K. 1978. *Unilever Overseas: The Anatomy of a Multinational: 1895–1965*. London: Croom Helm.

———. 1994. *Merchant Capital and Economic Decolonization: The United Africa Company 1929–1987*. Oxford: Clarendon Press.

Flint, John. 1960. *Sir George Goldie and the Making of Nigeria*. London: Oxford University Press.

———. 1973. Britain and the Partition of West Africa. In *Perspectives of Empire. Essays Presented to Gerald S. Graham*, ed. John E. Flint and Glyndwr Williams, 93–111. London: Longman.

Frankema, Ewout, Jeffrey Williamson, and Pieter Woltjer. 2018. An Economic Rationale for the West African Scramble? The Commercial Transition and the Commodity Price Boom of 1835–1885. *The Journal of Economic History* 78 (1): 231–267.

Freund, Bill. 1981. *Capital and Labour in the Nigerian Tin Mines*. Harlow: Longman.

Fry, Richard. 1976. *Bankers in West Africa: The Story of the Bank of British West Africa Limited*. London: Hutchinson Benham.

Getz, Trevor. 2004. *Slavery and Reform in West Africa: Toward Emancipation in Nineteenth-Century Senegal and the Gold Coast*. Athens, OH: Ohio University Press.

Greenhalgh, P.A.L. 1985. *West African Diamonds, 1919–1983: An Economic History*. Manchester: Manchester University Press.

Hargreaves, John. 1963. *Prelude to the Partition of West Africa*. London: Macmillan.

Headrick, Daniel R., and Pascal Griset. 2001. Submarine Telegraph Cables: Business and Politics, 1838–1939. *Business History Review* 75 (3): 543–578.

Hilson, Gavin. 2002. Harvesting Mineral Riches: 1000 Years of Gold Mining in Ghana. *Resources Policy* 28 (1): 13–26.

Hopkins, Anthony G. 1968. Economic Imperialism in West Africa: Lagos, 1880–92. *The Economic History Review* 21 (3): 580–606.

———. 1973. *An Economic History of West Africa*. London: Longman.

Howard, Rhoda. 1976. Economic Imperialism and Oligopolization of Trade in the Gold Coast: 1886–1939. *Ufahamu: A Journal of African Studies* 7 (1): 71–92.

———. 1978. *Colonialism and Underdevelopment in Ghana*. London: Croom Helm.

Hutchful, Eboe. 1979. A Tale of Two Regimes: Imperialism, the Military and Class in Ghana. *Review of African Political Economy* 6 (14): 36–55.

Ingulstad, Mats. 2015. Banging the Tin Drum: The United States and the Quest for Strategic Self-Sufficiency in Tin, 1840–1945. In *Tin and Global Capitalism: A History of the Devil's Metal, 1850–2000*, ed. Mats Ingulstad, Andrew Perchard, and Espen Storli, 89–122. New York: Routledge.

Ingulstad, Mats, Andrew Perchard, and Espen Storli. 2015. Introduction: 'The Path of Civilization Is Paved with Tin Cans': The Political Economy of the Global Tin Industry. In *Tin and Global Capitalism: A History of the Devil's Metal, 1850–2000*, ed. Mats Ingulstad, Andrew Perchard, and Espen Storli, 1–21. New York: Routledge.

Jones, Geoffrey. 1993. *British Multinational Banking, 1830–1990*. Oxford: Clarendon Press.

———. 2000. *Merchants to Multinationals: British Trading Companies in the 19th and 20th Centuries*. Oxford: Oxford University Press.

Kimble, David. 1963. *A Political History of Ghana: The Rise of Gold Coast Nationalism 1850–1928*. Oxford: Oxford University Press.

Leubuscher, Charlotte. 1963. *The West African Shipping Trade 1909–1959*. Leiden: A.W. Sythoff.

Lovejoy, Paul E., and Jan S. Hogendorn. 1993. *Slow Death for Slavery: The Course of Abolition in Northern Nigeria 1897–1936*. Cambridge: Cambridge University Press.

Lynn, Martin. 1989. From Sail to Steam: The Impact of the Steamship Services on the British Palm Oil Trade with West Africa, 1850–1890. *The Journal of African History* 30 (2): 227–245.

———. 1992. British Business and the African Trade: Richard & William King Ltd. of Bristol and West Africa, 1833–1918. *Business History* 34 (4): 20–37.

———. 1997. *Commerce and Economic Change in West Africa: The Palm Oil Trade in the Nineteenth Century*. Cambridge: Cambridge University Press.

Martin, Susan. 1988. *Palm Oil and Protest: An Economic History of the Ngwa Region, South-Eastern Nigeria, 1800–1980*. Cambridge: Cambridge University Press.

McCaskie, T.C. 1978. The Creation of Ashanti Goldfields Corporation, Ltd., ca. 1890–1910: An Episode in the Colonial Impact upon Asante. *Asantesem* 9: 37–55.

Müller, Simone M. 2016. *Wiring the World: The Social and Cultural Creation of Global Telegraph Networks*. New York: Columbia University Press.

Murillo, Bianca. 2011. 'The Devil We Know': Gold Coast Consumers, Local Employees, and the United Africa Company, 1940–1960. *Enterprise and Society* 12 (2): 317–355.

Newbury, Colin. 1978. Trade and Technology in West Africa: The Case of the Niger Company, 1900–1920. *The Journal of African History* 19 (4): 551–575.

Ochonu, Moses. 2013. African Colonial Economies: Land, Labor, and Livelihoods. *History Compass* 11 (2): 91–103.

Ofosu-Mensah, Emmanuel Ababio. 2011. Gold Mining and the Socio-Economic Development of Obuasi in Adanse. *African Journal of History and Culture* 3 (4): 54.

———. 2016. Mining in Colonial Ghana: Extractive Capitalism and Its Social Benefits in Akyem Abuakwa under Nana Ofori Atta I. *Africa Today* 63 (1): 22–55.

Olukoju, Ayodeji. 1992. Elder Dempster and the Shipping Trade of Nigeria during the First World War. *The Journal of African History* 33 (2): 255–271.

Pedler, Frederick. 1974. *The Lion and the Unicorn in Africa: A History of the Origins of the United Africa Company 1787–1931*. London: Heinemann.

Phillips, Anne. 1989. *The Enigma of Colonialism: British Policy in West Africa*. London: James Currey.

Phimister, Ian. 2000. Corners and Company-Mongering: Nigerian Tin and the City of London, 1909–12. *The Journal of Imperial and Commonwealth History* 28 (2): 23–41.

Porter, Bernard. 2012. *The Lion's Share - A History of British Imperialism 1850 to the Present*. 5th ed. London: Routledge.

Rathbone, Richard. 2004. West Africa, 1874–1948: Employment Legislation in a Nonsettler Peasant Economy. In *Masters, Servants, and Magistrates in Britain & the Empire, 1562–1955*, ed. Douglas Hay and Paul Craven, 481–497. Chapel Hill: University of North Carolina Press.

Reynolds, Edward. 1975. Economic Imperialism: The Case of the Gold Coast. *The Journal of Economic History* 35 (01): 94–116.

Robinson, Ronald Edward, and John Gallagher. 1968. *Africa and the Victorians: The Climax of Imperialism*. New York: Anchor Books.

Shenton, Bob, and Bill Freund. 1978. The Incorporation of Northern Nigeria into the World Capitalist Economy. *Review of African Political Economy* 5 (13): 8–20.

Sherwood, Marika. 1997. Elder Dempster and West Africa 1891–C. 1940: The Genesis of Underdevelopment? *The International Journal of African Historical Studies* 30 (2): 253–276.

Silver, Jim. 1981. The Failure of European Mining Companies in the Nineteenth-Century Gold Coast. *The Journal of African History* 22 (4): 511–529.

Stockwell, Sarah. 1995. Political Strategies of British Business during Decolonization: The Case of the Gold Coast/Ghana, 1945–57. *The Journal of Imperial and Commonwealth History* 23 (2): 277–300.

———. 2000. *The Business of Decolonization: British Business Strategies in the Gold Coast*. Oxford: Oxford University Press.

———. 2004. Trade, Empire, and the Fiscal Context of Imperial Business during Decolonization. *The Economic History Review* 57 (1): 142–160.

Thoburn, John. 2015. Increasing Developing Countries' Gains from Tin Mining: The Boom Years from the 1960s to 1985. In *Tin and Global Capitalism: A History of the Devil's Metal, 1850–2000*, ed. Mats Ingulstad, Andrew Perchard, and Espen Storli, 221–239. New York: Routledge.

Thomas, Roger G. 1973. Forced Labour in British West Africa: The Case of the Northern Territories of the Gold Coast 1906–1927. *The Journal of African History* 14 (1): 79–103.
Uche, Chibuike Ugochukwu. 1999. Foreign Banks, Africans, and Credit in Colonial Nigeria, c. 1890–1912. *Economic History Review* 52 (4): 669–691.
———. 2010. British Petroleum vs. the Nigerian Government: The Capital Gains Tax Dispute, 1972–9. *The Journal of African History* 51 (2): 167–188.

10

Central/Southern Africa

The British Colonization of Southern and Central Africa Until 1924

Central and Southern Africa experienced drastic changes during the nineteenth century. Starting in 1819, the *mfecane*, initiated by Zulu expansion, led to major migratory flows in the region. Around the same time, the Great Trek from the Cape northwards meant that a growing number of European settlers, primarily farmers, entered the area, putting pressure on local populations to move elsewhere (Keppel-Jones 1983, 2–4). This would later be followed by other settlers, searching for the great mineral riches that supposedly were to be found in the region (Robinson and Gallagher 1968, 221). British imperialist expansion northwards from South Africa began in the 1880s (Keppel-Jones 1983, 20). Bechuanaland was declared a British protectorate in 1885. In the wake of this, European companies started prospecting for minerals in the new protectorate. These attempts did amount to little at the time, as they found no major deposits of gold (Selolwane 1980).

The most important individual behind the drive to colonize the region was Cecil Rhodes. During the 1870s and 1880s, Rhodes made a considerable fortune for himself from diamonds in Kimberley (see Chap. 11). Rhodes' ambitions did, however, not stop there. Exactly what drove Rhodes' has been debated and suggestions include personal or political ambitions or failing investments on the Rand that needed compensation (Phimister 1974, 87; Loney 1975, 30–31). Regardless of Rhodes' ulterior motives, he pushed for further colonization northwards. He took part in establishing exploration companies to prospect for minerals and enter into agreements with local rulers for the right to develop any mineral findings (Gann 1958, 55–57). The most important, but also the most controversial, of these agreements were the agreements with King Lobengula of the Ndebele (the so-called Rudd Concession) and with King Lewanika of Barotseland (the so-called Lochner Concession). The concession by King Lobengula did, according to Rhodes' agent Rudd, grant exclusive land and mineral rights to the whole of his country, constituting a major part of current-day Zimbabwe, in exchange for a symbolic reimbursement. The contents of the treaty, and the extent to which King Lobengula understood the consequences of these, have been highly contested (see the drastically different interpretations in Robinson and Gallagher 1968, 234; Galbraith 1974, 71–73; Flint 1976, 104–7; Palmer 1977, 26–28; Schreuder 1980, 219–23; Keppel-Jones 1983, 78; Rotberg 1988, 262; Laurie 2008, chaps. 3–4; Mlambo 2014, 38–43). Already in February 1889, Lobengula made it clear to the British that the idea that he would have ceded to these rights was a misunderstanding and that no such concession had been made (Galbraith 1974, 72; Keppel-Jones 1983, 86; Rotberg 1988, 291; Laurie 2008, 59). That the king rejected having granted any concession was of little importance to the companies claiming the concession rights since, as John Galbraith has put it, the concession put 'a gloss of legitimacy to arbitrary dispossession' (Galbraith 1974, 74). In order to protect this legitimacy, Rhodes even went so far as to plot to murder Lobengula in December 1889, but the plot failed since the agent employed managed to reveal the plot beforehand (Flint 1976, 128). The concession by King Lewanika did, in a similar manner, supposedly grant exclusive land and mineral rights to the whole of Barotseland, in current-day Zambia, but the legitimacy of this concession has also been questioned (Gann 1958, 55–57; Slinn

Table 10.1 Real return on investment in selected portfolios in Central/Southern Africa, 1890–1969 (geometric mean per year)

Portfolio	Time period	Real return (%)
Total Central/Southern Africa	*1869–1969*	*2.2*
	1869–1923	−6.9
	1924–1969	9.4
Southern Rhodesia (Zimbabwe)	*1890–1969*	*2.3*
	1890–1923	−5.0
	1924–1969	8.0
Northern Rhodesia (Zambia)	*1905–1969*	*2.6*
	1905–1923	−11.5
	1924–1969	9.1
Mining sector	*1890–1969*	*1.5*
	1890–1923	−7.7
	1924–1969	8.9

Source: African Colonial Equities Database (ACED)

1971; Galbraith 1974, 102, 217–19; Flint 1976, 133–35; Rotberg 1988, 323–26; Larmer 2017, 172) (Table 10.1).

The British South Africa Company

The British government was reluctant to undertake further colonization of its own in the region. Leading figures in the government realized that the profits that private interests might gain were uncertain, whereas the government's cost for acquiring and governing the territory would be real from the start (Gann 1958, 47; Robinson and Gallagher 1968, 237; Porter 2012, 89). The vehicle for colonization of this region therefore came to be the chartered British South Africa Company (BSAC), itself effectively an amalgamation of a couple of exploration companies (Galbraith 1973, 1974, 83–86). The royal charter gave governmental powers to the BSAC and allowed it to profit from any agreements entered into with local rulers in the region, in exchange for administering the territory on behalf of the British crown (Flint 1976, 118; Schreuder 1980, 250–51; Keppel-Jones 1983, 134; Rotberg 1988, 285). BSAC's charter delimited the territory to be covered by the charter to the south, east and west, but left any delimitation to the north open for discussion and contestation (Coleman 1971, 2; Galbraith 1974, 111–12; Guene 2017).

Even though the charter stipulated borders east- and westwards, there were disputes with Portugal over where exactly to draw the border between the Portuguese colonies in the region and BSAC's territories (Flint 1976, 136–45; Mseba 2018).

The initial capital for the BSAC came from the South African company controlled by Cecil Rhodes and his partners Alfred Beit and Charles Rudd, through a couple of companies they controlled: De Beers, Gold Fields of South Africa, Wernher, Beit & Company and the Exploring Company. The capital was soon to be increased (Galbraith 1974, 122–23; Keppel-Jones 1983, 128–30).

Once the royal charter and finances had been secured, the actual colonization of the territory began. The occupation started in Matabeleland, the homeland of the Ndebeles, in 1890. The first wave was undertaken by the 'Pioneers Column', made up of 186 civilian Europeans, mainly prospectors themselves, in addition to some 500 policemen and around 350 Ngwato labourers (Keppel-Jones 1983, 164; Rotberg 1988, 299; Mlambo 2014, 43). The colonization quickly became violent and land and cattle were stolen *en masse* from the Ndebele (Ranger 1967, 102–10; Galbraith 1974, chap. 9; Flint 1976, 150–54; Keppel-Jones 1983, 286, 374, 395; Phimister 1988, 13; Rotberg 1988, chap. 16; Mlambo 2014, 44; Pilossof 2014, 339–40). The Ndebeles for a long time attempted to avoid a direct confrontation with the BSAC, but were eventually unable to avoid it once the BSAC initiated direct military attacks. Further uprisings in 1896 and 1897 were similarly brutally squashed by the colonizers (Ranger 1967, chaps. 4–8; Flint 1976, 150–54; Phimister 1988, 18–20; Rotberg 1988, chap. 20; Pilossof 2014, 339–40). In his orders to the BSAC's military forces, Cecil Rhodes himself was explicit to 'do the most harm you can' and 'kill all you can', in order to effectively repress any rebellion in the territory (quoted in Rotberg 1988, 557). In 1898, the British government issued Orders in Council to recognize the new colony (Mlambo 2014, 44).

Colonial rule under the BSAC had consequences for the local population. Starting in areas like Gwai and Shangani in 1890, land was expropriated through a number of laws and practices and sold to Europeans. In parallel, starting in 1898, members of the local population were forced to live in special 'native reserves' (Palmer 1977, 57–73; Phimister 1988, 65,

99; Mlambo 2014, 54–60). Inhabitants living in Matabeleland at the time of colonization were assured certain land rights in these reserves in the legislation imposed under company rule, but these rights did not accrue to the descendants of the Ndebele living at the time (Keppel-Jones 1983, 335).

The company also worked strategically to secure a labour force. A hut tax was introduced in Rhodesia in 1894, with the purpose of generating revenue. The tax did also have the purpose of generating a steady supply of labour since the tax was to be paid in cash and the hut owners therefore had to earn cash in some way (Keppel-Jones 1983, 400, 404; Phimister 1988, 50). The hut tax did not create a sufficiently large supply of labour on its own, but the BSAC also exploited different forms of coerced labour. This included rounding up potential labourers and forcing them to march to the destination where they were needed as well as directly burning huts and destroying food stores to 'give Africans no alternative but to seek wage labour' (quote from Butler 2007b, 44; see also Phimister 1988, 16–17; Mlambo 2014, 50). A Masters and Servants legislation introduced in the early twentieth century further reinforced discipline among the labourers (Gann 1965, 144; Loney 1975, 62).

In its role as a frontier exploration company, the BSAC also became deeply involved in a series of railway projects. On the face of it, these projects were important for the long-term success of the mining projects, but when looking into the historical details, a more complex pattern emerges. Firstly, railways were not only constructed for the long-term delivery of goods and men. Railways were also strategic projects which insiders used to signal to the financial market that their mining companies were developing in the right direction. For example, when the inner circle of the BSAC promoted the Ayrshire mine in Rhodesia in the last years of the 1890s, the construction of a cheap railway played an important role in making the prospects of the mine look brighter than they were (Phimister 2015). Secondly, railways were not a waterproof way to enhance corporate profits. Since public and private interests often shared the risks of the projects, some projects put considerable financial stress on the companies. This happened during the first years of the twentieth century when the BSAC was pushed to the brink of bankruptcy due to its guarantees of Rhodesian railway debentures (Slinn 1971, 367). Thirdly, railways were not simple conduits of transportation, rather they were the focal points of different political, economic and financial interests. So when the BSAC engaged in Rhodesian railways, the support from British government was not only about securing corporate profits. It was also part of a struggle for political control in Southern Africa in competition with other colonial powers like Germany, Portugal and Belgium (Katzenellenbogen 1973, 132).

All these policies notwithstanding, the company struggled to make ends meet economically. As Arthur Keppel-Jones put it, the company was, to a large extent, operating the 'government of a shell', with high administrative costs for governing the territory, but comparatively little economic activity that generated revenue (Keppel-Jones 1983, 296, 574; see also Slinn 1971, 367). A consequence of this was that the company did not start to pay out dividends to its shareholders until 1924. No wonder that the return on investment in the company was negative during the first decades: the annual real return on investment from 1893 to 1923 was −6.3 per cent (see Table 10.2).

Mining

The BSAC did not have enough capital of its own to actually develop mining activity, and would therefore grant concessions to other companies to prospect for minerals and develop mines in the territory it controlled (Gann 1958, 118; Galbraith 1974, 255–56; Van Onselen 1976, 14–33). In Southern Rhodesia, there were a number of attempts to develop mining operations, starting soon after the territory had been colonized by the BSAC. Some of the companies involved could, as Ian Phimister has argued, assume 'Potemkin-like form'. These were speculative ventures based on limited information about the ventures' actual operations since there was substantial asymmetrical information in favour of the founders of the company compared to the general investors in London (Phimister 2015). The mining industry was also hurt by the conflicts in the region during the 1890s and was even brought close to ruin as a consequence. Several companies did, however, manage to survive and experienced a period of reconstruction (Van Onselen 1976, 29–33; Phimister 1976c, 466).

Table 10.2 Real return on investment in selected companies in Central/Southern Africa, 1890–1969 (geometric mean per year)

Company	Time period	Real return (%)
British South Africa Company	*1893–1965*	*2.7*
	1893–1923	*−6.3*
	1924–1965	*9.9*
Bwana Mkubwa Copper Mining Company	*1914–1934*	*−3.6*
Cam & Motor Gold Mining	*1911–1959*	*5.1*
	1911–1923	*−8.1*
	1924–1959	*10.3*
Consolidated Diamond Mines of South West Africa	*1922–1947*	*12.4*
Globe and Phoenix Mine	*1900–1969*	*7.0*
	1900–1923	*7.5*
	1924–1969	*6.6*
N'Changa Consolidated Copper Mines	*1938–1969*	*6.9*
Rhodesian Anglo-American	*1929–1969*	*9.8*
Rhodesian Selection Trust	*1929–1969*	*8.6*
Rhokana Corporation	*1926–1969*	*10.2*
Roan Antelope Copper Mines	*1929–1962*	*−2.5*
Shamva Mines	*1910–1931*	*−12.9*
Tanganyika Concessions	*1905–1969*	*−0.5*
	1905–1923	*−13.2*
	1924–1969	*5.3*
Wankie Colliery	*1914–1969*	*0.5*
	1914–1923	*−9.9*
	1924–1969	*2.9*

Source: African Colonial Equities Database (ACED)

The Southern Rhodesian companies continued to face severe competition from the richer mines in South Africa. In order to compete, company managers employed cost-cutting strategies. Reducing labour costs was the most important strategy in terms of maintaining profitability (Van Onselen 1976; Phimister 1976c, 480). Another key was the implementation of the so-called compound system, imported from the South African mining industry (see Chap. 11). Since labour conditions generally were appalling, mining companies often faced high rates of desertion (Perrings 1979, 165–73). The compound system was therefore introduced to create a controlled environment in the mining districts (Van

Onselen 1975; Van Onselen 1976, chap. 5; Mlambo 2014, 71; Butler 2007b, 47–48). Other coercive mechanisms introduced for the same purpose included the Masters and Servants Ordinance of 1901 and pass laws regulating the mobility of the labour force. The pass laws were introduced in 1896 to control movement into towns and broadened in 1902 to include any movement between districts (Van Onselen 1976, 98–99; Raftopoulos 1997; Mlambo 2014, 71; Särkkä 2016, 335–36). Unsurprisingly, the companies also attempted to reduce costs by limiting investments in the housing units in the compounds, as well as by reducing the food rations distributed to the workers—sometimes even below the levels stipulated by legislation (Phimister 1975, 1976b; Van Onselen 1976, 34–45). In consequence, one of the most common diseases among African mineworkers was scurvy, evidence that workers were malnourished (Phimister 1976a, 176).

Three of the largest mining companies operating in Southern Rhodesia are the Cam & Motor Gold Mining Company, the Globe and Phoenix Gold Mining Company and Shamva Mines Ltd. The fate of these companies would differ substantially. Cam & Motor Gold Mining Company, incorporated in 1910, soon faced economic difficulties. The nature of the ore mines led to a much lower recovery rate than initially expected (Bowen 1980, 20–23). The return on investment was therefore negative during this period, as is shown in Table 10.2, but the company survived and continued its operations. Shamva Mines, incorporated in the same year as Cam & Motor, experienced similar problems as to the nature of the ore mines. The company was also rocked by several strikes during the 1920s (Phimister 1988, 160–61). The Shamva mine finally closed in 1930 (Bowen 1980, 76–79). The company was clearly not a good investment since the return on investment over the whole period it was traded on the London Stock Exchange amounted to −12.9 per cent per year on average, not the least due to massive capital losses during the last years of the company's existence. Globe and Phoenix Gold Mining Company, in contrast, turned out to be a successful investment early on, with an average real return on investment during this period of 8.3 per cent per year, as is shown in Table 10.2.

One company came to be of particular importance to the region—the Wankie Colliery. Cheap coal was a necessity for the gold-mining industry and Wankie Colliery developed into a major supplier in the region. Due to the strategic importance played by coal for the industry, the company was under heavy pressure to keep low prices for the coal (see, e.g. Phimister 1994, 92–93). Again, this created a pressure to minimize production costs by keeping wages low. A consequence of this low-wage policy was that the company often suffered from labour shortages (Van Onselen 1974; Phimister 1992, 1994, 11–13, 32–36, 103). Despite attempts to minimize costs, investments in the company were not successful during the company's initial years, as is shown in Table 10.2: the real return on investment in the company was even negative at −9.9 per cent per year during the period up to 1923.

Further north, the Zambezia Exploring Company was formed in the 1890s for the exploration of minerals in Northern Rhodesia, particularly focussing upon the region along the border to Katanga. The company acquired mineral rights to a major area in the region in 1898. In the following year, Tanganyika Concessions was established to develop the concession (*Union Minière Du Haut Katanga 1906–1956* 1956, 44; Coleman 1971, 7; Perrings 1979, 9; Lekime 1992, 26; Särkkä 2016, 318–19). Findings of copper in the Katanga region led to the establishment of the Union Minière du Haut-Katanga (UMHK) in 1906. Tanganyika Concessions became one of the major owners of this company, controlling 40 per cent of the shares. It soon pulled out of further mining activities in Northern Rhodesia in order to concentrate fully upon its holdings in UMHK (Bradley 1952, 62; *Union Minière Du Haut Katanga 1906–1956* 1956, 66–67; Coleman 1971, 12; Perrings 1979, 10; Lekime 1992, 40; Särkkä 2016, 338). After several years of preparations, mining operations in Katanga started in 1913. Despite the rich findings in Katanga and despite the continued widespread use of coerced labour practices in the Katangan mines at the time (Renton, Seddon, and Zeilig 2007, 52), it took until 1919 before the UMHK paid its first dividends (*Union Minière Du Haut Katanga 1906–1956* 1956, 109, 128). Investments in Tanganyika Concessions were, therefore, not a good investment during this period. As shown in Table 10.2, the average annual real return on investment was −13.2, up until 1923.

Meanwhile, the Bwana Mkubwa Copper Mining Company was established in Northern Rhodesia in 1910 and copper mining began for real in the colony at this time (Coleman 1971, 20; Perrings 1979, 27). A comparatively high population density in parts of Northern Rhodesia, along with the monetary taxation introduced which forced people to seek waged employment, created a situation where there initially was a comparatively large supply of labour available, despite the low-paid working opportunities offered by the mines (Gann 1958, 121; Perrings 1979, 14). Though there was increasing competition for labour between the mining companies, not the least between Tanganyika Concessions and the UMHK, on the one hand, and the BSAC, on the other (Perrings 1979, 14–24).

The End of Corporate Rule

The 1920s spelled major changes, both for the colonies of Southern and Northern Rhodesia in general, and for the BSAC in particular. In 1923, it was agreed that the British government would take over the administrative control of Northern Rhodesia. As compensation for its cost of administering the territory over the three decades since colonization, the BSAC received £3.75 million from the British government (Gann 1964, 231–50; Coleman 1971, 29; Slinn 1971, 370–72; Porter 2012, 225). Southern Rhodesia, for its part, was annexed by the United Kingdom in the same year, after an election in the colony showing major support for 'responsible government' (by and for the white settler population) instead of corporate rule (Gann 1965, 180–92; Phimister 1988, 100–1; Mlambo 2014, 105–6). Previous scholars have discussed what interests were driving these changes. The most common interpretation is to analyse it as the result of a conflict between mining and farming interests, where farming interests won (see e.g. Mseba 2016; Madimu, Msindo, and Swart 2018). The investors in the British South Africa nonetheless seem to have been positive to these changes, since the price of the share started to increase dramatically in 1924, almost trebling in a couple of years' time. As a consequence, investors benefitted from the British government taking over political control of Rhodesia.

Another important event in the 1920s was the discovery of the large and rich copper deposits north of the Zambezi River, marking the beginning of a new era for the region (Slinn 1971). It had been known for some time that there were copper deposits in the region but the exact geology of the region was largely unknown (Frederiksen 2013). The question was how rich these deposits were and whether it would be worthwhile to develop them (Bradley 1952, chaps. 1–2). In 1920, the American mining entrepreneur Alfred Chester Beatty's company, Selection Trust Limited, acquired a substantial share of the Bwana Mkubwa Company. The company had experienced economic difficulties for some time and investors experienced negative return (see Table 10.2). The share price dropped by almost two-thirds in 1920. Shortly after, the South African mining tycoon Ernest Oppenheimer (see Chap. 11) also invested in the same company. In 1922, the company was reconstructed and the mining operations at Bwana Mkubwa were relaunched (Bradley 1952, 78–79; Coleman 1971, 32; Berger 1974, 4–5; Butler 2007b, 15).

A new company, operating in neighbouring South West Africa (current-day Namibia), was also introduced on the London Stock Exchange in 1922: the Consolidated Diamond Mines of South West Africa. Production of diamonds had started some years before and the region quickly became the third most important player in the diamond business. In contrast to South Africa, the production was spread among several companies, and during the 1910s, an intense struggle for control commenced. Besides the business aspects of this process, it also entailed political dimensions, as South West Africa was a German colony and the diamond mines were taken over by the Custodian for Enemy Property following the South African occupation in 1915. In this complicated process, Ernest Oppenheimer—and his company, the Anglo-American Corporation—came to play a decisive role. With important connections, in both business and politics, Oppenheimer seized the opportunity to enter into secret negotiations with the German producers, which eventually led to the formation of the Consolidated Diamond Mines of South West Africa (Innes 1983, 98–101; Newbury 1989, 18–19; Davenport 2013, 264–65; Cleveland 2014, 88–89). The diamond market was weak in 1922, but the year after it started to recover and also did so during the remainder of the 1920s. This is also reflected in an extraordinary high return on investment: 15.4 per cent per year on average.

In 1922, finally, BSAC changed its policy for how to make agreements regarding mining concessions. The new policy allowed large corporations—able to actually establish substantial operations—to acquire concessions (Perrings 1979, 48; Butler 2007b, 15). This opened the door for further investments in the region and to what developed into the so-called Copperbelt of Northern Rhodesia. The mines on the Copperbelt had higher ore grade than other copper mines of the same magnitude of the deposits anywhere in the world (Schmitz 1986, fig. 2; Ross 2017, 173). During the 1920s, four new major mines were developed on the Copperbelt, aside from Bwana Mkubwa: Roan Antelope, Mufulira, Nkana and Nchanga (Coleman 1971, chap. 4; Butler 2007b, 15). Roan Antelope was primarily under the control of Beatty's Selection Trust (Bradley 1952, 80–81, 86, 92; Berger 1974, 5; Perrings 1979, 75; Roberts 1982, 349), whereas Nchanga primarily was controlled by Oppenheimer's Anglo-American (Berger 1974, 5; Perrings 1979, 74; Roberts 1982, 349; Parpart 1983, 21). Nkana and Mufulira were the shared interests of both Selection Trust and Anglo-American (Bradley 1952, 92; Berger 1974, 5; Perrings 1979, 75; Roberts 1982, 349; Parpart 1983, 20–21). The BSAC also owned a substantial number of shares in the newly established mining companies. The BSAC was in turn, to a large extent, owned by the Anglo-American Corporation (Berger 1974, 5). In 1928, Beatty's Selection Trust incorporated the Rhodesian Selection Trust, and in the same year, Oppenheimer's Anglo-American established the Rhodesian Anglo-American. Each respective company's assets in Northern Rhodesia were transferred to these new companies (Parpart 1983, 20–21; Innes 1983, 137; Butler 2007b, 16).

Southern Rhodesia, 1924–1969

Further institutional changes followed in the 1930s. In Southern Rhodesia, the Land Apportionment Act of 1930 codified one key aspect of racial discrimination by designating 49 million acres of the country's agricultural land as open for European settlers alone, while the vastly larger African population was designated to 'native reserves', totalling 29 million acres (Pollak 1975, 264–65; Machingaidze 1991, 558; Mlambo

2014, 61–67). Initially, population density in the 'native reserves' were not enormously high, but the population living in the reserves had increased by the 1960s to such a degree that there developed a severe land shortage (Bessant 1992, 64). This was one factor pushing people towards wage labour, driving a process of proletarization of large segments of the African population (Arrighi 1970). This was accompanied by the Industrial Conciliation Act of 1934, effectively introducing a 'colour bar', whereby the African population was prohibited from holding more qualified positions on the labour market in Southern Rhodesia (Phimister 1988, 192; Mlambo 2014, 107), like in South Africa (see Chap. 11).

Attracting labour to the Southern Rhodesian mines remained a serious problem, with the continuing competition from the South African mining industry, as well as the developing mines in Northern Rhodesia. By the 1930s, several Southern Rhodesian mining companies had at least invested some money in housing for labourers, enough to at least be able to compete with the South African mining companies on this account (Phimister 1975, 217). A perceived decline in the profitability of Southern Rhodesian mines during the 1930s led companies to try to cut labour costs, for example, by avoiding regulations stipulating minimum food rations for labourers (Phimister 1976b, 66). The global financial crash of 1929 also had direct repercussions on the Southern Rhodesian mines, with drastic losses for most investments in this particular year. This was to some extent counterbalanced by the same change that supported the South African gold mines during the 1930s: the abandonment of the Gold Standard (see Chap. 11). Overall, Southern Rhodesian investments were not performing very well during the 1930s: the average annual real return on investment in Southern Rhodesian companies during the decade was essentially zero. This was, to a large extent, a consequence of the BSAC still dominating the sample (exhibiting zero per cent real return on average during the 1930s). Some of the other companies operating in Southern Rhodesia were extraordinarily well, most importantly, some of the larger mining companies: the average annual return in Cam & Motor was, for example, 20.6 per cent, and in Globe and Phoenix, the annual return over the decade was a staggering 27.0 per cent per year.

In the years following the Second World War, trade unions started to grow substantially in Southern Rhodesia and a general strike was declared in 1948 (Raftopoulos 1997). The initial years after the war were also negative for several of the investments in the colony, though the outcome of the general strike does seem to have favoured capital owners. The return on investment increased for many companies in the sample following the end of the strike, and it remained high throughout the 1950s. One of the most successful companies during the latter decade was the Cam & Motor Gold Mining Company, with an average return on investment of 0.4 per cent during the 1940s, but 16.9 per cent per year during the 1950s.

The 1960s became a turbulent period for Southern Rhodesia. The colony was, for some years, part of the Central African Federation, together with Northern and North-Eastern Rhodesia, but this federation collapsed in 1963 (Mlambo 2014, 119, 127). The United Kingdom refused to grant political independence to Southern Rhodesia before the inevitability of majority rule at some future point had been recognized. The white minority regime controlling the colony refused to accept this, which eventually led to a unilateral declaration of independence from the United Kingdom in 1965. The United Kingdom responded by freezing further investments in Rhodesia and by imposing economic sanctions on Rhodesia, though these sanctions never became very effective (Mlambo 2014, 150–52; Nyamunda 2017). The final years of the decade also saw the outbreak of an armed struggle by the black population against the oppressive minority regime (Mlambo 2014, 160–61). At least one major company, the Wankie Colliery, managed to flourish economically despite all of these circumstances, exhibiting an average return on investment of 16.7 per cent per year during the 1960s, after several decades of essentially zero return on investment. For other investors, though, the 1960s was negative: the return on investment in the Globe and Phoenix Mine, for example, amounted to −13.6 per cent per year during the decade.

Northern Rhodesia, 1924–1969

The 1930s was a period of major development of mining on the Copperbelt of North Rhodesia with output from the mines growing at a fast pace, even though the Great Depression led to a temporary collapse of the copper industry (Butler 2007b, 18). The year 1930 was also the year that some of the previously established companies in the region merged to form the Rhokana Corporation. By this merger, the copper industry in the region essentially achieved the corporate structure that remained until the 1960s (Alford and Harvey 1980; Butler 2007b, 17). With increased mining activity, not only in Northern Rhodesia but also in neighbouring Katanga, there followed a rising demand for labour (Perrings 1979, 76; Parpart 1983, 32). The result was an increased dependence on migrant labour (Berger 1974, 12–16; Butler 2007b, 44). Many of these were voluntary recruits, but contemporary reports also showed that there were both deceptive practices and direct coercion when recruiting labour for the Northern Rhodesian mines (Henderson 1974, 296; Perrings 1979, 152). An attempt was also made in 1929 to establish a Native Labour Association for the recruitment of labourers to the Copperbelt mines, but the association never achieved a monopsony position similar to what was achieved in South Africa. It was therefore never as successful in pushing down the wage costs as the mine owners had hoped for (Parpart 1983, 33–34).

By the early 1930s, companies responded to decreasing copper prices during the Depression by trying to lower the wages (Parpart 1983, 46–47). This was one crucial factor behind early attempts to unionize the labour force on the Copperbelt (Henderson 1973, 292). Increased desperation and labour militancy in combination were also key factors behind the outbreak of a major strike on the Copperbelt in 1935 (Henderson 1975; Perrings 1977, 1979, 210; Parpart 1983, chap. 3). The strike seems to have had little or no effect on the return on investment, as it remained high in both this and following years. Indeed, 1936 seems to have been a particularly good year for the companies on the Copperbelt with the return on investment exceeding 100 per cent for all of the major companies (and exceeding 200 per cent for Rhodesian Anglo-American in particular). These figures were, perhaps, a consequence of the short-lived international copper cartel, where the Copperbelt companies participated. It was established to increase global copper prices (Roberts 1982, 350; Parpart 1983, 22). At the same time, 1936 was an outstanding exception during what for the investors otherwise was a bleak decade.

The weighted average return on investment for the companies in the colony amounted to −2.0 per cent per year during the 1930s.

A new strike—at Nkana, Rhokana and other mines—followed in 1940, to a large extent driven by rising living costs during the Second World War (Henderson 1975; Perrings 1979, 218–25; Parpart 1983, chap. 4; Butler 2007b, 70). Investments in the Copperbelt companies exhibited major losses this particular year—the return on investment in both Rhodesian Selection Trust and Rhodesian Anglo-American was around −40 per cent. Some of this might be attributable to the strike action by the labourers, but also an effect of the outbreak of the Second World War. Copper was perceived as a strategic input for the war effort, and therefore, it was regulated throughout the war through fixed prices and the British government buying the bulk of the product (Butler 2007b, 60–62). In neighbouring Katanga, recruitment of labour remained a similar problem, and while the Union Minière du Haut-Katanga had abandoned obviously coerced labour, it still resorted to similar practices as in Northern Rhodesia, such as the use of the compound system (Renton, Seddon, and Zeilig 2007, 54–55). For the major UMHK-owner Tanganyika Concessions, return on investment was fluctuating substantially between the years. By this time, new work routines had been introduced and labour productivity had consequently increased (Higginson 1988, 12) so that the rate of return on investment was 5.3 per cent per year, from 1924 onwards.

This period also saw the emergence of a 'colour bar' in Northern Rhodesian mining, just as had previously been introduced in South African and Southern Rhodesia (Berger 1974, chap. 4; Parpart 1983, 24; Cooper 1996, 337–38; Butler 2007b, 71–72). Because of the substantial wage differences between European and African workers (Perrings 1979, chap. 4), mining companies would have wanted to get rid of the 'colour bar' in order to replace highly paid skilled or semi-skilled European workers with low-paid African workers. Though, for a long period of time, companies did not want to challenge the power of the white workers' trade union (Butler 2007b, 137–39). While unionization of both the European and African labour forces had started prior to the Second World War, it took off after 1945 (Berger 1974, 137–58; Parpart 1983, 114, 1987; Butler 2007b, 132–37). This seems to have been most rewarding not the least for African workers, as their real wages were increased substantially from the 1940s onwards (Juif and Frankema 2018). In contrast, the 1940s was not a positive decade for the investors in Copperbelt mines: the average real annual return on investment for the Northern Rhodesian companies amounted to a mere 0.5 per cent.

The economic development of the Copperbelt enhanced the importance of the Lochner Concession—the treaty through which King Lewanika supposedly granted the BSAC the mineral rights in Barotseland. As was noted above, the BSAC had managed to maintain the right to profit from the concession even after the United Kingdom took over the administration of the colony (Slinn 1971; Butler 2007b, 35). This treaty would turn extremely lucrative, as the copper industry expanded in the region. After a couple of mere decades, from the company's point of view, royalties from mining skyrocketed from the 1940s onwards (Slinn 1971, 374; Butler 2007b, 154). As a consequence, the return on investment in the BSAC increased substantially, averaging a real return on investment of 8.0 per cent per year during the 1940s.

After 1945, several companies—spearheaded by the Rhodesian Selection Trust—started to challenge the industrial 'colour bar' in order to be able to cut wage costs by replacing skilled white workers with low-paid black workers (Butler 2007a, 472–75; Phillips 2009, 230–31; Phimister 2011). This was done under the slogan of enabling 'African advancement' in the companies (Cooper 1996, 338; Butler 2007b, 224–32). The trade unions by and for European workers in Northern Rhodesia responded with the slogan of 'equal pay for equal work'. From the union's perspective, this was a way of counteracting the mining companies' wage-dumping attempts (Cooper 1996, 338; Butler 2007b, 139–40). Initially, the African Mine Workers' Union supported the same policy of 'equal pay for equal work', but it soon started to move away from this position. Instead, it favoured a policy of enabling advancement for African workers too (Cooper 1996, 340–42; Butler 2007b, 139–40). This culminated in major strikes in 1955 and 1956, driven primarily by the twin issues of 'African advancement' and the discriminatory low wages paid to the African workers (Berger 1974, 137–58; Parpart 1983, 126–27, 144–45; Cooper 1996, 344–45). While the strikes temporarily affected the companies (and their investors) negatively, the average return on investment of the 1950s in total tells a different story. It amounted to an extraordinarily high annual average return of 15.3 per cent. Meanwhile, the BSAC's Lochner Concession was recurrently challenged by political interests in London, by white settlers and later also by interests representing the black majority in Northern Rhodesia (Slinn 1971, 384). There were, for example, discussions on whether the colonial government of Northern Rhodesia ought to purchase the BSAC's mineral rights (Butler 2007b, 177–87). In 1949, therefore, the BSAC chose to enter into an agreement with the colonial government. It stipulated that 20 per cent of the company's royalties for the mineral rights in Northern Rhodesia were to be handed over to the colonial treasury, in exchange for continued recognition of the concession as a whole (Slinn 1971, 377–78; Berger 1974, 10; Butler 2007b, 187). While the agreement initially was perceived negatively by the financial market, the share price of the BSAC turned up again in 1950, and during the 1950s, the average annual return amounted to an extraordinary 21.9 per cent per year.

The Lochner Concession was again challenged in the 1960s when the legality of the original treaty came under severe criticism (Butler 2007b, 280–87). The BSAC's position was weaker than ever in 1964 when the company received an ultimatum that the alternative to an agreement would be expropriation without compensation. On 24 October 1964, the very day before Zambia achieved political independence, BSAC therefore accepted to hand over its mineral rights in exchange for a limited reimbursement (Slinn 1971, 380–83; Butler 2007b, 291). The result was substantial losses for the investors in the company, with an average return of −6.1 per cent per year until the company was delisted from the London Stock Exchange in 1965.

There were fears among several other copper companies that they too would face nationalizations after decolonization, despite leaders of the nationalist movement declaring that this would not happen (Butler 2007b, 276–79). As a consequence of capital losses due to falling share prices, return on investment in the companies operating in what was henceforth called Zambia temporarily turned negative during the year of independence, but the share price seems to have recovered quickly following political independence. Only at the end of our study, in 1969, did the Zambian government decide to pursue nationalization of the mining industry, by taking over 51 per cent of all shares in the copper mines. The nationalization was negotiated, on what has been described as amicable terms, and investors were reimbursed in the form of bonds issued by the newly formed Zambia Industrial and Mining Corp (ZIMCO) (Stoever 1985, 137–38). The partial nationalization does therefore not seem to have created any immediate losses for the investors. In time, these bonds were traded below their initial value (Coulson 2012, 266), but this capital loss started after the end of the period of this study. Immediately after 1964, therefore, return on investment in Zambia remained extraordinarily high. Despite the formal nationalization, the annual return from 1964 to 1969 for the whole sample of Zambian companies was 34 per cent.

In neighbouring Belgian Congo, political independence was achieved rapidly in 1960, a few years after the birth of a nationalist movement in the colony (Renton, Seddon, and Zeilig 2007, 71–82). The region of Katanga seceded from the newly independent country, initiating a period of instability and unrest. The elected prime minister Lumumba was deposed and assassinated shortly after independence. In 1965, Joseph Mobutu seized power in a military coup. Even though Mobutu was considered an ally of the capitalist countries, the new rule had important implications for investors in the country. It soon moved towards nationalization, including the assets of the mining company UMHK in January of 1967. The nationalization was initially undertaken without any compensation to the previous owners, but within weeks, the US government had put pressure upon the Zaïrian government, forcing it to accept to pay compensation to the previous owners (Gibbs 1997, 175–76).

Return on Investment in Central/Southern Africa in the Long Run, 1869–1969

Figure 10.1 shows the weighted average rate of return on investment by decade for investments in the region.

The rate of return increased substantially over time. The importance of the BSAC has been emphasized in much historiography on Southern

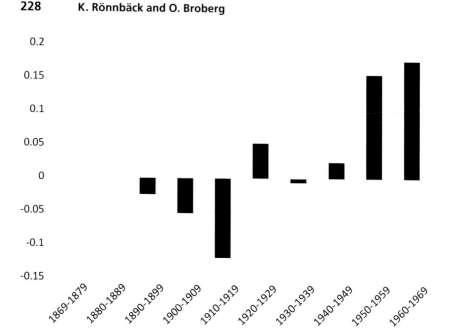

Fig. 10.1 Real return on investment in Central/Southern Africa, by decade, 1869–1969 (geometric mean per year). Source: African Colonial Equities Database (ACED)

Africa. In terms of return on investment, the company was unsuccessful during the chartered period. This was not the least attributable to the fact that one key purpose of the company was to develop the colonies of Northern and Southern Rhodesia, so that other companies—often with the same investors and entrepreneurs—could flourish.

Two factors would change the situation for the BSAC. Firstly, the company was relieved of (and compensated for) the costs for controlling and administering the territories of both Northern and Southern Rhodesia, when the British state took over this responsibility. Secondly, the mining industry grew substantially following the findings of copper in what became known as the Copperbelt. Once these two factors had been realized, the BSAC was able to present substantial return on investment for several decades, until decolonization put a halt to further exploitation of their concessionary rights. The development of the Copperbelt also led to the emergence of several new mining companies from the

1920s onwards, many of which with intimate connections to the South African mining industry. After initial investments and expansion, many of these companies exhibited very high return on investment throughout the remainder of the period studied in this book.

References

Alford, B.W.E., and Charles Harvey. 1980. Copperbelt Merger: The Formation of the Rhokana Corporation, 1930–1932. *Business History Review* 54 (3): 330–358.
Arrighi, Giovanni. 1970. Labour Supplies in Historical Perspective: A Study of the Proletarianization of the African Peasantry in Rhodesia. *The Journal of Development Studies* 6 (3): 197–234.
Berger, Elena L. 1974. *Labour, Race, and Colonial Rule: The Copperbelt from 1924 to Independence*. Oxford: Clarendon Press.
Bessant, Leonard Leslie. 1992. Coercive Development: Land Shortage, Forced Labor, and Colonial Development in the Chiweshe Reserve, Colonial Zimbabwe, 1938–1946. *The International Journal of African Historical Studies* 25 (1): 39–65.
Bowen, D.J. 1980. *Gold Mines of Mashonaland 1890–1980*. Salisbury: Thomson Publications.
Bradley, Kenneth. 1952. *Copper Venture: The Discovery and Development of Roan Antelope and Mufulira*. London: Mufulira Copper Mines Ltd and Roan Antelope Copper Mines Ltd.
Butler, L.J. 2007a. Business and British Decolonisation: Sir Ronald Prain, the Mining Industry and the Central African Federation. *Journal of Imperial and Commonwealth History* 35 (3): 459–484.
———. 2007b. *Copper Empire: Mining and the Colonial State in Northern Rhodesia, c.1930–64*. New York: Palgrave Macmillan.
Cleveland, Todd. 2014. *Stones of Contention: A History of Africa's Diamonds*. Athens, OH: Ohio University Press.
Coleman, Francis L. 1971. *The Northern Rhodesia Copperbelt 1899–1962: Technological Development up to the End of the Central African Federation*. Manchester: Manchester University Press.
Cooper, Frederick. 1996. *Decolonization and African Society: The Labor Question in French and British Africa*. Cambridge: Cambridge University Press.

Coulson, Michael. 2012. *The History of Mining: The Events, Technology and People Involved in the Industry That Forged the Modern World*. Petersfield: Harriman House.

Davenport, Jade. 2013. *Digging Deep: A History of Mining in South Africa, 1852–2002*. Johannesburg: Jonathan Ball Publishers.

Flint, John. 1976. *Cecil Rhodes*. London: Hutchinson.

Frederiksen, Tomas. 2013. Seeing the Copperbelt: Science, Mining and Colonial Power in Northern Rhodesia. *Geoforum* 44: 271–281.

Galbraith, John. 1973. Origins of The British South Africa Company. In *Perspectives of Empire. Essays Presented to Gerald S. Graham*, ed. John E. Flint and Glyndwr Williams, 148–171. London: Longman.

———. 1974. *Crown and Charter: The Early Years of the British South Africa Company*. Berkeley: University of California Press.

Gann, Lewis H. 1958. *The Birth of a Plural Society: The Development of Northern Rhodesia under the British South Africa Company 1894–1914*. Manchester: Manchester University Press.

———. 1964. *A History of Northern Rhodesia: Early Days to 1953*. London: Chatto & Windus.

———. 1965. *A History of Southern Rhodesia: Early Days to 1934*. London: Chatto & Windus.

Gibbs, David. 1997. International Commercial Rivalries & the Zaïrian Copper Nationalisation of 1967. *Review of African Political Economy* 24 (72): 171–184. https://doi.org/10.1080/03056249708704251.

Guene, Enid. 2017. *Copper, Borders and Nation-Building: The Katangese Factor in Zambian Political and Economic History*. Leiden: African Studies Centre.

Henderson, Ian. 1973. Wage-Earners and Political Protest in Colonial Africa: The Case of the Copperbelt. *African Affairs* 72 (288): 288–299.

———. 1974. The Limits of Colonial Power: Race and Labour Problems in Colonial Zambia, 1900–1953. *The Journal of Imperial and Commonwealth History* 2 (3): 294–307.

———. 1975. Early African Leadership: The Copperbelt Disturbances of 1935 and 1940. *Journal of Southern African Studies* 2 (1): 83–97.

Higginson, John. 1988. Disputing the Machines: Scientific Management and the Transformation of the WorkRoutine at the Union Miniere Du Haut-Katanga, 1918–1930. *African Economic History* 17: 1–21.

Innes, Duncan. 1983. *Anglo American and the Rise of Modern South Africa*. London: Heinemann Educational.

Juif, Dácil, and Ewout Frankema. 2018. From Coercion to Compensation: Institutional Responses to Labour Scarcity in the Central African Copperbelt. *Journal of Institutional Economics* 14 (s2): 313–343.

Katzenellenbogen, Simon. 1973. *Railways and the Copper Mines of Katanga*. Oxford: Clarendon press.

Keppel-Jones, Arthur. 1983. *Rhodes and Rhodesia: The White Conquest of Zimbabwe 1884–1902*. Kingston: McGill-Queen's University Press.

Larmer, Miles. 2017. Permanent Precarity: Capital and Labour in the Central African Copperbelt. *Labor History* 58 (2): 170–184.

Laurie, Alexander Charles. 2008. *Every Man Has His Price: The Story of Collusion and Corruption in the Scramble for Rhodesia*. Lanham: University Press of America.

Lekime, Fernand. 1992. *La Mangeuse de Cuivre: La Saga de l'Union Minière Du Haut-Katanga 1906–1966*. Brussels: Didier Hatier.

Loney, Martin. 1975. *Rhodesia: White Racism and Imperial Response*. Harmondsworth: Penguin.

Machingaidze, Victor. 1991. Agrarian Change from Above: The Southern Rhodesia Native Land Husbandry Act and African Response. *The International Journal of African Historical Studies* 24 (3): 557–588.

Madimu, Tapiwa, Enocent Msindo, and Sandra Swart. 2018. Farmer–Miner Contestations and the British South Africa Company in Colonial Zimbabwe, 1895–1923. *Journal of Southern African Studies* 44 (5): 793–814.

Mlambo, A.S. 2014. *A History of Zimbabwe*. New York: Cambridge University Press.

Mseba, Admire. 2016. Law, Expertise, and Settler Conflicts over Land in Early Colonial Zimbabwe, 1890–1923. *Environment and Planning* 48 (4): 665–680.

———. 2018. Late Precolonial Struggles, European Expansion, and the Making of Colonial Authority in Northeastern Zimbabwe, ca. 1840–1903. *International Journal of African Historical Studies* 51 (2): 243–262.

Newbury, Colin. 1989. *The Diamond Ring: Business, Politics and Precious Stones in South Africa, 1867–1947*. Oxford: Clarendon Press.

Nyamunda, Tinashe. 2017. Money, Banking and Rhodesia's Unilateral Declaration of Independence. *The Journal of Imperial and Commonwealth History* 45 (5): 746–776.

Palmer, Robin. 1977. *Land and Racial Domination in Rhodesia*. London: Heinemann.

Parpart, Jane L. 1983. *Labor and Capital on the African Copperbelt*. Philadelphia: Temple University Press.

———. 1987. Class Consciousness among the Zambian Copper Miners, 1950–1968. *Canadian Journal of African Studies/La Revue Canadienne Des Études Africaines* 21 (1): 54–77.

Perrings, Charles. 1977. Consciousness, Conflict and Proletarianization: An Assessment of the 1935 Mineworkers' Strike on the Northern Rhodesian Copperbelt. *Journal of Southern African Studies* 4 (1): 31–51.

———. 1979. *Black Mineworkers in Central Africa: Industrial Strategies and the Evolution of an African Proletariat in the Copperbelt 1911–41*. London: Heinemann.

Phillips, John. 2009. Alfred Chester Beatty: Mining Engineer, Financier, and Entrepreneur, 1898–1950. In *Mining Tycoons in the Age of Empire, 1870–1945: Entrepreneurship, High Finance, Politics and Territorial Expansion*, ed. Raymond Dumett, 215–238. Farnham: Ashgate.

Phimister, Ian. 1974. Rhodes, Rhodesia and the Rand. *Journal of Southern African Studies* 1 (1): 74–90.

———. 1975. African Labour Conditions and Health in the Southern Rhodesian Mining Industry, 1898–1953. Part One: Accommodation. *Central African Journal of Medicine* 21 (10): 214–220.

———. 1976a. African Labour Conditions and Health in the Southern Rhodesian Mining Industry, 1898–1953. Part Three: Health. *Central African Journal of Medicine* 22 (9): 173–179.

———. 1976b. African Labour Conditions and Health in the Southern Rhodesian Mining Industry, 1898–1953. Part Two: Diet. *Central African Journal of Medicine* 22 (4): 63–68.

———. 1976c. The Reconstruction of the Southern Rhodesian Gold Mining Industry, 1903–10. *The Economic History Review* 29 (3): 465–481.

———. 1988. *An Economic and Social History of Zimbabwe, 1890–1948: Capital Accumulation and Class Struggle*. London: Longman.

———. 1992. Coal, Crisis, and Class Struggle: Wankie Colliery, 1918–22. *The Journal of African History* 33 (1): 65–86.

———. 1994. *Wangi Kolia: Coal, Capital and Labour in Colonial Zimbabwe 1894–1954*. Johannesburg: Witwatersrand University Press.

———. 2011. Corporate Profit and Race in Central African Copper Mining, 1946–1958. *Business History Review* 85 (4): 749–774.

———. 2015. Late Nineteenth-Century Globalization: London and Lomagundi Perspectives on Mining Speculation in Southern Africa, 1894–1904. *Journal of Global History* 10 (1): 27–52.

Pilossof, Rory. 2014. Labor Relations in Zimbabwe from 1900 to 2000: Sources, Interpretations, and Understandings. *History in Africa* 41: 337–362.

Pollak, Oliver. 1975. Black Farmers and White Politics in Rhodesia. *African Affairs* 74 (296): 263–277.
Porter, Bernard. 2012. *The Lion's Share – A History of British Imperialism 1850 to the Present*. 5th ed. London: Routledge.
Raftopoulos, Brian. 1997. The Labour Movement in Zimbabwe: 1945–1965. In *Keep on Knocking: A History of the Labour Movement in Zimbabwe 1900–97*, ed. Brian Raftopoulos and Ian Phimister, 55–90. Harare: Baobab Books.
Ranger, T.O. 1967. *Revolt in Southern Rhodesia 1896–7: A Study in African Resistance*. London: Heinemann.
Renton, Dave, David Seddon, and Leo Zeilig. 2007. *The Congo: Plunder and Resistance*. London: Zed.
Roberts, Andrew D. 1982. Notes towards a Financial History of Copper Mining in Northern Rhodesia. *Canadian Journal of African Studies/La Revue Canadienne Des Études Africaines* 16 (2): 347–359.
Robinson, Ronald Edward, and John Gallagher. 1968. *Africa and the Victorians: The Climax of Imperialism*. New York: Anchor Books.
Ross, Corey. 2017. *Ecology and Power in the Age of Empire: Europe and the Transformation of the Tropical World*. Oxford: Oxford University Press.
Rotberg, Robert. 1988. *The Founder: Cecil Rhodes and the Pursuit of Power*. Oxford: Oxford University Press.
Särkkä, Timo. 2016. The Lure of Katanga Copper: Tanganyika Concessions Limited and the Anatomy of Mining and Mine Exploration 1899–1906. *South African Historical Journal* 68 (3): 318–341.
Schmitz, Christopher. 1986. The Rise of Big Business in the World Copper Industry 1870–1930. *The Economic History Review* 39 (3): 392–410.
Schreuder, D.M. 1980. *The Scramble for Southern Africa, 1877–1895: The Politics of Partition Reappraised*. Cambridge: Cambridge University Press.
Selolwane, O. 1980. Colonization by Concession: Capitalist Expansion in the Bechuanaland Protectorate. 1885–1950. *Pula: Botswana Journal of African Studies* 2 (1): 75–124.
Slinn, Peter. 1971. Commercial Concessions and Politics during the Colonial Period: The Role of the British South Africa Company in Northern Rhodesia 1890–1964. *African Affairs* 70 (281): 365–384.
Stoever, William A. 1985. A Business Analysis of the Partial Nationalization of Zambia's Copper Industry, 1969–1981. *Journal of International Business Studies* 16 (1): 137–163.
Union Minière Du Haut Katanga 1906–1956. 1956. Brussels: Éditions L. Cuypers.

Van Onselen, Charles. 1974. The 1912 Wankie Colliery Strike. *The Journal of African History* 15 (2): 275–289.

———. 1975. Black Workers in Central African Industry: A Critical Essay on the Historiography and Sociology of Rhodesia. *Journal of Southern African Studies* 1 (2): 228–246.

———. 1976. *Chibaro: African Mine Labour in Southern Rhodesia 1900–1933*. London: Pluto Press.

11

South Africa

The Dutch Legacy and British Imperial Control Until the 1860s

During the first decades of our study, the area under study in this chapter had not yet been unified into one single polity. The Union of South Africa was only established in 1910, incorporating the Cape Colony, Natal Colony, the Transvaal Colony and the Orange River Colony. The formation of a unified South African colony was thus a protracted process. In this chapter, we occasionally use the term 'South Africa', ahead of the unification, as a shorthand to talk about the whole region that falls within the boundaries of present-day South Africa.

The establishment of a financial link between European capitalism and southern Africa had begun already in the seventeenth century with the arrival of the Dutch East India Company. The company, an important forerunner to the modern corporation, left a limited imprint in terms of capital imports to the local economy. The Dutch initiated some mining ventures but without any lasting success (Webb 1983, 163–65; Thompson 2001, chap. 2; Davenport 2013, 5–11). The most important Dutch legacy was instead the flow of people who migrated to the interior areas surrounding the original colony. They developed into an important force in the formation of the South Africa nation (Visagie 2014).

The United Kingdom took control over the Cape Colony following the Napoleonic Wars. During the nineteenth century, the United Kingdom extended its imperial influence from the Cape Colony into the interior of the southern part of Africa. In the wake of this expansion followed a number of British settlers. Three independent Boer Republics—the Natalia Republic, the Orange Free State and the South African Republic (SAR, also known as the Transvaal Republic)—were also established around the middle of the nineteenth century, but the first of the three was annexed by the British Empire after only a few years (Thompson 2001, 100–109).

Dispossession of land from the local African populations was pursued by both European settler groups—from the British conquest of Griqualand West in 1871 in the wake of diamond findings, to the Boer's recurrent wars with African nations to form their own state (Newbury 1989; Feinstein 2005, 35; Wilson 2011).

In terms of connecting the local economy to an expanding international economy, wool became the first important South African export commodity (Katzenellenbogen 1975, 361; Thompson 2001, 53; L. Greyling and Verhoef 2015, 10). While the export-oriented wool production rested on a combination of domestic and foreign capital, it was the discovery of copper, diamonds and gold in the latter half of the nineteenth century that evoked major interest from international investors (S. Jones 1988, 2–5, 1996, 24:16; Verhoef 2013, 404–5).

The process of capital formation was slow. Failed attempts by British interests to pick up copper mining in the 1840s and 1850s illustrate that both the institutional framework and the infrastructural network were still limiting the transformational forces of capital. The problem became apparent during the expansion of copper mining in Namaqualand—in Northern Cape Colony—in the early 1850s, when the lack of a legislative framework was unable to supply mining entrepreneurs with clear rules for mining rights. What the boom did, however, was to initiate a political process so that an institutional framework had been introduced by the mid-1860s. This process included both formal institutions like the mining regulations of 1853 and 1865 and the political formation of mining interests into informal institutions (Webb 1983, 166–67; Davenport 2013, 17–35).

The New Beginning, 1860–1885

The 1860s marked the beginning of a new phase in the financial link between the United Kingdom and South Africa. One manifestation of this was the large number of companies established to undertake overseas mining ventures during the latter half of the nineteenth century in Britain. Among these were an increasing number of South African mining ventures traded on the London Stock Exchange. The shares of a large number of companies were also traded unofficially outside the formal exchange (Van Helten 1990, 161; Michie 2006, 92). Another manifestation was that a new type of organization saw the light at the London Stock Exchange in the 1860s: the exploration company. This was a joint stock syndicate where participants would pool their resources to prospect land for mining possibilities. Exploration companies became a popular investment vehicles for investors looking for opportunities to take part in the expansion of capitalistic ventures in distant locations of the British Empire (Wilkins 1988; Turrell and Van Helten 1986). The South African Goldfields Exploration Company was founded in 1868 as one of the first of its kind. The company's prospection in Northern Transvaal was futile, but it was soon followed by the more successful London & South African Exploration Company. This company was established in 1870 but only by the mid-1880s were its shares traded in London to such an extent that it appears in the sources underlying our database (Chapman 1988, 33–35; Ferguson 1998, 876–78).

The few mining companies present in our sample during this period were clearly performing well in terms of their return on investment, with a very high average return of 13.8 per cent per year, but the finance sector also showed a high return (9.6 per cent per year). Investments in some other sectors of the economy were, in contrast, not performing as well during this period, so that the return on investment in our whole sample of companies on average was 8.9 per cent per year (see Table 11.1).

Table 11.1 Real return on investment in selected portfolios in South Africa, 1869–1969 (geometric mean per year)

Portfolio	Period of data	Real return (%)
Total sample	*1869–1969*	*6.2*
	1869–1885	8.9
	1886–1899	12.2
	1900–1919	−0.9
	1920–1939	8.8
	1940–1969	5.1
Finance sector	*1869–1969*	*4.7*
	1869–1885	9.6
	1886–1899	7.4
	1900–1919	−0.8
	1920–1939	4.6
	1940–1969	4.6
Mining sector	*1869–1969*	*7.7*
	1869–1885	13.8
	1886–1899	16.0
	1900–1919	−1.0
	1920–1939	9.4
	1940–1969	5.4

Source: African Colonial Equities Database (ACED)

Copper

Namaqualand, a region in current-day Northern Cape Colony, had thus experienced a copper-mining boom in the 1850s, attracting substantial amounts of capital. The bubble did, however, burst and only two of the companies survived. In 1863, Cape Copper Mining Corporation was founded and purchased all copper interests in Namaqualand (Webb 1983, 165; Davenport 2013, 18–28; Nkosi 2011, 23). In the coming decades, Cape Copper grew into an established and successful mining company. This is also reflected in our data: from the start of our period of study in 1869 up until 1885 the average real return on investment was an extraordinary 16.7 per cent per year (see Table 11.2). Hence, Cape Copper was the first larger mining venture in South Africa to attract capital from London (Davenport 2013, 28–34).

Table 11.2 Real return on investment in selected companies in South Africa, 1869–1969 (geometric mean per year)

Company	Period of data	Real return (%)
African Banking Corporation	1898–1920	2.2
Anglo-African Diamond Mining	1881–1890	2.0
Anglo-American Corporation	1920–1969	7.0
	1920–1939	2.1
	1940–1969	10.4
Anglo-American Investment Trust	1943–1969	21.0
Bank of Africa	1879–1912	3.7
Blyvooruitzicht Gold Mining	1940–1969	7.8
Cape Copper	1869–1928	−0.3
	1869–1885	16.7
	1886–1899	19.3
	1900–1919	−4.8
	1920–1928	−37.8
Colonial Bank	1869–1925	6.1
	1869–1885	8.4
	1886–1899	3.2
	1900–1919	5.3
	1920–1925	9.2
Consolidated Goldfields	1893–1969	4.7
	1893–1899	23.5
	1900–1919	−7.4
	1920–1939	7.5
	1940–1969	7.5
De Beers Consolidated	1889–1969	8.9
	1889–1899	11.5
	1900–1919	5.6
	1920–1939	−4.7
	1940–1969	20.5
General Mining and Finance Corporation	1904–1969	1.2
	1904–1919	−16.9
	1920–1939	15.4
	1940–1969	3.0
Johannesburg Consolidated Investment	1895–1969	4.7
	1895–1899	−11.0
	1900–1919	−1.8
	1920–1939	7.6
	1940–1969	9.9
Kimberley North Block Diamond Mining	1881–1888	9.2
London and South African Bank	1869–1877	9.7

(continued)

Table 11.2 (continued)

Company	Period of data	Real return (%)
London & South African Exploration Co. Ltd.	*1886–1899*	*10.4*
Modderfontein Gold Mining	*1895–1927*	*7.5*
	1895–1899	−16.2
	1900–1919	9.0
	1920–1927	21.2
Premier Diamond Mine	*1904–1925*	*30.0*
Rand Mines	*1895–1969*	*2.3*
	1895–1899	−0.3
	1900–1919	−2.7
	1920–1939	10.8
	1940–1969	0.6
Standard Bank of South Africa	*1869–1969*	*6.8*
	1869–1885	16.4
	1886–1899	9.7
	1900–1919	1.7
	1920–1939	5.5
	1940–1969	4.5
Sub Nigel Mine	*1909–1969*	*12.9*
	1909–1919	24.1
	1920–1939	28.5
	1940–1969	1.9

Source: African Colonial Equities Database (ACED)

Diamonds

Diamonds were discovered in the Griqualand already in the late 1860s and the findings soon developed into a diamond rush (Nkosi 2011, 42). During the first phase of the rush, individual diggers staked out small claims that were worked manually with only limited capital needs (W. Worger 1987, chap. 1; Turrell 1987, chap. 1). During the 1870s, production was mechanized and steam engines were introduced for long-distance haulage (Newbury 1989, 31). The capital intensity of production rose sharply, and by 1881, no less than 71 joint stock companies had been established with a total capital of more than £8 million. This capital was primarily raised within South Africa. The capital came partly from the mines themselves, as many of them were profitable enough to provide the means of expansion from retained profits. Cape Colony banks also advanced considerable sums to the mines using share capital as collateral (Turrell 1987, 113; Ferguson 1998, 881; Katzenellenbogen 1975, 362; Nkosi 2011, 47–51). Hence, the financial link to the London City was, during this period, still only indirect, through the financial infrastructure provided by banks operating in the Cape Colony. British investors still remained hesitant about investing directly in South African mining (Chapman 1985b, 648–49). Due to the rules of the London Stock Exchange, the shares of these new mining ventures were initially mostly traded outside the Official List (Turrell 1987, 110). The first two diamond-mining companies to appear in our sample of companies— which happened during the 1880s—were therefore the relatively small companies Anglo-African Diamond Mining Company and Kimberley North Block. During the 1880s, they generated, respectively, 2.0 and 9.2 per cent in average real return (see Table 11.2), which is not outstanding if compared to the whole portfolio of mining companies.

The diamond rush in Kimberley set great social forces in motion, with long-term implications for the South African economy and society. The city of Kimberley developed rapidly in the wake of the rush (Roberts 1985). The influx of people from all over the world and the rapidly growing importance of a few leading diamond companies put great strain on the institutional framework surrounding the mining industry that had emerged in the 1860s. On the one hand, the discovery of diamonds set off a struggle between different interests over the control of land, not the least between the British Cape Colony, the independent Orange Free State and the local African populations. The Kimberley area was occupied by the British in 1871 and incorporated into the Cape Colony as the new province of Griqualand West (W. Worger 1987, 16). The original population in the area were subjected to British control which eventually led to increasing conflicts between the groups (Shillington 1982; Davenport 2013, 48; Cleveland 2014, 63). The eventual outcome was British supremacy, which secured protection of the mine owners' interests. So-called mining boards were set up and granted quasi-governmental authority in the mining area. These boards institutionalized a mixture of managerial, financial, legal and political powers (W. Worger 1987, 41–42; Newbury 1987a, 3–5).

The development of the diamond business in the 1870s led to the development of a white-owned, capitalist mining sector. Labour for this sector was to a large extent supplied by the African populations in the region. Before the onset of the mining activities, the local African population could compete on relatively equal terms with white settlers. With increasing scale of production and sharper racial conflicts among the labour force, the 1870s marked the beginning of institutionalized segregation in South Africa, with the aim of the mine owners to create an abundant, low-paid labour force (Trapido 1971, 311–14; Marks and Rathbone 1982, 6; Turrell 1987, 29–31; W. Worger 1987, 26–30; Terreblanche 2003, chap. 6.5; Nkosi 2017, chap. 3).

Banking

Yet another other important part of the financial link to London was the growth of British multinational banking. Boosted by the new company legislation in the United Kingdom in 1857–1858, nearly 30 new imperial banks were founded within a decade. While some of the new banks were short-lived speculative ventures, others delivered high returns to their investors in the long run (G. Jones 1993, 23–26). Six imperial banks entered South Africa in total, but it was the London and South African Bank (founded 1860), the Standard Bank of South Africa (1862) and the Colonial Bank (founded already in 1836, originally to cater for banking in the West Indies) that came to form the backbone of an emerging South African banking system (G. Jones 1993, 14; S. Jones 1996, vol. 24, chap. 2; Verhoef 2013, 413). These three banks were all also listed at the London Stock Exchange and hence included in our sample. The London and South African Bank was rather short-lived, as it was acquired by the Standard Bank in 1877 (G. Jones 1993, 25).

Our data shows that the banks delivered high returns to their investors during this period, but the Standard Bank of South Africa was outstanding with an average real return of 16.4 per cent for the years 1869–1885 (see Table 11.2). Such a level of return is extraordinary in a comparative perspective. To this must be added the fact that the volatility of the return in the South African banks was low. The relatively low risk and conservative business practices of the imperial banks shaped the South African banking sector for more than a century (S. Jones and Müller 1992, 94–95; Verhoef 2013, 403–5).

Part of a Global Mining Boom, 1886–1899

During the second half of the nineteenth century, interconnected stock exchanges around the world developed into central institutions of an emerging global capitalist economic structure. Old exchanges like London and New York channelled vast sums of capital to various ventures, both domestically and internationally. At the same time, new exchanges opened around the globe to exploit local economic conditions and to spur local industrialization processes, including places like Johannesburg. The number of South African mining companies traded in London rose sharply during three distinct booms in the 1890s and early 1900s. In our sample, the number of companies grew from 5 to 32 in 1889–1990, from 33 to 75 in 1894–1995 and from 88 to 143 in 1903–1904. The vast majority of these new companies were gold-mining companies. The three booms followed a well-known pattern in financial history—including company mongering, unscrupulous promoters and naïve investors (Phimister and Mouat 2003; Davenport-Hines and Van Helten 1986).

Our estimates of the annual return for the total South African portfolio for the period 1886–1899 was 12.2 per cent (see Table 11.1). While the financial sector continued to deliver a stable return (7.4 per cent per year), the mining sector exhibited an average extraordinary return of 16.0 per cent per year during this period. The Cape Copper Company (19.3 per cent per year) was clearly driving up the return in mining and the return of the whole portfolio. However, the relative importance of Cape Copper was in decline. In 1886, the market value of Cape Copper was 9.8 per cent of the total value of the South African mining companies in our sample. By 1899, this had fallen to 1.0 per cent. Instead, the entry of diamond and gold companies became increasingly important. By the mid-1890s, the sample was dominated by gold companies.

Exploration companies also continued to be of importance for the development of the mining industry. Between 1886 and 1899, the London & South African Exploration Company delivered an average return of 10.4 per cent per year to its investors (see Table 11.2). Its stable dividends derived from the large parcels of lands it had acquired in the diamond area around Kimberley. In 1899, the company was sold at a high price to De Beers Consolidated (see below). During the 1890s, the London Exploration Company (controlled by the Rothschilds) took over as the leading exploration company. This company focussed more on the promotion of gold companies on the official list of the London Stock Exchange (Chapman 1988, 33–35; Ferguson 1998, 876–78). By the turn of the century, investment trusts and investment groups replaced earlier ways of channelling capital to the mining industry. The reason, Chapman (1988) argues, was that they were able to combine the attractions of investment in lucrative new frontiers through foreign/colonial expertise with an aura of safety manifested by a familiar name and a London office.

Diamonds

During the 1880s, the diamond business went through an amalgamation process. In 1888, Kimberley's leading diamond producers—spearheaded by Cecil Rhodes—formed and floated the company De Beers Consolidated. The merger marked the end of almost two decades of company formations, mergers and acquisitions. De Beers managed to outmanoeuvre its main competitors through successfully combining skills in production, management and financial intelligence (W. Worger 1987, chaps. 5–6; Turrell 1987, chap. 10; Newbury 1989, 86–99). Our estimates show that the annual return on investment was 11.5 per cent during the company's first decade of existence (see Table 11.1). De Beers was thereby one of the best performing investment objects among the large companies in our sample. An important explanation for its success was that De Beers achieved an effective monopoly on the output of non-alluvial diamonds (W. Worger 1987, 191–236). An important strategic shift among the diamond magnates was that the earlier tradition to retain control by limiting outside capital was gradually abandoned in the 1880s and 1890s. De Beers expanded its contacts with merchant and financial interests in London and Paris, paving the way for the vertical integration of the diamond business (Newbury 1989, 86–99). Hence, when the company was listed, it was from a strong position. The trade in De Beers Consolidated started in London in December 1888, and by the end of 1889, the share price had risen from £14 to £23. Together with a £1 dividend (and negligible inflation), this amounted to a real return for the first year of 67 per cent.

During the 1890s, the size and performance of De Beers made it the most important share for investors in London who sought to exploit the potential of the South Africa mining boom. This was strengthened even further by the creation of the London Diamond Syndicate. When De Beers was floated at the London Stock Exchange, diamond dealers held 60 per cent of the capital. Because of divergent views on the pricing and marketing strategies, tensions built up within De Beers. Tensions were intensified as the price of diamonds fell over 50 per cent during the last decades of the nineteenth century (Newbury 1987a, 10).

The formation of the London Diamond Syndicate during the 1890s partially solved this tension by limiting production, creating a single-channel selling organization and dividing profits in an acceptable way to the involved producers and merchants. As the London Diamond Syndicate thereby came to be the sole dominant seller in diamonds, and largely was controlled by De Beers Consolidated, the latter company was more or less in control of both global production and distribution of diamonds by the turn of the century (Newbury 1987b, 1989, chap. 4). This enabled monopolistic price-setting and monopoly rents on the market for diamonds.

The possibility to realize monopoly rents is far from the whole explanation of the performance of De Beers in the 1880s and 1890s. The organization of production and the development of labour relations were also crucial for maintaining a profitable business, and thereby generating high returns to its investors. In 1883, the board concluded that the working expense per carat yield was higher than for most competitors, and therefore, initiated a process to reduce labour-related costs. The primary aims were to take control of recruiting, to reduce wages and to minimize diamond thefts. Between 1884 and 1886, closed compounds were built where all black workers were accommodated. This 'compound system' implied not only a change in lodging but included a new type of labour contract where black labour had to sign agreements where they agreed to be locked up and subjected to supervision. At the end of each contract period, there was also a scheduled stay at a detention centre where labours had to spend three to four days to be purged of any swallowed diamonds. Together with other changes in labour management, this institution allowed the management to cut labour-related costs (as share of total production costs) from 36 to 26 per cent. The new compound system spread, first among the other diamond producers in Kimberley, but later also to the gold mines in Witwatersrand (Turrell 1982; Levy 1982, 41; Lipton 1985, 125–26; Turrell 1987, 146–58; W. Worger 1987, 144; Newbury 1987a, 17–18), and later still to neighbouring colonies (see Chap. 10).

In parallel to the development of the compound system, there were also other important changes taking place during the 1880s. These changes not only transformed the production of diamonds, but also played a part in a larger transformation of social relations (Webb 1983, 171–72). Two aspects of this interdependent process will be highlighted here. First, the opening of the railway line between Cape Town and Kimberley in 1885. The railway, heavily lobbied for by the diamond interests through their political connections, shifted local economic conditions in favour of the mine owners. Cheap food (American grain) and energy (Cape coal) undermined local markets and thereby the economic opportunities for independent farmers. Farmers found the situation untenable, and they were forced to seek employment elsewhere. The mine owners could take advantage of this situation by reducing wages to recruited black labourers, often striking recruitment deals with local chiefs (W. Worger 1987, 106). Second, a series of initiatives against theft and illegal diamond trade were taken by politicians, courts and companies during the 1870s and 1880s. Workers recurrently protested against the more and more detailed inspections they were forced to endure. In 1884, a new instruction separated the workforce and the more intimidating inspections were henceforth not enforced on the white labour force (Simons and Simons 1969, 41). The intensified control over the entire production process, including the measures of control towards the black labour force, resulted in a long period of relative social stability in the diamond industry. Hence, the mid-1880s became something of a watershed in the relationship between the diamond companies of Kimberley and their black labourers (W. Worger 1987, 108–9; Newbury 1989, 68–76; Cleveland 2014, 56–58).

When De Beers was floated at the London Stock Exchange in 1889, its market value was 27 per cent of our total African portfolio. In terms of depth and breadth, the market matured around the turn of the century, as the number of flotations increased markedly. A direct effect of this was that the De Beers' share of the total market value decreased in relative terms to below ten per cent in 1899 (and to below five per cent in 1909)—despite the fact that the company's own market value increased substantially over the same period. Instead, the primary interest of international investors turned to gold.

Gold

Following the diamond rush in the late 1860s, there was a sharp increase in the efforts to find new mineral deposits in South Africa. When South African gold companies were floated in large numbers in the 1890s, investors at the London Stock Exchange were ready in terms of capital, risk appetite, financial organization and connections to mining expertise (Richardson and Van Helten 1984, 319; Turrell and Van Helten 1986, 181; Harvey and Press 1990, 98). Gold had been found in several places during the 1870s and 1880s, but none that proved viable for large-scale mining. Findings in eastern Transvaal in 1884–1885 showed some initial good prospects. Thousands of claims were pegged and a local Stock Exchange opened in Barberton for hastily floated companies. This boom was over in a year with most of the invested money lost. The interest of speculators quickly moved on when news of gold discoveries at the Witwatersrand—300 kilometres west of Barberton—spread like wildfire throughout Africa and the world. Within a year, more than 60 gold-mining companies had been formed and diggers were pouring in to the territory, which would turn into the city of Johannesburg in just a few years. The Standard Bank set up an office already in 1886, and in 1887, the Johannesburg Stock Exchange opened (Webb 1983, 173–74; Davenport 2013, 102–5; Lukasiewicz 2017, 719). In contrast to previous mining booms, the geology of the Witwatersrand could be mapped with greater accuracy, which made it potentially less risky (Richardson and Van Helten 1984). The following rapid development is reflected in our sample of companies: in the 1880s, only one single gold-mining company appears in our sample of South African companies. In 1890, this suddenly increased to 23 South African gold-mining companies traded on the London Stock Exchange, jumping to 65 by 1895 and peaking at 134 companies in 1905.

In contrast to earlier gold booms (where busts soon followed suit), a staggering increase in the actual gold production sets in. In 1885, the value of the annual South African gold production was £10,000. Thanks to the production at the Witwatersrand, this had risen to £6,000,000 in 1898, and by 1911, it reached £70,000,000. By the outbreak of the First World War, Witwatersrand was the largest gold-producing site in the world (S. Jones 1988, 8–9). Technological improvements, most importantly the MacArthur-Forrest method of cyanide leaching, increased the extraction of minerals from the ore and thereby enabled the mining of ever-lower ore grades (see Chap. 14). Hence, on the aggregated level, the Witwatersrand was a success beyond all expectations.

This dramatic increase in production points to the role capital played in the establishment of the gold mines around Johannesburg. In contrast to Kimberley, access to substantial amount of capital was necessary from the start, to be able to establish payable mines. Potential investors were sceptical about the euphoric reports of large gold discoveries and took a conservative stance against gold-mining shares due to the high risks involved (Chapman 1985a, 230, 1985b, 648–60). Several major diamond players nonetheless quickly established their presence in Johannesburg. Their involvement in the goldfields had several effects. Retained diamond profits, connections to commercial banks and other important networks gave the diamond magnates a competitive advantage when the struggle for control began (Richardson and Van Helten 1984, 332; Feinstein 2005, 100; Wheatcroft 1985, 84–86). These men were soon to be known as the Randlords—the nickname given to them by the

London press in the 1890s (Wheatcroft 41–42). Though they were competitors, they were also cooperating to a large extent. This cooperation took the form of joint ventures, but the collusive strategies also involved political lobbying through the Chamber of Mines (see Chap. 12).

Our estimates show that the wealth created by the gold mines was unevenly distributed (see Table 11.2). While, for example, the annual average return on investment was 23.5 per cent for Consolidated Goldfields during its first seven years, Modderfontein Gold Mining Company exhibited negative returns during the 1890s. Taken together, risks were high even though the underlying gold reef was promising. With an estimated average return of 3.8 per cent per year during this period, most of the flotations of gold companies in London were in fact not very successful (see further discussion on this in Chap. 12). It is a paradox that during the years when the world's largest gold deposit was found and mines were successfully established, the average return to investors was still below our total South African portfolio.

Banking

During the last 15 years of the nineteenth century, there was an increased competition among the banks in South Africa. The competition came neither from the first generation of local banks nor from the Colonial Bank. Though the Colonial Bank yielded 3.2 per cent to its investors during this period, it never established a strong foothold in South Africa. Instead the competition came from the entry of two additional imperial banks—the Bank of Africa and the African Banking Corporation—and from two banks more closely related to the South African Republic—the Netherlands Bank and the National Bank (S. Jones 1988, 11; G. Jones 1993, 76; Verhoef 2013, 414–16). The National Bank managed to get an important foothold in Johannesburg via its collaboration with the Corner House Group (Alan Patrick Cartwright 1965, 113).

Despite this competition, the Standard Bank now definitely established itself as the leading bank in South Africa. The bank also continued to be a successful investment during the period: between 1886 and 1899, the annual return on investment in Standard Bank was 9.7 per cent

(Table 11.2). The growth of the diamond- and gold-mining businesses was one reason for this. The Standard Bank was the first bank to establish a branch in Johannesburg, already in 1886. The main business in Johannesburg was the rapidly growing remittance business (Verhoef 2013, 415). Banking related to mining was almost as volatile as mining itself, and the business related to trade and agriculture continued to be the base for the Standard Bank—its operation in the Cape Colony continued to make up two-thirds of the profits throughout the 1890s. The Standard Bank also acted as the paymaster to the army, which was lucrative for the bank (S. Jones 1996, vol. 24, chap. 11).

A World at War: Human and Capital Destruction, 1900–1919

During the first decade of the new century, British overseas investment in global mining ventures continued to grow (Phimister and Mouat 2003, 1; Harvey and Press 1990, 100). As previously noted, the risks involved were high due to the inherent risks of exploration and the uncertainty involved when new mines were established. The general risk level also increased because of rising global political instability during the 1910s (Harvey and Press 1990, 99). We know from earlier research that the First World War resulted not only in widespread human tragedies but that it also shook the foundations of the international financial system when the Gold Standard crumbled and globally falling share prices resulted in capital destruction of an unprecedented magnitude (Michie 2006, 155–64; Reinhart and Rogoff 2009, fig. 16.2; Piketty 2014, 117).

From a South African perspective, the risks associated with political instability started even earlier. With the outbreak of the South African War in October 1899, South Africa quickly fell from first to seventh place among the world's gold producers (Dumett 2009, 12). This substantial decrease in gold supply was not only an issue of production, but it also pointed to the heart of British imperial ambitions. London's position as global leader in gold bullion trade, and as the anchor of the Gold Standard system, had been built up over a long time and it rested on a combination of financial and political institutions. Gold possessed a special lure to investors of all kinds, and at the same time, private investors enjoyed the benefits of an imperial power backing up their positions both politically and financially (Ally 1994; Ferguson 1998, 881–94; Cain and Hopkins 2001). The political turmoil in South Africa after the Jameson Raid in 1895–1896 threatened to spoil this balance of interests and the Witwatersrand was at the centre of the conflict. This is an issue we will return to in greater depth in Chap. 13, but the short-term consequences of the South African War for investors at the London Stock Exchange were actually positive as the return on the portfolio investments remained high throughout the war, despite the decrease in output.

In the following years, the South African mines performed much worse. The first two decades of the twentieth century were therefore a period of turmoil and instability for the South African-oriented investors at the London Stock Exchange. The overall picture is that of a falling market, which is in line with the global development at this time. In a global perspective, the negative return of −0.9 per cent per year (see Table 11.1) over the whole period from 1900 to 1919 was actually fairly decent, as the return on investment was negative around the world during this period (Dimson, Marsh, and Staunton 2002, 311–15; Grossman 2015, 484). The results also exhibit large variations among companies (see Table 11.2). While the Colonial Bank (5.3 per cent per year) and the Standard Bank (1.7 per cent per year) showed positive returns, some of the largest copper and gold companies exhibited negative returns. In the case of Cape Copper (−4.8 per cent per year) this was the beginning of the end, and the company was eventually delisted in 1928. The positive outlier was clearly the Premier Diamond Mine (30 per cent per year), for reasons which will be discussed below.

The establishment of the Union of South African in 1910 not only manifested independence from the United Kingdom, it was also the time when the issue of labour supply to the mines was institutionalized and exerted more directs effects of racial segregation on the South African society at large (Innes 1983, 57–71; Feinstein 2005, 74–80). On the one hand, the so-called 'colour bar' was first instituted in 1893 and successively extended in the coming decades, with the aim of excluding black workers from skilled and semi-skilled work. As the number of white mine workers in South Africa was relatively limited, this introduced an artificial scarcity among—and correspondingly high wages for—the skilled white workers. For the mining companies, this policy thereby increased the labour costs for skilled white workers (Lipton 1985, 112–16).

On the other hand, South African mining was still labour intensive, and the vast majority of that labour required limited skills. A key challenge for the mining companies was therefore to find ways of recruiting large enough numbers of unskilled labourers at a low cost. The need to secure labour for a growing mining sector had been an issue already in the 1870s, but it was the dramatic growth of the gold mines in the 1890s that put the issue centre stage. In numbers, this meant that the roughly 10,000 Africans working in the diamond fields in 1870s had grown to about 260,000 Africans working in different mining operations in 1911 (Feinstein 2005, 66).

One possible solution to meet the mines' increasing demand for labour would have been to offer higher wages to entice more black South African to accept to work in the mines. For several reasons, this was not the path chosen in South Africa. First of all, the international Gold Standard still put a ceiling on the gold price, which indirectly put a pressure on the gold companies to keep wages down (Bell 2001). Second, productivity growth could still have enabled room for wage increases, but development instead continued in the direction of a segregated labour market along racial lines. As Jeremy Seekings and Nicoli Nattrass put it, unskilled, black labour was 'the only cost component that could be controlled' (Nattrass and Seekings 2011, 522). Consequently, a number of institutions developed to secure a labour supply based on the logic of keeping black workers' wages down. One key institution was the Witwatersrand Native Labour Association, established in 1896 (and later transformed to the National Recruiting Corporation). The association acquired a monopsony position on the labour market for unskilled black workers, at times effectively managing to keep the mines from over-bidding each other in their hunt for black workers (Simons and Simons 1969; Wilson 1972, chap. 1; Legassick 1974; Johnstone 1976, chap. 1; Lacey 1981, chap. 5; Levy 1982, 50, 58, 72; Richardson and Van Helten 1982, 89–90; Lipton 1985, 120–22; Feinstein 2005, 74–77).

Apart from the monopsony recruitment strategy, the labour issue was also closely intertwined with other more indirect methods of exerting pressure on the black part of the population to work for the mines (for an overview over key policies, see Seekings and Nattrass 2005, table 1.2). One such method was taxation, which generated government revenues and at the same time pressed Africans to seek employment for white employers, most importantly in the mines (Feinstein 2005, 55–56). Another method was the enforcement of pass laws—the Native Labour Regulation Act was enacted shortly after independence in 1911. Different forms of pass laws had been deployed in the British Empire for a long time as a way of controlling the labour force, but in the South African case, the pass laws developed into one of the cornerstones of racial segregation (Levy 1982, 74–80; Chanock 2004; Feinstein 2005, 57–59; Clark and Worger 2016, 20–23). A third method was to limit the black population's access to land. 'Native reserves' were established which intentionally were too small to sustain all of their inhabitants. Large shares of the inhabitants of these reserves therefore found it necessary to seek work outside of the reserves in order to meet their subsistence needs as well as other consumer demands. The process reached its climax when the Native Lands Act was passed in 1913. The law made it illegal for the black population to own or rent land outside of specially designated areas, which reinforced pressures on the black populations to seek work outside of the reserves (Lipton 1985, 119–20; Thompson 2001, 163–64; Feinstein 2005, 42–44; Wilson 2011). The new law created major disruptions for farming activities among black peasants. It thereby also had the consequence of reducing the competition that white farmers faced when trying to sell their output as well as made it easier for white farmers to recruit farm workers among the former black peasants. This laid the foundation for the so-called maize and gold-alliance between white farmers and gold-mining companies (J. C. Greyling, Vink, and van der Merwe 2018).

Gold

Despite increasingly coercive institutions on the labour market driving down labour costs, the gold-mining companies were not performing very well (from the perspective of a London investor) during this period. Our estimates show that the South African gold companies exhibited an average negative return (−2.8 per cent per year) during the first two decades of the twentieth century. This can, to a large extent, be attributed to the international political-economic environment that the companies were operating in.

Major destruction during First World War was detrimental to investments all over the world. In addition, South African gold mining was an integral part of British foreign policy during this time, as South African gold played a pivotal role for the international Gold Standard (Ally 1994, 224–25). Shortly after the outbreak of the First World War, the Bank of England managed to negotiate a deal to secure the continued supply of gold and to ensure that no gold fell into enemy hands. The August Agreement in 1914 between the Bank of England and the South African gold producers stated that the entire gold production should be delivered to the African Banking Corporation, The National Bank of South Africa or the Standard Bank of South Africa. The gold was passed on to the Bank of England at a fixed price. Though at the time portrayed by the British as a voluntary agreement designed to help South Africa, the deal was, in fact, enforced by British interests by the use of informal pressure (Ally 1994, 221). The fixed price did not take war-time inflation into account with the effect that the investors in virtually all of the gold-mining companies faced major losses during the war. After the war, the gold producers of the Witwatersrand reached an agreement with the Bank of England which temporarily allowed them to sell their gold in London at market price. In combination with a suspended gold convertibility for the Pound, these measures gave a dramatic boost to the gold producers in the year 1919 (Feinstein 2005, 79). This so-called gold premium translated into temporarily rising share prices. The return to investors during 1919 soared for some companies, such as Rand Mines (+33 per cent), Modderfontein (+35 per cent) and Crown Mines (+63 per cent). The return in others were more moderate—the General Mining and Finance Corporation exhibited 6.6 per cent and Consolidated Goldfields 2.4 per cent (data was lacking for Johannesburg Consolidated Investment Company (JCI) for 1919). Increasing share prices and dividends once again made South African gold companies attractive to investors, and in January 1920, Rand Mines Corporation was introduced at the New York Stock Exchange—as the first South African gold-mining company (Alan Patrick Cartwright 1968, 103).

Besides the general market forces exerting pressure on the gold companies, the period 1900–1919 exhibits a combination of declining ore grades, new technology for deep-level mining and organizational innovations that induced a process of creative destruction. Taken together, these processes fundamentally changed the mining business in terms of organization and capital needs. Technological changes involved all levels of the excavation and production process—from diamond studded drills and new pumping devices to the cyanide process for gold and silver recovery. The organizational innovations included financial aspects, like the proliferation of 'mining houses' and specialized investment groups, but also the emergence of vertically integrated mining conglomerates that had the capacity to adapt to the new technical and financial requirements (Webb 1983, 185–86; Harvey and Press 1990, 105; Dumett 2009, 5–9). As some of the most easily mined findings close to the surface were the first to be exhausted, furthermore, new deposits of gold were to be found at increasingly deeper levels below ground. The effects of deep-level mining and the struggles to secure rights on new mining ground have been much debated, and the complexities of this process have spurred diverging historical interpretations (see Chap. 12) (Blainey 1968; Kubicek 1979; Innes 1983). What is beyond doubt is that deep-level mining required substantially larger capital investments than mining on the Witwatersrand previously had done.

Overall, our estimates show that the result for the investors of these transformations during the first two decades of the twentieth century varied greatly, as can be seen in Table 11.2. While Modderfontein was the best performing company among the larger mines during this period, with an average return on investment at 9 per cent per year, the return on investment in most of the gold-mining companies was negative: Consolidated Goldfields −7.4 per cent, Rand Mines −2.7 per cent and Johannesburg Consolidated Investment −1.8 per cent per year.

Diamonds

The market conditions for diamonds were a mirror image of the gold market—the price was potentially volatile as it was negotiated by market supply and demand, and the market demand was furthermore limited. So while production and labour costs were central to both diamond- and gold-mining companies, pricing and marketing strategies were crucial to diamond companies. As was noted earlier, the creation of the London Diamond Syndicate had enabled De Beers in particular to reap monopoly profits on the diamond market. This enabled the company to deliver an average real return of 5.6 per cent per year to its investors during the two first decades of the twentieth century (see Table 11.2), substantially better than most companies listed at the London Stock Exchange during this turbulent period.

The whole idea of the London Diamond Syndicate was to tackle the secular trend of falling prices. During the early years of the twentieth century, the syndicate seemed successful, as the diamond price showed signs of recovery. However, the price was volatile and sensitive to changes in output. Therefore, a central concern for De Beers was to limit the global supply of diamonds (Newbury 1987b). The biggest risk was, of course, that large deposits of diamonds would be discovered on sites outside the company's control. This is exactly what happened at the turn of the century (Cleveland 2014, 87). In 1902, the newly founded Premier Transvaal Diamond Mining Corporation started its mining operations 40 kilometres northeast of Pretoria. The site turned out to be the largest diamond deposit ever found in South Africa. When the company was introduced at the London Stock Exchange two years later, it had already developed into a serious rival to De Beers. Premier flooded the market with gems and set up an independent selling organization in London. The financial crises in 1907–1908 hit all actors on the diamond business hard, and late in 1907, the London Diamond Syndicate managed to negotiate a temporary deal with both De Beers and Premier. The agreement fell apart in the following year and Premier continued to challenge De Beers' hegemonic position (Newbury 1989, chap. 6). The richness of Premier's deposits and its low production costs nonetheless made it an extraordinary investment. During the 15 years up until 1919, the average real return was a staggering 31.6 per cent per year (see Table 11.2). In 1917, the power balance between the two contenders changed dramatically when the largest shareholders of Premier—the Barnato brothers—sold their controlling interest in Premier to De Beers (Davenport 2013, 254–58).

Yet another challenge to De Beers appeared in 1908, when a new diamondiferous area was found in South West Africa (Namibia) (see Chap. 10). An intense struggle for control commenced, where the diamond dealer Ernest Oppenheimer came to play a decisive role. With financial backing from the American investment banking firm JP Morgan, Oppenheimer managed to secure control of the diamond-mining operations in South West Africa. With the establishment of the Anglo-American Corporation in 1917, diamond and gold mining became the cornerstones of a new conglomerate, which would have profound effects on the South African economy, in general, and on the mining industry, in particular, for the rest of our period of investigation (Newbury 1987a, 18–19; Cleveland 2014, 88–89; Innes 1983, 90; Davenport 2013, 264–65).

Banking

In 1900, the Standard Bank was at the height of its power. Its most serious competitor, the National Bank, was on the brink of collapse and the South African War seemed to pave the way for an even stronger position for the Standard Bank. The bank was engaged in all kinds of economic sectors; it was the largest note issuer in South Africa and acted as the government's primary bank (in the absence of a proper central bank) (S. Jones 1996, vol. 24, chap. 12). Furthermore, its financial position was strong, and it had delivered good returns to its investors for four decades. Nonetheless, during the first two decades of the twentieth century, the Standard Bank actually experienced a relative weakening of its market position as the competition on the banking market increased when the National Bank revived and embarked on an expansionary strategy. During the 1910s, the National Bank acquired the Bank of the Orange Free State, the Bank of Africa and the Natal Bank. After Standard Bank's acquisition of the African Banking Corporation in 1920, the two banks dominated the South African banking sector completely (S. Jones and Müller 1992, 95–98; Verhoef 2013, 415). From an investor's point of view, the first two decades of the twentieth century were a disappointment. The Standard Bank yielded an annual average of 1.7 per cent during this period (see Table 11.2). Given the political and financial instability of the times and compared to the performance of the overall South African portfolio during this period (−0.9 per cent per year), the performance of the bank was not that bad.

The Interwar Period, 1920–1939

The First World War set off a series of events with implications for global securities markets in general, and for our South African portfolio in particular. A crumbling Gold Standard hampered international exchange and distrust spread among international financial markets. The global tendency during the interwar years was to handle an increasing instability and uncertainty with a more national focus and increasing government intervention. In London, for example, domestic war bonds alongside British industrial and financial blue chips filled up the vacuum of a weakened market for foreign securities (Michie 2006, 164–65).

In South Africa, the interwar years also meant an increased national focus and rising social tensions. The discriminatory practices against the black population described earlier were gradually intensified during this period (Nattrass and Seekings 2011, 535). Real wages for black South African workers seemed to have stagnated or even decreased in real terms (Lipton 1985, table 11; Nattrass and Seekings 2011, 533–35). When mine employers started to experience labour shortages, as too few from the black populations in South Africa were willing to seek employment in the mines at these low wages, recruitment of migrant workers from other countries was expanded in order to reduce the shortages (Crush, Jeeves, and Yudelman 1991; Harries 1994). Partly as a consequence of these developments, poverty levels among the black populations in South Africa seem to have increased; an indication of this can be an absolute decrease in bodily stature found among several black populations during this period (Mpeta, Fourie, and Inwood 2018, fig. 3).

At the same time, it was also a period of rapid industrialization and new openings not the least for the gold business (Alan Patrick Cartwright 1968, chap. 9; Innes 1983, chap. 5; Feinstein 2005, chap. 6). A direct effect of the war was also the costs incurred on German investors, which was a result of the appropriation of shares via the custodian of enemy property. The effect was a substantive transfer of wealth to the remaining shareholders of these companies (Alan Patrick Cartwright 1968, 123–24).

Our estimates show that the annual return on investment of the South African portfolio between 1920 and 1939 was 8.8 per cent per year, which was substantially higher than during the previous period. The main explanation for this was the mining sector, which yielded on average 9.4 per cent per year. Investments in financial and real estate companies yielded 4.6 per cent per year (see Table 11.1).

Gold

To understand the high return on mining during this period, one has to turn to gold. The interwar period was the time when the gold companies as a group matured enough to generate high returns to their investors in London. The aforementioned gold premium of 19191920 was a quick fix, but its effects faded quickly when the pound regained most of its value against the dollar in 1921–1922. The gold producers once again struggled with rising production costs. Wages and the 'colour bar' took centre stage in the political debate, as Duncan Innes has argued:

> *the mine-owners found themselves under attack from two quarters: by the increasing militancy and organization of black workers and by the spiraling cost structure in which white wage increases were the major factor. The long-term solution which they were to seek to impose on the industry was to shake the very fabric of white racial domination in South Africa society before its success was assured.* (Innes 1983, 78)

These tensions would lead to the so-called Rand Revolt. The revolt erupted in December 1921 when mine owners attempted to replace skilled white workers with black workers on a large scale. This breach of the 'colour bar' lowered the total wage bill of the gold companies to 20 per cent by replacing close to 5000 white workers with lower-paid black workers. The subsequent strike by white workers led to violent confrontations, but the government assisted the mining companies with a massive military force to put the revolt down. By March 1922, the Rand Revolt was over, around 250 lives had been lost, and the mine owners had won an important victory in restructuring the labour supply of the mines in their interest (Johnstone 1976, 125–36; Webb 1983, 189; Innes 1983, 80–83). The chairman of the Anglo-American Corporation, Ernest Oppenheimer, stressed in a speech to the shareholders in 1925 that the labour reorganization leading to the Rand Revolt was fundamental for the turnaround of the gold business' profitability (Gregory 1962, 499). Oppenheimer's word seems to be supported by the profitability and rising share prices of the leading gold companies. After low or negative returns in 1920 and 1921, the return on investment in the major gold companies in our South African portfolio skyrocketed in 1922, including for Consolidated Goldfields (+28 per cent), Modderfontein (+46 per cent), Rand Mines (+74 per cent) and Crown Mines (+94 per cent).

The gold business continued to be volatile during the interwar years, but overall, our estimates show that the business of the two leading gold companies developed much stronger than in the preceding two decades: Rand Mines and Consolidated Goldfields exhibited an average real return of roughly 10 per cent per year (see Table 11.2). The return on investment can be explained by a combination of several factors.

First, the companies managed to maintain low wages to the black labour force. As was noted above, the discrimination of the black labour force also seems to have increased during this period.

Second, the legacy of the early Randlords was taken over by Ernest Oppenheimer as he became the leading figure in South African business from the 1920s onwards through his chairmanship in the Anglo-American Corporation (Wheatcroft 1985, 249–56; Pallister, Stewart, and Lepper 1987). Collusion between the leading Randlords dated back to the opening of the Witwatersrand in the 1880s and to the formation of the politically important Chamber of Mines. By 1936, the six leading mining houses—Rand Mines, Johannesburg Investment Company, Anglo-American, Consolidated Goldfields, Union Corporation and General Mining and Finance Corporation—controlled 96 per cent of the output from the Witwatersrand—with extensive cross-ownership and interlocking directorates in the underlying mines (Innes 1983, 84–86; Feinstein 2005, 99–105; Nattrass and Seekings 2011, 523). The cooperation between the major mining companies continued to be of central importance to the development of the gold business during the interwar period, as they often used their collective political influence to shape institutionalized racial segregation in their interest, as demonstrated for example, in the Rand Revolt.

Third, the abandonment of the Gold Standard by the United Kingdom in 1931 was followed by 31 other countries. South Africa resisted the change, but in December 1932, they followed suit (Davenport 2013, 311–13; Padayachee and Bordiss 2015, 182). The price of gold was henceforth set by the interplay of supply and demand on the market, and in comparison to the gold premium of 1919–1920, the fall of the Gold Standard resulted in long-term upward movement of the gold price (Schmitz 1979, 274).

Fourth, the importance of the development of two new mining areas of Witwatersrand cannot be overestimated. In the early 1920s, the future of the gold-mining industry was uncertain. Several of the mines located at the central part of the gold reef were simply running out of gold. As it turned out, the central reef was far from the only findings of gold on the Witwatersrand. Some first positive news came from the Far East Rand (Innes 1983, 97–98; Richardson and Van Helten 1984, 338–39). Here, new mines started to develop quickly, particularly during the interwar period. With the expansion of mines like Springs, Brakpan, Nigel and Benoni, the eastern-most mines, by the late 1920s, produced more gold than the central mines. Nigel had initially been explored in the early 1890s, but it was after 1917 that the mine Sub Nigel developed into the most important mine for Consolidated Goldfields (Alan Patrick Cartwright 1967, 128–33). During its entire lifespan, from 1909 to 1969, Sub Nigel returned a yearly average of 12.9 per cent to its investors in London (see Table 11.2). An even greater change occurred at the other end of the Witwatersrand. The western-most part of the Rand had been explored during the first decades of the twentieth century, but none of the ventures had turned into profitable mines. The turnaround came in the initial years of the 1930s (Alan Patrick Cartwright 1967, 141–65).

The expansion of the gold industry also boosted the industrialization of the South African economy on several accounts. Machinery, electrical equipment, explosives, cables and cement were all industries that benefitted from a process of backwards linkages during the interwar period. At the same time, the gold export earned much needed foreign exchange, stabilizing the deficits created by imports to manufacturing and other industries (Feinstein 2005, 106–8; S. Jones and Müller 1992, 45–76). With the gold companies as locomotives, the interwar years developed into an industrial takeoff for South Africa. The industrial output increased fivefold in real value, while the number of employees rose from approximately 150,000 to 350,000 (Feinstein 2005, 121–23; Verhoef 2017, 73). The strong industrial growth also induced mining companies to invest outside their immediate sphere of interest. For example, the Anglo-American Corporation began a trajectory from being a holding company in gold and diamond shares into establishing oneself as the leading corporate conglomerate of South Africa (Innes 1983, 131). New political alliances were also formed which partially ran contrary to the interest of the mine owners. Starting with the Customs Tariff Act in 1914, South Africa embarked on an import-substitution path that gathered strong support among nationalistically oriented politicians. This path was strengthened in 1924 when the National and Labour parties jointly won the election and formed a coalition of urban and rural lower white working class (S. Jones and Müller 1992, 70–71; Feinstein 2005, 77–89).

Diamonds

While gold companies yielded an average of 11 per cent to their investors between 1920 and 1939, the diamond companies yielded only 0.6 per cent. The primary explanation for this was the weak performance of De Beers Consolidated. As explained in the previous section, the diamond business was drawn into a structural transformation process during the first two decades of the twentieth century, following the establishment of new mines and new actors in the business. The turbulence continued during the interwar period. Prior to 1920, De Beers had been one of the Imperial Blue Chips in London. However, after the First World War, the problems mounted for De Beers: the Spanish influenza hit Kimberley hard in 1918–1919 (with the consequence that production was shut down for five months), demand for diamonds fell sharply during the global recession in 1920–1922, and, at the same time, competition arose from new actors and new mines (Chilvers 1939, 219–22; Newbury 1989, chap. 6). As a result, De Beers lost its leading position in the diamond business. Not only did investors in London experience a negative return on investment (−4.7 per cent), volatility was also high and the stock lost two-thirds of its value three times (1920, 1930–1931, 1937–1939). A positive development was instead found among De Beers' competitors, such as The Premier Diamond Company and the Consolidated Diamond Mines of South West Africa (see Chap. 10 for the latter company).

The most important change during these years was the strategy pursued by the Anglo-American and its chairman Ernest Oppenheimer. The company expanded geographically by investing in diamond mines in multiple sites across the African continent. At the same time, Ernest Oppenheimer worked relentlessly to secure control over De Beers, which finally paid off in 1929. The Anglo-American was also the driving force behind the transformation of the old London Diamond Syndicate into a new form of monopsony/monopoly organization called the Central Selling Organization (Newbury 1989, chap. 11, 1995, 1996). The financial problems which followed for all diamond companies in the wake of the Great Depression were weathered more easily by the Anglo-American due to its large income from the booming gold industry. Hence, the Anglo-American used the turbulence of the 1930s to consolidate its position even further. The average return on investment was 2.1 per cent between 1920 and 1939 (see Table 11.2). This included a massive negative return (−71 per cent) for the particular year of 1920. From 1921 onwards, the Anglo-American stabilized its position as one of the leading Imperial Blue Chips at the London Stock Exchange—with an increasingly diversified portfolio in diamonds and gold, but later also including industrial and financial interests (Innes 1983, 101–8; Cleveland 2014, 89; Davenport 2013, 264–78).

Banking

In the finance sector, our estimates show that the average return on investment was 4.6 per cent per year between 1920 and 1939 (see Table 11.2). This was a relatively high figure in an international comparative perspective, given the global financial turbulence during the interwar period. The National Bank experienced serious problems in the wake of its expansionary strategy of the preceding decades, which opened up for the entrepreneurial chairman F.C. Goodenough of the Barclays Bank. In the early 1920s, Barclays acquired control over both the Colonial Bank and the National Bank. The result was the formation of the Barclays DCO and the delisting of Colonial Bank from the London Stock Exchange. The acquisitions were part of a diversification strategy pursued by Barclays to establish a truly multinational bank (G. Jones 1993, 148–53). Due to its different geographical locations around the world, the Barclays DCO is not included in our sample. Several smaller South African competitors also ceased to be included in the sources used for this study (due to either formal delisting or simply limited trading). From the mid-1920s, the two imperial banks—the Barclays DCO and the Standard Bank—completely dominated the South African bank market with a combined market share above 90 per cent. The oligopoly position benefitted the two banks and enabled them to build up large hidden reserves during the interwar period. The investors in London could also bear the fruit of this, as the average return on investment in the Standard Bank was 5.5 per cent throughout the interwar period (G. Jones 1993, 200; Verhoef 2013, 417). Hence, the banks also brought stability to the South African financial system during a period when the world's banking system was on the verge of collapse (S. Jones 1996, vol. 24, chap. 13).

Nationalism and Racial Segregation, 1940–1969

From the middle of the 1930s and through the Second World War, the South African economy experienced an economic boom. Acute labour shortages for a time increased the real wages of black workers (Nattrass 1990; Nattrass and Seekings 2011, 536–38). This development was, however, short-lived. The victory of the National Party in the general election of 1948 marked a watershed in the history of South Africa. One important aspect of this growing nationalism among white Afrikaners— the descendants of the Boer settlers—was a rise of so-called Afrikaner capitalism in the post-war decades, with a number of companies established by Afrikaner interests and with Afrikaner capital (O'Meara 1983; Feinstein 2005; Verhoef 2018). Afrikaner nationalism also became manifest in a further intensification of racial segregation. As noted earlier, racial segregation was nothing new to the South African society, but the National Party now used it as the basis for its *apartheid* election platform. During the 1950s and 1960s, the apartheid system was institutionalized in most policy areas and it became an overarching logic for political and economical domination of the white elite with far-reaching implications not only for social relations in South Africa but also concretely for business life (Thompson 2001, chap. 6; Terreblanche 2003, chap. 9; Seekings and Nattrass 2005, chaps. 3–4; Feinstein 2005, 149–51; Welsh 2009, chap. 3; Clark and Worger 2016, chap. 3).

A central tenet of the apartheid system was racial separation and a concomitant ambition to counteract urbanization of the black population. According to the ideology of separate development, black workers should preferably remain in the small 'native reserves' in the countryside and/or in mining compounds as long as there was a demand for their labour. On the one hand, this would ensure low-paid labour for the mining and agricultural sectors. On the other hand, it ran contrary to the process of industrialization wherein cities emerged as new engines of growth but then required a market for their output. The 'colour bar' regulations that reserved skilled jobs for white workers furthermore still hindered the companies from decreasing their labour costs by replacing white workers with black workers, despite the major victory of the mining companies during the Rand Revolt (see above). These particular aspects of the apartheid policies remained problematic for capitalist interests (Yudelman 1983; Lipton 1985, 112–16).

During the 1950s and 1960s, the real GDP per capita growth was around two per cent per year in South Africa. Such a growth was in line with the general development for African and Latin-American countries but was only half of what industrialized countries in Western Europe experienced at the same time. It is clear that the strong world economy helped South Africa, but it is also equally clear that the country did not manage to achieve any overall catching-up during these years (Moll 1991; Feinstein 2005, 144–; Nattrass and Seekings 2011, 541).

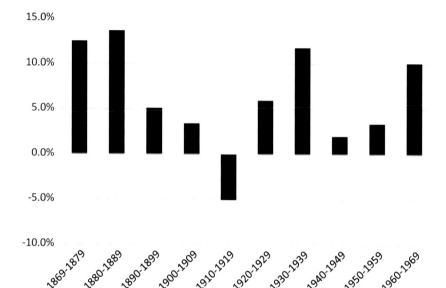

Fig. 11.1 Real return on investment in South Africa, by decade, 1869–1969 (geometric mean per year). Source: African Colonial Equities Database (ACED)

In previous research, it has been argued that profit rates declined during apartheid (Nattrass 1989, 1990, 2014; Seekings and Nattrass 2005, figs. 4.4 & 4.8). For the part of the period that we are able to study here (i.e. until 1969), any such development is not reflected in the return on investment in the companies in our sample. The South African investment portfolio exhibited an average return of 5.1 per cent per year between 1940 and 1969 (see Table 11.1). The rate of return actually increased over these three decades from 2.0 per cent during the 1940s, to 3.3 per cent during the 1950s and 10.1 per cent per year during the 1960s (see Fig. 11.1 below).

Gold and Diamonds

The average return to investment in the mining sector was 5.4 per cent during this period (see Table 11.1), but the internal disparities within the mining sector were considerable and the fluid boundaries of the companies' operations became even more apparent compared to previous periods. The development of the leading mining companies exemplifies the different trajectories within the mining sector. Among these companies, the Anglo-American Corporation stands out as the company that in itself epitomized the growth, transformations and contradictions of the South African economy in the post-war decades.

For investors in London, the Anglo-American Corporation continued to be one of the most important investment objects operating in Africa during this period. Between 1940 and 1969, the company grew into the largest South African conglomerate, while at the same time, it returned 10.4 per cent annually to its investors (see Table 11.2). The expansion and profitability rested on several legs. First, the Anglo-American managed to secure and develop holdings in both the Far West Rand in the 1930s and 1940s and in the Orange Free State in the 1940s and 1950s—the two most important gold-producing areas in the post-war period. The company secured its leading position in gold mining through vast investments, made possible, on the one hand, by resources channelled from its diamond holdings in De Beers and, on the other hand, from investors in Europe. The devaluation of the British Pound in 1949 further helped the company's business by raising the gold price to a high level, which was sustained until 1970. Second, Anglo-American took control of a whole range of industrial companies that developed strongly in the post-war years—such as AE & CI, Boart and Hard Metals and the Union Steel Corporation. Third, Anglo-American also developed the South African financial markets through its active ownership in corporations like the National Finance Corporation and Union Acceptances. Fourth, the Anglo-American invested heavily outside South Africa and thereby built up a large international portfolio. The Anglo-American Corporation continued to grow after our period of investigation, so that by the mid-1970s the Anglo-American Corporation included 139 subsidiaries, of which 69 were located outside South Africa, and by 1983, the group controlled over 50 per cent of the Johannesburg Stock Exchange in terms of market capitalization (Alan Patrick Cartwright 1968, 252; Innes 1983, chaps. 6 & 7; S. Jones 1992, 298; Davenport 2013, 329–40).

The Far West Rand developed rapidly during this period. The new company Blyvooruitzicht (established in 1937, in production since 1942) turned out to be one of the most lucrative gold mines in South Africa (Alan Patrick Cartwright 1967, 128–33; Alan Patrick Cartwright 1968, 229–44). In 1943, five years after it was floated at the London Stock Exchange, Blyvooruitzicht was the most highly capitalized gold mine in the South African portfolio. The return for the investors was high, though not extraordinary, with an annual return from 1943 to 1969 of 7.8 per cent (see Table 11.2). The profitability was a result of the rich gold-bearing reefs of the Far West Rand (Alan Patrick Cartwright 1968, 229–44; Webb 1983, 191–93). The mine also illustrates another important development of South African mining in the post-war years—its expansion into the mining of other metals. This expansion was partly due to the opening of new mines, like the copper mine of Phalabourwa in northeastern Transvaal, but equally important was the development of new techniques to extract other metals from already existing mines (Feinstein 2005, 172). In the case of Blyvooruitzicht, uranium developed as the most important by-product. With the support from a governmental agency, the first pilot plant for extracting uranium from slime was established at the Blyvooruitzicht in 1948. By 1960, there were seventeen uranium plants in South Africa, adding some £50 million in annual profits to the mining industry (Alan Patrick Cartwright 1968, 261–64; Webb 1983, 192).

Not all the gold-mining companies were equally successful. Most importantly, the former giant Rand Mines had not managed to acquire any major interests in the Far West Rand or in the Orange Free State. Consequently, it experienced a decline in the 1950s when its mines on the central reef slowly ran out of economically mineable ore. In 1959, Charles Engelhard became chairman of Rand Mines, and not before long, the company launched an ambitious industrial diversification programme. The industrial portfolio did not develop according to plan, and in 1971, Rand Mines merged with Thos. Barlow and Sons (Alan Patrick Cartwright 1968, 330–51; Innes 1983, 212–13). During the post-war years, Rand Mines therefore returned a meagre return of 0.6 per cent per year to its investors (see Table 11.2).

While the Rand Mines experienced a steady decline from its former top-position, De Beers made a spectacular comeback as an important investment object at the London Stock Exchange. Between 1940 and 1969, De Beers' annual return on investment was on average an extraordinary 20.5 per cent per year (see Table 11.2). During the turbulent 1930s, De Beers benefitted from its strong connection to the Anglo-American Corporation and the company weathered the depression. One effect of this was the hoarding of diamonds, which could be sold at highly profitable prices in the 1940s and 1950s, when global demand for diamonds grew strongly. Furthermore, De Beers embarked on a strategy from the 1940s onwards to exploit its position of producing high-quality gemstones and to move up the value chain. The new strategy involved a greater focus on how diamonds were sold and consumed—a shift marked by the unprecedented marketing campaign *Diamonds are forever*—launched in the United States in 1939 and resumed after the war. The strategy turned out to be profitable during the coming decades: the diamond business boomed in South Africa and the stock market valuation in De Beers and other diamond companies soared—peaking in 1969 (S. Jones 1992, 287; Feinstein 2005, 171; Cochrane 2015, 50–55).

Banking

The oligopoly of the South African banking system continued to the end of our period of study, though there were niches of the banking and financial market where new entrants started to challenge the Standard Bank and the Barclays DCO. Especially, the Netherlands Bank and the Volkskas changed the relative dependence on British banking in favour of more nationalist oriented interests (S. Jones and Müller 1992, 202–6). The result was that the imperial banking tradition continued throughout the period, but these banks were not the primary innovative force of the South African financial market (Verhoef 2013, 419–21). However, the Standard Bank of South Africa, now the only remaining bank in our sample, continued to the end of our period to maintain its position as an Imperial Blue Chips—with an average annual return of 4.5 per cent for the years 1940–1969 (i.e. including the Second World War).

Return on Investment in South Africa in the Long Run, 1869–1969

Figure 11.1 shows the development of the return on investment in South Africa over a hundred years. The composition of the sample and the return on investment varied substantially over the investigated period.

The average annual real return over the total period amounted to 6.2 per cent. The data series exhibits drastic fluctuations—in some years, the index increased in value by more than 60 per cent, whereas in some other years, it decreased by more than 40 per cent. As has been described in this chapter, these booms and busts can, to a large extent, be explained by fluctuations in the mining industry. We discern three phases when returns were particularly high. The first period stretches from 1869 to the outbreak of the South African War in 1899, the second is the 1930s and the third goes from the mid-1950s to the end of our period. In between these phases, returns were either negative (during the 1910s) or relatively low compared to the return from investments elsewhere in the world (see Chap. 6).

Up until 1889, there were about 10 companies in our sample. During this first period, The Cape Copper Mining Company, the Colonial Bank and the Standard Bank provided the financial market in London with the first long-term investment opportunities in South Africa—a kind of Imperial Blue Chips. During the 1870s and 1880s, the high return on investment was associated with the South African mining boom in copper and diamonds. This laid the foundation for the flotation and expansion of further diamond- and gold-mining companies at the London Stock Exchange in the 1890s. The importance of the diamond industry up until the late 1880s—though still negligible at the London Stock Exchange—was the way it shaped institutions and social relations and the profits it helped to create in other parts of the economy, not the least in the financial sector. The number of South African companies traded regularly on the London Stock Exchange soared during the mining boom of the 1890s—peaking at around 180 between 1904 and 1907. The companies that initially had dominated the sample in terms of their market capitalization were now dwarfed by newer mining companies like De Beers Consolidated and Rand Mines Limited.

The mining sector continued to expand from the 1920s and onwards when gold deposits were exploited on the far eastern and far western part of Witwatersrand and later also in the Orange Free State. In this process, the Anglo-American and Blyvooruitzicht became the most highly capitalized South African stocks in London, next to De Beers. Furthermore, the industrialization of the South African economy also came to the fore in our sample, as the Anglo-American Corporation transformed into an industrial conglomerate from the 1930s onwards. When we come to the late 1960s, the market capitalization of De Beers, Anglo-American and Consolidated Goldfields made up 30–35 per cent of the South African portfolio at the London Stock Exchange.

To conclude, our figures indicate that South Africa established itself as an important outlet for London investors around the turn of the century 1900. The long-run performance of South African companies also shows signs of a relatively mature market when compared to other peripheral markets. All of this occurred against the backdrop of continuously increasing racial segregation and discrimination of the black population in South Africa, as has been described in this chapter. These were processes that had been initiated already during the first mining booms in the late nineteenth century, but they were further intensified through various formal and informal institutions during the early twentieth century, and finally institutionalized on a national level under the name of *apartheid* in the late 1940s. These policies, undoubtedly, helped to keep the cost of land and labour lower in South Africa than they otherwise would have been. There is nonetheless no easily discernible relationship between the discrimination of the black population and the return on investment in South Africa. One key reason for this is that the discrimination had consequences for virtually all sectors of, and companies operating in, the South African economy. At the same time, there were several factors that impacted the return on investment in individual companies. These two factors complicate any attempt to empirically isolate any effects of discriminatory institutions from other factors influencing the return on investment. Though most importantly, London investors were surely aware of this discrimination and for long took it for granted—in some cases, even explicitly supporting it. The racial segregation, and the economic consequences it had, was thereby factored it in for the investors' decision whether to invest in South African ventures.

References

Ally, Russell. 1994. *Gold & Empire: The Bank of England and South Africa's Gold Producers, 1886–1926*. Johannesburg: Witwatersrand University Press.
Bell, Jocelyn A. 2001. The Influence on the South African Economy of the Gold Mining Industry 1925–2000. *South African Journal of Economic History* 16 (1–2): 29–46.
Blainey, Geoffrey. 1968. *The Rise of Broken Hill*. Melbourne: Macmillan.
Cain, Peter J., and Anthony G. Hopkins. 2001. *British Imperialism, 1688–2000*. Harlow: Longman.
Cartwright, Alan Patrick. 1965. *The Corner House. The Early History of Johannesburg*. Cape Town: Purnell & Sons.
———. 1967. *Gold Paved the Way*. London: Macmillan.
———. 1968. *Golden Age. The Story of the Industrialization of South Africa and the Part Played in It by the Corner House Group of Companies 1910–1967*. Johannesburg: Purnell & Sons.
Chanock, Martin. 2004. South Africa, 1841–1924: Race, Contract, and Coercion. In *Masters, Servants, and Magistrates in Britain & the Empire, 1562–1955*, ed. Douglas Hay and Paul Craven, 338–364. Chapel Hill: University of North Carolina Press.
Chapman, Stanley. 1985a. British-Based Investment Groups Before 1914. *The Economic History Review* 38 (2): 230–247.
———. 1985b. Rhodes and the City of London: Another View of Imperialism. *The Historical Journal* 28 (3): 647–666.
———. 1988. Venture Capital and Financial Organisation: London and South Africa in the Nineteenth Century. In *Banking and Business in South Africa*, ed. Stuart Jones. Cham: Springer.
Chilvers, Hedley A. 1939. *The Story of De Beers: With Some Notes on the Company's Financial, Farming, Railway and Industrial Activities in Africa and Some Introductory Chapters on the River Diggings and Early Kimberley*. London: Cassell and Co.
Clark, Nancy, and William Worger. 2016. *South Africa: The Rise and Fall of Apartheid*. 3rd ed. London: Routledge.

Cleveland, Todd. 2014. *Stones of Contention: A History of Africa's Diamonds*. Athens, OH: Ohio University Press.
Cochrane, David Troy. 2015. What's Love Got to Do with It? Diamonds and the Accumulation of De Beers, 1935–55. York University. http://bnarchives.yorku.ca/469/.
Crush, Jonathan, Alan Jeeves, and David Yudelman. 1991. *South Africa's Labor Empire: A History of Black Migrancy to the Gold Mines*. Boulder: Westview Press.
Davenport, Jade. 2013. *Digging Deep: A History of Mining in South Africa, 1852–2002*. Johannesburg: Jonathan Ball Publishers.
Davenport-Hines, R.P.T., and Jean-Jacques Van Helten. 1986. Edgar Vincent, Viscount D'Abernon, and the Eastern Investment Company in London, Constantinople and Johannesburg. *Business History* 28 (1): 35–61.
Dimson, Elroy, Paul Marsh, and Mike Staunton. 2002. *Triumph of the Optimists: 101 Years of Global Investment Returns*. Princeton, NJ: Princeton University Press.
Dumett, Raymond. 2009. *Mining Tycoons in the Age of Empire, 1870–1945: Entrepreneurship, High Finance, Politics and Territorial Expansion*. Farnham: Ashgate.
Feinstein, Charles. 2005. *An Economic History of South Africa: Conquest, Discrimination and Development*. Cambridge: Cambridge University Press.
Ferguson, Niall. 1998. *The World's Banker: The History of the House of Rothschild*. London: Weidenfeld & Nicolson.
Gregory, Sir Theodore. 1962. *Ernest Oppenheimer and the Economic Development of Southern Africa*. Cape Town: Oxford U.P.
Greyling, Lorraine, and Grietjie Verhoef. 2015. Slow Growth, Supply Shocks and Structural Change: The GDP of the Cape Colony in the Late Nineteenth Century. *Economic History of Developing Regions* 30 (1): 23–43.
Greyling, Jan C., Nick Vink, and Emily van der Merwe. 2018. Maize and Gold: South African Agriculture's Transition from Suppression to Support, 1886–1948. In *Agricultural Development in the World Periphery: A Global Economic History Approach*, ed. Vicente Pinilla and Henry Willebald, 179–204. Cham: Springer International Publishing.
Grossman, Richard S. 2015. Bloody Foreigners! Overseas Equity on the London Stock Exchange, 1869–1929. *The Economic History Review* 68 (2): 471–521.
Harries, Patrick. 1994. *Work, Culture and Identity: Migrant Laborers in Mozambique and South Africa, c. 1860–1910*. London: J. Currey.
Harvey, Charles, and Jon Press. 1990. The City and International Mining, 1870–1914. *Business History* 32 (3): 98–119.

Innes, Duncan. 1983. *Anglo American and the Rise of Modern South Africa*. London: Heinemann Educational.

Johnstone, Frederick A. 1976. *Class, Race and Gold: A Study of Class Relations and Racial Discrimination in South Africa*. London: Routledge.

Jones, Stuart. 1988. *Banking and Business in South Africa*. New York: Palgrave Macmillan.

———. 1992. The Johannesburg Stock Market and Stock Exchange., 1962–87. In *Financial Enterprise in South Africa Since 1950*, 273–301. London: Macmillan.

Jones, Geoffrey. 1993. *British Multinational Banking, 1830–1990*. Oxford: Clarendon Press.

Jones, Stuart. 1996. *The Great Imperial Banks in South Africa: A Study of the Business of Standard Bank and Barclays Bank, 1861–1961*. Vol. 24. Pretoria: University of South Africa.

Jones, Stuart, and André Müller. 1992. *The South African Economy, 1910–90*. New York: Palgrave Macmillan.

Katzenellenbogen, Simon. 1975. The Miner's Frontier, Transport and General Economic Development. In *Colonialism in Africa, 1870–1960: The Economics of Colonialism*, ed. P. Duignan and L.H. Gann, 360–426. Cambridge: Cambridge University Press.

Kubicek, Robert. 1979. *Economic Imperialism in Theory and Practice*. Durham, NC: Duke University Center for International Studies Publication.

Lacey, Marian. 1981. *Working for Boroko: The Origins of a Coercive Labour System in South Africa*. Johannesburg: Ravan Press.

Legassick, Martin. 1974. South Africa: Capital Accumulation and Violence. *Economy and Society* 3 (3): 253–291.

Levy, Norman. 1982. *The Foundations of the South African Cheap Labour System*. London: Routledge & Kegan Paul.

Lipton, Merle. 1985. *Capitalism and Apartheid: South Africa, 1910–84*. Hounslow: Maurice Temple Smith.

Lukasiewicz, Mariusz. 2017. From Diamonds to Gold: The Making of the Johannesburg Stock Exchange, 1880–1890. *Journal of Southern African Studies* 43 (4): 715–732.

Marks, Shula, and Richard John Alex Reuben Rathbone. 1982. *Industrialisation and Social Change in South Africa: African Class Formation, Culture, and Consciousness, 1870–1930*. Harlow: Longman.

Michie, Ranald C. 2006. *The Global Securities Market a History*. Oxford: Oxford University Press.

Moll, Terence. 1991. Did the Apartheid Economy 'Fail'?: Journal of Southern African Studies: Vol 17, No 2. *Journal of Southern African Studies* 17 (2): 271–291.

Mpeta, Bokang, Johan Fourie, and Kris Inwood. 2018. Black Living Standards in South Africa before Democracy: New Evidence from Height. *South African Journal of Science* 114: 1–2): 1–8.

Nattrass, Nicoli. 1989. Apartheid & Profit Rates: Challenging the Radical Orthodoxy. *Indicator SA* 7 (1): 33–37.

———. 1990. Wages, Profits and Apartheid: 1939–1960. In *History Workshop*. Johannesburg: University of Witwatersrand.

———. 2014. Deconstructing Profitability under Apartheid: 1960–1989. *Economic History of Developing Regions* 29 (2): 245–267.

Nattrass, Nicoli, and Jeremy Seekings. 2011. The Economy and Poverty in the Twentieth Century. In *The Cambridge History of South Africa*, ed. R. Ross, A. Mager, and B. Nasson, 518–572. Cambridge: Cambridge University Press.

Newbury, Colin. 1987a. Technology, Capital, and Consolidation: The Performance of De Beers Mining Company Limited, 1880–1889. *Business History Review* 61 (1): 1–42.

———. 1987b. The Origins and Function of the London Diamond Syndicate, 1889–1914. *Business History* 29 (1): 5–26.

———. 1989. *The Diamond Ring: Business, Politics and Precious Stones in South Africa, 1867–1947*. Oxford: Clarendon Press.

———. 1995. South Africa and the International Diamond Trade Part One: Sir Ernest Oppenheimer, De Beers and the Evolution of Central Selling, 1920–1950. *South African Journal of Economic History* 10 (2): 1–22.

———. 1996. South Africa and the International Diamond Trade-Part Two: The Rise and Fall of South Africa as a Diamond Entrepôt, 1945–1990. *South African Journal of Economic History* 11 (1): 251–284.

Nkosi, Morley. 2011. *Mining Deep: The Origins of the Labour Structure in South Africa*. Claremont, South Africa: David Philip.

———. 2017. *Black Workers White Supervisors: The Emergence of the Labor Structure in South Africa*. Trenton: Africa World Press, Inc.

O'Meara, Dan. 1983. *Volkskapitalisme: Class, Capital and Ideology in the Development of Afrikaner Nationalism, 1934–1948*. Cambridge: Cambridge University Press.

Padayachee, Vishnu, and Bradley Bordiss. 2015. How Global Geo-Politics Shaped South Africa's Post-World War I Monetary Policy: The Case of Gerhard Vissering and Edwin Kemmerer in South Africa, 1924–25. *Economic History of Developing Regions* 30 (2): 182–209.

Pallister, David, Sarah Stewart, and Ian Lepper. 1987. *South Africa Inc.: The Oppenheimer Empire*. London: Simon & Schuster.

Phimister, Ian, and Jeremy Mouat. 2003. Mining, Engineers and Risk Management: British Overseas Investment, 1894–1914. *South African Historical Journal* 49 (1): 1–26.

Piketty, Thomas. 2014. *Capital in the Twenty-First Century*. Cambridge: Belknap Press of Harvard University Press.

Reinhart, Carmen M., and Kenneth S. Rogoff. 2009. *This Time Is Different: Eight Centuries of Financial Folly*. Princeton, NJ: Princeton University Press.

Richardson, Peter, and Jean-Jacques Van Helten. 1982. Labour in the South African Gold Mining Industry, 1886–1914. In *Industrialisation and Social Change in South Africa: African Class Formation, Culture, and Consciousness, 1870–1930*, ed. Shula Marks and Richard Rathbone, 77–98. New York: Longman.

———. 1984. The Development of the South African Gold-Mining Industry, 1895–1918. *The Economic History Review* 37 (3): 319–340.

Roberts, Brian. 1985. *Kimberley: Turbulent City*. Cape Town: David Philip.

Schmitz, Christopher J. 1979. *World Non-Ferrous Metal Production and Prices, 1700–1976*. London: Cass.

Seekings, Jeremy, and Nicoli Nattrass. 2005. *Class, Race, and Inequality in South Africa*. New Haven: Yale University Press.

Shillington, Kevin. 1982. The Impact of the Diamond Discoveries on the Kimberley Hinterland: Class Formation, Colonialism and Resistance among the Tlhaping of Griqualand West in the 1870s. In *Industrialisation and Social Change in South Africa: African Class Formation, Culture, and Consciousness, 1870–1930*, ed. Shula Marks and Richard Rathbone, 99–118. New York: Longman.

Simons, Harold J., and Ray E. Simons. 1969. *Class and Colour in South Africa, 1850–1950*. Harmondsworth: Penguin.

Terreblanche, Sampie. 2003. *A History of Inequality in South Africa, 1652–2002*. Pietermaritzburg: University of Natal Press.

Thompson, Leonard. 2001. *A History of South Africa*. 3rd ed. New Haven: Yale University Press.

Trapido, Stanley. 1971. South Africa in a Comparative Study of Industrialization. *The Journal of Development Studies* 7 (3): 309–320.

Turrell, Robert Vicat. 1982. Kimberley: Labour and Compounds, 1871–1888. In *Industrialisation and Social Change in South Africa: African Class Formation, Culture, and Consciousness, 1870–1930*, ed. Shula Marks and Richard Rathbone, 45–76. New York: Longman.

———. 1987. *Capital and Labour on the Kimberley Diamond Fields 1871–1890.* Cambridge: Cambridge University Press.

Turrell, Robert Vicat, and Jean-Jacques Van Helten. 1986. The Rothschilds, the Exploration Company and Mining Finance. *Business History* 28 (2): 181–205.

Van Helten, Jean-Jacques. 1990. Mining, Share Manias and Speculation: British Investment in Overseas Mining, 1880–1913. In *Capitalism in a Mature Economy: Financial Institutions, Capital Exports and British Industry, 1870–1939*, ed. Jean-Jacques Van Helten and Youssef Cassis, 159–185. Aldershot: Edward Elgar.

Verhoef, Grietjie. 2013. Financial Intermediaries in Settler Economies: The Role of the Banking Sector Development in South Africa, 1850–2000. In *Settler Economies in World History*, ed. Christopher Lloyd, Jacob Metzer, and Richard Sutch, 403–433. Leiden: Brill.

———. 2017. *The History of Business in Africa. Complex Discontinuity to Emerging Markets.* Studies in Economic History. Cham: Springer.

———. 2018. *The Power of Your Life: The Sanlam Century of Insurance Empowerment, 1918–2018.* Oxford: Oxford University Press.

Visagie, Jan. 2014. The Emigration of the Voortrekkers into the Interior. In *A History of South Africa. From the Distant Past to the Present Day*, ed. Fransjohan Pretorius. Pretoria: Protea Book House.

Webb, Arthur. 1983. Mining in South Africa. In *Economic History of South Africa*, ed. Francis Coleman. Pretoria: Haum.

Welsh, David. 2009. *The Rise and Fall of Apartheid.* Johannesburg: Jonathan Ball Publishers.

Wheatcroft, Geoffrey. 1985. *The Randlords: The Men Who Made South Africa.* London: Weidenfeld and Nicolson.

Wilkins, Mira. 1988. The Free-Standing Company, 1870–1914: An Important Type of British Foreign Direct Investment. *The Economic History Review* 41 (2): 259–282.

Wilson, Francis. 1972. *Labour in the South African Gold Mines 1911–1969.* London: Cambridge University Press.

———. 2011. Historical Roots of Inequality in South Africa. *Economic History of Developing Regions* 26 (1): 1–15.

Worger, William. 1987. *South Africa's City of Diamonds: Mine Workers and Monopoly Capitalism in Kimberley, 1867–1895.* New Haven: Yale University Press.

Yudelman, David. 1983. *The Emergence of Modern South Africa: State, Capital, and the Incorporation of Organized Labor on the South African Gold Fields, 1902–1939.* London: Greenwood Press.

Benjamin Disraeli buys Suez Canal shares. A caricature showing Benjamin Disraeli purchasing the key to India—shares in the Suez Canal Company—on behalf of the English lion from the *khedive* Isma'il Pasha of Egypt. © Mary Evans Picture Library

Part IV

Thematical Studies

12

On the Ground Floor: The Corner House Group

The Traditional Narrative Versus Quantitative Estimates

By 1913, the exploitation of the gold deposits around Johannesburg had turned South Africa into the largest producer of gold in the world. The production at the Witwatersrand was to 95 per cent controlled by eight larger groups (a.k.a. mining houses), via direct and indirect ownership. The dominant player was the Corner House group, which on its own accounted for 37 per cent of the gold produced at the Witwatersrand and 11 per cent of the total world output of gold (Kubicek 1979, 54; Wheatcroft 1985, 8). The flagship of the Corner House group was the company Rand Mines Limited. This was one of the larger gold companies in our sample from the 1890s to the 1960s (see Chap. 11). In previous literature, Rand Mines has mostly been described as a success. This narrative rests on the combination of two factors. First, the company was a spearhead in implementing deep-level mining techniques at Witwatersrand. Second, the traditional narrative describes the company as generating financial wealth to its investors (Cartwright 1965, 125–33;

Kubicek 1979, 53–84; Richardson and Van Helten 1984, 321–26; Innes 1983, 55–56; Wheatcroft 1985, 162; R. V. Turrell and Van Helten 1986, 188). We know, for example, that Cecil Rhodes benefitted greatly in financial terms from his cooperation with The Corner House (Newbury 1981, 29). Kubicek furthermore stated that Alfred Beit (the primus motor of Rand Mines) left an estate worth £8 million when he died in 1906, and Kubicek continued to argue that immensely profitable gold mines provided investors in Rand Mines with very high dividends during the 1890s (Kubicek 1979, 53). Cartwright made a similar argument in his book about the Corner House where he details the wealth created for the original partners of Rand Mines, claiming that everyone who was associated with them did equally well (Cartwright 1965, 132; R. V. Turrell and Van Helten 1986, 188).

This wealth-creation claim of the traditional narrative stands in contrast to the findings in the previous chapters of this book. Despite the meteoric rise of Johannesburg as the city of gold around 1900, the average return on investment in the South African gold companies floated at the London Stock Exchange around the turn of the century proved a relative disappointment (see Chap. 11). Even the biggest companies—like Rand Mines—seem to have underperformed. The average annual return on investment in Rand Mines between 1895 and 1913 was 1 per cent according to the figures that can be arrived at using the data in sources such as the *Investors' Monthly Manual*. To understand this discrepancy between the traditional narrative of a successful company and the quantitative estimates of the return on investment in the company, we need to turn to the background of the company formation, the strategy of the Corner House and the actual trade on the financial markets in London and Johannesburg.

Inside and Outside the Network: The Formation of the Corner House

The Corner House was the brainchild of financier Alfred Beit, though it quickly developed into a network of companies and individuals. Aside from Rand Mines Limited, the group consisted of a number of mining

12 On the Ground Floor: The Corner House Group

and financial companies, including, for example, The Central Mining and Investment Corporation, The Consolidated Goldfields of South Africa, Wernher, Beit & Company and Eckstein & Company. By formally and informally connecting these companies and their leading individuals, the Corner House formed a diverse network. It was active in South African mining, but it was also an important financial actor in international financial centres like London and Paris (Cartwright 1965; Kubicek 1979, 53–85; Davenport 2013, 180–82). The correspondence between the group's offices in London and Johannesburg testifies to the character of its business.[1] A letter from Johannesburg to London illustrates this international connection:

> *The list of transactions will show you that an active business, has been doing this week, and we think that had it not been for some anxiety about the internal affairs in France, owing mainly to the Dreyfus case, and to the possibility of some unrest owing to the possible negotiations between England and France in Fashoda, it would have remained more active still. The undertone, however, is exceedingly good.*[2]

Hence, the Corner House illustrated international business during the first wave of globalization—where information and capital flowed freely in the world of the telegraph and the international Gold Standard. Over the years, the group also operated in a number of different locations in Africa and Europe. The goldfields of Witwatersrand and the financial markets in London, nonetheless, remained as the two main centres of activities. The financial control remained in London during its initial decade and the lion share of the profits went to the London partners, even though the Corner House became known as a South African mining house (Cartwright 1965, 118; Wheatcroft 1985, 118–19).

Alfred Beit was a typical Randlord in the sense that he had made his first fortune in diamonds during the 1870s. He became partner of the diamond merchant Jules Porges & Co during the 1880s and when Porges retired in 1890, Alfred Beit and Julius Wernher took over and renamed

---

[1] WB 118, 940119; WB 121, 951025; HE 61, 951101; WB 173, 960317.
[2] HE 65, 980916.

the company to Wernher, Beit & Co. Next, Beit recruited Hermann Eckstein from the Phoenix Diamond Mining Company and the successful Barberton-speculator Jim Taylor to develop a gold business at the Rand (Wheatcroft 1985, 111). Together with Lionell Phillips, yet another Kimberley veteran, they formed the inner circle of the emerging mining house. The office in Johannesburg was located at the corner of Commissioner and Simmond's Street and Eckstein's name also meant 'corner' in German—so in the 1890s, the whole group became referred to as the 'Corner House'. Beit and Wernher worked primarily from London, while Eckstein and Taylor ran the Johannesburg office (under the name Eckstein & Company). Phillips was recruited in 1889 as a mining advisor to the group, but he quickly became important in designing the structure of the new mining house (Fraser 1977, 10–11; Cartwright 1965, 9–17). The contacts between London and Johannesburg were close, even when they divided their attention in terms of work. Wernher and Beit managed more of the contacts with the international financial markets, while Eckstein, Taylor and Phillips primarily developed their local networks in terms of buying up claims and setting up new mining companies (Wheatcroft 1985, 113; Fraser 1977, 29).

In order to exploit both long- and short-term business opportunities, Beit and Eckstein shared the view that it was important to build a financial structure that would strike a balance between securing profits for the inner circle and at the same time be open enough to attract necessary capital in all forms—be it human, social and financial. To do this, the group employed several of the techniques and financial instruments that were popular in the City of London around the turn of the century.

One of the most important tools employed by the Corner House was to invite certain individuals (or companies) to 'come in on the ground floor'—that is, to buy shares at nominal value when a new company was formed, before the initial public offering. With a deliberately low original valuation, shares often increased in value when they started to trade publicly, and the people initially invited could capitalize on this by selling off their part, if they wished to do so. This was a way for the founders to create an interest for the company, and at the same time, it was a technique to maintain and extend valuable networks without having to put up a lot of cash (Cartwright 1965, 20; Van Helten 1990, 163–68; Dumett

2009, 17–18). The position of the specially invited could also be leveraged further with so-called founder's shares. These special shares gave the owners an exclusive right to a specified part of a company's profits, before ordinary shareholders would receive any dividends. Not everyone invited in on the ground floor would necessarily get access to founders' shares. The special rights of such shares were, furthermore, not always communicated clearly to outside investors, and sometimes, it resulted in conflicts between the original partners and outside investors. This usually happened a couple of years after the flotation of a successful company, when such a clause made the value of the founders' shares skyrocket (Cartwright 1967, 69–70; Fraser 1977, 10–11; Wheatcroft 1985, 146–47; Davenport-Hines and Van Helten 1986, 45–47; R. V. Turrell and Van Helten 1986, 181–85; Newbury 1987, 21–23; Harvey and Press 1990, 112–13; Hannah 2007, 666–70; Dumett 2009, 23–24). Yet another tool was the use of so-called vendor's interest. The valuation of new mining companies was mostly based on the underlying claims to gold-bearing ground. When such claims were acquired to float a new company, the former owners were often compensated with shares in the new company. This enabled the partners to secure a large share of the company's capital for themselves. It also enabled financial actors to engage in company promotion without supplying much new capital to the actual mining business. The result was that mines ran out of working capital before they had entered a productive stage.[3]

The outer circle of the Corner House network consisted of other Randlords, mining engineers, journalists and politicians. The connection to the political sphere was of particular importance for the long-term development of the mining industry (Gwaindepi 2019). These people were also occasionally invited to participate on the ground floor, though generally on a smaller scale and without any founder's shares.[4] An illustrative example is the report from London to Johannesburg in February 1895, where common interests in Randfontein and Tribute Block with

---

[3] Authors use slightly different terminology when they refer to the same technique: vendor's interest, vendor's capital and vendor' shares (Cartwright 1967, 29–33; Wheatcroft 1985, 116; Phimister 1988, 63–64; Katzenellenbogen 1975, 362; Van Helten 1990, 163–68; Dumett 2009, 23–24).

[4] HE 124, 871109; HE 124, 871219; WB 117, 930203; HE 64, 980311. See also (Cartwright 1967, 127; Fraser 1977, 56).

Robinson and Bailey (long-term antagonists of the Corner House) were discussed. The report is an illustration of the networks' wider circle since it mentions several other leading figures in Johannesburg and also connections to the financial markets of United Kingdom, France and Germany.[5] Despite the fact that the Randlords were competitors and to some extent personal enemies, the letters between London and Johannesburg contained jointly planned and implemented ventures. The engineers were also vital for success of the Corner House, especially after the turn to deep-level mining in the early 1890s. In the correspondence, we see two clear marks of this. First is the search for competent and loyal engineers. People recurrently asked for and sent off recommendations, and when new ventures were planned, engineering competence was much discussed. Second, different kinds of financial remuneration were on the table. The engineer's salaries were mentioned, but the strategic use of shares and ground floor participation was also discussed. For example, when the Corner House took part in the H F Syndicate in 1893, the London office recommended that one of the chief engineers' participation on beneficial terms:

> *Mr Hamilton Smith would like to have an interest of 4 to 5 shares, after a good deal of conversation we told him we would recommend the sale of £500, which is £150 below market price. Mr Smith is a very good friend of ours, and we could afford to be generous and take credit for letting him have the shares.*[6]

Beit and Eckstein used all these techniques and financial instruments to ensure the access of the Corner House to future profits in the companies they got involved. On a general level, they were also important in order to establish and maintain a network that would ensure access to valuable information, relating to both mining and financial matters. In a letter to London, Eckstein explained that '*in the long run it will pay better to let other people earn something as well. It will bring grist to the mill in the shape of timely information*' (quoted in Cartwright 1965, 119). This strategy—to be able to make connections to people with different skills and

---

[5] HE 61, 950208.
[6] HE 58, 930215.

12 On the Ground Floor: The Corner House Group

formal powers—was crucial to the success of the Corner House. The strategy was pursued, for example, in cooperation with Cecil Rhodes, who was not only a leading diamond magnate but also a politically important figure in the Cape Colony (see Chap. 11). Cecil Rhodes, Charles Rudd and their company Consolidated Goldfields became long-term allies to the inner circle of the Corner House during the late 1880s (Cartwright 1967, 13; Wheatcroft 1985, 50). During the negotiations to start up Rand Mines in 1892, Beit remarked in a letter:

> *I shall make some arrangements with Rhodes and Rudd, selling them 2.5 per cent our 25 percent at a moderate price, probably £8000, so as to make their interests fall in with ours. Rhodes' brains are not to be despised and if we had interests apart there would always be friction.*[7]

In the end, this cooperation proved mutually beneficial, as the offer to participate on the ground floor in Rand Mines proved lucrative for both Consolidated as a company and for Rhodes and Rudd personally. The quote also points to the fact that strategic networking was also about handling risks. The fundamental risk was of course the risk of losing too much capital in individual ventures. Inviting others to join on the ground floor was a way of balancing the investment portfolio of the Corner House.[8] Another risk was people acting in a way that would impute the reputation of the network. The so-called Lippert scandal in 1889–90 was such an example, when Beit's cousin William Lippert was trying to cover up losses in the 1889 crisis by forging the signature of his cousin. In the end, Beit distanced himself from Lippert and witnessed in court against his cousin in order to clear himself, and the network, from any further suspicion.[9]

The Corner House consisted of individuals and companies that in different ways benefitted from their participation in the network—through inside information, share allotments, access to membership in company

---

[7] Quoted in (Cartwright 1965, 130).
[8] HE 124, 871108; HE 124 980506. See also (Kubicek 1979, 58).
[9] HE 58, 930210. See also (Cartwright 1965, 120–42; Fraser 1977, 39).

boards, social status, etc.[10] Another example was when the London office wrote to Johannesburg in 1898 about the development of the Ferreira Deep mine:

> We have been besieged with so many applications for shares at £4, that we have decided not to make any issue at all on this side at present, but authorised you to give away to friends of the Rand Mines in Johannesburg and Pretoria 5 000 shares at £4. According to our valuation the shares should be worth at least £8, and whilst the Rand Mines may be justified in distributing a number of shares at very cheap rates to local people, either in recognition of loyalty or services rendered, or for the purpose of giving a little impetus to local dealing, we do not think that they would be justified in supplying at that price anything like the quantity which would be necessary to at all satisfy aspirants at this end.[11]

Their relationship with the press was also important for Corner House, right from the start. In 1889, Hermann Eckstein participated in a venture to take over the Johannesburg-based newspaper *The Eastern Star*. The paper was renamed *The Star* and became one of the leading papers in the city throughout the twentieth century and 'forcefully expressed the views of the mining community', as Cartwright has put it (Cartwright 1965, 64). Eckstein and others had a well-founded fear of negative press. Throughout the 1890s, negative publicity reappeared in both local and international newspapers (often referring to each other as sources). It is clear that information flowed relatively quickly between the continents. Even large corporate entities had to face the fact that the press was critically scrutinizing its operations. The letters and the press clippings in the corporate archive show that the corporate image painted by the press was an issue that was followed up and acted on by the company.[12] Wheatcroft's conclusion seems plausible—Corner House could and did buy the South African and the Paris press when it suited them, but the London press was less biddable (Wheatcroft 1985, 134–35).

---

[10] HE 124, 871108; HE 58, 930311; WB 120, 941229; WB 122, 960908; HE 140, 970830; HE 65, 980722; HE 65, 980916.

[11] HE 65, 980916.

[12] HE 5, 900707; HE 5, 930930; HE 5, 931105; HE5, 931110; HE 5, 940602; HE 950118, WB 122, 960912, WB 173, 960317; WB 173, 960318; WB 173, 960321; HE 64, 980107; HE 64, 980520.

The Information Race for Short-Term Speculation and Long-Term Development

During the autumn of 1887, the Corner House group increased its activity in Johannesburg. The letters sent to London were filled with reports on possible claims to buy and on technical issues relating to the actual gold production.[13] Eckstein noted to Beit that the working capital was running out for several mines, which could open up for takeovers.[14] Because the widespread use of vendor's interests did not supply the mines with working capital, this was not a big surprise (Wheatcroft 1985, 116; Van Helten 1990, 163–68). In November 1887, there were plans together with the Randlord J.B. Robinson for a large-scale amalgamation of different interests into one large gold company. In the end, however, Beit was not happy with the proposal and advised Eckstein to form a syndicate instead and to continue to buy up shares of mining companies with a wish to carrying on an amalgamation scheme on its own.[15]

In the spring of 1888, the Corner House had taken control of eight mines at the Witwatersrand, either through formations of new mines or through acquisitions of controlling interests in existing ones.[16] Furthermore, it held extensive claims and options through participating in syndicates, which were formed among the local mining interests—with Rhodes, Adolf Goerz and Sigmund Neumann as important allies among other Randlords (Fraser 1977, 10–11; Kubicek 1979, 60). This expansion was done at the same time as a speculation in gold-related shares was taking off in both Johannesburg and London (Davenport 2013, 173; Wheatcroft 1985, 114). The letters between the members of the Corner House group during the autumn of 1887 reveal that they were in agreement that the gold deposits at the Witwatersrand were both large and uniform enough to justify their long-term strategy.[17]

---

[13] HE 124, 871109; HE 124, 871125; HE 124, 871202; HE 124, 871221.
[14] HE 124, 871118.
[15] HE 124, 871118; HE 124, 871119.
[16] Baantjes, Langlaagte, Robinson, Ferreria, Henry Nourse, Jubilee, Salisbury and Wolhuter.
[17] HE 124, 871119.

It is clear that the group strategically built up holding positions in terms of gold production. It is also clear that insiders of the Corner House could draw on their advantageous situation in terms of information flow to exploit the potential for short-time speculation (Fraser 1977, 8; Wheatcroft 1985, 113). There was continuous buying and selling of positions in companies relating to short-term profits.[18] After the opening of the Johannesburg Stock Exchange in August 1887, the market for short-term speculation could be conducted both in London and in Johannesburg (Davenport 2013, 174–75). Hence, speculation was not in opposition to a long-term production strategy, but rather a profitable side effect. The information flowing through the Corner House group gave access to first-hand information on technological development, the latest mining reports and price information from different financial markets where gold shares were traded.[19] A precondition for the possibility of exploiting this information was access to fast and reliable information and communication technology. This was achieved by a combination of personal travels, letter writing and telegraph. Eckstein & Company was not only a major postal customer; they also designed combinations of different technologies to stay ahead in the information race. For example, letters fleshed out news originally transmitted by cables (Cartwright 1965, 51–54). Sometimes different conduits of information were directly brought together to speed things up, for example, combining the use of telegraph and dispatch riders on certain routes, to circumvent the need to use other, choked-up telegraph lines (Cartwright 1965, 53). Hence, the Corner House was well equipped to exploit the information flows transmitted by the telegraph, but it also became clear that it was an ongoing struggle to stay on top. All types of market participants used the telegraph, and the business press was quick to transmit information between the continents and between geographically dispersed financial centres.[20] Hence, with a continuous development of the telegraph system, the competitive situation changed accordingly. In one example, Alfred Beit wrote to Hermann Eckstein complaining about the situation:

---

[18] HE 124, 871103; HE 124, 871105; HE 124, 871108; HE 124, 871119.
[19] HE 124, 871103; HE 124, 871105; HE 56, 901017. See also (Kubicek 1979, 62).
[20] See, for example, FT 940529.

12 On the Ground Floor: The Corner House Group

We wish again to draw your attention to the fact that your telegraphic information about important matters is generally behind others. When we received your cable that the monthly return of the Geldenhuis would be better, this news was known two days before in Paris, and Mr Kahn informed us before the arrival of your cable. The news about the strike in the French Rand was known 24 hours before your cable. The Bonanza crushing was published 24 hours before the receipt of your news, and there were long articles in the Financial Times *and other papers on Salisbury matters. We had good many enquiries by the letter on the subject, and the only answer we could give was that we knew nothing about it. This places us in a very awkward position. Please cable before anybody else or not at all, as news of common knowledge is published in all the papers.*[21]

When a crisis hit the goldfields of Witwatersrand in 1889, it tested the capabilities of the Corner House. The crisis emerged from a combination of financial- and mining-related issues (Davenport 2013, 177). Financially, it was a classic example of a speculative boom, ending when profits did not materialize as fast as promised in the flood of optimistic prospectuses. Technically, the situation was aggravated by mining reports showing that at depths starting at around 120 feet below ground, the ore was different in structure. The gold content was the same, but it resisted traditional methods of treatment. The result was that gold-related shares fell quickly in value and forced hundreds of companies in Johannesburg to wind up (Kubicek 1979, 43). Though this was bad news for the business, the Corner House managed to use the situation to its own benefit, both in the short and long run (Cartwright 1967, 64–66). The pyritic ore was first discovered at the premise of the Percy Company (a subsidiary to Eckstein & Co). Taylor sent a confidential telegram to London, and the Corner House managed to sell off substantial amounts of their short-term holdings prior to the fall of the share prices. However, the news soon leaked out and by the beginning of 1890, the total market value of Johannesburg gold companies was down by more than 50 per cent (Davenport 2013, 175–77; Wheatcroft 1985, 116–18).

The long-term challenge for Corner House was now to find technical solutions to the challenges of continued gold exploitation (see also

---

[21] WB 122, 961212.

Chap. 14). The challenge of pyritic ore was overcome by the introduction of the MacArthur-Forrest process. The challenge of relatively low (but uniform) gold content that continued in long vertical reefs was overcome by the introduction of large-scale deep-level mining. Hence, after selling off shares early in the crisis at reasonable prices, the Corner House now took the lead in both of these processes (Kubicek 1979, 43–46). Lionel Phillips was actively pushing the argument towards Beit for Corner House to embark on an ambitious deep-level investment strategy (Fraser 1977, 50). This development put the issue of capital intensity at centre stage, as the emerging deep-level mining technique demanded a working capital on a completely different scale than outcrop mining (Dumett 2009, 15; Wheatcroft 1985, 163). It also stressed the role of skilled engineers for putting these large sums of capital into productive use. Lionell Phillips has already been mentioned, and from 1889 onwards, the Corner House recruited several other recognized engineers. Several of them came to serve Corner House, thanks to the strategic alliance with the Rothschild family and the London Exploration Company. Hennen Jennings was typical in this respect. He was an American mining engineer who had won his spurs from managing mines in Venezuela. He was engaged as a consultant to Corner House from 1889 to 1905 and his early work in Johannesburg was vital in quickly introducing the MacArthur-Forrest process (Cartwright 1965, 95–98).

In 1891, the worst part of the crisis was over, and when a general recovery of the gold business began, the Corner House could continue its path of expansion from a strong position (Wheatcroft 1985, 120–23). By now, the inner circle had come to believe in the necessity of deep-level mining in order to make gold mining at the Witwatersrand profitable—while the most bitter competitor of the Corner House, Joseph Benjamin Robinson, still denounced deep-level mining as a fraud (Fraser 1977, 60–62; Wheatcroft 1985, 122). The emergence of this insight also made it clear that a long-term strategy was needed to include the realization of economies of scale and scope on an unprecedented level. Furthermore, the industrialization of the gold business also recurrently included expensive lawsuits, political lobbying and the need to ensure a steady growth of labour supply (Wheatcroft 1985, 120; Fraser 1977, 78–79). The stage was set for the formation of new and bigger gold companies. At the same time, it was obvious that higher stakes also meant higher risks. Therefore, while Lionell Phillips argued for an ambitious deep-level investment plan, there were also other considerations. Alfred Beit, still the leading person in Corner House, was convinced that deep-level mining was the way to go, but he continued to argue for extensive risk-sharing when the discussions on forming Rand Mines took off: *I think we must on no account be able to retain more than fifty percent for ourselves. It would be too much for our firm to invest £100 000 in this enterprise.*[22]

The Rand Mines Limited: The Insiders, the Critics and the Wealth Created

The preparations for establishing a new gold-mining company took off after the crisis of 1889–91 was overcome, and the planning process intensified during 1892 (Fraser 1977, 55). The involved persons negotiated the size and scope of the new company. They also decided whom to invite in on the ground floor and the extra benefits to be awarded to the original founders. The challenge was to form a company that would include promising claims, trusted investors and competent engineers—but without giving away too much of the original shares in compensation, in order to secure a decent profit for the members of the Corner House group.[23] By late 1892, there was an agreement in place with important external interests like the Rothschild's (via the Exploration Company). The result combined a controlled level of risk-taking on the part of Corner House, with a strategic shift towards a system with a leading mining house as a holding company and the productive mines as partially or wholly owned subsidiaries. This way of organizing the relationship between the mining and the financial interest came later to be known as the group system (Cartwright 1965, 230, 1967, 126–30; Fraser 1977, 70).

---

[22] Quoted in (Cartwright 1965, 127).
[23] HE 58 n.d.; WB 117, 930117; HE 58, 930311; Annual report of Rand Mines 1894, p. 13.

Rand Mines Limited was launched in February 1893 with a nominal capital of £400,000 in £1 shares.[24] The stated purpose of Rand Mines was to acquire and to develop mining claims and shares in mining companies. The single largest owner was Lionell Phillips (50,000 shares) who was also appointed as the chairman. The Johannesburg interests were also represented by Hermann Eckstein (42,600 shares) and by most of the well-known Randlords (with 500–23,000 shares each). Furthermore, four mining engineers were together allotted 15,000 shares in total. The London interests were represented both by Beit (25,000 shares) and Wernher (25,000 shares) but also by external investors like the Rothschild family (24,000 shares) and Ernest Cassel (6000 shares). The editor of the Johannesburg newspaper *The Star*, Francis Dormer, was also invited in on the ground floor (200 shares). Besides the distribution of ordinary shares, there was also a clause giving Wernher, Beit and Eckstein personally the right to 25 per cent of future profits, after a 100 per cent dividend had been paid out (Kubicek 1979, 64–71; Wheatcroft 1985, 134). Hence, the original ownership was highly concentrated to the Corner House network—with its connections both in the City and in Johannesburg.

By being invited in on the ground floor, and thereby able to acquire shares in the company before the initial public offering, these individuals stood the chance of making substantial economic gains already before the company became publicly traded. Though Rand Mines Limited was not floated at the London Stock Exchange when it was formed, the share seems to have attracted the interest of the financial market. The London Exploration Company was eager to make Rand shares available on the unofficial market in London.[25] There are no official quotations of Rand Mines from this time, but the letters between Johannesburg and London refer to an ongoing (albeit limited) trade.[26] This enables us to reconstruct the development of the company's stock before it was publicly traded (see Fig. 12.1). Given the prices mentioned in these letters, the price of Rand

---

[24] 332,708 shares (out of the 400,000) was issued and fully paid up when the company was formed. The rest of the shares were kept as a reserve. To provide further working capital, debentures were created in 1897 to a value of £1,250,000 (at 5% interest). In 1898, another 4436 shares were issued (at £32), in order to acquire the shares in Rose Deep and Glen Deep (Cartwright 1967, 127–31).
[25] HE 58, 930210.
[26] HE 58, 930303; WB 117, 930602; WB 118, 931202.

12 On the Ground Floor: The Corner House Group

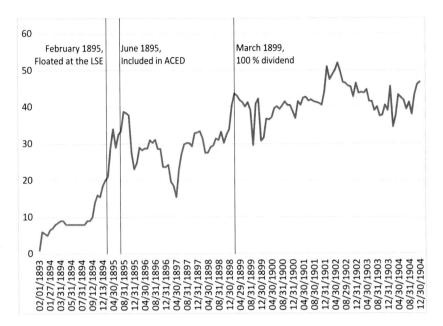

Fig. 12.1 Price quotations for the Rand Mines Limited in London, by month, 1893–1904 (£ sterling, current prices). Source: Letters (February 1893–February 1894), *Financial Times* (FT) (March 1894–May 1895), African Colonial Equities Database (ACED) (June 1895–December 1904). Note: The time series has been adjusted for the split of the stock in 1901. The series are interpolated February 1893 to February 1894 based on letters found in March 1893, June 1893, December 1893 and February 1894)

Mines hovered around £6 after registration—an increase of 500 per cent within a month. The year after, in March 1894, *The Financial Times* included Rand Mines in its reports of African mining shares and under the heading 'Deep-levels to the front' the trade in Rand Mines was now reported to make up a substantial part of the trade conducted.[27]

After its first year of existence, the company had acquired controlling interests in five mines, totalling 1357 claims. After the initial surge in the share price, Rand Mines levelled out during 1894, at around £8.[28] This coincided with a period of highly critical press. In January 1894, *The Economist* published a letter which detailed the background to several of

---
[27] FT 940320.
[28] FT 940305; FT 940530; FT 940815.

the claims owned by the Rand Mines, specifically the Ferreira Gold Mining Company and the Robinson Company. The letter is long and the author is critical of how 'the Rand financiers' enriched themselves at the expense of outside investors.[29] The issue surfaced at the annual meeting of Rand Mines in February 1894, where the well-known Randlord Carl Hanau defended the management and instead accused the press of spreading unjustified critique.[30] It turned out, the critique was not a one-off. It reappeared all the way until September in both local and international press.[31] *The Economist* published an article where the basic argument was that the original allotment of capital in Rand Mines (and most of the Witwatersrand gold companies) was out of proportion and that insiders had been able to dispose much of these shares to unknowing investors in London and on the continent:

> *To take the most flagrant case, that of Rand Mines. [...] This is certainly a novel system of mining finance, and its novelty will scarcely appeal to prudent investors. We have no wish to discourage legitimate mining enterprise, but it is necessary to warn investors and speculators not to rush into a new and dangerous gambling at the bidding of the men who have already enriched themselves so enormously by their connection with the Rand district.*[32]

The bottom line was that the press accused insiders of the Rand Mines to actively hide information from shareholders—for example, the clause that Wernher, Beit & Company were entitled to 25 per cent of the profits (after the owners of the original shares had their first dividend amounting £1 per share). *The Financial Times* also developed a general argument about the asymmetric information position between the insiders in Johannesburg—called 'the ring'—and the outside investors in London. Again, Rand Mines and the Corner House group were identified as the primary examples of these malpractices.[33]

---

[29] *The Economist* 940106. See also (Cartwright 1965, 120–25).
[30] Annual report of Rand Mines 1894, p. 8.
[31] ECO 940310; FT 940320; FT 940407; FT 940621; FT 940628. See also HE 5, 940602.
[32] ECO 940310.
[33] FT 940628.

12 On the Ground Floor: The Corner House Group

During the autumn of 1894, there was a shift in how *The Financial Times* portrayed Rand Mines (and other mines at the Witwatersrand), away from issues of speculation towards a larger emphasis on mining. There was less of overt criticism and the paper stated that the ore in Witwatersrand seemed to be relatively homogenous and possible to mine with large-scale industrial techniques.[34] At the same time, the prices of South African mining shares in general, and Rand Mines in particular, once again soared—from £8 in August to £20 by the end of the year. This was part of the feverish mining mania of the time in the City and other European financial centres. *The Financial Times* noted that there were grounds for optimism, but at the same time, it cautioned against too sharp increases, for the high volatility of mining shares and for the asymmetric information which pertained to all investments in mining ventures.[35] Paris was, according to *The Financial Times*, specifically disadvantaged in terms of access to reliable information. At the same time, *The Financial Times* pointed out the French market as driving the rally in South African mining shares.[36]

The boom was timely for the formal registration of Rand Mines at the London Stock Exchange (see Fig. 12.1). The share stood at £20 when official trading began in February 1895. By the time the company's shares were traded regularly enough to be included in the *Investors' Monthly Manual* in June 1895, the price of the share had increased even further. While the nominal share price was £1, the first observed price of the share at the date it entered our database was a staggering £32.5, and by August 1895, the price peaked at £39. Among all the large companies in our sample, Rand Mines exhibit the largest difference between the market value at the point of introduction in our data and nominal share price. Most other of the large companies in our sample have a first observed price much closer to the nominal share price (with the median ratio, among the large companies, of first observed price relative to the nominal share price approximately three). Only the West African company Ashanti

---

[34] FT 940905; FT 940907.
[35] FT 941030; FT941119.
[36] FT 950108; FT 950924.

Goldfields exhibits a ratio between first observed price and nominal share price of the same magnitude (see Chap. 9).

From September 1895 onwards, financial turbulence increased and prices fell in all mining-related shares in Johannesburg, London and Paris (Wheatcroft 1985, 166). In November, Rand Mines was down to £28 and in December, the Jameson Raid made things even worse. The Johannesburg Stock Exchange virtually ceased to function during January 1896 due to a combination of political turmoil and an interrupted information flow.[37] The weekly letters to London recurrently commented on the unstable telegraphic connection: *East Rands are 93s. this morning, we could have bought a few at this price on your quotation of £5, but in view of the unsatisfactory way the cables are, we thought is better to abstain.*[38] The situation created large uncertainties in the financial market. Different telegraphic routes could be used and the speed varied significantly due to the increased traffic. Already in October, the Johannesburg office wrote to London urging them to use the eastern most connection because it had proven to be 2 to 3 hours faster.[39] Besides technical problems, the British authorities took control of the cables during the height of the crisis:

> *The Stock Exchange was practically closed during the whole time and very little business was transacted. We have been entirely without cable news as regards the condition of the market on your side. And it seems to us tolerably probable that the authorities are keeping our cables back.*[40]

The share price of Rand Mines was down to £23 in December 1895, but in February, the price stabilized again, at around £29. Compared to other mining shares, Rand Mines actually fared relatively well, despite the fact that leading individuals of the Corner House group were deeply involved in the Jameson Raid (Meredith 2007, 323–34). So, while the direct financial effects of the Raid disappeared surprisingly quickly, the general downturn of the mining market continued and affected Rand Mines more. The share price fell back to a low of £15 in April 1897,

---

[37] HE 307, 951220; HE 307, 960111.
[38] HE 307, 951225.
[39] HE 306, 951026.
[40] HE 307, 960111.

before the price recovered. From late 1898 and during the first years of the new century, Rand Mines was again traded at levels around £40.

Though the shareholder register showed signs of dispersal, the original partners retained large holdings of the company throughout the 1890s (Kubicek 1979, 65). Furthermore, the weekly correspondence between the offices in London and Johannesburg for 1895 and 1896 goes into great detail on market conditions and lists the buying and selling of shares of each office.[41] A striking feature of these reports was the relative absence of Rand Mines Limited: the letters rarely mention trade and prices for the company. Instead, companies like East Rand, Randfontein, Jumpers, Ferreira and Bonanzas were frequently reported on. These were companies directly involved in gold mining. After initial financial profits were reaped by the founders in 1893–95, Rand Mines developed into a holding company for a limited circle of mining interest, rather than an object for general speculation. The cautious investment strategy of the Corner House group after 1895 and the relatively stable portfolio of Rand Mines would strengthen such a conclusion.[42] Rand Mines Limited also became an important node for an information flow between London and Johannesburg, regarding both mining development and financial transactions.[43] This is not to say that Rand Mines was marginalized after the 1895–96 boom, but the management of the company seems to have focussed more on the mining business in its portfolio companies (Fraser 1977, 13).

This dual purpose of the company—on the one hand, to act as a vehicle for speculation in mining shares and, on the other hand, to actually develop mining activities—came clearly to the front at the annual meetings of Rand Mines during the 1890s. On the one hand, the managers and the chairman spoke at length on technical issues relating to the development of deep-level mining and the technical competence of its engineers. They went into great detail about boreholes, crushing techniques and how to valuate different claims.[44] On the other hand, the numbers

---

[41] HE 307, various letters.
[42] Annual report of Rand Mines 1896, p. 7 and 1897, p. 7. See also (Kubicek 1979, 82).
[43] HE 58, 930310; HE 306, 950511; HE 140, 970830; HE 64, 980406; HE 64, 980513.
[44] See annual reports of Rand Mines 1893–99.

they presented also showed clearly that the development of the mines took longer than expected and that the profits presented to a large degree came from profitable buying and selling of shares.[45] This was particularly true for the year 1895, when the company declared its first big profit. Of the £952,091 in declared profit, no less than £941,955 came from buying and selling of claims and shares.[46] This is not to say that the actual mining development faired bad, but to develop the deep-level programme was a time- and resource-consuming project. As noted at the annual meeting in January 1897:

> *It will be observed that the past year's estimate of expenditure on the subsidiary mines have been considerably exceeded. The principal causes of this are the longer period of mine development, delays in delivery of machinery, and, in some instances, additions to general plant. Interest charges, which were not included in the estimates, have also been an important factor in causing extra costs. The Native Labour difficulties have also had their effect.*[47]

The Black Labour Question

A profitable mining business demanded different kinds of labour and there was a steady increase in the gold mines' demand for labour during the last decades of the nineteenth century (see Chap. 11). The access to skilled engineers has already been mentioned. Discussions on appropriate candidates for different positions within the Corner House group were a recurrent theme in the London-Johannesburg correspondence.[48] At the other side of the spectrum was the need for manual labour. The strategic problem from the mine owners' point of view was how to secure a steady stream of willing (or forced) workers to dig the mines for low pay (Feinstein 2005, 55).

Given the labour-intensity of the business and the fixed price of gold within the international Gold Standard, the supply of black labour

---

[45] See annual reports of Rand Mines 1893–99.
[46] Annual report of Rand Mines 1895, p. 7.
[47] Annual report of Rand Mines 1897, p. 17.
[48] HE 124, 871219; WB 117, 930203; HE 167, 970730.

12 On the Ground Floor: The Corner House Group

received high priority within the mining community from the 1890s onwards (Webb 1983, 183–84; Feinstein 2005, 55). However, as for the Corner House group, the question did not primarily involve the London office. The company did admit 'difficulties' with the black mine-labourers in some of its annual reports, as noted above. The issue also surfaced a couple of times in the London-Johannesburg correspondence, but mostly in sweeping formulations when there was a general scarcity of black labour.[49] One exception was the correspondence in August 1897, describing an attempt at Witwatersrand mines to substitute skilled miners (often foreigners drawn to South Africa for good pay) with domestic white labour.[50] From the miners' point of view, the possibility to access low-paid white labour was attractive:

> *From this point of view the experiment is a most instructive one and if we can only induce the poor whites of South Africa to take to mining there are quite enough of them in the country to make us wholly independent of the imported miner and to enable us to the solve the question of white wages.*[51]

Though these experiments continued and expanded, these matters were not much discussed between Johannesburg and London. The labour question was instead mostly dealt with as a local South African issue.

This points to another important nexus in the development of the Corner House group—the role played by political lobbying through the Chambers of Mines. Hermann Eckstein was elected as the Chamber's first chairman in 1887—a position he would hold to his resignation in 1893. Lionel Phillips was elected as his successor, and by then, the Corner House had established itself as the leading mining house. Phillips became one of the most powerful men in Johannesburg, until the catastrophic Jameson Raid in 1895–96. During Phillips' chairmanship, the Corner House used the Chamber to consolidate its position further. The Chamber was an important entity for organizing the voice of the often antagonistic mine owners and Corner House developed a strategy in the early years of

---

[49] HE 307, 960215; HE 307, 960222.
[50] HE 140, 970823; HE 140, 970830. See also annual report of Rand Mines 1897, pp. 33–34.
[51] HE 140, 970830.

the 1890s where it sought to strengthen its position by acting as a bridge between the different mines (Cartwright 1965, 103; Fraser 1977, 4–6, 69).

The Chamber of Mines challenged the dynamite monopoly and acted as a lobby force for the building of railways (Fraser 1977, 56,77). Furthermore, the cost of labour was an issue where the Chamber acted to unite the mine owners (Fraser 1977, 38,41; Kubicek 1979, 80; Wheatcroft 1985, 129; Davenport 2013, 233). During the booming years of the late 1880s, the wages for black workers in the mines had risen and during the crisis of 1890, the Chamber took active part in trying to cut down on wages in order to sustain the profitability of the mines. In August 1890, the Chamber agreed with the mine managers of a maximum monthly wage of 40s (down from 63 s per month prior to the crisis). Phillips continued this hard line towards black labour, and the Chamber also persuaded the Boer government in Pretoria to enforce the pass system, which required Africans to obtain a pass that his employer would hold until he was discharged (Wheatcroft 1985, 131; Feinstein 2005, 64). However, the involvement of the Corner House in the Jameson Raid changed the power balance in the Chamber of Mines. Lionel Phillips had to resign from his duties and leave the country (Fraser 1977, 14; Meredith 2007, 323). A few years later, in 1899, the Chamber of Mines was reorganized and the position of the Corner House was not as strong as it had been—though the Chamber of Mines continued to play an important role in South African politics throughout the twentieth century (Davenport 2013, 234).

The First Dividend, the Beginning of the End

In retrospect, the last years of the 1890s became a watershed in the development of Rand Mines, not only because it lost its leading position in the most important lobby organization. These years were also the time when the company's gold production took off. The company had one mine in production in 1896, the year after three more opened, and by 1898, there were in total nine mines in production. The Geldenhuis Deep had opened in late 1892.[52] In a few years, it turned into the first successful deep-level

---

[52] Annual report of Geldenhuis Deep 1893.

project of Rand Mines. The mine was used as an illustrative example in the external communications, and from 1896 onwards, The Geldenhuis Deep paid stable dividends to Rand Mines. To speed up the development of the mines in the portfolio, Rand Mines issued £1 million in 5 per cent bonds in 1897. The issue was placed in both London and Paris.[53]

On the face of it, Rand Mines was on the right track. However, concomitant to the takeoff in gold production, there were several signs of a general weakening of the Corner House group. While the network had used the financial crisis of 1889 to strategically expand and strengthen its position, the Corner House acted more cautiously from the mid-1890s onwards. The leadership of the network was further weakened by the death and retirement of several leading individuals. The effect of this more risk-averse strategy had the long-term effect that the Corner House missed out on the move to new mining sites during the early twentieth century. Besides specific explanations, general trends also affected the Corner House. South African mining, in general, awoke less interest in the City from the turn of the century and the reputation of the Randlords deteriorated (Fraser 1977, 13–14; Kubicek 1979, 69, 84–85).

These processes had financial effects that were important for the analysis of this chapter. The annual meeting in March 1899 accepted the board's suggestion of a dividend of £1 per share. This was the first dividend paid out by Rand Mines. With a share price of around £40, it was not an impressing dividend, but for ground floor participants, it still meant a 100 per cent refund. Even more important, the size of the dividend activated the clause of the original partners' profit-sharing. Furthermore, the share price developed strongly in the year following the dividend. Several of the early investors in Rand Mines sold out in 1899 and in the share-split of 1901. Hence, when the tide started to turn against the Corner House during the first years of the new century, Rand Mines Limited was, in most aspects, a different company compared to what it had been in 1895, and the first generation of insiders had already pocketed substantial profits (Cartwright 1967, 77; Kubicek 1979, 71,77). Cartwright thus estimates that Eckstein & Co made a gross profit of

---

[53] HE 58, 930115; HE 58, 930117; HE 58, 930224; HE 140, 970830; Annual report of Rand Mines 1897, p. 25 and 1898 p. 28. See also (Kubicek 1979, 68).

£10,000,000, when the different sources of income related to Rand Mines were summed up (Cartwright 1965, 132). This was a profit of a totally different magnitude than what an average investor in the company would have been able to pocket.

Conclusion

On the one hand, a picture emerges of a company that was representative of the vibrant, but also highly speculative, London Stock Exchange of the 1890s. On the other hand, Rand Mines was unique in the way the Corner House built up its positions in both Johannesburg and London. The traditional narrative of Rand Mines Limited is that it was a great success. This narrative stands in contrast to the experience of an average investor at the London Stock Exchange, for which the annual return was negative (−0.4 per cent per year) during the first 25 years after the company was officially listed in February 1895.[54] We show in this chapter that the overall explanation to this seemingly contradictory result has to do with the issue of inside and outside investors. We know from earlier research that several of the leading individuals and companies in the Corner House network made fortunes from its investments in Rand Mines. We show in this chapter that this wealth creation rested on positions that were built up during the years leading up to the flotation. Key people were invited to the inner network of the Corner House and to invest on the ground floor in Rand Mines because they possessed some kind of valuable capital. Some were persons with financial capital, such as rich mining magnates and bankers, some were persons with social capital, such as politicians or journalists, and some were also engineers with valuable human capital, such as engineers. All of these groups could make considerable economic gains through various instruments and techniques, such as the allotment of vendor's interests and a founders' shares-clause.

---

[54] This figure is based on the augmented time series which was presented in Fig. 12.1. If our original data is used (starting in June 1895) and if 1920 would be included, then the return would drop to an average of −4.5%. For the whole period 1895–1969, the average return to investors in Rand Mines was 2.3 per cent, well below the return of our overall South African portfolio, see Chap. 7.

We also show why informational asymmetries are yet another key to understand the outcome for different kind of investors. The early access of the Corner House to technical, organizational and financial information could be exploited by those invited in on the ground floor. We know from earlier research that such inside practices were widespread during the South African mining booms around the turn of the century (R. Turrell 1986, 70–72; Van Helten 1990, 166–67; Katzenellenbogen 1990, 128–29). At the same time, insiders did not have a monopoly on the information. There were several other informed agents who resided on the outskirts of the network, including dealers and brokers that the Corner House made frequent business with. The Corner House was, furthermore, as we have shown in this chapter, examined in the contemporary business press and the network was recurrently criticized for its business practices in both London and Paris.

While some inside investors no doubt made great fortunes, it is also beyond doubt that the manual labour force was exploited in terms of poor wages and horrible working conditions (see Chap. 11). But there also existed a number of different layers of actors in between these two extremes, ranging from the supervisors or engineers working in the mines, to the journalists or the stockbrokers working in London. They all benefitted from the operations of Rand Mines through their different associations with the company. Sometimes, these benefits took the form of well-paid jobs, while in other circumstances, the association paid off in the possibility to make money on the financial market thanks to privy information. To fully grasp the return on investment in a company such as Rand Mines, we need to acknowledge this multitude of actors.

References

Cartwright, Alan Patrick. 1965. *The Corner House. The Early History of Johannesburg*. Cape Town: Purnell & Sons.
———. 1967. *Gold Paved the Way: The Story of the Gold Fields Group of Companies*. London: Palgrave Macmillan.
Davenport, Jade. 2013. *Digging Deep: A History of Mining in South Africa, 1852–2002*. Johannesburg: Jonathan Ball Publishers.

Davenport-Hines, R.P.T., and Jean-Jacques Van Helten. 1986. Edgar Vincent, Viscount D'Abernon, and the Eastern Investment Company in London, Constantinople and Johannesburg. *Business History* 28 (1): 35–61.

Dumett, Raymond. 2009. *Mining Tycoons in the Age of Empire, 1870–1945: Entrepreneurship, High Finance, Politics and Territorial Expansion*. Farnham: Ashgate.

Feinstein, Charles. 2005. *An Economic History of South Africa: Conquest, Discrimination and Development*. Cambridge: Cambridge University Press.

Fraser, Maryna. 1977. *All That Glittered. Selected Correspondence of Lionel Phillips 1890–1924*. Cape Town: Oxford University Press.

Gwaindepi, Abel. 2019. *Serving God and Mammon: The 'Minerals-Railway Complex' and Its Effects on Colonial Public Finances in the British Cape Colony, 1810–1910*. African Economic History Network Working Paper Series # 44.

Hannah, Leslie. 2007. Pioneering Modern Corporate Governance: A View from London in 1900. *Enterprise and Society* 8 (3): 642–686.

Harvey, Charles, and Jon Press. 1990. The City and International Mining, 1870–1914. *Business History* 32 (3): 98–119.

Innes, Duncan. 1983. *Anglo American and the Rise of Modern South Africa*. London: Heinemann Educational.

Katzenellenbogen, Simon. 1975. The Miner's Frontier, Transport and General Economic Development. In *Colonialism in Africa, 1870–1960: The Economics of Colonialism*, ed. P. Duignan and L.H. Gann, 360–426. Cambridge: Cambridge University Press.

———. 1990. Southern African Mining Interests in Australia Before 1939. *Business History* 32 (3): 120–132.

Kubicek, Robert. 1979. *Economic Imperialism in Theory and Practice*. Durham, NC: Duke University Center for International Studies Publication.

Meredith, Martin. 2007. *Diamonds, Gold and War: The Making of South Africa*. London: Simon & Schuster.

Newbury, Colin. 1981. Out of the Pit: The Capital Accumulation of Cecil Rhodes. *The Journal of Imperial and Commonwealth History* 10 (1): 25–49.

———. 1987. The Origins and Function of the London Diamond Syndicate, 1889–1914. *Business History* 29 (1): 5–26.

Phimister, Ian. 1988. *An Economic and Social History of Zimbabwe, 1890–1948: Capital Accumulation and Class Struggle*. London: Longman.

Richardson, Peter, and Jean-Jacques Van Helten. 1984. The Development of the South African Gold-Mining Industry, 1895–1918. *The Economic History Review* 37 (3): 319–340.

Turrell, Rob. 1986. Sir Frederic Philipson Stow: The Unknown Diamond Magnate. *Business History* 28 (1): 62–79.

Turrell, Robert Vicat, and Jean-Jacques Van Helten. 1986. The Rothschilds, the Exploration Company and Mining Finance. *Business History* 28 (2): 181–205.

Van Helten, Jean-Jacques. 1990. Mining, Share Manias and Speculation: British Investment in Overseas Mining, 1880–1913. In *Capitalism in a Mature Economy: Financial Institutions, Capital Exports and British Industry, 1870–1939*, ed. Jean-Jacques Van Helten and Youssef Cassis, 159–185. Aldershot: Edward Elgar.

Webb, Arthur. 1983. Mining in South Africa. In *Economic History of South Africa*, ed. Francis Coleman. Pretoria: Haum.

Wheatcroft, Geoffrey. 1985. *The Randlords: The Men Who Made South Africa*. London: Weidenfeld and Nicolson.

Additional Sources

Archive (Barlow Rand Archive, Johannesburg, South Africa).
WB (Wernher, Beit & Co), volume 117 to 173.
HE (H. Eckstein & Co), volume 5 to 307.
Annual Reports of Rand Mines Limited, 1893 to 1899.
Annual Report of Geldenhuis Deep Limited, 1893.

Business Press

ECO (*The Economist*), various issues 1894.
FT (*Financial Times*), various issues 1894 and 1895.

13

Imperial Profit

The Colonization of Egypt

As described in Chap. 8, British forces occupied Egypt in 1882. Egypt has been given an important role in the historiography of the Scramble for Africa, as scholars have claimed that this particular occupation opened the gates for further colonization. The reason why the United Kingdom occupied Egypt has been debated. Early scholars claimed that Egypt was occupied largely in the interest of foreign bondholders (see Platt 1968, 154–55, for an overview of the discussion). This thesis was criticized by scholars who believed that financial interests were of little or no importance for the British decision to occupy Egypt. Instead, they argue that the decision to do so was taken primarily based on the strategic interest in controlling the Suez Canal. Desmond Platt was one of the most outspoken critics of the thesis of economic imperialism in Egypt, arguing that it merely was 'folk-lore' (Platt 1968, 156, see also pp. 179–180; Tignor 1966, 11; Robinson and Gallagher 1968, 156–59; Schölch 1976, 776; Harrison 1995, 98; B. Porter 2012, 83). More recent scholars have, despite such criticism, maintained that financial interests—that is, banks engaged in Egypt—were in favour of the British occupation of Egypt and

© The Author(s) 2019
K. Rönnbäck, O. Broberg, *Capital and Colonialism*, Palgrave Studies in Economic History, https://doi.org/10.1007/978-3-030-19711-7_13

actively influenced the decision to do so. They argue that there was no strategic motive for Britain to occupy Egypt at the time. As Cain and Hopkins have put it, 'The disorder they [the British government] feared was financial; and fiscal anarchy was a moral issue, not just an economic one. Resolving the confusions of Egyptian finances became, for Gladstone, a "holy subject"—and thus a matter of principle. The Suez Canal was not at risk in 1882' (Cain and Hopkins 2001, 316; see also others, e.g. Farnie 1969, 292; Chamberlain 1976, 240–41; Galbraith and al-Sayyid-Marsot 1978, 473–74; Hopkins 1986, 377; Vatikiotis 1991, 139–41; Pakenham 1991, 124; see also Platt 1968, 154–56, for an overview over previous scholars arguing along similar lines).

The scholarly debate on why Egypt was occupied can be boiled down to a discussion over the relative importance of financial and geopolitical/strategic motives. Data from the London Stock Exchange can potentially shed further light on this debate.

Figure 13.1 shows data on the closing price the last day of every month for the three most important Egyptian stocks traded on the London

Fig. 13.1 Price quotations for Egyptian equity on the London Stock Exchange, by month, 1870–1885 (index 1881 m1 = 100, current prices). Source: African Colonial Equities Database (ACED)

Stock Exchange—the Suez Canal Company and the two major foreign-owned Egyptian banks. Both of the latter were involved in the lending of money to the Egyptian government. The period in the figure covers the critical period leading up to the occupation and the years immediately following the occupation.

The Egyptian government's lending spree during the 1860s was apparently positive for the investors in Egyptian banks lending to the Egyptian government—share prices were increasing until the early 1870s. However, as government debt reached unsustainable levels, share prices in these companies stagnated or started to decline around 1873–1874. In November 1875, the Egyptian government sold off its shares in the Suez Canal Company (see Chap. 8). According to Douglas Farnie, this led to a massive rush for Egyptian stocks (Farnie 1969, 233)—though no such rush is apparent in our dataset. The share prices of both banks increased marginally during that particular month compared to the month of October, before they started to decrease. In the case of the Anglo-Egyptian Bank, there was in contrast a drastic decrease of the share price in the following months, as can be seen in Fig. 13.1. Investors did possibly not consider the sell-off of Suez Canal Company shares enough to get public finances in order and feared that debt repayments would be reneged upon. In November 1876, Dual Control was imposed on the Egyptian economy (see Chap. 8). The share prices of the banks nonetheless continued to drop. The decrease in their share prices was—at least in the case of the Anglo-Egyptian Bank—not as drastic as in the previous years. This might be an indication that the intervention was considered positive but insufficient by the British investors.

Through most of these events, the share price of the Suez Canal Company remained remarkably stable. The British government purchased the Egyptian government's shares in the company in November 1875. Contemporary observers did not miss the significance of this event. In 1875, Gladstone criticized the purchase of shares in the company, believing that this in time could become a cause for intervention in, to be followed by colonization of, North Africa—a policy with which Gladstone did not particularly agree (Robinson and Gallagher 1968, 92). Disraeli's Lord Chancellor argued along similar lines. The fact that the British government henceforth owned shares in the company would make a military occupation—should any such be necessary—a matter of 'defending our own property', rather than a matter of taking possession of the property of others, as would otherwise have been the case (quoted in B. Porter 2012, 82). This intervention, as well as the Dual Control imposed in the following year, had minor effects upon the company's share price. The share price fluctuated around £27–30 from 1875 to January 1880. There is no evidence of any rush in November 1875 for this stock either. At the same time, the following stability is perhaps not so surprising, as there is no indication in the previous literature that the Suez Canal Company was under any threat of nationalization during this period, despite the Egyptian government's troubled finances.

In April 1879, the *khedive* (vice king) of Egypt, Isma'il Pasha, attempted to regain control over Egyptian public finances by ousting the Dual Control, only to be formally deposed by the Ottoman authorities—after an imperialist intervention by the British government—in June the same year. He was replaced by the new khedive Tewfik Pasha (see Chap. 8). This, finally, changed the downward trend for the share prices of the major Egyptian banks, as can be seen in Fig. 13.1. The share prices of the banks started to increase already during the second half of 1879, an indication that the investors held hopes that the new khedive also would be more agreeable to their interests. By 1880, any positive effects that the investors anticipated from the imposed regime change had been exhausted, and the share prices of the banks stagnated.

The British-imposed regime under Tewfik Pasha was, in contrast, positive for the investors in the Suez Canal Company. As is shown in Fig. 13.1, the share price of the Suez Canal rose drastically during the spring of 1880 and continued to do so until December 1881. But the imposition of the khedive created resistance and an Egyptian nationalist movement started to rise already in 1879. By 1881, the movement was so influential that it again stoked fears among the foreign investors that a nationalist regime would not only repudiate any foreign debt repayments, and thereby inflict major losses upon the banks that had lent the money to the Egyptian regime, but potentially also renege upon other agreements—including the agreements concerning Suez Canal. This was unacceptable to foreign interests. In November and December 1881, the British and French governments started to talk about taking action to uphold the khedive Tewfik, if necessary. This ended with the famous

Joint Note of January 1882, where the two governments expressed their support for the khedive Tewfik (see Chap. 8).

The threat of a British-French intervention impacted the companies differently. The share prices of the Egyptian banks fell slowly during this period. The share price of the Suez Canal Company, in contrast, experienced a remarkable rush—with the share price almost doubling in the two final months of 1881. This can partly be explained by over-optimistic expectations, which is shown by the fact that the share price fell back in the following month of January 1882. Even when accounting for this, the increase in the share price was substantial. The eventful spring of 1882 caused considerable fluctuations in the price of Egyptian equity, most importantly of the Suez Canal Company.

The military occupation of Egypt in July and August 1882 coincided with an immediate increase in the price of all three stocks shown in Fig. 13.1. The rise was not as drastic as the sudden spike experienced by the Suez Canal Company in November-December of 1881, but still not negligible. In the following months, share prices for all three Egyptian companies studied in Fig. 13.1 declined, as the conflict created much uncertainty for the investors. By mid-1884, investors seemed confident that the occupation was successful from the British imperial point of view. The decline in share prices was turned around, and the prices of Egyptian equity started to experience a long period of increase (see Chap. 8). Figure 13.2 shows monthly data on the accumulated return on investment before and after the occupation of Egypt, in a somewhat longer perspective.

The sudden increase in the market value of the Suez Canal Company, beginning in early 1880, some months after the imposition of Tewfik Pasha, shows up clearly in Fig. 13.2. As investors started to anticipate a further British intervention in Egypt during the last months of 1881, share prices skyrocketed (as was shown in Fig. 13.1)—something which also becomes apparent in the accumulated return on investment in Fig. 13.2. This development in 1880 and 1881 provided a massive, but temporary, boost to the accumulated return on investment in Egypt. This was followed by a few years of declining share prices of the Egyptian companies, following the actual occupation of Egypt, which again is reflected in the accumulated return on investment shown in Fig. 13.2.

Fig. 13.2 Accumulated return on investment in Egypt, by month, 1874–1890 (index, January 1882 = 100, logarithmic scale). Source: African Colonial Equities Database (ACED)

From 1884 onwards, the trend turned positive again. The long-term trends to the return on investment were, from this time onwards, not drastically different from the trend in the data during the time prior to the imposition of Tewfik Pasha. The share prices of the Egyptian companies did never drop back down to pre-intervention levels, but they remained on a significantly higher level than before the imposition of Tewfik Pasha. Seen over a longer period, the British interventions in Egypt clearly boosted the return on investment in the country.

The Suez Canal's strategic position was, undoubtedly, an important factor behind the British decision to intervene in Egyptian politics and finally to occupy the country. The previous literature's controversy between geopolitical/strategic or financial interests as the ultimate driving force behind the occupation of Egypt has largely neglected one key aspect of the process: the major investments involved in the Suez Canal Company, and in particular, the fact that the British Government itself became a major investor in the company. Interventions in, and the following occupation of, Egypt to safeguard the canal from being expropriated by Egyptian nationalists became an issue of defending British investments in general, and the investments of the British Government in particular.

The South African War

The South African War of 1899–1902 was used already by Hobson as the archetype of an imperialist war driven by financial interests (Hobson 1900, 229–40, 1988, 98). The control over the gold-mining complex in Witwatersrand was a key issue in the conflict, according to this line of thought. The gold-bearing region was under the jurisdiction of the Boer-controlled South African Republic and therefore outside British jurisdiction, despite the substantial British interests in the mining ventures (see Chap. 11). The role that 'uitlanders' (foreigners) were allowed to play in the republic became a bone of contention between the British and the Boers. What role different interests played for the outbreak of the war has since generated considerable debate among scholars (see, e.g. Robinson and Gallagher 1968, 457–61; Pakenham 1979, 111–14; Hobsbawm 1987, 66; Pakenham 1991, 558–64; Jeeves 1996; Wesseling 1996, 316–19; Darwin 1997, 641; A. Porter 2000, 637; Cain and Hopkins 2001, 324–27; Pretorius 2014, 239–41).

What has been lacking in this debate is a quantitative analysis of what the South African War actually implied for British investors in South Africa. Our data can help shed light on this issue. Figure 13.3 shows the accumulated return on investment in South African finance and gold companies, monthly from January 1895 (i.e. some months prior to the Jameson Raid of December 1895) to December 1905 (a couple of years after the end of the South African War).

The Jameson Raid took place from 29 December 1895 to 2 January 1896, with the aim of rousing a rebellion among the 'uitlanders' against the Boer regime (Pakenham 1991, 489–90; Wesseling 1996, 305–9). As the raid failed, it does not seem to have had much discernible impact for the London investors. Share prices dropped around this time, but this can primarily be explained by the general turning tide of the London

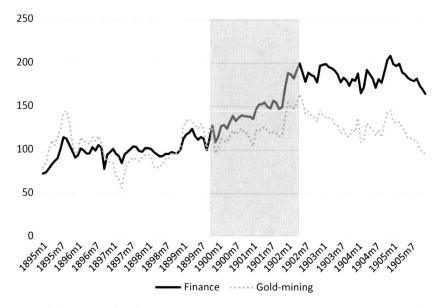

Fig. 13.3 Accumulated return on investment in South Africa, by month, 1895–1905 (index, September 1899 = 100). Source: African Colonial Equities Database (ACED). Note: The shaded area shows the period of the South African War, from October 1899 to May 1902

Stock Exchange which set in prior to the raid—when the previous boom in South African mining companies came to a full stop during the autumn of 1895. Not even the gold company which was most heavily involved in the actual execution of the raid—the Rand Mines Limited—suffered to any great extent in terms of share price during the raid (see Chap. 12). The 18 months following the raid was a period when share prices readjusted downwards in the wake of 1894–1895 mania. The general price fall in South African mining equity happened, despite the fact that the gold mining as a business was in an expansionary phase, with rapidly increasing production figures for each year (see Chaps. 11 and 12).

The outbreak of the South African War occurred on 11 October 1899, after a period of building up for a war (Wesseling 1996, 321). The immediate outbreak of the war seems to have been received positively by London investors in South African equity, as share prices increased substantially in that particular month. Investors in South

African gold-mining companies earned a return of 26 per cent in October 1899, and investors in South African finance companies earned a 14 per cent return on their investments in the same month.

These gains were short-lived, as can be seen in Fig. 13.3. In the following two months, the Boer forces were advancing on the British (Pakenham 1991, 567–70; Wesseling 1996, 321–23). The British military losses were directly reflected in the share prices of South African companies, and the quick profits following the outbreak of the war were consequently obliterated in the following months. This was particularly salient for investments in gold-mining companies, where share prices dropped below pre-war levels.

The Boer victories were short-lived. From January to September 1900, the tide of the war changed, and British forces started to advance on the Boers (Pakenham 1991, 571–75; Wesseling 1996, 323–25). Again, share prices of South African stocks followed suit, as British investors again started to hope for what, from their perspective, would be a positive outcome. By June 1900, Johannesburg and Pretoria had been captured by the British. From an investor's perspective, the war was essentially won, and the Rand had largely been saved from any sabotage—which had been a plan in case the British would be victorious (Pakenham 1979, 432). After this began the third phase of the war—the protracted guerilla warfare by the Boers—which continued until peace finally was agreed upon in May 1902 (Wesseling 1996, 325–26). Despite the atrocities of the imperial warfare, which was acknowledged and criticized in the press all over Europe, London investors seem to have remained positive throughout this phase of the war. The accumulated return on investment in South African mining equity continued to grow, in particularly between December 1901 and January 1902, when it became increasingly clear that the British forces eventually would come out victorious from the guerilla war as well. This was also the time when the horrible conditions in the British concentration camps used against the Boers were revealed—facts that obviously had limited impact on the sentiments of the financial market (Pakenham 1991, 578–79).

Hence, no wonder that London stockbrokers could be found to be jubilant by the end of the war, as the London Illustrated News depicted them (see picture on page 379). Not only did the British come out victorious, thereby safeguarding British investors from destruction or expropriation. They had also been able to gain a high return on investment during the years of war. When peace was finally declared on 31 May 1902, investors in South African gold companies had earned a nominal accumulated return on investment of 64 per cent relative to September 1899, that is, prior to the outbreak of the war. Investors in South African financial companies (heavily involved directly and indirectly in the mining business) made even larger gains, earning a nominal return on their investments of 100 per cent relative to the pre-war level of September 1899. Given the low rate of inflation in these years, the average real annual rate of return translated into 8 per cent per year for South African gold-mining companies and 17 per cent per year for investments in South African finance companies. These private gains had come at an enormous cost to the British Treasury, which had to foot the £217 million bill for the massive military intervention as well as to more than 20,000 dead British soldiers (Pakenham 1979, 572; A. Porter 2000, 635).

In hindsight, it is possible to see that, had the London investors been able to foresee the future better, they would not have been as jubilant. Victory in the war would not be enough to safeguard the profits of the gold-mining companies. Despite continued increases in production, the declaration of peace in May 1902 marked the zenith in terms of the accumulated return on investment for investments in South African gold mining for years to come. By the end of 1905, losses had accumulated due to falling share prices to such an extent that all the gains that the London investors had made during the South African War were gone.

The Value of a Royal Charter

Direct military intervention, as in Egypt, was not necessarily the United Kingdom's first-hand choice during the Scramble for Africa. Sometimes, the UK government allowed private interests to undertake the actual process of colonization by granting special charters to specific companies. The costs of colonization could thereby be privatized. This had been common practice at earlier times in British imperial history, with the most famous example being the British East India Company. The value of such a charter varied considerably. Some charters enabled companies to earn considerable economic rents, while there are also examples of chartered companies that failed to make any substantial profits (Carlos and Nicholas 1988; Jones and Ville 1996). The value of receiving a charter did depend upon the context and the content of the charter.

During the Scramble for Africa, the United Kingdom most importantly granted charters to three companies: the Royal Niger Company, operating in current-day Nigeria (Flint 1960; Baker 1996); the Imperial British East Africa Company, operating in current-day Kenya (Galbraith 1972), and the British South Africa Company, operating in current-day Zambia and Zimbabwe (Galbraith 1973, 1974; Flint 1976). Of these three companies, two appear in our sample of companies—the Royal Niger Company and the British South Africa Company.

The charters of both these companies bore similarities (Flint 1960, 85–87; Galbraith 1974, 121–22; Flint 1976, 118–19; Rotberg 1988, 285–87). The companies were charged with administrative powers to maintain law and order in the occupied territories. They were given certain specific tasks, such as to abolish the slave trade. The companies were also granted the right to expand their territories geographically, if local rulers agreed to this. As for the companies' privileges, these were actually few: the charters did not include any clauses creating legal monopolies in either territory. One economic boon of receiving the charter seems to have been that the companies were allowed to levy customs duties in order to pay for any necessary costs of governing the territory. Both companies were also allowed to retain the full benefits from any agreement entered into with local rulers in their respective regions of operation.

Eventually, both companies were to lose their charters. In the case of the Royal Niger Company, this occurred in January 1900 when the British government took over administrative control of the Nigerian territory and declared it a protectorate. In the case of the British South Africa Company, this occurred during the autumn of 1923 after demands for self-government by the white settler minority. In both cases, the companies were compensated economically for the loss of their charters and for the administrative costs that they had carried for several years: £0.865 million to the Royal Niger Company, and £3.75 million to the British South Africa Company (Flint 1960, 307–8; Slinn 1971, 370–72; Pedler 1974, 137).

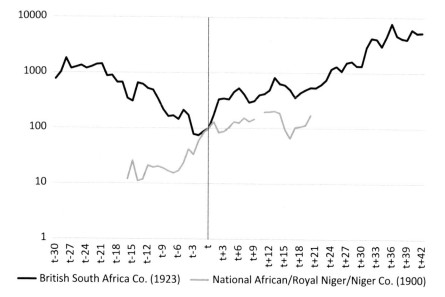

Fig. 13.4 Accumulated return on investment for the British South Africa and Royal Niger Companies during chartered and post-chartered periods, by year, 1883–1965 (index, year charter ended = 100, logarithmic scale). Source: African Colonial Equities Database (ACED). Note: In the case of RNC, 1899 is treated as the last year of the charter, whereas in the case of BSAC, 1923 is treated as the last year of the charter, as the charter in the latter case was revoked effectively first by the end of the year

So, how valuable were the charters to these companies? In Fig. 13.4, we show the accumulated return on investment in these two chartered companies, before and after the charters were revoked.

As can be seen in the figure, investments in the two companies experienced drastically different historical trajectories. In the case of the Royal Niger Company, the return on investment was initially around zero, before taking off during the 1890s, when the company was able to gain monopoly profits after having entered into a cartel agreement regarding trade in the Nigerian territory with its main competitor (see Chap. 9). After the charter was revoked, the return on investment fell to a lower level, but the return did at least remain positive for some time after the charter had been revoked.

In the case of the British South Africa Company, the period of chartered rule of Rhodesia was catastrophic from the perspective of the investors. High administrative costs and limited economic activity that could generate economic rents to the company meant that the company was operating at a loss for several decades (see Chap. 10). Once the company had been relieved of the administrative burden of the territory, things changed drastically. Actually, the company turned into a highly profitable investment once the charter had been revoked.

At a glance, the charters do therefore not seem to have had any direct importance for neither of the two chartered companies. This conclusion would be too simplified. What the charters most importantly did for the companies was to recognize treaties that the companies supposedly had entered into with local rulers. The hundreds of agreements that the Royal Niger Company's predecessor (the National African Company) had entered into with local rulers supposedly granted the company substantial land and mineral rights in the territories in question and the right to exclude foreigners from these territories (see Chap. 9). The British South Africa Company had likewise entered into several agreements, including the so-called 'Rudd Concession' and 'Lochner Concession', which supposedly granted land and mineral rights to that company (see Chap. 10). Even though these agreements were seriously contested already at the time, and might seem highly dubious to a modern-day observer, the UK government in practice accepted the claims of the companies that they were legitimate. In both cases, the negotiated land rights were not revoked along with the charters. It was also, to a great extent, thanks to these rights that the companies—and most prominently the British South Africa Company—were able to make substantial profits even after the charters had been revoked.

Different Types of Colonies

As was described in Chap. 5, scholars have suggested classifying colonies into different types. A crucial distinction has been between settler and non-settler colonies, since it has been argued that the governments established in African settler colonies as a rule tried to impose low-paid labour policies, often including various measures of coercion, in contrast to non-settler colonies where this was of less importance (Austin, Frankema, and Jerven 2017, 13; Austin 2016, 324–25). It has been argued by other scholars—most importantly, scholars from the dependency school—that these coercive measures were also important for the profitability of the companies involved in such types of colonies (see Chap. 3). Hence, the distinction might be fruitful for an analysis of these institutions' impact upon our estimated return on investment. Figure 13.5 therefore shows the accumulated return on investment in settler versus non-settler colonies in Africa.

As can be seen in the figure, the return on investment did not seem to differ much between the settler and non-settler colonies during the first two decades, with estimated average return on investment in the range of 12–14 per cent per year for settler and non-settler colonies alike. In the case of the non-settler colonies, this is largely attributable to the high return of the Suez Canal Company, which at the time dominated the

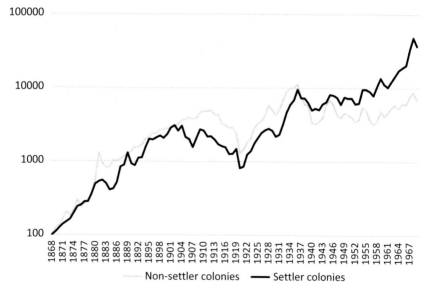

Fig. 13.5 Accumulated return on investment by type of colony, by year, 1869–1969 (index, 1868 = 100). Source: African Colonial Equities Database (ACED)

sample. As was noted previously in this chapter, the return on investment was particularly high in connection with the British occupation of Egypt. This can be seen in the figure on accumulated return on investment in the form of the sudden jump in the series in 1881–1882. In the settler colonies, the high rate of return on investment is mainly attributable to the South African mining boom and the high return on investment associated with this boom in other sectors of the economy, such as the financial sector, as well (see Chap. 11). One consequence of this mining boom was that the accumulated return on investment in settler colonies caught up with the accumulated return on investment in non-settler colonies during the second half of the 1880s.

During the 1890s, the rates of return on investment were similar in the settler and non-settler colonies. This changed in the first decade of the twentieth century. The estimates for non-settler colonies were still dominated by the return on investment in the Suez Canal Company. The company experienced a steady growth in the number of passages through the Canal during the first decade of the twentieth century, and thereby growth in the revenues received (see Chap. 8). The South African mining industry, in contrast, experienced a more problematic start of the new century, which lowered the return on investment for our sample of settler colonies. To a lesser extent, the costly early development of the Rhodesian colonies by the British South Africa Company during the same period also reduced the average return on investment in settler colonies (see Chap. 10). The return on investment in settler colonies therefore decreased to around 3 per cent per year during the first decade of the 1900s, compared to 5 per cent for non-settler colonies.

In the 1910s, the return on investment was again similar between the two types of colonies. The First World War thus inflicted substantial losses for investors in ventures throughout the continent, so that the average return on investment during the 1910s was around −6 per cent per year for both types of colonies. The interwar period in contrast exhibited substantial recovery in many of the colonies—not the least in Egypt, and several settler colonies (see Chaps. 8, 9, 10 and 11). The recovery was the strongest in Egypt, which is why the return on investment averaged almost 8 per cent per year during the decade in the non-settler colonies compared to the settler economies' average of 6 per cent per year. In the

West African non-settler colonies, the return to peace after the First World War did mainly led to a situation of fierce competition between some of the major trading companies, with the results of a continued negative average return on investment (−2 per cent per year) during the period.

From the 1930s onwards, the pattern shifted substantially. The return on investment in non-settler colonies deteriorated drastically compared to the previous decade, exhibiting a real rate of return of 1 per cent per year on average during the 1930s and decreasing even further to −2 per cent per year on average during the 1940s. The rate of return recovered in the 1950s and 1960s, reaching a moderate average rate of return of 3.5 per cent per year during the 1960s. This is attributable to a number of factors. One the one hand, one key factor increased the return on investment in non-settler colonies: a shift towards investments in mining. By the 1930s, the nature of the investment in the West African non-settler colonies had changed compared to the nature of the portfolio in previous years. Virtually all of the old trading and shipping companies had been merged into larger companies before being incorporated as a branch of a major multinational company by the late 1920s, leading to their disappearance from the sample. The limited number of these companies that remained in our sample played a marginal role. The portfolio of investments in the West African non-settler colonies were dominated by investments in mining from this time onwards—gold and diamond mines on the Gold Coast and tin mines in Nigeria (see Chap. 9). There were, on the other hand, factors decreasing the return on investment in the non-settler colonies, most importantly (the fear of), decolonization. Investments in Egypt experienced drastic losses on average from the 1930s onwards, to a large extent, due to the major losses experienced by the Suez Canal Company in the run up to the Second World War. The fear of nationalizations in post-war Egypt, and the fact that the Suez Canal was de facto nationalized in the 1950s ascertained that investments in Egypt would continue to make a loss for several decades further (see Chap. 8).

At the same time, investments in the settler colonies developed strongly, with an average rate of return of 9 per cent per year during the 1930s. The

Second World War decreased the rate of return during the 1940s (down to 2 per cent per year on average during this decade), but the rate of return recovered in the 1950s (to 6 per cent) and increased further in the 1960s (to 11 per cent per year). This very high rate of return is partly attributable to the development of new ventures, such as the development of the Copperbelt in Northern Rhodesia and new locations for gold mining in South Africa (see Chaps. 10 and 11). Other explanations were the definite abandonment of the Gold Standard and the development of the Central Selling Organization in diamonds, both of which further benefitted the investors in settler colonies.

The return on investment was also an effect of the coercive industrial relations in the settler colonies. Over time, the level of coercion increased substantially (see Chaps. 10 and 11). In South Africa, the Native Lands' Act of 1913 severely curtailed the economic options available for large segments of the black population in South Africa. At the same time, discrimination of black labourers increased, for example, by monopsony hiring of labourers through the Witwatersrand Native Labour Association. Similar processes took place in both Southern and Northern Rhodesia beginning in the 1930s with institutional changes imposed in order to provide white-run companies with low-paid labour. With wage costs being kept down by discriminatory institutions, it does not seem far-fetched to interpret these figures as if these institutions should have impacted upon the rate of return on investment in the settler colonies (see, e.g. Feinstein 2005, 109–12).

Over the whole period, there is no straightforward pattern of higher return on investment in settler colonies compared to non-settler colonies. On the contrary, return on investment was similar in both types of colonies for much of the period, with some temporary exceptions for particular events (e.g. the British occupation of Egypt discussed above). From the 1940s onwards, the accumulated return on investment started to diverge. It does not seem far-fetched to conclude that this divergence, at least partially, was associated with the more widespread and intensified coercion of the labour force developing in both South Africa and Rhodesia during that period.

Decolonization in Africa and the Return on Investment

Decolonization had substantial implications in several of the countries studied here. In countries like current-day Zimbabwe and South Africa, decolonization was a complex and drawn-out process. Political independence might have been achieved on paper but hardly in reality, making it problematic to date when actual independence was achieved (Wickins 1986, 204). In South Africa, for example, the Union of South Africa was established in 1910, self-governance was achieved in 1931, the Republic of South Africa declared in 1961, but majority rule was first achieved in 1994. These institutional changes impacted the companies operating in South Africa in different ways. As the self-governing, and later completely independent, pre-democratic governments were staunchly pro-capitalist, there were hardly any fears that self-governance or political independence from the British government was any threat to foreign investors. During the period of our study, the return on investment in South Africa therefore seems to have been affected more by other types of external shocks—such as the First and Second World Wars, or the abandonment of the Gold Standard—than by these institutional changes (see Chap. 11).

In other cases, it is easy to pinpoint a particular breaking point when political independence was achieved, for example, in Egypt after the revolution in 1952, in Ghana in 1957, in Nigeria and Belgian Congo in 1960 and in Zambia in 1964. Current-day Zimbabwe achieved real political independence after the period of our study, but in 1965, the white minority regime unilaterally declared independence from the British Empire. The process of decolonization in these countries was widely anticipated by foreign actors. There was also a widespread fear that political independence might spell the end of operations in Africa, as radical nationalists might be inclined to expropriate foreign assets—in particular, assets owned by agents from the imperial power. Companies operating in different colonies therefore attempted to 'africanize' their operations in various ways, as a means to safeguard their operations against nationalizations (see, e.g. Chaps. 8 and 9).

Since political independence generally was anticipated by the investors, and because they all exhibited a distinct political break at independence, stock exchange data can shed light on what impact the process of decolonization had on the investors in the respective colonies. In previous research on Belgian Congo, Buelens and Marysse have shown that falling share prices during the last years of Belgian rule entailed substantial losses for Belgian colonial investors (Buelens and Marysse 2009, table 2). Figure 13.6 shows data on the accumulated return on investment for British investors for the ten years prior to and following political independence in three key states in North and West Africa: Egypt, Ghana and Nigeria.

The United Kingdom unilaterally declared Egypt independent in 1922, but in reality the United Kingdom remained in control of several aspects of Egyptian politics, and in particular, in control of the Suez Canal. Egypt therefore did not achieve effective independence until the political revolution in 1952 (see Chap. 8). The end of the Second World

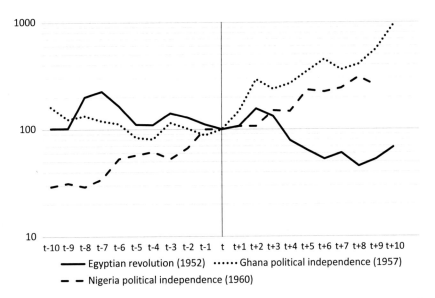

Fig. 13.6 Accumulated return on investment prior to and following political independence in Egypt, Ghana and Nigeria, by year (index, year of independence = 100, logarithmic scale). Source: African Colonial Equities Database (ACED)

War in North Africa improved the economic conditions for Egyptian companies listed in London (particularly the Suez Canal). Soon after the war, however, the anticipation of a coming political independence put the accumulated return on investment in Egypt on a downward trend. The portfolio seems to have recovered in the immediate aftermath of the political revolution. Once the new Egyptian regime started to nationalize foreign companies in 1956, the accumulated return on investment dropped again. The payment of compensation for the assets expropriated from the Suez Canal Company would finally put a stop to the drop in the share price.

Ghana achieved political independence in 1957, and the Convention People's Party that got into power was officially a socialist party (see Chap. 9). Investors in the colony would reasonably have feared that nationalizations might start to occur once independence was achieved. The accumulated return on investment therefore also decreased substantially over the decade prior to independence—at a time when economies were recovering in the aftermath of the Second World War. However, the Nkrumah government did not nationalize any foreign assets coercively. When investors realized (and trusted) this, share prices started to increase. The effect was a rapid increase in the accumulated return on investment in the period after political independence in Ghana.

In Nigeria, many foreign companies had 'africanized' their operations substantially by the time of independence. Companies present in the colony were furthermore operating businesses with comparatively few geographically fixed assets that easily could be nationalized (such as banking, trading and shipping) (see Chap. 9). It is for these reasons not surprising that investors do not seem to have anticipated any major disruptions from political independence in Nigeria; the accumulated return on investment in the colony continued to increase up until political independence. No financial disruptions seem to have been forthcoming after independence either, and the accumulated return on investment thereby continued to increase after independence as well.

In Fig. 13.7, we study the impact of decolonization in three countries in Central/Southern Africa: Belgian Congo, Zambia and Southern Rhodesia. In Belgian Congo, decolonization indeed had substantial effects. Few people seem to have anticipated decolonization until a few

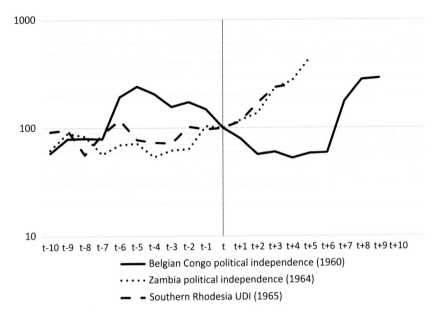

Fig. 13.7 Accumulated return on investment prior to and following political independence in Belgian Congo, Zambia and Southern Rhodesia, by year (index, year of independence = 100, logarithmic scale). Source: African Colonial Equities Database (ACED). Note: All data are for portfolios representing all equity investments in each respective colony/country, except in the case of Belgian Congo, which is based on the sole company of Tanganyika Concessions. As was shown in Fig. 6.8, the return on investment in this particular company seems to match the return on investment for the Belgian portfolio of investments studied by Buelens and Marysse quite well

years prior to its realization. This fits well with what is known about the independence movement, making its first appearances in 1956 (see Chap. 10). It is also from this time onwards that the accumulated return on investment in the colony took a turn downwards. After independence, demands for Katangan secession, general political instability during the Congo Crisis and further fears of nationalizations meant that the return on investment in Belgian Congo continued to be negative for some years, with accumulated return on investment reaching nadir by 1962. These results mirror the results arrived at by Buelens and Marysse in their previous study on the return on investment in Belgian Congo. As their study ended in 1962, they were unable to study what happened to the investments in the following years. In 1967, the new military regime under Joseph Mobutu went ahead with nationalizations of foreign assets. As the Zaïrian government (as the country now was called) was pressured by the United States to pay compensation to the owners, the accumulated return on investment in Tanganyika Concessions actually exhibited a drastic recovery that year.

In Zambia, political independence was achieved in 1964. On the day before independence, the British South Africa Company lost its mineral rights in the colony. Since the company, by that time, had no other major assets, it was eventually dissolved. For investors in that company, decolonization thus had a major negative impact. For fear of antagonizing foreign investors, the Zambian nationalist movement explicitly promised not to nationalize any foreign-owned mining industries. Though the newly formed government reneged on this promise in 1969, the investors were compensated for this expropriation in the form of bonds in the newly established state-owned mining company Zambia Industrial and Mining Corp (ZIMCO) (see Chap. 10). During the period of our study, the return on investment was therefore not negatively impacted by decolonization, but on the contrary, experienced a high return on investment still in the years following independence. It was only in the following decade, after the end of our study, that the compensation paid to the previous owners turned out to be less valuable than originally anticipated, with deteriorating bond values as a result.

In Southern Rhodesia, finally, increasing tensions in the 1950s and 1960s seem to have led to stagnating return on investment. The white minority regime's unilateral declaration of independence in 1965—and the following sanctions against the regime and the outbreak of the guerilla war—does not seem to have had any direct negative impact upon the London investors. The return on investment soared in the years immediately following independence.

Conclusion

Colonization was not a process with a homogenous or straightforward impact on the return on investment. The outcomes were, on the contrary, highly diverse between different colonies in Africa.

In the case of Egypt, prior to colonization, foreign investors seem to have feared what nationalist sentiments could do to their investments. Investors in the Egyptian financial sector seem to have been satisfied with the Dual Control imposed upon Egypt in the 1870s. Investors in the Suez Canal Company, on the other hand, did apparently put greater trust in the British government's statements to intervene—if necessary—on behalf of the khedive Tewfik Pasha. This created a rush in the company's share price and an extraordinary return for investors for a short period. The actual occupation, on the other hand, created a period of uncertainty for the investors. At the same time, the occupation safeguarded their investments against a nationalist government reneging upon any agreements. A few years after the occupation of Egypt, investors again experienced high return on their investments.

The South African War has been used by many scholars as a leading example of finance-driven imperialism. The war favoured London investors, with share prices increasing drastically during the war, leading to extraordinarily high rates of return for investors as soon as the tides of the war had turned in favour of the British side, some months after the outbreak of the war in October 1899. When the war ended in 1902 with a British victory, London investors could celebrate that their interests in the Witwatersrand goldfields had been safeguarded and also the high return on investment during the war itself. The return on investment fell shortly after the war, as the mining sector of South Africa experienced several structural problems during the first decades of the twentieth century.

For the two chartered companies—the Royal Niger Company and the British South Africa Company—the main value of their charters was the right to profit from any agreements entered into with local rulers. The fact that many of these agreements were highly contested and dubious was never recognized by the British imperial authorities. In the case of the Royal Niger Company, there was an already comparatively highly developed economy in the region, and the company had conducted trade there already prior to receiving its charter. With the charter, the RNC increased its profits through de facto monopoly rents and delivered a high return to its investors. In Rhodesia, in contrast, the BSAC experienced a comparatively less developed economy, and at the same time, faced substantial administrative costs. The return on investing in that company was therefore negative during the chartered period. When the charters were revoked, both companies were able to negotiate settlements with the British imperial authorities. They not only received a compensation for the loss of their charters (and/or for the costs that they had incurred for the administration of the territories during the chartered period). They also managed to keep the most valuable claim from the charters: the right to profit from agreements entered into with local rulers. The most important content of such agreements referred to land and mineral rights. This meant that both the RNC and the BSAC could earn substantial profits from land rents extracted from mining companies starting to operate in the respective regions from the 1920s onwards.

Previous scholarship has made use of a distinction between settler and non-settler colonies. Our figures indicate that the return on investment over a long period was similar in both types of colonies. However, during the last decades studied here, the return on investment diverged substantially between the two types of colonies. We argue that an important explanation to the higher return in settler economies can be attributed to differences in the development of colonial institutions. Local populations were dispossessed from the land to a much higher degree in settler colonies. Various coercive institutions were also more frequently put in place in settler economies in order to secure a low-paid labour force. The coercion generally intensified over time, most importantly after First World War, in both South Africa and Rhodesia. It would be too simplified to attribute any differences in the return on investment solely to the type of colonialism imposed, as other factors also played a role for this development—not the least the different fates during decolonization. In our view, it is likely that coercive measures in the settler colonies, to some extent, contributed to an increase in company profitability, and thereby to a higher return on investment.

The process of decolonization, finally, exhibited paradoxical results. Foreign investors did anticipate that decolonization was imminent and tried to deal with this proactively in different ways, such as Africanizing their operations. Investors nonetheless undoubtedly feared what decolonization actually would entail. This was also reflected in the price of the equity portfolios of the independent countries, which often decreased when the investors had reason to fear that a decolonization threatened their investments. In reality, decolonization often played out in unexpected ways. In Egypt, the nationalist revolution expropriated foreign assets, which caused major losses for the investors. The self-proclaimed socialist Nkrumah, around the same time, caused investors to fear for a nationalization of foreign assets in advance of political independence, but the government never went ahead with any forced nationalizations of foreign assets. Thus, the threat of nationalizations was not realized (during our period of study) and the anticipated negative return on investment turned into positive return on investment in the years after independence. In Nigeria, Southern Rhodesia and Zambia, investors did generally not seem to have feared any nationalizations during the period under study. Independent Zambia did nationalize foreign-owned mines, but investors were paid some compensation, and it was not until after the end of our study that it was found out how little this compensation actually was worth. In Belgian Congo, finally, decolonization arrived suddenly, but when it came, it had large effects. During the last few years of colonial period, investors' confidence decreased substantially. Political independence soon degenerated into civil war and a military coup. Following the coup, Belgian assets in the former colony were nationalized, but paradoxically by a pro-capitalist Western ally. Imperialist intervention—but now by the United States—ascertained compensation for the former owners, including the one found in our sample. A few years after independence, the return on investment in that former colony was therefore high again.

References

Austin, Gareth. 2016. Sub-Saharan Africa. In *A History of the Global Economy 1500 to the Present*, ed. Joerg Baten, 316–350. Cambridge: Cambridge University Press.

Austin, Gareth, Ewout Frankema, and Ewout Morten Jerven. 2017. Patterns of Manufacturing Growth in Sub-Saharan Africa: From Colonization to the Present. In *The Spread of Industrialization in the Global Periphery*, ed. Kevin O'Rourke and Jeffrey Williamson, 345–374. Oxford: Oxford University Press.

Baker, Geoffrey. 1996. *Trade Winds on the Niger: The Saga of the Royal Niger Company, 1830–1971*. London: The Radcliffe Press.

Buelens, Frans, and Stefaan Marysse. 2009. Returns on Investments During the Colonial Era: The Case of the Belgian Congo. *The Economic History Review* 62 (s1): 135–166.

Cain, Peter J., and Anthony G. Hopkins. 2001. *British Imperialism, 1688–2000*. Harlow: Longman.

Carlos, Ann M., and Stephen Nicholas. 1988. 'Giants of an Earlier Capitalism': The Chartered Trading Companies as Modern Multinationals. *Business History Review* 62 (3): 398–419.

Chamberlain, M.E. 1976. Sir Charles Dilke and the British Intervention in Egypt, 1882: Decision Making in a Nineteenth-Century Cabinet. *Review of International Studies* 2 (3): 231–245.

Darwin, John. 1997. Imperialism and the Victorians: The Dynamics of Territorial Expansion. *The English Historical Review* 112 (447): 614–642.

Farnie, D.A. 1969. *East and West of Suez: The Suez Canal in History 1854–1956*. Oxford: Clarendon Press.

Feinstein, Charles. 2005. *An Economic History of South Africa: Conquest, Discrimination and Development*. Cambridge: Cambridge University Press.

Flint, John. 1960. *Sir George Goldie and the Making of Nigeria*. London: Oxford University Press.

———. 1976. *Cecil Rhodes*. London: Hutchinson.

Galbraith, John. 1972. *Mackinnon and East Africa 1878–1895: A Study in the 'new Imperialism'*. Cambridge: Cambridge University Press.

———. 1973. Origins of The British South Africa Company. In *Perspectives of Empire. Essays Presented to Gerald S. Graham*, ed. John E. Flint and Glyndwr Williams, 148–171. London: Longman.

———. 1974. *Crown and Charter: The Early Years of the British South Africa Company*. Berkeley: University of California Press.

Galbraith, John, and Afaf Lutfi al-Sayyid-Marsot. 1978. The British Occupation of Egypt: Another View. *International Journal of Middle East Studies* 9 (4): 471–488.

Harrison, Robert. 1995. *Gladstone's Imperialism in Egypt: Techniques of Domination*. Westport: Greenwood Press.

Hobsbawm, Eric. 1987. *The Age of Empire, 1875–1914*. London: Weidenfeld and Nicolson.

Hobson, John Atkinson. 1900. *The War in South Africa: Its Causes and Effects*. London: J. Nisbet.

———. 1988. *Imperialism: A Study*. London: Unwin Hyman.

Hopkins, Anthony G. 1986. The Victorians and Africa: A Reconsideration of the Occupation of Egypt, 1882. *The Journal of African History* 27 (2): 363–391.

Jeeves, Alan H. 1996. The Rand Capitalists and the Coming of the South African War 1896–1899. *South African Journal of Economic History* 11 (1): 55–81.

Jones, S.R.H., and Simon P. Ville. 1996. Efficient Transactors or Rent-Seeking Monopolists? The Rationale for Early Chartered Trading Companies. *The Journal of Economic History* 56 (4): 898–915.

Pakenham, Thomas. 1979. *The Boer War*. London: Weidenfeld and Nicolson.

———. 1991. *The Scramble for Africa 1876–1912*. London: Weidenfeld and Nicolson.

Pedler, Frederick. 1974. *The Lion and the Unicorn in Africa: A History of the Origins of the United Africa Company 1787–1931*. London: Heinemann.

Platt, D.C.M. 1968. *Finance, Trade, and Politics in British Foreign Policy 1815–1914*. Oxford: Clarendon Press.

Porter, Andrew. 2000. The South African War and the Historians. *African Affairs* 99 (397): 633–648.

Porter, Bernard. 2012. *The Lion's Share – A History of British Imperialism 1850 to the Present*. 5th ed. London: Routledge.

Pretorius, Fransjohan. 2014. Everyone's War: The Anglo-Boer War (1899–1902). In *A History of South Africa: From the Distant Past to the Present Day*, ed. Fransjohan Pretorious, 239–259. Pretoria: Protea Book House.

Robinson, Ronald Edward, and John Gallagher. 1968. *Africa and the Victorians: The Climax of Imperialism*. New York: Anchor Books.

Rotberg, Robert. 1988. *The Founder: Cecil Rhodes and the Pursuit of Power*. Oxford: Oxford University Press.

Schölch, Alexander. 1976. The 'Men on the Spot' and the English Occupation of Egypt in 1882. *The Historical Journal* 19 (3): 773–785.

Slinn, Peter. 1971. Commercial Concessions and Politics during the Colonial Period: The Role of the British South Africa Company in Northern Rhodesia 1890–1964. *African Affairs* 70 (281): 365–384.

Tignor, Robert. 1966. *Modernization and British Colonial Rule in Egypt, 1882–1914*. Princeton: Princeton University Press.

Vatikiotis, P.J. 1991. *The History of Modern Egypt from Muhammad Ali to Mubarak*. 4th ed. London: Weidenfeld and Nicolson.

Wesseling, Hendrik Lodewijk. 1996. *Divide and Rule: The Partition of Africa, 1880–1914*. Westport: Praeger.

Wickins, Peter. 1986. *Africa 1880–1980: An Economic History*. Cape Town: Oxford University Press.

14

African Mining in Global Comparison

New Frontiers for Mining

Imperial policies contributed to shaping the socio-economic development of many colonial societies, for example, policies favouring the development of large-scale plantations producing export crops. However, whereas plantations could be developed in a variety of different settings—albeit some more suitable than others—the location of particular ore deposits was determined solely by nature. This had important implications for imperial policy. As Corey Ross has put it: 'The fact that they had to be extracted in situ meant that mining tended to shape the geography of modern empire rather than the other way around' (Ross 2017, 136).

During the nineteenth century, new frontiers of mining were opening up all over the world. In the 1840s, California experienced a gold rush following the finding of gold in the Sierra Nevada mountains (Lynch 2002, 120–27; Coulson 2012, 95–100). This was followed by a gold rush in Australia, in Victoria and New South Wales, in the 1850s (Blainey 1964, chap. 3; Lynch 2002, 134–40; Coulson 2012, 115–22), as well as in Colorado (the United States) and Klondike (Canada) and other places, in the following decades (Lynch 2002, 245–46; Coulson 2012, 123–28).

As investors saw investment opportunities open up abroad, British investments in mining became more globalized. Some British investors became involved already in some of the early gold rushes in the United States and Australia (Woodland 2014). The global export of capital to the mining sector would nonetheless remain limited prior to the 1870s. By 1869, mining companies operating in Europe still accounted for two-thirds of the total market capitalization of (non-ferrous) mining companies traded on the London Stock Exchange. The share decreased during the 1870s, as investments became more prominent in North American mining companies, followed in the 1880s by investments in Latin American mining companies. As can be seen in Fig. 14.1, the major change came when British investors got involved in the South African gold and diamond mines on a large scale, particularly from 1889 onwards. This led to a major increase in the market capitalization of the mining sector on the London Stock Exchange, at an average rate of 12 per cent per year, during the period from 1889 to the peak in 1904. The mining

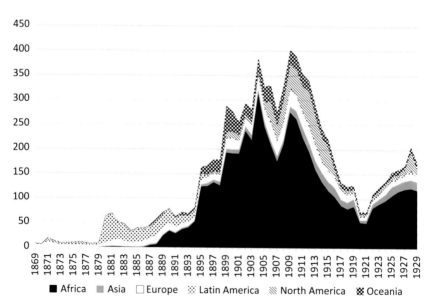

Fig. 14.1 Market capitalization of companies in the Global Mining Equities Database, by continent of operation, 1869–1929 (£ million, constant 1868 prices). Source: Global Mining Equities Database (GMED)

boom peaked during the first decade of the twentieth century, after which the market capitalization of the industry decreased substantially until the interwar period, most particularly in Southern Africa. The data reported in Fig. 14.1 therefore fits well with Charles Harvey and Jon Press' claim that Southern Africa accounted for about half of the capital employed by British overseas mining companies in 1913 (Harvey and Press 1990, 105).

As Harvey and Press have noted, British investors 'did not enjoy the same degree of success in countries with ample local supplies of capital and know-how', such as the United States, as they did in British colonies (Harvey and Press 1990, 113). After the end of the First World War, South African mines therefore continued to dominate British investments in mining, throughout the period under study here. No wonder then that, as Raymond Dumett has argued, African minerals came to be crucial for the Allied war effort during the Second World War, both for some base metals and for several metals of more recent interest (Dumett 1985).

The aggregate market capitalization of mining companies traded on the London Stock Exchange experienced a slow growth in real terms, averaging around 3 per cent per year from the 1930s to the 1950s, as shown in Fig. 14.2. The 1960s, finally, exhibited a renewed boom in mining, primarily driven by mining companies in Africa and Australia. The real total market capitalization of the sector increased at a rate of around 10 per cent per year.

Adding the data from the previous two figures together, Fig. 14.3 shows the respective market share of investments in (non-ferrous, non-coal) mining in British colonies (including Dominions and ex-colonies/ex-dominions in the British Commonwealth) and in other polities that were not British colonies.

As can be seen in the graph, British colonies were initially of limited importance for investments in the mining industry, accounting for around 10 per cent of the total market capitalization. Most investments at this time still went to independent countries either in Europe or in the Americas. This picture shifted drastically with the development of the mining industry in South Africa, particularly from the late 1880s onwards, increasing the share of investments going to British colonies to up to 90 per cent of the total market capitalization for a period. Following

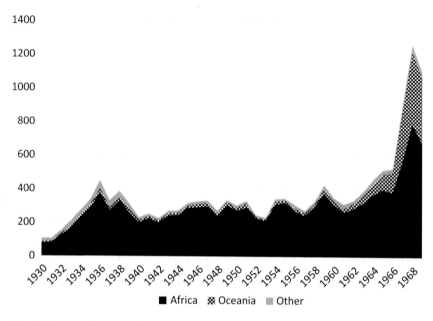

Fig. 14.2 Market capitalization of companies in the Global Mining Equities Database, by continent of operation, 1930–1969 (£ million, constant 1868 prices). Source: Global Mining Equities Database (GMED)

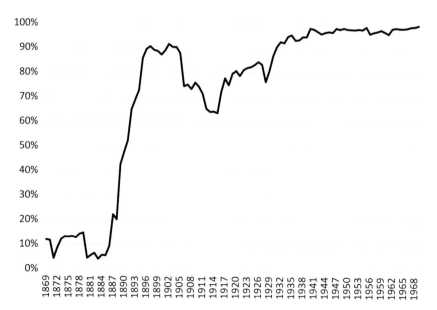

Fig. 14.3 Relative market capitalization of companies in the Global Mining Equities Database operating in British colonies, 1869–1969 (per cent of market capitalization of all companies in the database). Source: Global Mining Equities Database (GMED)

the structural problems of the South Africa mining sector in the early twentieth century, the importance of colonial mining was reduced to around 60 per cent—particularly in favour of North American mining. Colonial mining made a strong comeback following the First World War and continued to increase in importance until the end of the period under study here. These results fit well with Fieldhouse's claim that British investments from the interwar period onwards increasingly were directed to British colonies (Fieldhouse 1999, 97). Indeed, by the end of the period, colonies (and ex-colonies) accounted for more than 99 per cent of the market capitalization of British investments in the (non-ferrous, non-coal) mining industry.

Technological Development and Falling Ore Grades

A crucial aspect to the economy of mining is how rich the body of ore is. Attempts to establish mining operations have recurrently failed simply because the ore was not rich enough to establish payable mines (see, e.g. Mollan 2009 for an African example). South African mines were often claimed to suffer from extraordinarily low ore grade (amount of extractable metals relative to the amount of ore mined)—an idea that also has been repeated by modern-day scholars (see, e.g. Webb 1983, 174). This was something that the South African Chamber of Mines—as well as South African colonial administration—considered to be a major challenge for the industry's development. Special so-called Low Grade Ore commissions were therefore appointed, both in 1920 and in 1930, to suggest means of dealing with this supposed fact.

In reality, the idea that South Africa suffered from particularly low grade ore is not supported by the empirical evidence. Figure 14.4 reports data on the weighted average ore grades of the gold ore mined in various countries and states, from 1886 to 1969.

As can be seen in the figure, South African gold mines were at virtually no time the mines with the lowest ore grades in the world. On the contrary, Canadian gold mines exhibited a considerably lower ore grade already from the start of the period under study here, and ore grades in

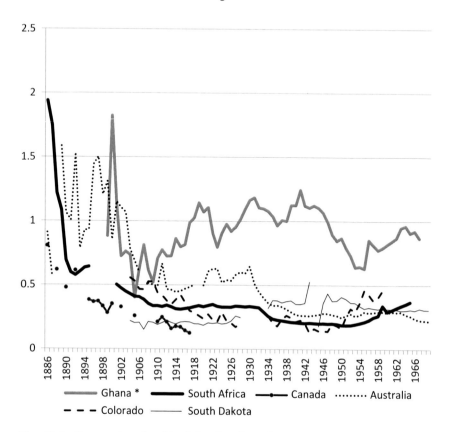

Fig. 14.4 Ore grades of gold mining in selected parts of the world, 1886–1969 (ounce gold per metric ton ore, weighted averages by year). Sources: for Ghana: (Afrifa-Taylor 2006, appendix 3); for South Africa: (Charles Sidney Goldmann (1895) South African Mines: Their Position, Results & Developments. London: Effingham Wilson & Co.; Notes and Proceedings of the House of Assembly; Vol. V, Colonial and Provincial Papers Transvaal; Mining Engineer, report for the year ending 30th June 1910, table 13; Annual report of Mining Engineer 1947, table 10; Annual report of Mining Engineer 1965, unnumbered table); for Canada: (Geological Survey of Canada. Annual Report 1886–1905; A General Summary of the Mineral Production of Canada 1910–1917); for Australia: (A Statistical Account of the Seven Colonies of Australasia, 1897–1898; The Wealth and Progress of New South Wales 1887–1901; Statistical Register of the Colony of Western Australia 1899–1905; Report of the Department of Mines, Western Australia, Mining Statistics 1906–1970); for Colorado and South Dakota in the United States: (Mineral Resources of the US 1904–1928; United States Bureau of Mines—Minerals Yearbook 1932–1969). Note: The data from Ghana is based on only one company, the major producer Ashanti Goldfields

the United States were likewise much lower at least from when comparable data started to become available from that country. It is, rather, Australian and most importantly the Ghanaian Ashanti goldfields that seem to have had particularly rich ores.

What is also striking in the figure is that most of the countries experienced a drastic decline in ore grades of the ore mined. Canadian ore grades declined from 0.8 ounce of gold per ton in the 1880s to around 0.1 ounce per ton by the First World War when our data series ends. Australian ore grades declined from 0.9 ounce per ton in 1886 to around 0.25 ounce per ton in the 1960s. South African gold mined in the 1880s had an average ore grade of almost two ounces of gold per ton, decreasing to one-tenth of this concentration by the middle of the twentieth century. We have only been able to find data from the United States starting in 1904. By this stage, the ore grade of the ore mined was already at very low levels in most of the main gold-producing states: 0.13 ounce per ton in Alaska, 0.26 ounce per ton in California and 0.22 ounce per ton in South Dakota. Only some of the by then minor gold-mining states, such as Colorado and Nevada, exhibited somewhat higher ore grades (0.56 and 0.83 ounce per ton, respectively). Across the United States, the ore grades of the ore mined also decreased to around 0.1–0.3 ounce per ton during the middle of the twentieth century. The Ghanaian Ashanti Goldfields Corporation was clearly an exception. The ore grade was much higher than what was found in other parts of the world. Furthermore, the ore grade of the Ashanti goldfields did not decline as sharply as it did over time in other parts of the world.

Declining ore grades were the consequence of a combination of factors. One key factor was reasonably that many of the companies—as they increasingly came to know the geology of the ore deposits—ought to have chosen to first mine richer sections of the ore deposits that they controlled, turning to mine ore deposits with lower ore grades when the richer deposits had been exhausted. New innovations in the industry also made it profitable to mine increasingly lower ore grades (Harvey and Press 1989, 72; Schodde 2011, 8). One innovation was the automatic rock drill, which reduced the heavy work of drilling holes for explosives (Blainey 1964, 78; Alexander 2006, 41). Another innovation was the development of dynamite, patented in 1867, a stronger but at the same time more safely manageable explosive than those that had been available previously (Meyers and Shanley 1990, 186–87; Lynch 2002, 181). For the gold-mining industry, another innovation was of the outmost importance: the MacArthur-Forrest method of cyanide leaching. Ancient methods of extracting gold from ore, such as mercury amalgamation, were ineffective, at best extracting around 55 per cent of the gold present in a deposit of ore (Gray and McLachlan 1933, 375; Lougheed 1989, 62). The cyanide process was developed in Scotland, and experiments showed that it had a much higher extraction rate—virtually all gold from a sample was extracted using cyanide leaching (Lougheed 1989, 63–64). The first field trials were made in Australia in 1888, followed by trials in New Zealand in 1889 and South Africa in 1890 (Gray and McLachlan 1933, 376; Rockoff 1984, 628–29; Lougheed 1989, 64–65). The effects were dramatic for the gold-mining industry. Estimates reveal that the yield per ton of ore might have increased by about 50 per cent from this process (Rockoff 1984, 628–29). The process also particularly favoured gold mining in some specific places, including Witwatersrand in South Africa, as it made it possible to mine low grade ore profitably. In South Africa, the breakthrough of this innovative method was therefore almost instantaneous. Already by 1891, a year after the first trials, many South African mining companies had started to employ cyanide leaching (Lougheed 1989, 66; Lynch 2002, 229–30). Increasingly lower ore grades and the new methods of extracting the metals from the ore would unfortunately also lead to an increasingly heavy environmental degradation in the wake of the mining (see, e.g. Smith 1993; McNeill and Vrtis 2017).

In the twentieth century, new scientific and technological improvements continued to develop the global mining industry. With the development of geology as a science, geophysics became an ever more important aspect of prospecting. The sorting of ore became automatized. Shafts could, on the one hand, be sunk deeper, but large-scale mechanization did also enable the growth of open-pit mining (Coulson 2012, 221–29).

Developments on the market, not the least the abandonment of the Gold Standard and the following appreciation of the value of gold (see Chap. 11), also made it profitable to mine gold deposits of lower ore grade. It is striking that the ore grades in some parts of the United States, as well as, for example, in South Africa, actually improved by the end of the period under study. This might be explained by the development of new mining fields, such as the Orange Free State in South Africa (see Chap. 11). This increase was temporary, as the trend of declining ore grades in the gold-mining industry have since continued to decline until modern days (Schodde 2011, 8).

What is possibly unique in the case of South Africa is the drastic drop in ore grades: starting with ore grades of almost 2 ounces of gold per ton of ore in 1886, dropping to 0.6 ounces per ton five years later and continuing a steady decline thereafter. It is possible that some of the other mining areas, for example, in Canada or the United States, might have exhibited similar drastic drops prior to when comparable historical data on ore grades became available. There were continuously new areas opening up for new development elsewhere, particularly in the United States. In South Africa, ore grades started to increase again in the 1950s after new mining sites had opened (Pretorius 1987, 410–11).

The South African mines were in essence not mining ores of particularly low grade in international perspective. Nonetheless, the perception that they did remained with the representatives both of the industry and the government, and it was considered a challenge that needed to be dealt with. The Low Grade Ore Commissions were therefore appointed to find ways of countering this problem. The main proposal to solve the perceived problem was to cut the labour costs. The working day of the African labourers was to be extended, the use of migrant labourers expanded, the higher-paid white workers were to be replaced by lower-paid African workers and both wages and compensation for phthisis to be reduced substantially for all workers ('Low Grade Ore Commission' 1932, 11–18). The (incorrect) idea that the ore in the South African gold mines were of particularly low grade thus came to be used as a means to exploit the mine workers even harder.

The Return on Investment in Global Mining

Table 14.1 reports data on the estimated return on investment in mining companies globally, and by the continent where the company in question mainly operated. As was discussed in Chap. 3, classifying according to

Table 14.1 Nominal and real return on investment in (non-ferrous) mining companies, 1869–1969 (geometric mean per year)

Continent	N (companies)	Average annual return (%) Nominal	Average annual return (%) Real	Standard deviation of annual return (percentage points)
Total	1035	5.0	2.7	21
By continent of operation				
Africa	518	9.9	7.1	26
Asia	88	2.6	0.0	41
Europe	144	4.7	2.1	31
Latin America	59	3.1	1.0	36
North America	84	5.7	3.5	36
Oceania	143	5.3	3.0	28
By colonial status of country of operation[a]				
British colonies (incl. former colonies)	741	7.7	5.4	22
Not British colonies	294	3.8	1.5	27

Source: Global Mining Equities Database (GMED)

[a]Countries have been categorized by a dummy variable for the whole period based on if it was a British colony at some time during the period 1869–1969. Colonies that became politically independent during the period (e.g. South Africa) have hence been classified as 'British colonies' throughout the period under study, while the United States is classified as not being a British colony here, as it became independent long before 1869

the geographical location of companies can, in some cases, be complicated as some companies might have operations in several countries but has here been based upon where a company is considered to have had its main operations.

The total return on investment in the mining industry was not particularly high: a nominal (geometric) mean annual return of 4.9 per cent per year, translating into a real return of 2.6 per cent per year. This is, to a large extent, a reflection of the large amounts of speculative capital that were invested in the industry without ever achieving the profits hoped for by the investors. As Charles Harvey and Jon Press have noted, more than 8000 mining companies were established during the mining booms of the late nineteenth and early twentieth centuries, but only a minority of them ever managed to become profitable

(Harvey and Press 1990, 99; see also Van Helten 1990). Information asymmetries between the potential investors and people with inside information (e.g. company managers and promoters) increased the risk that the investors could be the victim of frauds (Phimister and Mouat 2003). Many investors therefore tried to spread the risks, and therefore often involved financial intermediaries such as Rothschild's Exploration Company (Turrell and Helten 1986). The inherent uncertainties of mining also propelled the development towards the group system, whereby large mining companies diversified their holdings into several different mines (see Chap. 12 for one such example, the Corner House group).

While the total return on investment in mining globally was not impressive, there were large geographical differences but also large differences over time. This is illustrated in greater detail in Fig. 14.5, showing the average return on investment by continent and by decade.

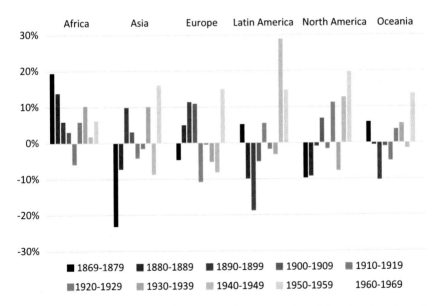

Fig. 14.5 Average annual real return on investment in mining, by decade and continent of operations, 1869–1969 (geometric mean per year). Source: Global Mining Equities Database (GMED)

Asia

Asian mining companies—in terms of market capitalization, most importantly, companies such as the Mysore Gold Mining Limited, Champion Reef Gold Mines and the Central Provinces Manganese Ore Company in India, as well as the Burma Corporation—were in total performing the worst in our sample of global mining companies: the regional weighted average nominal return of 2.6 per cent per year was completely countered by inflation, so that the real return on investment in the Asian mining companies essentially amounted to zero over the whole period studied. The bad overall performance is, to a large extent, explained by major losses for the early investors, during the 1870s and 1880s, which were turbulent decades, with the annual return on investment fluctuating drastically between the years. Return on investment was much more stable during the following period and also turned into losses only during the odd year, which also shows up in the form of a positive real return during the period 1889–1913. Investments in one particular group of companies—Malayan tin-mining companies—would continue to experience substantial losses during this period, averaging a negative return (−20 per cent per year) until 1920. Malayan tin mining had boomed in the 1860s and 1870s, making Malaya the main producer of tin in the world (Drabble 2000, 39, 55). European investors started to get involved in the 1890s. By this time, however, much of the readily accessible ores had already been exploited, so that demands for capital investments increased substantially (Drabble 2000, 58, 70–71). Despite these investments, production stagnated during the first decades of the twentieth century (Drabble 2000, 107–8), leading to major losses for British investors, as can be seen in Table 14.2.

Asian mining companies were negatively affected by the First World War as the return on investment was negative during all the years of the war. The 1920s would be a period of recovery for some of the companies, including for several of the Malayan tin-mining companies (Drabble 2000, 130), turning into a crash following the financial crash of 1929. The 1930s remained turbulent, turning into major losses again during the Second World War. Following the stabilization of tin prices

Table 14.2 Real return on investment for selected mining companies, 1869–1969 (geometric mean per year)

Company	Main metal mined	Main country of operation	Time-period	Real return (%)
Malayan tin-mining companies[a]	Tin	Malaya	1890–1969	−2.6
			1890–1920	−20.5
			1921–1945	6.9
			1946–1969	13.0
St. John d'el Rey Mining	Gold	Brazil	1869–1969	5.0
			1869–1888	−6.4
			1889–1929	11.4
			1930–1969	4.7
Tongoy Mine	Copper	Chile	1880–1897	−18.7
Rio Tinto	Copper	Spain (later various countries)	1873–1969	5.8
			1873–1928	8.6
			1929–1969	2.1
Broken Hill Proprietary	Silver	Australia	1892–1969	2.3
			1892–1929	0.8
			1930–1969	4.4
Mount Morgan Gold Mining Co.	Gold	Australia	1896–1929	−3.9
Mount Lyell Mining	Gold	Australia	1897–1969	−0.2
Cassel Cyanide Company	(Cyanide leaching)	(Global)	1895–1927	1.4
Emma Silver Mining Company	Silver	USA	1872–1879	−47.1
Anaconda Copper Mining	Copper	USA	1896–1940	14.5
Amalgamated Copper Company	Copper	USA	1907–1915	−4.4
Utah Copper Company	Copper	USA	1906–1915	19.7
Selection Trust Limited	Various[b]	Various[b]	1934–1969	14.3

Source: Global Mining Equities Database (GMED)

[a]Weighted average of all tin-mining companies operating in the region of current-day Malaysia

[b]Selection Trust Limited was originally based in the United States and is in the geographical disaggregation employed here, hence classified as coming from that region, but in time, the company came to acquire substantial interests in a number of different mining ventures, including in Yugoslavia, the Soviet Union, Northern Rhodesia and West Africa (Phillips 2009, 226)

from the International Tin Agreements in the 1930s (Drabble 2000, 130–31), the Malayan tin-mining industry would finally turn profitable for the investors—which is also reflected in the data in Fig. 14.5. The post-war period was again more stable with higher return on investment overall and only a few odd years exhibiting a negative return on investment in Asian mining. By this time, Malayan tin-mining also turned into a lucrative investment opportunity, not the least attributable to the successive International Tin Agreements from 1956 onwards (Drabble 2000, 230), exhibiting average return on investment of 13.0 per cent per year.

Latin America

The search for gold and other precious metals had been one of the key drivers of the colonization of Latin America. Vast deposits of silver had been found at Potosí, in current-day Bolivia, and gold was later found in Brazil (Brown 2012, chaps. 2–3). In the early nineteenth century, the newly independent republics on the continent attempted to reinvigorate the mining industry in their respective countries. To a large extent, this entailed foreign—and most importantly British—investments (Rippy 1952, 341–42; Brown 2012, 91–100). British investors invested substantial amounts in companies such as St. John d'el Rey Mining in Brazil, Aramayo Mines in Bolivia, the Tongoy Mine and Consolidado de Minas del Cobre (both in Chile) and Mines of El Oro and the San Francisco Mines (both in Mexico).

One of the first, but also most long-lasting British companies established in the region, was the St. John d'el Rey Mining Company, first established in 1834 to mine for gold in Minas Gerais, Brazil (Eakin 1986, 706–7, 1989, 24). Throughout most of the nineteenth century, the company relied on slave labourers. The slaves made up between 50 and 80 per cent of the labour force until the 1870s, when employed (free) labourers started to become more important for the company (Eakin 1986, fig. 3, 1989, fig. 2). During this time, investors experienced substantial capital gains, as the share price increased from £80 each in 1869 (after adjusting for splits) to well over £400 each in 1875.

The time of abolition of slavery was approaching in Brazil just as it had in other parts of the Americas earlier in the century. During the second half of the 1870s, the price of the company's shares decreased to around £200 each. In 1882, furthermore, a court ordered that the vast majority of the remaining slaves were to be set free (Eakin 1986, 713–14, 1989, 36). By the middle of the 1880s, the share price was down to £60 each. To further add to the company's financial difficulties, the mine collapsed completely in 1886 (Eakin 1986, 715), which drove the share price down even further, reaching a low of around £10 each by the time slavery was abolished in Brazil in 1888. During this first phase of the company's history, the return on investment in the company was therefore negative, on average −6.4 per cent per year.

The investors of the St. John d'el Rey Mining Company were not alone in experiencing losses during this period. On the contrary, the Latin American investments were performing badly overall during the late nineteenth century with many very bad years for investors during the 1880s and 1890s. The year 1896 was particularly disastrous, since the stock that dominated the regional sample at the time in terms of market capitalization—Tongoy Mine—experienced a drastic decline in the price of its shares, from £8.75 per share in January 1896 to £0.75 one year later.

The board of St. John d'el Rey Mining Company managed to successfully reorganize the company after the collapse of the mine in 1886. Large sums of capital were injected to reopen the collapsed mine (Eakin 1986, 715–18, 1986, 42–46). The first attempts in Latin America to utilize cyanide leaching for the extraction of precious metals from the ore were undertaken in Mexico in 1894, and the process started to come into widespread use on the continent during the first decade of the twentieth century (Brown 2012, 111–13). This would improve the performance of several gold- and silver-mining companies—not the least the performance of the St. John d'el Rey Company (Eakin 1989, 134, 140). Return on investment in this particular company was, during this second phase of the company's existence, therefore very high in comparison, averaging 11.4 per cent per year.

The First World War did not impact investments in Latin American mining as negatively as it did investments in other parts of the world. In contrast to other parts of the world, furthermore, the outbreak of the

Second World War seems to have led to major gains for investments in Latin American mining, as the weighted regional average return on investment boomed in both 1941 and 1942. From the interwar period onwards, the investments that remained in Latin American mining companies were therefore profitable, though volatility was also high. Starting in the 1930s, trade unions gained in strength in many countries in Latin America. One country where this happened was Brazil, partly due to assistance from the government's Ministry of Labour. A union was organized at the mine of St. John d'el Rey in 1934. The company's confrontational response to unionization led to highly disruptive conflicts, which turned out to be costly for the company, almost causing it to collapse financially (Eakin 1986, 729–33, 1989, 99–100, 218–29). During the third phase of the company's existence, the return on investment was therefore down to more conventional levels, averaging about 4.7 per cent per year.

In total, over the whole period studied, the investments in Latin American mining companies were performing marginally better than the Asian mines over the whole period, with a nominal return of 3.1 per cent per year, amounting to a real return of 1.0 per cent per year on average.

Europe

The European sample of mining companies traded on the London Stock Exchange was, in terms of market capitalization, completely dominated by one single company, Rio Tinto Limited. This company had been established in 1873, when the Spanish government sold the then state-owned copper-mine at Rio Tinto (Harvey 1981, 4–5; Lynch 2002, 165–67). The company's profits increased up to the First World War, primarily driven by the positive return on its copper sales (Harvey 1981, 197–98). This is also reflected in the figures reported in Table 14.2, with large impact on the average return on investment in European mining during this period, shown in Fig. 14.5.

Charles Harvey and Peter Taylor have studied the performance of British investments in Spanish mining in particular, during the period 1851–1913. Many of the companies, the authors find, were short-lived, with an average lifespan of around ten years (Harvey and Taylor 1987, 190). Their results furthermore show that the profits on capital employed were in the range of 7–15 per cent, with a total average of 11 per cent over the whole period, with slightly higher figures by the end of the period than at the beginning (Harvey and Taylor 1987, table 5). Though their figures are not directly comparable to ours, the figures are still well in line with the nominal figures that can be estimated using the London Stock Exchange data employed in this book, amounting to a (geometric) mean nominal return of around 13 per cent per year during the period 1869–1913.

For the period from 1914 onwards, the Spanish mines were, in contrast, generally non-performing—with an average nominal return of 1.1 per cent per year (equivalent to a real return of −3.6 per cent per year). Even these figures might give a biased impression of the return on investment in European mining. In the 1920s, Rio Tinto Limited started to diversify its operations geographically. Most importantly, in 1929, it increased the company's capital in order to be able to get involved in the quickly developing ventures on the Copperbelt in Northern Rhodesia (see Chap. 10). Rio Tinto consequently managed to acquire a substantial share of the company Minerals Separation, which was one of the leading companies on the Copperbelt, as well as the Rhokana Corporation (Harvey 1981, 215). At the same time, the return on the company's investments in Europe was on the decline (Harvey 1981, 223). The Spanish Civil War, during the 1930s, was considered to pose a serious threat of nationalization of Rio Tinto's assets in Spain. The perceived risk was associated with the democratically elected government. The fascist side did, however, conquer the region and thereby hinder any nationalization of the company's assets (Harvey 1981, chap. 10). Fascist rule over Spain from 1939 onwards would instead lead to a number of regulations of the company's operations (Harvey 1981, 294–95). In 1954, the original Rio Tinto mine in Spain was sold by the company, and this enabled a new wave of global diversification not least in Australia (Harvey 1981, 304–7). As was noted in Chap. 5, it is for methodological reasons that it is not possible to capture the company's geographical diversification in the crude geographical disaggregation employed here. This probably introduces an upward bias in the regional estimates (i.e. higher return on investment in Northern Rhodesian or Australian mines here being included under the umbrella of the mother company still mainly operating in Spain).

Because Rio Tinto dominated the sample for most of the period in terms of market capitalization, the weighted average return on investment in European mining companies is, to a large extent, similar to Rio Tinto's figures. The British investors in European mining, on average, faced major losses during all the years of the First World War. There was some recovery, with several years of positive return on investment, during the 1920s, followed by a major decline following the financial crash of 1929. The 1930s exhibited high volatility in European mining companies, not the least due to Spanish investments being negatively impacted by the civil war and following the fascist rule in Spain. The outbreak of the Second World War also leads to drastic losses for investors in European mining. Overall, the period from the First World War until the end of the Second World War remained disastrous from an investor's point of view. It is only in the last period, during the 1950s and the 1960s, that the return on investment in European mining companies turned positive again. Over the whole period studied, the real return on investment in European mining companies amounted to a bare 2.1 per cent per year.

Oceania

The most important mining companies traded on the London Stock Exchange and operating in Australia and New Zealand were the companies mining in Broken Hill (Broken Hill Proprietary (BHP), North Broken Hill, Broken Hill South and New Broken Hill), Mount Morgan Gold Mining Company, Waihi Gold Mining Company, the Cassel Cyanide Company, Mount Lyell Mining and Railway and—following a merger in 1962—also a reconstructed Rio Tinto plc. In a global comparison, the return on investment in this region was considerably less volatile. The single most important company in this regional sample was the silver-mining company Broken Hill Proprietary. The company was first established in Australia in 1885, with shares sold at £9 each on the Melbourne Stock Exchange. The share price skyrocketed after introduction, reaching

14 African Mining in Global Comparison

£175 per share at the end of 1887, £275 in January of 1888 and peaking at £409 per share at the end of February 1888 (Blainey 1964, 147–50, 1968, 29). The boom was short and already by the initial years of the 1890s, Broken Hill Proprietary's 'halo faded', according to Geoffrey Blainey, as both the ore grade and the international silver price declined (Blainey 1964, 157–58). By the time the company was regularly traded on the London Stock Exchange from 1892 onwards, the price of the share had dropped to levels slightly below what the shares initially had been sold for, £7.3 per share. In the same year, a major strike further rocked the company's finances (Blainey 1968, 59–62). The share price continued to decline, reaching a low around £2 per share by the end of 1894. Nonetheless, BHP came to have a dominant position in this region's sample of companies, in terms of market capitalization. Given the importance that this single company had for the weighted sample average for this region, the major losses exhibited by investments in this company translate into a major decline in the weighted average return on investment in mining in this region during this period. To make matters worse, by the early twentieth century, investors started to fear that Broken Hill essentially had been exhausted. It was only by diversifying into several different other ventures that the company managed to stay afloat (Blainey 1964, 273; Coulson 2012, 194). Furthermore, the company experienced two major strikes, in 1909 and 1919–1920 (Blainey 1968, 120–21, 140–44). The latter strike was a particular loss for the company, as it is 'doubtful if any strike in Australia ever won so much' (Blainey 1968, 142). Blainey's words are also reflected in the depressed return on investment, as the price of the shares decreased from around £3 in early 1919, to a low of around £1.5 two years later. Up until the financial crash of 1929, the return on investment in BHP shares was, therefore, in real terms not even 1 per cent per year on average, and it was only in the period from the 1930s onwards that investments in this company started to exhibit a higher return on average.

The leading Australian gold-mining companies, including the Mount Morgan Gold Mining Company or the Mount Lyell Mining and Railway, exhibited patterns similar to those exhibited by BHP: initial booms in the share price, followed by severe slumps once the mines started to face difficulties (Blainey 1964, 215–24, 232–40, 284–90). This is also reflected in the return on investment in these companies up until 1929: −3.9 per cent per year, on average, in real terms for investments in the Mount Morgan Company and −0.2 per cent per year, on average, in real terms for investments in the Mount Lyell Company.

Another company with its base in Australia, but in practice operating in many parts of the world was the Cassel Cyanide Company. As was mentioned previously in this chapter, this company had developed and patented the process of cyanide leaching which became of such major importance for the global gold-mining industry from the 1890s onwards. The company did not manage to make any substantial profits from the innovation, since its patent rights soon were challenged on the ground that the chemistry essentially was known already before the development of the patent. The patent was hence revoked by court order (Gray and McLachlan 1933, 378–94; Lougheed 1989, 71). The return on investment in the Cassel Cyanide Company was therefore on average low, amounting to a mere 1.4 per cent per year in real terms.

The investments in the region as a whole were seemingly not yielding as badly following the outbreak of the First World War as investments in European or Asian mining were, but they did, on the other hand, experience a drastic decline following the financial crash of 1929 as well as the outbreak of the Second World War. Mining in Australia and New Zealand would in total not turn out to be very profitable for the investors until the end of the period under study here, in the 1950s and 1960s, when the industry was able to finally achieve a high return on investment—but then at the price of a high volatility in comparison with investments elsewhere in the world.

North America

The early North American gold rushes, for example, in California in the 1840s, required comparatively little capital (though there were some British involvements already at this stage) (Woodland 2014). Capital needs increased when the industry developed, particularly from the 1860s onwards, and the access to British investors, therefore, became of increasing interest (Spence 1956, 482, 2000, 5–7). After the Californian gold rush, new mineral deposits containing gold, silver, copper and other metals were found in states like Colorado, Nevada, Idaho, Utah and Arizona. Hundreds of new mining companies were established, with a large share of them being introduced on the London Stock Exchange (Spence 2000, appendix III).

One of the perceived obstacles to British investments in the region was the Native American population at the time still living in several of these states—the Cheyenne, Comanche, Navajo/Diné, Apache and several others. Early mining explorations in the Western states often intruded into Native American lands and hence came into conflicts with the Native American nations in question (Wilson Paul 2001, 253–60). This occasionally led to casualties among the explorers which often was used as an excuse by the American federal and state authorities to instigate wars against the Native Americans. Indeed, as Rodman Wilson Paul has put it, 'virtually every Indian war began with a mining boom and its consequences' (Wilson Paul 2001, 282). The power relationships were such that the core mining interests rarely were threatened by the Native American resistance. On the contrary, it was the Native Americans that faced massive repression by state-level and federal authorities (Thornton 1987, 104–23; Michno 2009). Early explorations in California during the 1840s faced some resistance from Native Americans—but the response by American settlers and authorities was genocidal (Trafzer and Hyer 1999, 17–20; Wilson Paul 2001, chap. 2; Lindsay 2012). A similar history occurred after the finding of the Comstock Lode silver deposits in Nevada in the 1850s. By 1860, relations between the settlers and explorers, on the one hand, and the Native American population in the region (the Paiute), on the other, had deteriorated to a point that war eventually was declared by the provisional governor in 1860. Though some early skirmishes were won by the Paiute, the federal government—accompanied by a militia of volunteers—soon mustered a superior force able to win a total victory over the Paiute. During the war, mining activities in the district ceased temporarily, but as soon as the war had been won, mining was resumed (R. M. James 1998, 42–44; Wilson Paul 2001, chap. 4). The finding of gold in the Black Hills of South Dakota in 1874 also led to war. The Native American population, the Sioux, refused to comply with demands to relocate from the Black Hills territory, in order to enable miners to exploit the deposits. In the war that followed, the Sioux were defeated by federal military forces (Clow 1976). Several of the Native American nations continued with their resistance for several decades (Utley and Washburn 2002, chaps. 7–11; Michno 2009; Dunbar-Ortiz 2014, 145–50). North American company promoters would nonetheless try to convince early British investors that what they called the 'Indian menace' was no problem anymore and posed no real risk to any investments in the region (Spence 2000, 10–11).

The return on investment in the early mining investments in North America was volatile and investors faced substantial losses during the first period, as was shown in Fig. 14.5. However, the historiography of the mining industry in Western United States does not suggest that losses experienced by the investors in these years were directly associated with any of the conflicts with the Native Americans (e.g. Arrington and Hansen 1963; Spence 2000; Whitley 2006; Caldwell Hawley 2014). The promoters thus seem to have been correct—the conflicts with the Native Americans posed no real risk to the investors since the American government bore the cost of these wars and that the government (and the mining interests) eventually came out victorious from the 'Indian Wars'.

Instead, the British investors faced other problems when investing in North American mines, most importantly, highly deceptive practices and misleading prospectuses issued by company promoters (Spence 1956, 485–91, 2000, 51–57). One of the largest early Anglo-American mining ventures was at Emma Hill in Utah. Silver was found in 1869, and it led to a minor rush of prospectors and miners. Already in 1871, the manager of the most important mine at Emma Hill warned the owners that the deposit soon would be depleted (L. James and Fell 2006, 276–77). Instead of ending mining operations, the owners decided to try to sell the mine in England. The Emma Silver Mining Company Limited was established in November 1871 and introduced on the London Stock Exchange with 50,000 shares of £20 each (Spence 2000, 145; L. James and Fell 2006, 277–78). Following generous promises in the prospectus and a glowing external inspection by an independent expert in the field, the share price increased in the following months, peaking at almost £30 in April of 1872. Already by mid-1872, news was spreading about problems at the mine; the ore was not as rich as claimed, costs, on the other hand, higher than expected, and to make matters even worse, cave-ins and flooding of the mine had stopped all operations for several months (Spence 2000, 165–66; L. James and Fell 2006, 279). By the end of the year, the share price was down to £10. The share price continued the downwards spiral: reaching £3 each by December 1873, £1 each by December 1874 and £0.1 each by the middle of 1877. The losses to the investors in the Emma Silver Mining Company amounted to an average return on investment of −47.1 per cent per year until the company finally was wound up. There were nonetheless several attempts to reconstruct the company and resume mining at the site, and it would take more than two decades before any such plans were definitely shelved (Spence 2000, 180–81).

High volatility continued to characterize all investments in the region throughout the period under study. One of the newcomers by the end of the nineteenth century was the Anaconda Copper Company, operating out of Butte, Montana. Silver had first been found here in 1875, followed later by copper (Richter 1927, 254–55; Lynch 2002, 172–73). In 1882, the Anaconda Copper Mining Company was born and remained a privately held company until 1896 when it first started to be traded publicly (Toole 1954, 23, 104). Already from an early stage, the company attempted to control the market for copper, for example, by entering into cartel agreements and by acquiring a dominant market position (Toole 1954, chap. XI). One of the major owners of the Anaconda Copper Company was the Amalgamated Copper Company, established in 1899 (but appearing regularly on the London Stock Exchange from 1907 onwards). The company held interests in a number of copper-mining ventures (Richter 1916, 387–88; Lynch 2002, 191). Dreams of establishing a monopoly on copper drove the establishment of the Amalgamated Copper Company, but the company never managed to achieve such a position (Richter 1916, 405; Toole 1954, 116–53). After several years of economic difficulties, the company was finally dissolved in 1915 (Richter 1916, 387). The return on investment was a mere 1.6 per cent per year on average in nominal terms, which translates into −4.4 per cent per year in real terms. Its main holding, the Anaconda Copper Mining Company, survived, and it later thrived economically.

A few years after the incorporation of the Amalgamated Copper Company, a competitor was born: the Utah Copper Company, incorporated in 1903 and holding claims in the Bingham Canyon of Utah (Arrington and Hansen 1963, 38; B. Whitehead and Rampton 2006, 228; Caldwell Hawley 2014, 38). The company was listed at the London Stock Exchange in 1906, in order to enable major capital investments (Alexander 2006, 43; B. Whitehead and Rampton 2006, 229). Following these capital injections, the company improved its efficiency considerably, which also translated into very high return on investment, see Table 14.1. The Utah Copper Company had a comparatively short lifespan as an independent company. In 1910, it was merged with the Boston Consolidated Company which held neighbouring claims in the Bingham Canyon (Arrington and Hansen 1963, chap. 4; B. Whitehead and Rampton 2006, 230). This was followed by the formation of the Kennecott Copper Corporation in 1915, which from the outset acquired a quarter of the Utah Copper Company's shares. By this time, the company was also delisted from the London Stock Exchange. Kennecott Copper Company continued to increase its ownership, so that by 1923 it controlled the vast majority of all shares in the Utah Copper Company (B. Whitehead and Rampton 2006, 236; Caldwell Hawley 2014, 212–14). For the investors that managed to invest in the company in time, before it was taken over by the Kennecott Copper Company, doing so was extraordinarily lucrative: an estimated real average return on investment of 19.7 per cent per year.

In the meanwhile, the Anaconda Copper Mining Company continued to grow as an independent company. One crucial aspect of this growth can be attributed to the fact that the company managed to keep labour costs low by resisting unionization of the labour force. The radical union I.W.W. (Industrial Workers of the World) had made several attempts to unionize the labour force in the state already prior to the First World War but met fierce and violent resistance from the Anaconda Copper Company, as well as from other mining companies (Toole 1954, chaps. XVI–XVII; Chester 2014, chap. 2). In 1917, a union organizer—Frank Little—was lynched. Even though five security guards employed by the Anaconda Company were accused of the crime, the county attorney never initiated any prosecution (Toole 1954, 185–86; Chester 2014, 98–104; Stacy 2017, 207). The company's violent reaction against unionization continued after the end of the First World War, culminating in what was dubbed the 'Anaconda Road Massacre', when Anaconda's security guards fired into a mass of strikers, killing one striker and injuring several more (Chester 2014, 113–14; Stacy 2017, 208).

Compared globally, mining investments in North America were not as negatively impacted by the outbreak of the First World War. The North American market boomed at the end of the 1920s, especially the Anaconda Copper Mining Company. The company successfully worked towards both horizontal and vertical integration by expanding its holdings in many companies operating in different places around the world, including in Chile, Mexico and Poland (Toole 1954, 235–42). This profitable period was followed by major losses for Anaconda—as for virtually all North American mining companies in the sample—following the financial crash of 1929. In the aftermath of this crash, furthermore, the labour force at Anaconda finally managed to unionize, with the support of the government during the Roosevelt Administration of the 1930s (Stacy 2017, 208). The unionization of the labour force is most certainly also one factor explaining why the return on investment in the company, on average, remained negative during the 1930s (until the company was delisted from the London Stock Exchange).

The Second World War as well as the post-war decades were, again similar to Latin America, beneficial for investors in North American mining. The return on investment was very high from 1941 onwards and though the post-war period exhibited high volatility, it also had the highest return on investment in a global comparison. This figure is, to some extent, misleading since the company completely dominating the sample in the 1950s and 1960s—Selection Trust Limited—had large interests in mining all over the world. Aside from its holdings in North America, the most important mines were located in Western and Southern Africa. These African investments have furthermore been described as having been the most lucrative of the company's ventures (Phillips 2009, 226–27, for more on these companies see Chaps. 9 and 10 of this book).

African Mining in Comparative Perspective

The return on investment in African mining companies was, in comparison to mining companies operating in other regions of the world, both higher and less volatile. The latter is, to some extent, potentially a consequence of the fact that there were a larger number of companies traded on the London Stock Exchange operating in Africa and that several of these companies came to constitute a substantial share of the total market capitalization of the region, so that no single company dominated the sample to the same extent as single companies did in some of the other continental portfolios. What is more striking is the fact that, in contrast to all other regions of the world, investments in African mining remained positive during every decade except the 1910s. There were individual years when the weighted average return on African investments also turned negative, but these individual years of negative return were countered by high positive return other years. Return on investment boomed during the late 1880s when several diamond companies in Kimberley merged into what would become the major player: De Beers Consolidated (see Chap. 11). It remained high until the mining boom collapsed during the first decade of the twentieth century. The First World War was a period of negative return on investment in the region, but this was largely recovered during the 1920s. As for all the other parts of the world, return on investment in African mining turned negative following the financial crash of 1929, but again the companies quickly recovered particularly following the abandonment of the Gold Standard. Investments in Africa were also less hurt by the outbreak of the Second World War: return on investment turned negative during the first years of the war but became positive during the second half of the war. The post-war period was a period of uncertainty for many investors in Africa, as potential nationalizations following decolonization were perceived as a threat to the investments made. As was shown in Chap. 13, there were in reality few cases where mining industries actually became nationalized during the period under study here. Share prices therefore often dropped when investors started to anticipate that decolonization would become a reality, but the price in many cases recovered once political decolonization had happened without nationalizations taking place.

14 African Mining in Global Comparison

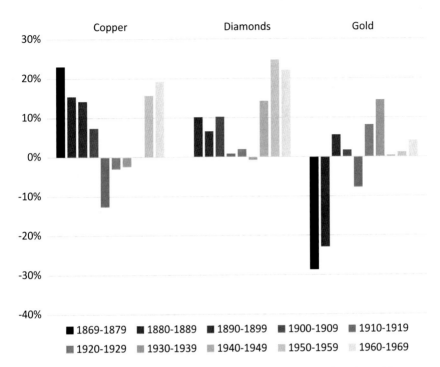

Fig. 14.6 Real return on investment in mining in Africa, by decade and by type of ore mined, 1869–1969 (geometric mean per year). Source: African Colonial Equities Database (ACED)

The type of ore mined also had major implications for the return on investment in mining in Africa. Figure 14.6 shows data on the return on investment in African mining by what was mined.

Copper mining was the oldest type of mining activity in Africa, with Cape Copper (in what would become South Africa) present in our sample of companies from when our study begins chronologically. African copper mining was during the early years of our study time also very successful. As new copper findings were developed elsewhere in the world, not the least in the United States, as was described earlier in this chapter, competition increased. The return on investment in African copper mining did consequently decrease substantially over time, as is shown in Fig. 14.6. With the development of the Copperbelt in Northern Rhodesia, copper mining in Africa took on a second life, returning to a high rate of return on investment by the last decades of our study. Overall, the rate of return on investment in African copper mining amounted to an average real return of 7.3 per cent per year during the whole century under study.

The most profitable type of mining in Africa was undoubtedly diamond mining, exhibiting a high real average annual return on investment of 9.7 per cent per year for a whole century. As can be seen in the figure, the return was high during the period from the 1880s to the 1900s, approaching 10 per cent per year. The period from the First World War until the end of the Second World War was not very successful, with real return approximately zero. After the end of the Second World War, diamond mining was extraordinarily profitable, with an average return on investment exceeding 20 per cent per year. This was in no small part due to the fact that De Beers and the Central Selling Organization, by this time, finally managed to stabilize the global diamond monopoly (Newbury 1989, chaps. 10–11; Coulson 2012, 243–44).

In contrast, investing in African gold mining was not very profitable. Certainly, there were some companies that were engaged in different mining activities—most importantly, the successful Anglo-American Corporation of South Africa (see Chap. 11), which was engaged in both gold and diamond mining, as well as other industrial activities. Including companies operating both gold and other mines under the category of gold-mining companies only increases the return on investment marginally for this category of companies during the last decades of the study (i.e. when the Anglo-American Corporation in particular had achieved a more important market capitalization). There is also an issue of downward bias in the estimates, as the shares of two of the key gold-mining companies (Rand Mines Limited and Ashanti Goldfields) experienced major speculative booms just prior to being included in the sources underlying our dataset (see Chaps. 9 and 12). Nonetheless, the return on investment in gold mining was low in comparison.

This low return is perhaps surprising, given the importance that the gold-mining industry had. The industry was of utmost importance for the South African economy (see Chap. 11). The Witwatersrand gold mines were also crucial for the development of the international Gold Standard, as it enabled an expansion of the gold base, and thereby a liquidity increase on international markets. The importance that these mines had for the development of the Gold Standard made it, in turn, all the more important for the British Empire to control them (Van Helten 1982; Richardson and Van Helten 1984; Ally 1991, 1994).

The scale and the importance of the operations, and the return on investment in them, must not be confused. While the gold-mining industry was crucial for the South African economy and important for the British Empire at large, it was not very profitable for the investors. Over the whole period under study, the average real rate of return on investment in all African gold mining was actually negative (−1.8 per cent per year). As shown in Fig. 14.6, this is, to a large extent, a consequence of the major losses experienced in the tiny gold-mining ventures started in South and West Africa during the 1870s and 1880s. Once gold had been found on the Rand (see Chap. 11), the rate of return on investment in gold at least turned positive. Due to the large number of gold-mining companies failing to make any profits at all from their operations, however, the return on investment in gold mining was rarely high.

What is more, there is no simple relationship between the grade of the ore mined and the return on the investment in the mining (see Fig. 14.7). The low return in the late 1880s is perhaps attributable to a number of failing start-ups at this time. There existed a tenuous relationship between the ore grades and the return on investment, in the sense that falling ore grades might help to explain the decline in the return on investment from the 1890s to the 1910s. It must be borne in mind that the results for the last decade mainly are driven by effects of the First World War, as described in Chap. 11. The high return on investment in South African gold mining during the 1920s and 1930s can, on the other hand, not be attributed to the ore grades, as the average grade of the ore continued to decline during this period. Other crucial factors, discussed further in Chap. 11, were instead that the Gold Standard was abandoned, and an increasing exploitation of the black labour force. Like the First World War, The Second World War had a substantial negative effect upon the return on investment in South African gold mining. The recovery after the war might largely be attributed to the new minefields (with higher ore grades) that were opened.

One of the most striking differences between African mining and mining elsewhere in the world was the low wages paid to the African workers.

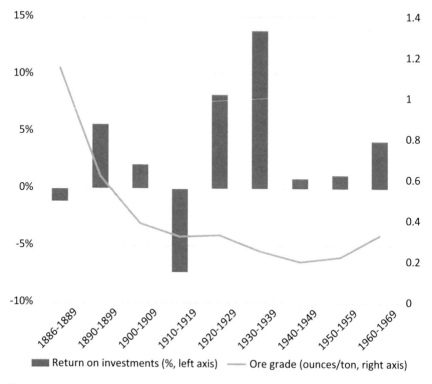

Fig. 14.7 Return on investment in South African gold mining and ore grade of the gold deposits mined, by decade, 1886–1969 (geometric mean per year). Source: African Colonial Equities Database (ACED) and Fig. 14.4

In 1914, a report of a special Economic Commission was presented to the Houses of Parliament in the Union of South Africa. In the report, the commission compared the wages paid to black and white mine workers in South Africa to the wages paid to mine workers in a number of different mining regions elsewhere in the world. It is not entirely transparent how the figures were collected and to what extent they ascertained the comparability of the data collected. The data is, nonetheless, informative of what the magnitudes of the wages might have been. Key figures from the commission's report are shown in Table 14.3.

What the data in the table clearly shows is that white mine workers in South Africa could earn a higher wage than mine workers in most other parts of the world around the same time, including the mining frontiers

Table 14.3 Wages paid to mine workers in various places around the world in 1914 (British shillings per shift)

Region	Wage (British shillings per shift)
South Africa	
White workers on Witwatersrand gold fields	19
White workers in Cape diamond mining	22
Black workers on Witwatersrand goldfields	2
Black workers at Premier mine	3
Metalliferous miners globally	
USA (various regions)	14.3–15
Canada (various regions)	7.3–15.6
Australia (various regions)	8–17.3
Gold Coast	1.8

Source: All data from ('Report of the Economic Commission' 1914, 26–27, 37) except for data from the Gold Coast, from (Crisp 1984)

in the United States, Canada and Australia. What the data also shows is that black mine workers in Africa, in contrast, were extremely low-paid compared to the wages paid to mine workers elsewhere in the world. While a black worker in South Africa at best could earn around 3 shillings per shift, even the lowest wages paid elsewhere in the world at the time (in some of the eastern parts of Canada or in Tasmania in Australia) were much higher, at around 7–8 shillings per shift. At the main mining frontiers, for example, in the frontier mining regions in the United States, Canada and Australia, the wages to mine workers fluctuated around 15 shillings per shift—five times the highest wages paid to black workers in Africa. The Commission's data provides data from one point in time. The development was not one where African wages caught up with the wages paid in the developed countries. It seems safe to assume that wages paid to the mine workers increased in real terms in both Australia, Canada and the United States for much of the remainder of the twentieth century. In Africa, there was a different development. Wages increased in the Gold Coast mines—but only from the 1.75 shillings per shift shown in the Table to around 4 shillings per shift by the 1960s (Crisp 1984; see also Frankema and Waijenburg 2012), so still only half of the lowest wages paid to white mine workers elsewhere in the world in 1914. Meanwhile, the wages paid to black workers in South Africa even declined in real terms all the time from the First World War until the 1960s (Lipton

1985, table 11; Wilson 2011, 103). What data there is thus suggests that the wage gap between black mine workers in Africa and mine workers elsewhere in the world was substantial already in 1914 and diverged even further in the course of the twentieth century.

The low wages paid to African workers were at the time explained in different ways. On the one hand, many European colonialists and white settlers for a long time claimed that African societies exhibited a backward-sloping (or backward-bending) supply curve of labour. The supposed reason for this was that the workers had a target income in mind when entering the formal labour market (e.g. to raise a certain amount of cash to pay for taxes), but preferred to return to traditional occupations as soon as the target income had been earned. A logical deduction of this hypothesis was that a higher wage only would lead the workers to reduce the number of hours they would be willing to work. The hypothesis has since been shown to be fundamentally flawed (Miracle and Fetter 1970; Miracle 1976), but at the time, it became a convenient excuse for employers not to raise the wage of black African workers. That African mine workers were paid low wages could, on the other hand, also be a reflection of a low level of productivity in general. It was sometimes argued that African workers were not 'cheap' labour if one takes into account the (supposedly low) output they produced. A commonly held stereotype among many representatives of the colonial authorities, as well as among many white employers, was that black Africans' low labour productivity could be explained by them being innately lazy and idle (Atkins 1993; A. Whitehead 1999, 2000; Rönnbäck 2014). This was also a commonly used argument by those employers who had an interest in defending the low wages paid to African workers. It was, however, a claim made largely without any empirical evidence supporting it.

Moving beyond such stereotypes is at the same time not easy as it would require taking the Habakukk thesis into consideration: that there are strong incentives to invest in machinery that economize on labour (by raising labour productivity), primarily when labour costs are high (Habakkuk 1962, 4–10; see also same argument in Allen 2009). Even if it could be shown that African workers were less productive than mine workers elsewhere in a static comparison, this could have been the dynamic outcome of the existing industrial relations, rather than a reflection of the innate productivity of the labour force. It might simply not have been worth it for the mining companies to invest in advanced mining machinery in the African mines as long as there were hundreds of thousands of manual workers, equipped with simple drills and other basic tools, who could be employed at low costs.

Conclusion

Investments in global mining boomed during the end of the nineteenth century. Africa became a focal point for such investments. The return on investment in the African mines was, as this chapter has shown, on average higher than the mining investments anywhere else in the world. This is attributable to a number of factors. The most important is the nature of the findings of valuable mineral deposits, most prominently in South Africa. The African mining industry would not have been so profitable over such a long period, had it not been for the diamonds around Kimberley and the gold around Johannesburg. That said, the geological factor cannot explain the high profitability all on its own. As shown in this chapter, the South African gold deposits were not in any way particularly rich in terms of ore grade if compared to other important gold-mining regions in the world. Nonetheless, several highly profitable mining ventures evolved from the exploitation of these deposits.

Institutional factors clearly played an important part in explaining the high return on investment. For a long period, the Gold Standard limited the profitability of gold-mining companies. In contrast, monopoly pricing (as occurred in the case of the diamond industry) or cartel cooperation (as occurred at times in the tin and copper industries) for the output, or monopsony pricing of inputs (as for the recruitment of labour in the South African mining industry) certainly improved the profits for the companies involved. More contentious were various forms of exploitative institutional arrangements. The land to be mined was often simply taken from native populations in several parts of the world, including both in independent nations (such as in the United States) and in colonies in Africa (such as in South Africa and the two Rhodesias) with no—or at most a symbolic—economic compensation. Had the land in question been purchased or leased on contractual terms, without any coercion involved, the price of or rent for the land would most certainly have been much higher than it turned out to be. This would in turn have decreased the profitability of mining the land in question. Labour relations were, furthermore, in many cases, highly exploitative. In the United States, several mining companies fiercely opposed unionization of the labour force, as this would have increased the labour costs. The well-known Anaconda Copper Mining Company, for example, managed to stay non-unionized (and also highly profitable) well into the 1920s. In the Brazilian gold-mining industry, slavery had formed the backbone of the industry, ever since its beginnings in the eighteenth century. Around the time when our study begins, slavery was slowly being phased out from the industry, which contributed to the declining profitability of gold mining in the country. In Africa, slavery was, in general, not an important part of the mines' labour supply during the period under study in this book. However, wages paid to the mine workers, in both South and West Africa, were much lower than the wages paid to mine workers in most other parts of the world, by an order of magnitude. This undoubtedly helped the bottom line for the mining companies operating in Africa.

References

Afrifa-Taylor, Ayowa. 2006. An Economic History of the Ashanti Goldfields Corporation, 1895–2004: Land, Labour, Capital and Enterprise. PhD Dissertation, London School of Economics and Political Science.

Alexander, Thomas. 2006. Generating Wealth from the Earth 1847–2000. In *From the Ground up: The History of Mining in Utah*, ed. Colleen Whitley, 37–57. Logan: Utah State University Press.

Allen, Robert C. 2009. *The British Industrial Revolution in Global Perspective*. Cambridge: Cambridge University Press.

Ally, Russell. 1991. War and Gold – The Bank of England, the London Gold Market and South Africa's Gold, 1914–19. *Journal of Southern African Studies* 17 (2): 221–238.

———. 1994. *Gold & Empire: The Bank of England and South Africa's Gold Producers, 1886–1926*. Johannesburg: Witwatersrand University Press.

Arrington, Leonard, and Gary Hansen. 1963. *'The Richest Hole on Earth': A History of the Bingham Copper Mine*. Logan: Utah State University Press.

Atkins, Keletso E. 1993. *The Moon Is Dead! Give Us Our Money!: The Cultural Origins of an African Work Ethic, Natal, South Africa, 1843–1900*. London: Heinemann.

Blainey, Geoffrey. 1964. *The Rush That Never Ended: A History of Australian Mining*. Melbourne: Melbourne University Press.

———. 1968. *The Rise of Broken Hill*. Melbourne: Macmillan.

Brown, Kendall. 2012. *A History of Mining in Latin America: From the Colonial Era to the Present*. Albuquerque: University of New Mexico Press.

Caldwell Hawley, Charles. 2014. *A Kennecott Story: Three Mines, Four Men, and One Hundred Years, 1897–1997*. Salt Lake City: University of Utah Press.

Chester, Eric. 2014. *The Wobblies in Their Heyday: The Rise and Destruction of the Industrial Workers of the World during the World War I Era*. Santa Barbara: Praeger.

Clow, Richmond L. 1976. The Sioux Nation and Indian Territory: The Attempted Removal of 1876. *South Dakota History* 6: 456–473.

Coulson, Michael. 2012. *The History of Mining: The Events, Technology and People Involved in the Industry That Forged the Modern World*. Petersfield: Harriman House.

Crisp, Jeff. 1984. *The Story of an African Working Class: Ghanaian Miners' Struggles 1870–1980*. London: Zed books.

Drabble, John. 2000. *An Economic History of Malaysia, c. 1800–1990: The Transition to Modern Economic Growth*. Basingstoke: Macmillan.

Dumett, Raymond. 1985. Africa's Strategic Minerals during the Second World War. *The Journal of African History* 26 (4): 381–408.

Dunbar-Ortiz, Roxanne. 2014. *An Indigenous Peoples' History of the United States*. Boston: Beacon Press.

Eakin, Marshall. 1986. Business Imperialism and British Enterprise in Brazil: The St. John d'el Rey Mining Company, Limited, 1830–1960. *The Hispanic American Historical Review* 66 (4): 697–741.

———. 1989. *British Enterprise in Brazil: The St. John d'el Rey Mining Company and the Morro Velho Gold Mine, 1830–1960*. Durham: Duke University Press.

Fieldhouse, D.K. 1999. The Metropolitan Economics of Empire. In *The Oxford History of the British Empire: The Twentieth Century*, ed. Andrew Porter, 88–113. Oxford: Oxford University Press.

Frankema, Ewout, and Marlous Van Waijenburg. 2012. Structural Impediments to African Growth? New Evidence from Real Wages in British Africa, 1880–1965. *The Journal of Economic History* 72 (4): 895–926.

Goldmann, Charles Sidney. 1895. *South African Mines: Their Position, Results & Developments*. London: Effingham Wilson & Co.

Gray, James, and J.A. McLachlan. 1933. A History of the Introduction of the MacArthur-Forrest Cyanide Process to the Witwatersrand Goldfields. *Journal of the Southern African Institute of Mining and Metallurgy* 33 (12): 375–397.

Habakkuk, Hrothgar John. 1962. *American and British Technology in the Nineteenth Century*. Cambridge: Cambridge University Press.

Harvey, Charles. 1981. *The Rio Tinto Company: An Economic History of a Leading International Mining Concern: 1873–1954*. Penzance: Alison Hodge.

Harvey, Charles, and Jon Press. 1989. Overseas Investment and the Professional Advance of British Metal Mining Engineers, 1851–1914. *The Economic History Review* 42 (1): 64–86.

———. 1990. The City and International Mining, 1870–1914. *Business History* 32 (3): 98–119.

Harvey, Charles, and Peter Taylor. 1987. Mineral Wealth and Economic Development: Foreign Direct Investment in Spain, 1851–1913. *The Economic History Review* 40 (2): 185–207.

James, Ronald M. 1998. *The Roar and the Silence: A History of Virginia City and the Comstock Lode*. Reno: University of Nevada.

James, Laurence, and James Fell. 2006. Alta, the Cottonwoods, and American Fork. In *From the Ground up: The History of Mining in Utah*, ed. Colleen Whitley, 272–298. Logan: Utah State University Press.

Lindsay, Brendan C. 2012. *Murder State: California's Native American Genocide, 1846–1873*. Lincoln: University of Nebraska Press.

Lipton, Merle. 1985. *Capitalism and Apartheid: South Africa, 1910–84*. Hounslow: Maurice Temple Smith.

Lougheed, Alan L. 1989. The Discovery, Development, and Diffusion of New Technology: The Cyanide Process for the Extraction of Gold, 1887–1914. *Prometheus* 7 (1): 61–74.

'Low Grade Ore Commission'. 1932. Union of South Africa, Estimates of Expenditure from Revenue Funds U.G. 1–2, 5–17, 19–22.

Lynch, Martin. 2002. *Mining in World History*. London: Reaktion books.

McNeill, J.R., and George Vrtis. 2017. *Mining North America: An Environmental History Since 1522*. Oakland: University of California Press.

Meyers, Sydney, and Edward S. Shanley. 1990. Industrial Explosives – A Brief History of Their Development and Use. *Journal of Hazardous Materials* 23 (2): 183–201.

Michno, Gregory. 2009. *Encyclopedia of Indian Wars: Western Battles and Skirmishes 1850–1890*. Missoula: Mountain Press Publishing Company.

Miracle, Marvin P. 1976. Interpretation of Backward-Sloping Labor Supply Curves in Africa. *Economic Development and Cultural Change* 24 (2): 399–406.

Miracle, Marvin P., and Bruce Fetter. 1970. Backward-Sloping Labor-Supply Functions and African Economic Behavior. *Economic Development and Cultural Change* 18 (2): 240–251.

Mollan, S.M. 2009. Business Failure, Capital Investment and Information: Mining Companies in the Anglo-Egyptian Sudan, 1900–13. *The Journal of Imperial and Commonwealth History* 37 (2): 229–248.

Newbury, Colin. 1989. *The Diamond Ring: Business, Politics and Precious Stones in South Africa, 1867–1947*. Oxford: Clarendon Press.

Phillips, John. 2009. Alfred Chester Beatty: Mining Engineer, Financier, and Entrepreneur, 1898–1950. In *Mining Tycoons in the Age of Empire, 1870–1945: Entrepreneurship, High Finance, Politics and Territorial Expansion*, ed. Raymond Dumett, 215–238. Farnham: Ashgate.

Phimister, Ian, and Jeremy Mouat. 2003. Mining, Engineers and Risk Management: British Overseas Investment, 1894–1914. *South African Historical Journal* 49 (1): 1–26.

Pretorius, Desmond A. 1987. The Depositional Environment of the Witwatersrand Goldfields: A Chronological Review of the Speculations and Observations. In *Gold: History and Genesis of Deposits*, ed. R.W. Boyle, 409–436. New York: Van Nostrand Reinhold Company.

'Report of the Economic Commission'. 1914. Pretoria: Union of South Africa.

Richardson, Peter, and Jean-Jacques Van Helten. 1984. The Development of the South African Gold-Mining Industry, 1895–1918. *The Economic History Review* 37 (3): 319–340.

Richter, F. Ernest. 1916. The Amalgamated Copper Company: A Closed Chapter in Corporation Finance. *The Quarterly Journal of Economics* 30 (2): 387–407.

———. 1927. The Copper-Mining Industry in the United States, 1845–1925. *The Quarterly Journal of Economics* 41 (2): 236–291.

Rippy, J. Fred. 1952. A Century of British Investments in Chile. *Pacific Historical Review* 21 (4): 341–348.

Rockoff, Hugh. 1984. Some Evidence on the Real Price of Gold, Its Costs of Production, and Commodity Prices. In *A Retrospective on the Classical Gold Standard, 1821–1931*, ed. Michael Bordo and Anna Schwartz, 613–650. Chicago: University of Chicago Press.

Rönnbäck, Klas. 2014. The Idle and the Industrious – European Ideas About the African Work Ethic in Precolonial West Africa. *History in Africa* 41 (June): 117–145.

Ross, Corey. 2017. *Ecology and Power in the Age of Empire: Europe and the Transformation of the Tropical World*. Oxford: Oxford University Press.

Schodde, Richard. 2011. Recent Trends in Gold Discovery. Presented at the NewGenGold Conference, Perth, Australia.

Smith, Duane. 1993. *Mining America: The Industry and the Environment, 1800–1980*. Niwor: University Press of Colorado.

Spence, Clark. 1956. When the Pound Sterling Went West: British Investments and the American Mineral Frontier. *The Journal of Economic History* 16 (4): 482–492.

———. 2000. *British Investments and the American Mining Frontier, 1860–1901*. London: Routledge.

Stacy, Robert. 2017. Anaconda Mining Company. In *Reforming America: A Thematic Encyclopedia and Document Collection of the Progressive Era*, ed. Jeffrey A. Johnson, 206–209. Santa Barbara: ABC-CLIO.

Thornton, Russell. 1987. *American Indian Holocaust and Survival: A Population History Since 1492*. Norman: University of Oklahoma Press.

Toole, Ross. 1954. *A History of the Anaconda Copper Mining Company: A Study in the Relationships Between a State and Its People and a Corporation 1880–1950*. Los Angeles: University of California.

Trafzer, Clifford E., and Joel Hyer. 1999. *Exterminate Them: Written Accounts of the Murder, Rape, and Enslavement of Native Americans during the California Gold Rush*. East Lansing: University of Michigan Press.

Turrell, Robert Vicat, and Jean-Jacques Van Helten. 1986. The Rothschilds, the Exploration Company and Mining Finance. *Business History* 28 (2): 181–205.

Utley, Robert, and Wilcomb Washburn. 2002. *Indian Wars*. Boston: Mariner Books.

Van Helten, Jean-Jacques. 1982. Empire and High Finance: South Africa and the International Gold Standard 1890–1914. *Journal of African History* 23 (4): 529–548.

———. 1990. Mining, Share Manias and Speculation: British Investment in Overseas Mining, 1880–1913. In *Capitalism in a Mature Economy: Financial Institutions, Capital Exports and British Industry, 1870–1939*, ed. Jean-Jacques Van Helten and Youssef Cassis, 159–185. Aldershot: Edward Elgar.

Webb, Arthur. 1983. Mining in South Africa. In *Economic History of South Africa*, ed. Francis Coleman. Pretoria: Haum.

Whitehead, Ann. 1999. Lazy Men', Time-Use, and Rural Development in Zambia. *Gender & Development* 7 (3): 49–61.

———. 2000. Continuities and Discontinuities in Political Constructions of the Working Man in Rural Sub-Saharan Africa: The 'Lazy Man' in African Agriculture. *The European Journal of Development Research* 12 (2): 23–52.

Whitehead, Bruce, and Robert Rampton. 2006. Bingham Canyon. In *From the Ground up: The History of Mining in Utah*, ed. Colleen Whitley, 220–249. Logan: Utah State University Press.

Whitley, Colleen. 2006. *From the Ground up: The History of Mining in Utah*. Logan: Utah State University Press.

Wilson, Francis. 2011. Historical Roots of Inequality in South Africa. *Economic History of Developing Regions* 26 (1): 1–15.

Wilson Paul, Rodman. 2001. *Mining Frontiers of the Far West 1848–1880*. Albuquerque: University of New Mexico Press.

Woodland, John. 2014. *Money Pits: British Mining Companies in the Californian and Australian Gold Rushes of the 1850s*. Farnham: Ashgate.

Jubilant stockbrokers. A caricature of stockbrokers dancing for joy at the news of the Boers' surrender in 1902, after the South African War. © Illustrated London News/Mary Evans Picture Library

15

Conclusions

In this book, our aim has been to analyse the role of imperialism and colonialism in the development of modern capitalism. More specifically, we have studied the interplay between financial markets and actors, on the one hand, and imperial policies and colonial institutions, on the other—in short, between capital and colonialism. To do this, we have analysed the return on investment in companies listed on the London Stock Exchange and operating in Africa from 1869 to 1969. This was a period of rapid transformation in the world economy. It also covers the colonial period for most of the African countries under study in the book. Previous research into capital exports and foreign investments had studied investments in various parts of the world, using a variety of methods, but had not been able to arrive at conclusive results. Whereas some research suggests that there was substantially higher return on investment (so-called super-profits) in colonies than in other parts of the world, other research suggests that there was no significant difference in the return on investment related to colonial status.

One key result of our study, as shown in Chap. 6, is that the average return on investment in Africa was not particularly high when compared to the return on investment elsewhere in the world during the whole

© The Author(s) 2019
K. Rönnbäck, O. Broberg, *Capital and Colonialism*, Palgrave Studies in Economic History, https://doi.org/10.1007/978-3-030-19711-7_15

period under study. On the aggregate level, our results thus lend support to the theories and previous research that has argued that there was no significant difference between the return on investment in colonies or in other parts of the world. Theories arguing that there were 'super-profits' to be made from investing in colonies find little support in our aggregate data. Disaggregating the data reveals a more complex pattern, as was also shown in Chap. 6. First, there were significant geographical differences. Investments in South Africa exhibited the highest return in the long run. Investments in several other parts of Africa were, in contrast, on average, not very successful at all. In the case of East and West Africa, investments even exhibited negative returns in real terms.

Long-term average figures hide important changes over time. In our complete sample of companies, investors were able to earn very high return on investment during a couple of decades in the late nineteenth century—essentially coinciding with the famous 'Scramble for Africa'. This is well in line with previous research in the field. Most of this literature has, however, focussed upon the period of 'high imperialism' until the First World War. What our results add here is that investments in several more mature colonial economies from the 1920s onwards also exhibited a most respectable return on investment. This has largely been missed by earlier research, due to its focus on the pre-1914 period.

When the spatial and temporal aspects are combined, different trends emerge in the respective regions. Investments in North Africa yielded extraordinarily high returns until the 1890s, while they incurred substantial losses for investors during the last decades under study, particularly in the 1950s and 1960s. Investors in both West and Central/Southern Africa, on the other hand, experienced an opposite trend, with major losses for investors during the first decades of investment, but increasing return on investment over time, particularly high during the last two decades of our study. Finally, investors in South Africa experienced no clear long-term trend over the whole period under study; instead, there were sizable fluctuations between the decades.

These shifts in the return on investment are, naturally, attributable to a whole number of factors influencing the profitability of the companies involved. One key factor was the monopoly positions that some of the companies occasionally were able to achieve in their respective markets, for longer or shorter periods. Examples include the trading operations in West Africa by the Royal Niger Company and the African Association. Another example is the diamond monopoly operated by the London Diamond Syndicate and later the Central Selling Organization (in turn largely controlled by De Beers Consolidated). Technological development was also important for the return on investment in particular industries. No example from our study is more telling here than the development of the MacArthur-Forrest process of cyanide leaching, which enabled gold-mining companies to extract a larger share of the gold present in the ore than had previously been possible. Institutional changes furthermore had important consequences for our estimates—not least when the Gold Standard was abandoned, as this led to a rise in the price of gold, and hence, to a higher return on investment in gold-mining companies.

The profitability of some high-profile companies—De Beers Consolidated, Consolidated Goldfields of South Africa, the Anglo-American Corporation and others—has been used by earlier scholars to argue in favour of 'super-profits' from colonial ventures. As the key results of this study show, drawing such conclusions from the previous literature is highly problematic. The selection of companies in case studies generally suffers from a bias in that the more successful companies are more likely to be selected, as their success creates a perception that they are of interest to study. However, for every successful business venture in Africa, there were several unsuccessful ones. This risk was naturally something that every investor, whether investing in Africa or elsewhere in the world, would have been aware of. As has been shown in Chaps. 6 and 7 of this book, almost half of the companies in the sample never managed to yield a positive return on the investment. There were almost three times as many unsuccessful companies, exhibiting a negative return on investment on average, as there were highly successful companies in our sample. Not surprisingly, it was mining ventures in particular that created losses for their investors. The geographical distance to the African continent might have aggravated these problems, as information asymmetries might have been more serious for investors in Africa than for investors engaged in regions where information flowed more easily.

One line of scholarship has focussed upon particular individuals, emphasizing how rich they became as a consequence of business ventures in colonial Africa. Their wealth has been used as evidence for the supposed 'super-profits' of colonialism and imperialism. No one has received more scholarly attention than Cecil Rhodes and the several companies that he was involved in. Drawing inferences from such individuals is, however, also problematic. As has been shown in Chap. 12 of this book, it is more proper to distinguish between the average investor and particularly invited agents. Aside from a number of entrepreneurs operating in their respective fields (such as Cecil Rhodes and other so-called Randlords), there was a larger group of people that got involved in the key companies from an early stage. These people were invited to get in 'on the ground floor', prior to the initial public offering of the company. As a rule, the invitees possessed certain assets that early entrepreneurs required in order to make their venture successful, such as social capital and political influence, technical skills or claims to land. In return for putting these assets at the disposal of the company, the invitees were offered valuable compensation in the form of various incentives, including founders' shares and/or vendors' interests. Such early movers could thus earn substantially higher return on their investments (if, indeed, they were even expected to invest any capital at all) than the average investor on the London Stock Exchange. Being invited in 'on the ground floor' could also mean that the invitee received preferential access to information, not just about the particular company in question, but also about other companies. Insiders could thereby make further gains from these information asymmetries.

From the perspective of London investors, Africa was an emerging market during the period of our study. This entailed an elevated risk compared to more mature markets. The market risk of investing in Africa, as measured by the annual fluctuation in the return on investment—volatility—was slightly higher than the equivalent risk of investing domestically in the United Kingdom during the same period. The slightly elevated return on investment in the region could thus be argued to correspond to its market risk. On an aggregate level, these findings fit well with what would be expected from theories of financial risk. The pattern is the opposite when the data is disaggregated geographically: it then becomes apparent that the average return on investment was the highest in the part of the continent where market risk was the lowest—South Africa. Thus, many investors were not compensated even in the long term for the elevated risk of investing in other parts of Africa.

Our results also suggest large differences in the return on investment in different sectors of the economy. One sector, mining, completely dominated our sample in terms of market capitalization. Mining was also, over the long run, the highest-yielding sector. Investors might have targeted specific sector investments, or even special commodities, since they might have possessed sector- or commodity-specific expertise. To shift from investments in a mining company to investments in a completely different type of business activity might therefore not have been a likely alternative for many investors. In Chap. 14, we therefore compared the return on investment in the African (non-ferrous, non-coal) mining industry with the return on investment in mining elsewhere in the world during the same period. Many South African companies and public officials alike complained about the supposed low grade of the auriferous ore of Witwatersrand. This is a claim that receives limited support in a comparative perspective. Our results show that the return on investing in African mining was strikingly higher than the return on investing in mining anywhere else in the world during the period under study. Unsurprisingly, the African portfolio became ever more dominant in terms of market capitalization, and—along with investments in (the former British colony) Australia—therefore completely dominated all investments in mining emanating from the London Stock Exchange by the end of the period under study in this book. Investments in mining in other parts of the world suffered from the same problems of asymmetric information and high 'mortality' among the companies established. There were, on the other hand, wide variations in the return on investment from mining companies, depending on the type of mineral they mined. The most profitable investments in the long run were to be found among companies involved in diamonds. This is unsurprising, given that the diamond industry established a monopoly sales organization that successfully managed the selling price of the diamonds produced. During the period under study, Africa hosted the vast majority of all commercial diamond producers in the world. Furthermore, in Northern Rhodesia and Belgian Congo, the copper findings were not the richest in the world in terms of ore grade, but they were the largest findings of copper in their class of mines (based on ore grade). Likewise, the ore grade in South African gold mines was not particularly high compared to the most successful gold-mining company in Ashanti, in current-day Ghana. The key to its success was instead the sheer scale of the total findings and the realization of economies of scale and scope.

That the aggregate return on investment in Africa was more or less on a par with the return on investment elsewhere in the world over the whole period studied should not be interpreted as suggesting that there was no economic exploitation of the African colonies. On the contrary, as much previous research referred to in this book has made clear, the colonization of the African continent was generally a brutal process. It entailed violence, colonial appropriation of land and coercion of labour. What little development there was in the form of public investments in infrastructure, health and education was to a large extent paid for through taxation of the local population. So, while in our minds it is beyond doubt that the colonization of Africa entailed economic exploitation on a grand scale, this did not translate into systematically higher return on investment for investors at the London Stock Exchange. How can that be?

Exploitative institutions, we suggest, were important for the operations of many of the companies under study in this book. Coercive labour institutions drove down the reservation wage—and hence the labour costs—of the workers. The appropriation and redistribution of land to colonial agents likewise reduced the cost of acquiring land, and hence any resources that could be extracted from it. In some cases, where companies faced a competitive international market for their products, the coercively lowered factor costs for land and labour translated into lower prices for the companies' output. In such cases, colonial policies would have favoured the consumers of the output, rather than the investors in the company. But by driving down the costs of these production factors, colonial institutions could, and in many cases probably did, enable an increase in static terms in the return to the third major production factor, capital. For many of the successful companies in our sample, we have shown how crucial particular colonial institutions and imperial policies could be for their bottom line. In Egypt, studied in Chap. 8, the Suez

Canal Company benefitted from the low-paid corvée labour. Had the company not had access to this cheap labour for several years during the costly construction of the canal (or not received compensation from the Egyptian government once this institution was abolished), the bankruptcy that the company was on the verge of by the end of the canal's period of construction could very well have become a reality. A bankruptcy at that time would have caused a massive loss of capital for its investors without the company even having begun actual operations.

In British West Africa, studied in Chap. 9, coercive labour institutions were not as widespread as in many other African colonies. Rights to land and minerals were, on the other hand, in several cases appropriated under highly dubious terms, but were nonetheless recognized by the colonial authorities, and came to be crucial for several of the key companies operating in the region, including the Royal Niger Company and its successor, and for the Ashanti Goldfields Corporation.

In Central/Southern Africa, as studied in Chap. 10, land rights were of key importance for several companies, not least the infamous British South Africa Company. As we show, the British South Africa Company was not a high-yielding investment for the London investor prior to the 1920s. The administration of the colony of Rhodesia, which was entrusted to the chartered company, was simply too costly relative to the limited turnover of the economic activities in the colony. Once the company had been freed from this burden, and the costs of administering the colony had been shifted to other parties, it became a hugely successful target for investment, since it managed to keep its rights to land and minerals in the colony. It also so happened that this process coincided with massive new copper findings in the colony. Over time, labour institutions became increasingly coercive in these colonies, and outside options became more limited for many local populations as colonial land appropriation continued in the first half of the twentieth century. During the 1950s and 1960s, investments in Central/Southern Africa therefore exhibit a very high rate of return on investment.

In South Africa, studied in Chap. 11, major land appropriation occurred in tandem with the introduction and strengthening of coercive labour institutions. These processes started as early as the late nineteenth century and intensified throughout most of the twentieth century. Many of the major mining companies operating in South Africa made frequent use of various types of coercive labour institutions. They also benefitted from the reduction in the reservation wages entailed by the creation of so-called 'native reserves' and by the monopsony price setting on the labour market. Without these institutions enabling access to a supply of low-paid labour, the major South African mining companies would undoubtedly not have been as profitable as they were. As the twentieth century progressed, new findings of gold outside Witwatersrand also had large implications on the performance of individual companies. This also coincided with an intensified oppression of the black labour force in South Africa, continuing to drive down the factor costs of production in the country. Both these factors in tandem influenced investors' return on investment in South Africa. Companies, such as Rand Mines, which did not manage to participate in the development of the mining frontier, ended up substantially less successful from the perspective of their investors.

Many readers will recognize that several of the leading companies have received a lot of attention in the previous literature, not least in the field of business history. In this study, we call them Imperial Blue Chips because they were relatively stable and high-yielding investment objects. In addition, because of their combined market capitalization, they exerted a big influence on the total performance of the African Colonial Equities Database (ACED) portfolio from 1869 to 1969. Some of these companies were operating ventures that most likely would have been successful even under 'normal' conditions in a capitalist society, that is, even if no particularly exploitative colonial institutions had been in place. Given that such institutions were in place, the investors in these companies gained higher return on investment than they otherwise would have.

However, Imperial Blue Chips were not the only companies attracting investors to Africa, and all investments were made based upon the investors' expectations of future profits. Investors undoubtedly factored in the existence of these colonial institutions. Investments in the colonies were for a long time made on the expectation that colonial authorities would come to consider the land or other natural resources appropriated by settlers as theirs by right, and that various coercive practices would remain in place or even be developed further in favour of the colonial agents. These institutions were taken as the 'rules of the game' when investors decided whether to invest in an African venture or not. This is also how in Chap. we interpret the fact that the issue of the mines' labour supply played such a limited role in the correspondence between the London and Johannesburg offices of the Rand Mines Limited. The London office did not consider the issue worth much attention, as they took the institutional setup as given, or as something that local representatives could solve on their own.

Investments were therefore made in a number of ventures where the expected return on investment—assuming the continued existence of these coercive institutions—was more or less on a par with the return on investment to be expected from investing anywhere else in the world. In a counterfactual scenario, if no such coercive colonial institutions had been in place, the returns on these investments would presumably have been lower than what they actually turned out to be. Some investments in these companies would in such a scenario not even have exhibited a positive return on investment. In a counterfactual scenario, where exploitative colonial institutions would have been absent (and the costs of labour or land consequently would have been higher), one would expect that capital exports from the United Kingdom would have been lower, as fewer British investors would have considered it economically rational to invest in the colonies. This would, in turn, potentially have affected the return on investment both domestically in the United Kingdom and potentially elsewhere in the world. A standard theoretical assumption in economics is that there is diminishing marginal return on capital within any single economy (or, as Marxists would have it, a tendency for the profit rate to fall). A decrease in the capital exported from the United Kingdom to Africa would therefore theoretically have meant that investors either would have had to invest in less-profitable ventures domestically (or in other parts of the world), and would therefore have gained a lower return on their investments, or would have refrained from investing in the first place. Both these factors could potentially have reduced the growth rate of the total economy. Imperialism might thus have increased the amount of capital exported—acting as a vent against diminishing marginal return on capital in the more mature capital markets in Europe.

Another aspect of colonialism was that it could be a way of reducing the risk of investing. One risk of investing in a foreign country is that the foreign sovereign may not recognize the investors' property rights. Colonization might thus be a policy intended to minimize this risk, as argued in some previous literature studying the bond spreads in colonies and non-colonies. The British occupation of Egypt in 1882 would be a case in point. In Chap. 13, we describe how the British government not only protected private British interests from the risk of nationalization by intervening in Egyptian politics, but most crucially also defended its own substantial financial investments in the Suez Canal (as is also illustrated in the picture on page 279). This issue has largely been ignored in the previous research. Much has, likewise, been written on the South African War of 1899–1902. British investors in South Africa did not lose out economically from the war. On the contrary, as we also show in Chap. 13, the return on investment during years of war was high. Many investors might, nonetheless, have considered the eventual British victory in the war as a relief, since they might have feared what a victory for the Boer Republics would have implied for British investors' chances of operating in the vast Witwatersrand goldfields. No wonder, then, that the London stockbrokers could be depicted as jubilant—see the picture on page 379—when British victory was declared.

The variety of colonial institutions also had different results for investors. One crucial distinction in the previous literature has been between settler and non-settler colonies. It has been argued that settler colonies in general enforced substantially more exploitative institutions. When we compare the return on investment in settler and non-settler colonies in Africa, the results indicate that they were actually on a par for most of the period under study. However, from the 1940s onwards, the different types of colonies start to diverge, with return on investment in settler colonies systematically higher than in non-settler colonies. There were certainly a number of factors that contributed to this trend, including several mentioned previously, such as the expanding mining frontier and the development of new findings, the technological development of various industries or the development of output markets. We also believe that the institutional changes that occurred in the settler colonies—most importantly for our study in South Africa and Rhodesia—with increased

15 Conclusions

oppression and exploitation of the black population living there contributed to this divergence between settler and non-settler colonies.

The risk of expropriation of assets became more imminent particularly after the Second World War, as processes towards political independence gained momentum in many African countries. Decolonization increased the risk that a company's assets would be nationalized by the young sovereign nations of Africa. The actual process of decolonization played out differently across the African continent. South Africa experienced several institutional changes as it moved from being a colony with substantial self-rule by the late nineteenth century to a sovereign republic under white minority rule by the end of our period under study. None of these institutional changes challenged the property rights of the investors. In other countries, such as Nigeria and Northern Rhodesia, political independence implied a distinct political break with the past, but it did not have any substantial impact on the return enjoyed by investors in London. In other parts of Africa, the process of decolonization had severe consequences for foreign investors. In Egypt, the independent nation soon moved to nationalize foreign assets, largely without compensation, so that foreign investors experienced major losses during the last two to three decades of our study. In Ghana, many foreign investors feared that their assets would be nationalized by the self-proclaimed socialists leading the struggle for independence. The return on investment in Ghana consequently turned negative in the years preceding independence as stock prices dropped. When no such nationalization occurred in the years immediately following independence, the capital values actually recovered (at least up until 1969, i.e. the years covered here). In Belgian Congo, investors similarly feared that nationalization would follow in the wake of political independence and share prices consequently tumbled in anticipation. The civil war that broke out following independence also decreased the capital value of investments even further. When nationalization finally occurred, swift intervention and political pressure from the United States led to the independent Zairian government paying compensation to investors. As a result, the accumulated return on investment actually returned to its pre-independence level.

In all, our research shows no straightforward relationship between capital and colonialism. Specific imperialist policies and colonial institutions certainly impacted the return on investment, but this did not automatically translate into higher average long-term return for all types of investors. In some cases, capital investors were clearly supportive of, or even actively pursued, imperialist policies, or helped to develop colonial institutions. In many other cases, investors were simply taking advantage of the fact that policies and institutions were imposed for various reasons without necessarily having to work actively in their favour. In yet other cases, imperialist policies or colonial institutions meant little for investors, as they might have had little impact upon their particular line of business. Over time, new investors anticipated and factored in such policies and institutions when making their investment decisions. More often than not, particular policies favoured investors in informationally advantageous positions, enabling them to anticipate and act on the policies that were about to be put into place. For investors that were able to exploit such opportunities, imperialism and colonialism could be highly rewarding.

Index

A
African and Eastern Trade Corporation, 183, 186, 187
 See also African Association
African Association, 180, 183, 185, 186, 383
 See also African and Eastern Trade Corporation
African Banking Corporation, 178, 239, 249, 254, 257
African Colonial Equities Database (ACED), 89, 105, 117, 318, 322, 331
 definition of, 81
African Direct Telegraph Company, 180
Africanization of foreign businesses, 166, 169, 194, 328
African Selection Trust, 192
African Steam Ship Company, 177, 178, 183, 187
Agricultural Bank of Egypt, 158, 162, 163, 167
Algeria, 21, 23, 83, 85
Amalgamated Copper Company, 351, 361, 362
Amalgamated Tin Mines of Nigeria, 183, 197, 199
Anaconda Copper Mining, 351, 361–363, 372
Anglo-African Bank, 188
Anglo-African Diamond Mining, 239, 241
Anglo-African Exploration Limited, 192
Anglo-American Corporation, 56, 106, 107, 219, 220, 239, 257, 260, 262, 263, 267, 269, 271, 366, 383
Anglo-American Investment Trust, 239
Anglo-Boer War, *see* South African War

Index

Anglo-Egyptian Banking Co Ltd., 156–158, 162, 167
Anglo-Oriental Trust, 197
Angola, 20, 83, 85
Asante, 176, 183, 184, 189
Ashanti Goldfields Corporation, 56, 104, 182–184, 189–191, 195, 196, 199, 201, 344, 345, 366, 387
Associated Tin Mines of Nigeria, 197
Asymmetric information, 48, 286, 298, 299, 385

B

Bank of Abyssinia, 158, 163, 167
Bank of Africa, 239, 249, 257
Bank of (British) West Africa, 178, 183, 187, 188, 194, 198
Bank of Egypt, 156, 158, 162, 163, 167
Bank of England, 58, 254
Bank of Nigeria, 188
Barclays (Dominion, Colonial and Overseas), 167, 188, 264, 269
Barlow Rand Archive, 91
Barnato Brothers, 256
Beatty, Alfred Chester, 220
   See also Selection Trust Limited
Bechuanaland, 209
   See also Botswana
Beit, Alfred, 284–286, 288, 289, 291, 292, 294–296, 298
   See also Rand Mines
Belgian Congo, 60, 61, 64, 85, 117, 118, 128, 227, 328–331, 335, 386, 391
Bentham, Jeremy, 39

Black Star Lines, 198
Blyvooruitzicht Gold Mining, 239, 268, 271
Boer War, *see* South African War
Botswana, 83
   See also Bechuanaland
British & African Steam Navigation Company, 177, 178, 183
British Empire, 4, 18, 19, 22, 24–26, 30, 31, 41, 44, 58, 119, 120, 133, 143, 176, 236, 237, 253, 328, 367
British Petroleum, 195
British South Africa Company, 56, 103, 106, 112, 211–215, 218, 220, 221, 225–228, 321–323, 325, 332–334, 387
Broken Hill Proprietary, 351, 356, 357
Bwana Mkubwa Copper Mining Company, 215, 217, 219, 220

C

Cade, Edwin, 183, 184, 190
Cain, P.J., 45, 46, 103, 104, 133
Cam & Motor Gold Mining, 215, 216, 221, 222
Cape Colony, 20, 23, 73, 235, 236, 238, 240, 241, 250, 289
   See also South Africa
Cape Copper, 238, 239, 243, 251, 270, 365
Capital exports, 26, 27, 30, 31, 39, 40, 42, 43, 381, 389
   recipients, 27, 43
   sector of investment, 27

Index

Cassel Cyanide Company, 351, 356, 358
Cassel, Ernest, 296
Central Mining and Investment Corporation, 285
Central Selling Organization, 196, 263, 327, 366, 383
Chamberlain, Joseph, 30
Chartered companies, 320–323, 333, 387
　The Value of a Royal Charter, 320–323
　See also Royal Niger Company, British South Africa Company
City of London, 25–32, 286
　Connecting the World, 25–32
　See also London Stock Exchange
Coercion, *see* Labour, coercion of
Colonial Bank, 188, 194, 239, 242, 249, 251, 264, 270
Colonialism
　definition of, 4, 5
　settler colonies *vs.* non-settler colonies, 85–86, 323–327
　different types of colonies, 85–86
Compagnie Universelle du Canal Maritime de Suez, see Suez Canal Company
Compounds
　in Rhodesia, 215, 216, 224
　in South Africa, 246, 265
Consolidated African Selection Trust (CAST), 183, 192, 196, 199, 200
　See also Selection Trust Limited
Consolidated Diamond Mines of South West Africa, 215, 219, 263

　See also Anglo-American Corporation
Consolidated Goldfields of South Africa, 141, 212, 239, 249, 254, 255, 260, 271, 285, 289, 383
Convention People's Party (CPP) (Ghana), 198, 330
Copperbelt, 103, 220, 222–225, 228, 327, 355, 365
　See also Northern Rhodesia
Corner House, 10, 90–91, 168, 249, 283–307, 349
　See also Rand Mines
Côte d'Or Mining Company, 182, 184
Crédit foncier de France, 159

D

Davis, Lance, 43–45, 58, 62, 64, 119–121, 190, 191
De Beers Consolidated, 56, 90, 106, 107, 141, 196, 212, 239, 244, 245, 247, 256, 262, 263, 267, 269, 271, 364, 366, 383
Decolonization, 25, 73, 326, 328–332, 334, 335, 364, 391
Decolonization in Africa and the Return on Investment, 328–332
de Lesseps, Ferdinand, 151, 152
　See also Suez Canal, construction of
Decolonization of Egypt, 166, 169, 326, 328–330, 391
Decolonization of Gold Coast, 25, 194, 196, 198, 326, 328–330, 391

Decolonization of Nigeria, 64, 194, 198, 326, 328–330, 391
Decolonization of Northern Rhodesia, 226, 327, 328, 331, 332, 391
Decolonization of Southern Rhodesia, 25, 73, 222, 228, 328, 330–332
Dormer, Francis, 296

E

Eckstein & Company, 285, 286, 292, 293, 305
Eckstein, Hermann, 286, 288, 290–292, 296, 303
Economic exploitation, 6, 18, 19, 42, 43, 367, 371, 386, 389–391
The Economist, 57, 61, 77, 91, 297, 298
Edelstein, Michael, 57, 62, 64, 119–121, 125, 128, 132, 133
Egypt, 8, 19, 22, 24, 27, 65, 83, 86, 88, 103, 111, 115, 149–172, 311–317, 329, 386
  Caisse de la Dette Publique, 157, 159
  The Colonization of Egypt, 311–317
  decolonization of, 326, 328 (*see also* Suez Canal)
  Dual Control of, 157, 159, 160, 313, 314, 333
  labour in, 151–153
  occupation of, 115, 157, 160–163, 172, 311, 313, 315–317, 325, 327, 333, 390
  The Colonization of Egypt, 311–317
  Unilateral Declaration of Independence of, 24, 163, 329
Egyptianization of foreign businesses, *see* Africanization of foreign businesses
Elder Dempster Company, 177, 178, 187
Emma Silver Mining Company, 351, 360, 361
Equity Risk Premium, 131–134
Ethiopia, 22, 73, 83, 163, 167

F

Ferreira Deep mine, 290
The Financial Times, 91, 293, 297–299
First World War, 21, 22, 31, 61, 76, 102, 106, 109, 110, 122, 127, 129, 163–168, 171, 185, 187, 188, 192, 193, 248, 250, 254, 258, 262, 325, 326, 334, 341, 343, 345, 350, 353, 354, 356, 358, 362–364, 366, 367, 369, 382
Foreign direct investments (FDI), 69
Founders' shares, 151, 287, 306, 384
Franco-Egyptian Bank, 158
Frankel, Herbert, 56, 57, 62, 116, 117

G

Geldenhuis Deep, 292, 304, 305
General Mining and Finance Corporation, 239, 254, 260

Ghana, 19, 20, 25, 65, 83, 86, 88, 193, 196, 198, 199, 328–330, 344, 386, 391
  See also Gold Coast
Global Financial Data (GFD), 77–82, 86, 87
Global Mining Equities Database (GMED), 87, 340, 342
Globe and Phoenix Mine, 215, 216, 221, 222
Goerz, Adolf, 291
Gold Coast, 80, 104, 175–201
  colonization of, 22, 23, 175, 176
  decolonization of, 196
  labour in, 23, 176, 181, 182, 190, 192, 195, 196
  land rights in, 23, 176, 177, 184
  Mine Managers' Association, 189
  See also Ghana
Gold Standard, 27, 30, 110, 117, 164, 195, 221, 250, 252, 254, 258, 261, 285, 302, 327, 328, 346, 364, 366, 367, 371, 383
Griqualand, 240, 241
  See also Kimberley
Ground floor, on the, 283–307, 384

Hanau, Carl, 298
Harvey, David, 42, 43
Hobson, John, 41, 42, 317

Hopkins, A.G., 45, 46, 103, 104, 133, 312
Huttenback, Robert, 44, 45, 58, 62, 64, 119–121, 190, 191

Imperial British East Africa Company, 321
Imperialism, definition of, 3–5
Investors' Monthly Manual, 57, 60, 61, 77, 79, 136, 191, 201
Isma'il Pasha, khedive, 153, 155, 157, 159, 279, 314

Jameson Raid, 251, 300, 303, 304, 317
Johannesburg, 28, 30, 91, 116, 243, 247–250, 255, 260, 267, 283–288, 290–294, 296, 298, 300, 301, 303, 306, 319, 371, 389
  See also Witwatersrand
Johannesburg Consolidated Investment Company, 141, 239, 254
Jones, Alfred, 178, 188

Kenya, 23, 83, 85, 321
Kimberley, 28, 103, 210, 241, 244, 246–248, 262, 286, 364, 371
Kimberley North Block Diamond Mining, 239, 241

Index

L

Labour
  coercion of, 6, 18, 23, 24, 42, 152, 153, 176, 181, 190, 193, 197, 213, 216, 217, 223, 253, 324, 327, 334, 386–388
  corvée, 23, 151–153, 181, 387
  enslaved, 18, 23, 175, 176, 181, 189, 190, 193, 352, 353, 372
  recruitment of, 176, 181, 182, 189, 190, 196, 223, 224, 245, 246, 252, 253, 258, 371
  scarcity of, 181, 217, 252, 258, 264, 303
  unionization of, 195, 197, 199, 201, 221, 223–225, 354, 362, 363, 372
  wages to, 6, 152, 189–191, 193, 197, 213, 217, 221, 223–225, 245, 246, 252, 258–260, 264, 303, 304, 307, 327, 347, 367–370, 386, 388
Land rights, 5, 18, 19
  See also Gold Coast; Nigeria; Northern Rhodesia; South Africa; Southern Rhodesia
Lewanika, king, 210, 225
Lippert, William, 289
Lobengula, king, 210
Lochner Concession, 210, 225, 226, 323
London and South African Bank, 239, 242
London & South African Exploration Company Limited, 237, 240, 244
London Diamond Syndicate, 245, 256, 263, 383
The (London) Exploration Company, 244, 294–296
London Stock Exchange Daily List, 77, 78
London Stock Exchange Yearbook, 79
London Tin Corporation, 197, 198

M

MacArthur-Forrest process, 294, 383
Malawi, 83
Market capitalization, 71, 74, 75, 102
Market concentration, 104–106
  decreasing market concentration, 104–106
Marx, Karl, 41, 42
Marxism, 41–43
Mauritius, 83
Mill, John Stuart, 39
Mineral rights, *see* Land rights
Mining
  in Belgian Congo, 118, 223, 224
  investments in, 27–29, 56, 57
  ore grades of, 343–347, 368
  technological development and falling ore grades, 343–347
  return on investment in, 112, 347–363
  The return on investment in global mining, 347–349
  in Rhodesia, 209–229, 327
  in South Africa, 28, 101, 109, 116, 117, 235–272, 285, 299, 305, 307, 317–320, 325, 327, 333, 367, 368, 371

technological development of, 292, 343–347
technological development and falling ore grades, 343–347
in West Africa, 175–201
Mobutu, Joseph, 227, 332
Modderfontein Gold Mining, 240, 249, 254, 260
Mount Lyell Mining, 351, 356, 357
Mount Morgan Gold Mining Co, 351, 356, 357
Mozambique, 20, 83, 85

N
Namaqualand, 238
See also Cape Copper
Namibia, 83, 219, 257
National African Company, 179, 183, 192
See also Royal Niger Company
National Bank of Egypt, 156, 158, 162, 163, 167
National Bank of South Africa, 249, 254, 257, 264
National Recruiting Corporation (South Africa)
See also Witwatersrand Native Labour Association
N'Changa Consolidated Copper Mines, 215
Neumann, Sigmund, 291
Niger Company, 183, 185, 186, 192, 193
See also Royal Niger Company
Nigeria, 8, 19, 24, 65, 72, 80, 83, 86, 88, 104, 175–201, 321, 328–330, 335, 391
colonization of, 22, 23, 175, 179

decolonization of, 326, 328–332
labour in, 23, 193, 197
land rights in, 23, 192
Nigerian National Shipping Line, 198
Nkrumah, Kwame, 198, 199, 330, 335
Northern Rhodesia, 88, 209–229, 327, 351, 355, 365, 385
colonization of, 210
"colour bar" in, 224, 225
copper in (see Copperbelt)
decolonization of, 226, 327, 328, 331, 332, 391
labour in, 218, 223, 224
land rights in, 210, 225, 226, 387
Native Labor Association, 223
See also Zambia

O
Oppenheimer, Ernest, 219, 220, 257, 260, 263
See also Anglo-American Corporation
Orange Free State / Orange River Colony, 236, 241, 257, 267, 268, 271, 347
See also South Africa

P
Pass laws, see South Africa & Southern Rhodesia
Phillips, Lionell, 286, 294–296, 303, 304
Porges, Jules, 285
Portfolio Investments, 69
Premier Diamond Mine, 240, 251, 256, 263

R

Randlords, 248, 260, 285, 287, 288, 291, 296, 305, 384
Rand Mines Limited, 90, 191, 240, 254, 255, 260, 268, 269, 271, 283, 284, 289, 295–302, 304–307, 318, 366, 389
Rand Revolt, 259–261, 265
Register of Defunct Companies, 88, 136, 139, 140
Return on investment
  aggregate estimates, 101–123
  in Central/Southern Africa, 110–112, 211, 227–229, 387
  in comparative perspective, 115–122, 386
    African mining in comparative perspective, 364–371
    return on British investments in Africa vs. other Investments, 115–122
  definition of, 74
  in East Africa, 110, 111, 382
  in the mining sector, 112, 181, 193
    the return on investment in global mining, 347–349
  in North Africa, 110, 111, 157, 170–172
  and relation to company profits, 69–72
    company profits and return on investment, 69–72
  in South Africa, 56, 57, 110–112, 116, 123, 130, 131, 133, 238, 270, 317, 318
  in West Africa, 110–112, 182, 200–201, 382

Rhodes, Cecil, 3, 90, 103, 190, 209, 210, 212, 244, 284, 289, 291, 384
  See also DeBeers Consolidated, Consolidated Goldfields of South Africa
Rhodesian Anglo-American, 215, 220, 223, 224
  See also Anglo-American Corporation
Rhodesian Selection Trust, 215, 220, 224, 225
  See also Selection Trust Limited
Rhokana Corporation, 215, 223, 355
Ricardo, David, 40
Rio Tinto, 84, 351, 354–356
Risk, and company survival, 134–141
  survival and death of African ventures, 134–141
Risk, and return on investment, 46–48, 125–143, 384, 390
  risk, return and the Empire Effect, 46–48
Roan Antelope Copper Mines, 215, 220
Robinson, Joseph Benjamin (J.B.), 291, 294
Rothschilds, 244, 294–296, 349
Royal Dutch Shell, 195
Royal Niger Company, 179, 180, 183, 185, 186, 200, 321–323, 333, 383, 387
  See also National African Company, and Niger Company
Rudd, Charles, 210, 212, 289
Rudd Concession, 210, 323

S

Sa'id Pasha, khedive, 151, 155
St. John d'el Rey Mining, 351–353
Scramble for Africa, 4, 19–25, 28, 73, 109, 123, 311, 320, 321, 382
　The European Colonization of Africa, 19–25
Second World War, 25, 72, 73, 106, 110, 122, 123, 139, 164–167, 172, 193, 194, 197, 221, 224, 264, 269, 326–330, 341, 350, 354, 356, 358, 363, 364, 366, 367, 391
Selection Trust Limited, 192, 219, 220, 351, 363
Shamva Mines, 215, 216
Sierra Leone, 24, 83, 104, 189, 199
Sierra Leone Selection Trust (SLST), 196
Smith, Adam, 23, 39, 41
South Africa, 20, 23, 27, 28, 30, 81, 83, 86, 106, 110, 113, 114, 117, 123, 130–133, 142, 168, 189, 195, 235–272, 283, 303, 317, 327, 328, 334, 341, 343, 346–348, 365, 368, 369, 371, 385, 387, 388, 391
　apartheid in, 265, 266, 271
　Chamber of Mines, 249, 260, 304, 343
　"colour bar" in, 251, 259, 265
　compounds in, 246, 265
　copper in (*see* Cape Copper)
　diamonds in (*see* Kimberley)
　gold in (*see* Witwatersrand)
　labour in, 242, 245–247, 251–253, 256, 258–260, 264, 265, 271, 302, 327, 334, 388
　land rights in, 23, 236, 241, 253, 271, 327, 387
　National Recruiting Corporation (*see also* Witwatersrand Native Labour Association)
　Native Lands Act in, 253, 327
　native reserves in, 253, 265, 388
　pass laws, 253
　Republic of, 328
　Union of, 24, 328
　Witwatersrand Native Labour Association, 252, 327
South African Republic, *see* Transvaal Republic
The South African War (1899–1902), 31, 250, 317–320, 390
Southern Rhodesia, 25, 73, 112, 209–229, 330–332, 335
　"colour bar" in, 221
　colonization of, 214
　compounds in, 215, 216, 224
　decolonization of, 25, 73, 222, 228, 328, 330–332
　labour in, 213, 215, 217, 221, 327, 334
　land rights in, 23, 210, 212, 213, 220, 387
　pass laws, 216
　Unilateral Declaration of Independence of, 222, 332
　See also Zimbabwe
South-West Africa, *see* Namibia
Standard Bank of South Africa, 131, 240, 242, 248–251, 254, 257, 264, 269, 270
Sub Nigel Mine, 240, 261

Sudan, 83, 149, 167
Sudan Plantation Syndicate, 158, 167, 168
Suez Canal
  construction of, 150, 152, 155, 387
  nationalization of, 169, 172, 330
Suez Canal Company, 56, 102–104, 106, 113, 115, 126, 131, 133, 151–159, 161, 164–166, 168–172, 279, 313–316, 324–326, 333, 386–387
Swaziland, 83

T

Tanganyika Concessions, 118, 119, 215, 217, 218, 224, 331, 332
Tanzania, 83
Taylor, Jim, 286, 293
Tewfik Pasha, khedive, 314–316, 333
The Times of London, 78, 82, 86
Tongoy Mine, 351–353
Transvaal Republic, 236
  See also South Africa

U

Uganda, 83
Union Corporation, 260
Union Minière du Haut-Katanga (UMHK), 118, 119, 217, 218, 224, 227
United African Company, 178, 179, 186, 187, 194, 197, 199
  See also National African Company; Niger Company; and Royal Niger Company
Utah Copper Company, 351, 362

V

Vendor's interest, 287, 291, 306, 384
Volatility, 46, 47, 61, 76, 108, 119, 125–132, 142, 161, 242, 263, 299, 354, 356, 358, 361, 363, 384

W

Wages, *see* Labour
Wakefield, Edward Gibbon, 39, 40
Wankie Colliery, 215–217, 222
Wernher, Beit & Company, 212, 285, 286
Wernher, Julius, 285, 286, 296
West African Shipping Conference, 178
West African Telegraph Co. Ltd., 180, 183
Witwatersrand, 28, 103, 246–248, 251, 254, 255, 260, 261, 271, 283, 285, 291, 293, 294, 298, 299, 303, 317, 333, 346, 366, 385, 388, 390

Z

Zambezia Exploring Company, 217
Zambia, 10, 65, 83, 85, 103, 210, 226, 227, 321, 328, 330–332, 335
  See also Northern Rhodesia
Zambia Industrial and Mining Corp (ZIMCO), 227, 332
Zimbabwe, 10, 23, 25, 65, 73, 83, 85, 210, 211, 321, 328
  See also Southern Rhodesia